POLITICAL BELIEF IN FRANCE, 1927-1945

POLITICAL BELIEF
IN FRANCE, 1927–1945

GENDER, EMPIRE, AND FASCISM IN THE
CROIX DE FEU AND PARTI SOCIAL FRANÇAIS

CAROLINE CAMPBELL

Louisiana State University Press
Baton Rouge

Published by Louisiana State University Press
Manufactured in the United States of America
First printing

Portions of chapter 2 first appeared in "Building a Movement, Dismantling the Republic: Women and Political Extremism in the Croix de Feu/Parti Social Français, 1927–1940." *French Historical Studies* 35, no. 4 (Fall 2012): 691–26.

Portions of chapter 4 first appeared in "'Our Body Doesn't Have to be Ugly': Physical Culture, Gender, and Racial Rejuvenation in the Croix de Feu/Parti Social Français." In *The French Right between the Wars: Political and Intellectual Movements from Conservatism to Fascism,* edited by S. Kalman and S. Kennedy. 163–79. New York: Berghahn Books, 2014.

Designer: Barbara Neely Bourgoyne
Typeface: Sina Nova
Printer and binder: Maple Press (digital)

Library of Congress Cataloging-in-Publication Data
Campbell, Caroline, 1977–
    Political belief in France, 1927–1945 : gender, empire, and fascism in the Croix de feu and Parti social français / Caroline Campbell.
        pages cm
    Includes bibliographical references and index.
    ISBN 978-0-8071-6097-8 (cloth : alk. paper) — ISBN 978-0-8071-6099-2 (pdf) —
ISBN 978-0-8071-6100-5 (epub) — ISBN 978-0-8071-6101-2 (mobi)
    1. Croix de feu (Organization : France) 2. Parti social français. 3. Fascism—France—History—20th century. 4. Right-wing extremists—France—History—20th century. 5. Women—Political activity—France—History—20th century. 6. Political culture—France—History—20th century. 7. France—Politics and government—1914–1940. 8. France—Politics and government—1940–1945. I. Title.
    DC389.C27 2015
    324.244′02—dc23

                                                                      2015019891

For My Parents

CONTENTS

Acknowledgments | ix

Abbreviations | xiii

Introduction: Republicanism, Imperialism, and Political and Social
Action in Metropolitan France and the Empire | 1

1 The Culture of War and the Masculine World of the Early Croix de Feu,
   1927–1934 | 27

2 Building a Social Action Movement: Women, Catholicism, and the
   Croix de Feu/PSF's Social First! Strategy, 1934–1939 | 49

3 Challenges to Women's Autonomy and Authority: Health, Financing,
   and Civic Action, 1934–1939 | 86

4 Transforming French Physical Culture: Social Darwinism, Bodily Fitness,
   and Gender, 1934–1939 | 106

5 Women, Race, and Culture in the Croix de Feu/PSF: Entertainment,
   Enlightenment Values, and the Civilizing Mission, 1934–1939 | 123

6 Social and Political Action in North Africa: The Fascism of the Croix
   de Feu/PSF in the French Maghreb, 1927–1940 | 147

7 "The Army of the Good": Vichy and the Feminization of the Croix de Feu/
   PSF, 1939–1945 | 178

Conclusion: Gender, Race, and Empire in the Sociocultural Action of the Croix de Feu/PSF | 203

Notes | 207

Bibliography | 247

Index | 273

Illustrations appear after page 122

ACKNOWLEDGMENTS

I am incredibly fortunate to have met many people inside and outside of academe who believe in "the life of the mind" and the richness that such a life offers.

Writing this book has been a long process and could not have happened without various forms of support. Funding that allowed me to finish it was provided by the National Endowment for the Humanities Summer Stipend; the American Philosophical Society's Franklin Award; the University of North Dakota's Arts, Social Sciences, and Humanities Award; the University of Iowa College of Liberal Arts and Science's Marcus Bach Fellowship for research related to religion and ethics; and the University of Iowa History Department's William Aydelotte Fellowship. In France, the staffs at the Archives nationales, Archives d'histoire contemporaine de la Fondation Nationale des Sciences politiques, Archives de la préfecture de police, Archives nationales d'outre mer, Centre des Archives contemporaines, and Centre des Archives diplomatiques de Nantes all helped me to navigate each archive. I am grateful to Hugues de La Rocque, who gave me access to his grandfather's archives and granted me permission to see everything I requested at the AN and Sciences Po. Finally, I would like to thank Alisa Plant at LSU Press for supporting this project, being highly responsive to all of my queries, and guiding me through a smooth publishing process.

The History Department at Iowa was an encouraging and intellectually invigorating place to enter into the historical profession, learn about women's and gender history, and develop a feminist consciousness. Most importantly, Jen Sessions offered wonderfully incisive feedback and guided me through the often mystifying process of finding sources of funding. Jen is incredibly generous with her time and energy. Lisa Heineman provided highly intelligent and invaluable guidance on how to think deeply about complex issues. Sarah Hanley offered warm encouragement. Linda K. Kerber pushed me to consider the intersections between women's history and moral and ethical behavior. At the University of

Colorado, Martha Hanna showed me that kind people could flourish in academia. Her unending patience with my writing and astute guidance through major historiographical debates was extremely valuable.

In addition to wonderful mentors, I was fortunate to enter the profession with a cohort that was dedicated to learning the craft of becoming a historian. The group made my years at Iowa enjoyable and fulfilling. Specifically, I want to thank Margie Cook Andersen, Christy Clark-Pujara, Justus Hartzok, Karissa Haugeberg, Anglea Keysor, Sharon Lake, Sharon Romeo, Sue Stanfield, Kate Stewart, and Charissa Threat for engaging in numerous discussions about history, reading and commenting on my writing and ideas, challenging me to reconsider aspects of my thinking that needed to be more refined and providing insights and new ways for me to think about women's history.

Life as a junior faculty member has been an interesting and enlightening experience. The College of Arts and Sciences at the University of North Dakota has provided research funding that has allowed me to go to Europe on multiple occasions. One of the best parts about being at UND was the ease with which I met colleagues in other departments when I first arrived, which made interdisciplinary discussions fun and invigorating. In particular, Melissa Birkhofer and Paul Worley broadened my perspectives on indigenous studies, Jeff Langstraat helped me understand better the relationship between sociology and history, and Robin Runge was unfailing in analyzing the law through a feminist lens. Several of my colleagues from UND's History Department provided useful comments on my project, including Cindy Prescott, Bill Caraher, Hans Broedel, Kim Porter, and Nikki Berg-Burin. My colleagues in French history have been equally generous, even when we disagree over points of interpretation, which demonstrates the vibrancy of the field of the French Right. I had the good fortune to meet Chris Millington when we were researching topics on French history that were quite similar. Over the years we have had many opportunities for wonderful conversation and good meals. Sam Kalman and Sean Kennedy have been especially welcoming of a junior faculty member entering the profession. Moreover, I am grateful for helpful comments on my work and tips about archives provided by Margie Cook Andersen, Geoff Read, Cheryl Koos, Richard Hopkins, Rebecca Scales, and Rachel Chrastil. Kevin Passmore, in particular, has used his deep knowledge of French history and historiography to provide profoundly insightful feedback that pushed me to think well beyond the limits of how I originally envisioned my book.

I do not know where to begin to thank my family for their confidence in me, except to say that I could not have written this book without them. My grandparents, Helene and Del Premer, gave me endless unconditional support and much wisdom. My brother, Tom, appreciates why pursuing creative endeavors can be so fulfilling (and maddening). I admire his strength. As public school teachers, my parents understand the value of education in terms of how it enriches one's life, but also, the ways in which teaching enriches the lives of others. My mom introduced me to feminism and my dad, believing that girls and boys were equally athletic and competitive, introduced me to sports. They never once questioned my decision to pursue a life in academia. I hope they recognize that they have provided me with nothing but support, encouragement, and love. They have inspired me to think independently and make my own way in life. This is why I dedicate this book to them.

ABBREVIATIONS

ADP	Artisans du Devoir Patriotique
AMSJA	L'Association Médico-Sociale Jeanne d'Arc
ANOM	Archives nationales d'outre-mer
ALP	Action Libérale Populaire
AP	Archives Privés
APP	Archives de la préfecture de police
ATP	Musée des Arts et Traditions Populaires
AUMA	Association des Ulama Musulmans Algériens
CAC	Le Centre des Archives Contemporaines
CADN	Centre des Archives diplomatiques de Nantes
CARAN	Le Centre d'accueil et de recherche des Archives nationales
CF	Croix de Feu
CGTT	Confédération Générale des Travailleurs Tunisiens
CHSP	Centre d'histoire de Sciences Po
CVIA	Le Comité de Vigilance des Intellectuels Antifascistes
ENA	Etoile Nord-Africaine
FEM	Fédération des Elus Musulmans
FFCF	Fils et Filles des Croix de Feu
JOC	Jeunesse Ouvrière Chrétienne
LADAPT	Ligue pour l'Adaptation du Diminué Physique au Travail
LFACF	Ligue Féminine d'Action Catholique Française
LFDF	Ligue Française pour le Droit des Femmes
LFF	Ligue des Femmes Françaises
LICA	Ligue Internationale Contre l'Antisémitisme
LPDF	Ligue Patriotique des Françaises
MRP	Mouvement Républicain Populaire
MSF	Mouvement Social Français

NSF	Nationalsozialistische Frauenschaft
PCF	Parti Communiste Français
PPA	Parti du Peuple Algérien
PPF	Parti Populaire Français
PSF	Parti Social Français
RAD	Reichsarbeitsdienst
RADwJ	Reichsarbeitsdienst-weibliche Jugend
RNCF	Regroupement National autour des Croix de Feu
RPF	Rassemblement du Peuple Français
SFIO	Section Française de l'Internationale Ouvrière
SPES	Société de Préparation et d'Education Sportive
STO	Service du Travail Obligatoire
UFCS	Union Féminine Civique et Social
UFSF	Union Française pour le Suffrage des Femmes
UNC	Union Nationale des Combattants
UNVF	Union Nationale pour le Vote des Femmes
VN	Volontaires Nationaux

POLITICAL BELIEF IN FRANCE, 1927–1945

INTRODUCTION

REPUBLICANISM, IMPERIALISM, AND POLITICAL AND SOCIAL

ACTION IN METROPOLITAN FRANCE AND THE EMPIRE

In the spring of 1938, amidst international turmoil concerning Nazi Germany's annexation of Austria, news about the high-profile show trials in the Soviet Union, and an increasingly bitter divide between anticolonial nationalists and French supporters of empire, nineteen Parisian university students traveled to Algeria for their Easter break. The young women were sent by the far Right Croix de Feu/PSF, which at the time was the largest political movement in French history.[1] Upon seeing Algeria's rich history and the beauty of its countryside for the first time, one of them, Marivic Duval, remarked, "We were at last able to measure and understand the colonizing efforts of so many generations of French who came here to make a Greater France."[2] She went on to express awe at the lush grasslands of the Mitidja plain, the Catholic basilica in Algiers, Roman ruins, and a fifth-century Christian mausoleum at Tipasa. She also made derogatory comments about the "dirty" and "veiled and prattling women" at an Arab cemetery and a souk in Algiers. Duval's travel descriptions echoed tropes common in travel writing, yet the university students' experiences were remarkable for several reasons. They were sent as emissaries by the Croix de Feu/PSF's metropolitan leadership to quell discord between the movement's Algerian and metropolitan sections, much of which stemmed from the Algerian Croix de Feu/PSF's violence, virulent anti-Semitism, and hatred of Algerian nationalism. While metropolitan leaders believed that the young, educated, nationalistic women best represented the movement, the extremism of the Algerian sections marginalized women to such an extent that settler women lacked the clout of their metropolitan counterparts. The travels thus reflected the prominent and influential place of women in the metropolitan Croix de Feu/PSF and the lack of settler women's authority and autonomy. It was opportunities such as these to participate in the political culture of Greater France that played a key role in why metropolitan women flocked to the Croix de Feu/PSF.

The university students' "vacation" raises several lines of inquiry. First, why did the Croix de Feu/PSF, which was founded in 1927 by far Right veterans and infamous for its militaristic parades and demonstrations, paramilitary violence, and hatred of communism, come to be dominated by women in metropolitan France but not the Maghreb? Why were metropolitan women able to obtain high rates of autonomy and authority, and what role did men have in this transformation? Finally, if women were able to transform the Croix de Feu/PSF, what role did the massive movement play in the conservative shift of French political culture in the late–Third Republic and Vichy period? The answers to these questions are rooted in the ways in which the conservative and reactionary women and men who participated in the Croix de Feu/PSF viewed their role in the politics, culture, and society of Greater France. Indeed, they operated in the political cultures of French republicanism, seeking to appropriate the principles of universalism and popular sovereignty for their own ends. One prominent Croix de Feu/PSF supporter, Nadine de La Rocque, explained it this way in 1934: "'Republic' is a very large word, which leaves considerable space for different modes of government." Depending on the general will of the people, she maintained, "the 'Republic' can comport itself to dictatorship, fascism, or socialism."[3] To examine the key role that empire and gender played in the Croix de Feu/PSF's use of republican principles at this critical moment in French history, we must first understand the historical context in which they operated.

HISTORICAL CONTEXT: THE ETHNORELIGIOUS AND GENDERED HIERARCHIES OF GREATER FRANCE

One of the most significant aspects of the 1789 French Revolution was the ways in which revolutionaries sought to create a new way of thinking about nationhood that was based upon universalist ideas. In 1792 the revolutionary government issued two decrees that formed the basis of French republicanism. One promised "fraternity and help to all peoples who wish to recover their liberty," while the other stated that France would establish "free and popular governments in any territory it occupied."[4] In articulating the principles of the republic—*liberté, égalité, fraternité*—in this way, revolutionary leaders sought to spread republican values beyond the borders of France and thus created a civilizing mission that centered around universalism and assimilation. In 1798 Napoleon Bonaparte led the French invasion of Egypt and justified his actions by using these principles.[5] However, the practicalities of subjecting indigenous people to French control undermined Napoleon's universalist claims that the French sought to preserve individual liberty. These events helped shape France's development in the nineteenth and twentieth centuries. The legacy of the revolutionary years—both that of republican imperialism and Bonapartism—established the frameworks for the ways in which generations of French people would understand their role in the nation and the world.

The French conquest of Algeria, which began in 1830, derived in part from the revolutionary era's ideas about liberty, the civilizing mission, and assumptions of French cultural superiority. Haunted by the Atlantic revolutions and the collapse of slavery in Haiti, a new generation of French believed they could create a different type of empire that allowed social and civic virtue to flourish by lifting up indigenous people and teaching them the value of work. However, French encroachments into Arab territories sparked a prolonged resistance beginning in 1839, which, for soldiers and the metropolitan public alike, reinforced "racist views of Algeria's supposedly ferocious native inhabitants."[6] The French military used brutal tactics, especially the *razzia,* to terrorize local populations by raiding their homes and villages, killing their livestock, and destroying their land, which led to the decimation and dislocation of many communities. As Jennifer Sessions points out, war became intertwined with ideas about France's civilizing abilities.[7]

As the conquest proceeded violently, metropolitan officials encouraged emigration by male citizens to settle the new land and build up its labor force for state-planned infrastructure and agricultural projects. There were cases of women's migration as well, especially women religious, although they faced barriers that were unique to colonial spaces. For example, Emilie de Vialar established a new religious order in Algeria that, following postrevolutionary trends, broke with the traditions of cloister to provide welfare and educational services. Vialar believed that aiding women and children from all ethnoreligious backgrounds was especially important.[8] However, disregarding protests from settlers and indigenous residents, the bishop of Algiers expelled Vialar over disagreements about episcopal authority and the bishop's aggressive efforts to convert Muslims despite a French governmental ban against such actions.[9] Believing that good works were the best way to bring people to Catholicism, Vialar moved to Tunisia, where her order remained the only one for over forty years. After her expulsion, Church leaders supported orders that were more compliant to diocesan authority and worked in settler rather than in Muslim communities, which the Church generally regarded as religiously intransigent.[10] In Tunisia, while Vialar's order served as a model for providing social services, it remained the only source of organizing for women religious, which reflected wider trends in religiously inspired social action.[11] Throughout the nineteenth and twentieth centuries, the Church cast missionary work as a crusade and thus a masculine endeavor.[12] The delay in women's emigration to North Africa, combined with the hypermasculine political culture carved out by war and the state's emphasis on male emigration, would have significant ramifications on the development of social action in the French Maghreb well into the twentieth century.

Algeria became France's most important settler colony and was designated an integral part of France by the Second Republic (1848–1851), which forced colonial administrators to grapple with the status of European migrants and indigenous people. A key part of the process of making Algeria French was the 1865 *senatus consulte,* which contributed to the creation of ethnoreligious hierarchies between settlers, indigenous elites who benefited from French rule, and the majority indigenous community. The law granted Muslim and Jewish men citizenship, but only if they were willing to cede their personal status, which amounted to apostasy. The modification of the law in 1870, which granted practicing Jews citizenship, drove a wedge between Jewish and Muslim communities and reflected the sentiments of many French: being a practicing Muslim was incompatible with being a French citizen. While the law institutionalized the assimilationist intent of the republican civilizing mission, it also reflected the long-standing tradition of viewing non-French people as backward and subjugating them to French rule.[13] Perhaps most significantly, the law had the unintended consequence of making the personal status a colonial construct and point of vigorous debate among indigenous activists, colonial reformers, and pro-empire activists through the Second World War.

When the Third Republic came to power in 1870, its leaders used the idea of the civilizing mission to establish civilian rule in Algeria and expand France's colonial holdings in sub-Saharan Africa, southeast Asia, the South Pacific, and North Africa. Greater France now included the metropole, colonies for settlement, and colonies for economic exploitation. By 1900, proponents of empire emphasized that Greater France was one hundred million strong, which included forty million citizens and sixty million colonial subjects. At the heart of the French colonial state was the *indigénat,* a set of administrative sanctions that were first established in Algeria in 1881 and applied throughout the colonies in the early twentieth century.[14] Gregory Mann explains that the *indigénat* was "based on rule by decree, enacted in often arbitrary and sometimes spectacular punishments, and concerned primarily with asserting administrative power."[15] In its original iteration in Algeria, the *indigénat* comprised thirty-three infractions that included sanctions against Muslims who were supposedly disrespectful to French officials or the French Republic, were accused of challenging forced labor, refused to "fight forest fires or grasshoppers," and allegedly failed to express goodwill when paying taxes.[16] Over time, the sanctions comprising the *indigénat* expanded and contracted, thus shifting the boundaries between the statuses of subject and citizen, which made the *indigénat* a primary (and changing) marker of difference between indigenous people and the "French."[17] Moreover, while the *indigénat* was not technically applied to protectorates like Tunisia (established in 1881) and Morocco (established in 1912), some of the codes that set limits on behavior were transferred. For this reason, reforming the "laws of exception"—codes that applied to Muslim subjects but not to the French or their indigenous elite collaborators—were primary goals for indigenous reformers in North Africa.

Such systematically discriminatory practices contributed to the French public's support for imperial expansion. Rates of migration increased and colonial explorers and administrators achieved celebrity status as heroes who spread the glories of French civilization.[18] Masculinity was one of the defining features of colonialism; many French defined Europeanness through the self-control of a civilized gentleman who was a father and the head of the family, which perpetuated long-standing stereotypes of Arabs as supposedly savage natives.[19] In Algeria the passing from military to civilian control transformed settler communities by increasing the rates at which the colonial state appropriated land from Arabs and Berbers, which in turn increased women's emigration from France.[20] While some women traveled independently, most joined male family members and entered a hypermasculine culture marked by ethnoreligious hierarchies.

While metropolitan women used republican conceptions of social rights to expand their spheres of influence, the delay in women's emigration to North Africa altered the development of a metropolitan-style civil society. Catholic social services, for instance, played a key role in civil society in metropolitan France. In Algeria, however, reflective of Vialar's struggles, such services were smaller in scale and aimed at settlers.[21] Moreover, professional opportunities for women, namely nursing and social work, were also limited. Well into the twentieth century, public health campaigns in Algeria required metropolitan medical personnel because there were not enough indigenous and settler women to provide services.[22] Despite these limitations, women in the colonies nevertheless played key roles as cultural vectors in disseminating French values through modes of sociability and interaction with indigenous elites.[23] In gaining access to domestic spaces that were off-limits to men, women became critical agents of empire. Colonial officials and women's groups alike believed that women's domestic influences would prevent miscegenation and promote racial purity by safeguarding Europeanness. Both groups maintained that marriage would regulate men's sexual desires, making them more suitable for citizenship.[24] Proponents of women's emigration thus believed that it would enable the foundation of settler families, which, as in the metropolitan context, provided the basic "cell" of French society. Organizations were subsequently created that promoted women's emigration. By the interwar period, the sex ratios were essentially even.[25]

The 1930s were the apogee in the history of metropolitan support for empire and settler society in North Africa.[26] Many settlers in Algeria, Morocco, and Tunisia thought of themselves as fundamentally different from their metropolitan counterparts. Settler communities in Algeria, for instance, were characterized by a vibrant urban culture and literary scene dominated by the popular authors who contributed to the *algérianité* movement.[27] *Algérianiste* writers—mostly men but some women—claimed that generations of contact with Algerian soil made European Algerians a distinct race. They looked back to the migrants who settled Algeria, most of whom came from Italy, Spain, and Malta, to claim that they represented a "unique racial fusion" that was more Latin than French. This view of race contributed directly to settler extremism, which was so profound that Samuel Kalman has argued that it represented a specific form of sociopolitical action: colonial fascism. Pointing to settlers' xenophobia, anti-Semitism, authoritarianism, and frequent use of violence, Kalman maintains that race and gender were at the heart of colonial fascism.[28]

Interwar Tunisia and Morocco also had powerful settler communities, and although the *algérianiste* movement was absent, the ethnoreligious backgrounds of settlers led many of them to believe that they were superior to Arabs, Jews, and Berbers. Neither protectorate pursued assimilation, favoring instead association and indirect rule whereby a resident general ruled in consultation with indigenous elites and the monarch.[29] In practice, the French systematically marginalized the ruling bureaucracies and the Tunisian Bey and Moroccan Sultan. French emigration to Tunisia was slow, which prompted authorities to offer naturalization to other European settlers, especially Italians, who, until the interwar period, were the dominant European nationality. By 1926 the French population counted 71,000 although it was outnumbered by 90,000 Italians, a significant number Maltese British, and 50,000 Jews; the population of nearly two million Muslims dwarfed European settlers.[30] In Morocco in 1936, 202,500 Europeans comprised 3 percent of a total population of roughly 6,245,000.[31] The Algerian settler community was much bigger; in 1926, 833,000 settlers comprised nearly 10 percent of the population.[32]

The demographic imbalances and ethnoreligious hierarchies played a key role in mobilizing indigenous reformers to demand legal equality, greater educational access, land protections, and indigenous language advocacy. Tunisia, historically a crossroads of the Mediterranean due to its geographical location, was home to one of the strongest and best-organized indigenous nationalist movements in Greater France.[33] Indigenous nationalism was strong in Morocco as well, as reformist sentiment united around the National Action Bloc in 1931.[34] Algeria's unique status as an integral part of France led directly to a large and diverse indigenous reform movement, which included activists who demanded reforms that would allow Muslims to integrate into French society, Muslim scholars who promoted Islamic revitalization, and, most radically, secular Arabs and Berbers who demanded independence.[35]

Another major group of reformers were French feminists living in metropolitan France and North Africa, many of whom believed that settlers and the state were more in need of "civilizing" than Arabs and Berbers.[36] Metropolitan feminist groups created sections throughout North Africa, which increased women's prominence in Maghrebi public spaces. Feminist activism was most influential in the early 1930s before declining at mid-decade in the face of settler extremism. The North African sections of metropolitan feminist groups were more humanistic than suffragist due to the complexities of suffrage at the local level.[37] While some feminists contended that in comparison to the French Civil Code, the Quran granted women "considerable financial and legal autonomy," others demanded that the French continue their civilizing work and apply the Civil Code to Algeria to end polygyny and child marriage, and increase Muslim women's access to education.[38]

Settler intransigence combined with indigenous and feminist demands for reform put colonial officials in a precarious position. In Algeria a key way that administrators responded was to redress the decades-long neglect of social ser-vices by strengthening state-provided welfare. In metropolitan France, such services were decentralized and marked by the civil activities of social Catholics, republican solidarists, and mutual aid societies. However, the delay in women's emigration played a role in the decision of Algerian officials to tie welfare services to hospitals and assign doctors to oversee their organization, which acknowledged the lack of private services and limited the authority of the few social workers and nurses in Algeria.[39] This masculinized social model differed from the one in metropolitan France, where social action was one of the few spheres of activity in which women had more influence than men. Moreover, the virility and strength that formed many settlers' self-identification increased their hostility to social workers and psychiatrists, whose mere presence suggested weakness in one's body and spirit. Tensions between social service providers and settlers, combined with inefficiencies in the organization of aid, led the government to restructure the Algerian public health system in the 1930s, which privileged medical therapies rather than metropolitan-style social interventions.[40] While settler women obtained higher profiles in the public sphere due to increasing employment opportunities in the service sectors, professions dominated by women remained marginalized by the structure of the Algerian public health system.[41] Authorities dedicated large sums of money for programs to educate the European population about the dangers of madness and death that "plagued the urban poor," while leaving the social welfare systems to languish because they were housed in underfunded mental hygiene dispensaries.[42]

The reform efforts of indigenous activists, feminists, and the state, combined with the intransigence of far Right settlers, have led several historians to call 1936 a watershed year in the history of Algeria.[43] In May the Popular Front, an "antifascist" coalition of Communists, Socialists, and Radical Republicans, was elected in metropolitan France. The Popular Front was committed to enacting reforms that broadened protections for the working classes and eased some of the most draconian restrictions on colonial subjects. The prospect of such reforms sparked intense backlash by extreme Right settlers and encouraged indigenous reformers to believe that finally, the French government might be willing to consider substantive reforms. Indeed, the rise of communism had galvanized secular indigenous activists, as some colonial subjects identified with communist conceptions of oppression and revolution. Immediately after the election of the Popular Front, Muslim reformers organized the first gathering of its kind in Algeria—the Algerian Muslim Congress—to demand equality before the law, the protection of Muslim personal status, freedom of religion and the press, and equitable access to citizenship. The Popular Front was committed to empire and proposed a more moderate set of reforms that became known as the Blum-Violette Bill. But the prospect of such change was too much for many settlers, who essentially declared war on Muslims and the Popular Front.

HISTORIOGRAPHICAL CONTEXT:

THE RISE OF THE CROIX DE FEU/PSF, REPUBLICANISM,

AND THE CIVILIZING MISSION IN THE 1930S

The group that galvanized settlers in Algeria, Tunisia, and Morocco during this critical time was the Croix de Feu/PSF. In 1937, its widely read North African newspaper, *La Flamme,* declared that the threat to Greater France was existential and had shifted from "red to green … from the sickle to the crescent."[44] Not only would such fear of Islam characterize the politics of the far Right for the remainder of the century, but the role of the Croix de Feu/PSF in French political culture reflected long-standing tensions in French republicanism itself. The complexity of republicanism was revealed in the Third Republic's status as what Gary Wilder has called an "imperial nation-state."[45] For Wilder, the Third Republic was more than Frederick Cooper's "empire-State" because it was governed by a parliamentary system based upon popular sovereignty.[46] Indeed, Wilder argues that metropolitan and colonial societies were a part of an integrated social and political system characterized by the flow of ideas, people, and goods, which demonstrated France's "dual character" as a parliamentary republic and authoritarian colonial power.[47] Following Wilder's work, some scholars have argued that republicanism and exclusion were not paradoxes, but that exclusions based upon one's particular background were built into republicanism itself and operated alongside universalism.[48] In contrast, others defend republicanism by contending that it was rejected in the colonial context.[49]

The concept of a "dual character" Third Republic was especially clear in the role that the Croix de Feu/PSF played in the political cultures of Greater France. Indeed, Nadine de La Rocque maintained that republicanism was defined by the will of the people; the university students believed that their travels revealed the civilizing mission of republican imperialism. In these ways, Croix de Feu/ PSF supporters appropriated republicanism according to what they believed it to be. While supporters may have rejected the ideal of individual rights as it was embedded in the *Rights of Man* they supported the declaration's emphasis on popular sovereignty so long as elites represented and led the people.[50] In metropolitan France such distinctions led members to support what they considered to be authoritarian republicanism. In North Africa, however, pervasive hostility to universal individual rights played a key role in settlers' use of systematic violence to defend racially based hierarchies. Although in some cases French settlers, Arabs, Berbers, and Jews believed that the acculturation of Muslims and Jews into France was possible, the North African Croix de Feu/PSF's denial of integration on the basis of ethnicity and religion was more typical. The standards for assimilation that settlers expected were so rigid that they precluded participation in the movement by practicing Muslims and Jews. By comparison, the metropolitan Croix de Feu/PSF championed French cultural superiority yet accepted that it was possible for assimilated Jews and Muslims to be French so long as they accepted that France was a Christian civilization.

This book is framed by two primary lines of argument that contribute to these debates over French republicanism. First, it seeks to show that the Croix de Feu/ PSF's conception of integration was in the republican tradition of universalist assimilation but recast in religious rather than secular terms. As Nadine de La Rocque argued, if the general will of the people held that France was a Christian civilization, it was the republic's duty to reflect that belief. For many supporters, it was not simply that Catholicism was a marker of French identity, but something more transcendent—that French identity itself was revealed by France's status as the primordial Christian civilization. This belief structured the Croix de Feu/PSF's ethnoreligious nationalism, which was a "mystique" that supporters claimed was self-evident and provided them with the language to undermine assertions by indigenous reformers and the Popular Front that it was possible to champion one's own ethnoreligious particularism and be French. Second, historians generally agree that while the metropolitan Croix de Feu/PSF was authoritarian, it transitioned away from paramilitarism as its supporters worked within a democratic framework to achieve their goals.[51] This book argues that women played the determinate role in transforming the league from a paramilitary veterans group to a social reform movement, as they convinced male leaders that social action would garner more popular support than paramilitary violence. By 1935, "Social First!" was one of the movement's most prominent slogans and revealed its social mission. However, empowering women as agents of social action was difficult in the hypermasculine political cultures of North Africa, where the professional and civil structures that metropolitan women used to expand their spheres of influence were underdeveloped. Indeed, the violence and ethnoreligious hierarchies that defined colonial rule undermined the egalitarian aspects of French republicanism that metropolitan women used to expand their social and civic rights.

The Croix de Feu/PSF's key role in contemporary debates over integration and the politics of the French imperial nation-state—or what its supporters called Greater France—raises the question of why so few studies exist on the French Right and empire. Given the influence of conservatives, it is important to understand their views of the relationship between republicanism and empire. A key reason for the scholarly neglect of this critical topic is due neither to a lack of sources nor the notion that conservatives had little to say about the empire, but to the development of multiple fields. First, Alice Conklin and Julia Clancy-Smith have shown that historians of Africa, informed by the methods of social history, tended to emphasize anticolonial nationalism and independence from European colonizers. Second, the work of historians of France and historians of French colonialism tended not to overlap except in dramatic cases such as the Algerian War.[52] Third, scholarship on the French Right was mired in the question of whether fascism was strong in France, a debate that hinged on differing definitions of fascism and had wide-ranging implications for French conceptions of their own national identity.[53] The Croix de Feu/PSF serves as a critical and as yet unexplored way to bridge the fields of the Right, empire, and women and gender. As we shall see, women were marginalized in the North African Croix de Feu/PSF, which had significant implications for the extremity of its politics. This argument supports Kalman's findings that there was a colonial type of fascism, extending the concept of colonial fascism to Tunisia and Morocco. Indeed, while metropolitan male Croix de Feu/PSF leaders were willing to cede control of policy formation and implementation to women, the movement's North African supporters refused to grant women the same influence as their metropolitan counterparts.

The ways in which Croix de Feu/PSF supporters viewed political and social action reflected the circulation of the movement's ideas, organizing strategies, and membership across borders. Because the Croix de Feu/PSF operated within the imperial nation-state, it played a central role in contributing to contemporary debates over republican imperialism, and its two major doctrinal components, assimilation and association. While at one time historians believed that French colonial policy shifted from assimilation in the nineteenth century to association in the twentieth century, scholars now emphasize that both operated at the same time alongside each other.[54] A key component of universalism, assimilation emphasized that the French could facilitate the process by which indigenous people became French by absorbing their political, economic, and judicial institutions. Association, on the other hand, was based upon the notion that indigenous people were incapable of becoming French and thus their political, agricultural, legal, and cultural traditions needed to be preserved.

While the Croix de Feu/PSF was consistent in championing the civilizing mission, it is difficult to classify the movement's approach to empire as assimilationist or associationist. First, in policy statements, metropolitan leaders aligned with the majority of French in promoting the civilizing mission and the universalist presumptions therein; they often argued that it took centuries to make the provinces "French" and that patience was needed in the case of Arabs, Berbers, sub-Saharan Africans, and others who comprised the vast empire. More progressive positions according to the standards at the time included the Blum-Violette proposal, which recognized that elite practicing Muslims could be full citizens, and the demands of the Algerian Muslim Congress to extend full citizenship rights to all Muslims. Critically, the Croix de Feu/PSF's nominal support for assimilation made it one of the period's premier defenders of empire, as its supporters sought to maintain Greater France in perpetuity while combatting all reform efforts. Second, metropolitan Croix de Feu/PSF supporters used culture to undermine growing anticolonial critiques of forced labor and discrimination, brought about by the *senatus consulte* and *indigénat,* by celebrating the glories of the civilizing mission. Much like the metropolitan policy pronouncements, the movement's cultural productions sought to ensure that Greater France would remain permanently in its contemporary state. Third, while ideas about empire were important in the metropolitan Croix de Feu/PSF, it was in the colonies that the movement's precepts took their most extreme form. The Croix de Feu/PSF became the leading proponent among settlers of the view that neither Muslims nor Jews could be French *and* maintain their ethnoreligious particularism. Such exclusion combined strong elements of association with exceedingly tepid support for eventual assimilation through what policy makers called "adapt and assimilate." The leadership of the North African Croix de Feu/PSF appropriated the movement's Social First! mission by claiming that Muslim society needed to evolve in its own time. Only after it "adapted" socially to the precepts of France's Christian civilization could it then begin the process of assimilation. In this way, the movement's leaders appeased associationist settlers while maintaining the universalist intent of the civilizing mission.

HISTORICAL CONTEXT: WOMEN'S SOCIAL AND POLITICAL ACTION IN METROPOLITAN FRANCE

The legacy of 1789 was as complex for the ways in which women and gender shaped metropolitan France as it was for France's relationship with its empire. During the Revolution, women earned citizenship that entitled them to civil rights such as equal inheritance and equal access to divorce.[55] A loosening of restrictions on the press enabled women to create over fifty political clubs that published newspapers and pamphlets demanding equal political rights. Literature written by women increased dramatically as well.[56] Despite these gains, women were denied full citizenship; they were designated as "passive" citizens bereft of voting rights and all of the benefits therein. When "universal" suffrage was instituted in 1792 to elect the First Republic, women were the only group of marginalized people—Jews, Protestants, free blacks, the working classes—to be excluded from voting. Moreover, when strong supporters of the idea of a republic, the Jacobins, came to power, they sought to diminish the Catholic Church's privileged status by initiating a dechristianization campaign. The dechristianization movement exacerbated tensions between supporters of the Republic and Catholics, many of whom were women, and hastened the "feminization of religion" that would continue throughout the nineteenth century.[57]

After Napoleon crowned himself emperor in 1804, the state instituted the highly restrictive Civil Code, which stripped women of the civil rights that they had earned during the Revolution. Originating in Roman law, the Civil Code declared that the family was the fundamental social unit and designated the father as the head of the family.[58] The Civil Code defined women as minors before the law and required them to obey their husbands, which denied married women's civil capacity and would relegate them to secondary legal status well into the twentieth century. In addition to assigning women to the same status as children and the cognitively disabled, Napoleon further stripped the Catholic Church of its political power by subordinating it to the state. In creating spaces for women as social and civic actors while denying their political rights the republican tradition coming out of the Revolution cast full citizenship as masculine. However, in the context of the deeply regressive nature of Bonapartism, republicanism's emphasis on women's social and civic rights led many women to support republican ideas as the best path toward emancipation.[59]

Religion also played a central role in women's activism in the nineteenth and twentieth centuries. Women religious, for example, challenged notions of paternal authority and inequitable property relations, and in doing so, undermined women's secondary status in civil law as it pertained to marriage and the family.[60] While some women used religion to challenge patriarchal hierarchies, others used it to broaden their own spheres of influence within such hierarchies. In the Nord, for example, bourgeois Catholic women helped shape civil society by organizing educational programs and charity networks that provided aid to the needy and included *crèches, ouvroirs,* kindergartens, and recreational opportunities.[61] Against the backdrop of industrialization, these women contested republican secularism by drawing the working classes to Catholic domestic values. Sylvie Fayet-Scribe has demonstrated that this charity moved toward social action in the 1890s with the papal encyclical *Rerum Novarum,* which established the Church's official response to socialism: the doctrine of social Catholicism.[62] Seeking to alleviate the miseries of industrialization by addressing the social concerns of the burgeoning working classes, the Church promoted access to education, social protections with regard to work, unemployment aid, and welfare provisions. Because Catholic women had traditionally devoted themselves to such services, they were at the front lines of social action.

The rise of social Catholicism combined with the Vatican's official acceptance of republicanism in 1892—known as the first *ralliement*—transformed Catholics' relationship with democratic politics.[63] As many Catholics sought to integrate themselves into the political structures and government of the Third Republic, the most staunch supporters of the Republic—now called the Radicals—took steps to regulate the ability of the Church to influence politics. One of the most important examples of republican anticlericalism was the 1901 Law on Associations. While the government sought to regulate the religious congregations by subjecting them to state authority (prefectoral authorization), the law had the adverse effect of galvanizing Catholics, of whom 70 percent of the practicing faithful were women.[64]

Indeed, many Catholic women viewed the law as further evidence of republican oppression, which spurred a new era of organizing.[65] Shortly after the law's passage, Catholic women created the Ligue des Femmes Françaises (LFF). Looking to influence politicians ahead of the 1902 elections, LFF women dispensed funds and distributed tracts, brochures, and posters.[66] The elections failed to meet the LFF's goals, and while the Parisian LFF wanted to continue their engagement in politics (and thus accept the legitimacy of the Republic), the Lyon sections did not and focused instead on monarchism and spiritual pursuits, leading some sections to affiliate with the royalist Action Française.[67] The Paris branch broke off and formed the Ligue Patriotique des Françaises (LPDF). The LPDF was allied with the new Catholic party the Action Libérale Populaire (ALP), and sought to integrate Catholics into the Republican regime. The LFF and LPDF would be the primary vehicles for Catholic women's organizing into the 1930s, with the LFF growing to half a million supporters on the eve of the Great War and the LPDF growing to 1.5 million in 1932.[68] Women in these groups were further galvanized when the Third Republic officially separated Church and state in 1905 by pulling state funding from Catholic education, hospitals, and charities, which had the unintended consequence of leading them to become more autonomous.

World War I accelerated the changing relationship between Catholics and the Third Republic. Much of the nation mobilized in support of the war effort, as Catholics fought alongside republicans to defend France from the German invasion and provide aid to the people and communities devastated by the war.[69] France's most valuable territory was occupied, huge areas of land were destroyed, and the human cost of the war was horrific: 2.5 million casualties and 1.4 million deaths, which constituted 10 percent of the male population and a significant portion of the male youth. Republican officials used Catholic social service networks to gain access to a variety of communities, which helped ease some of the tensions between Catholics and the Republic. Continuing reconciliation between the two groups was especially important when the Bolshevik revolution broke out in Russia, raising the specter of a workers' revolution in France.

After the war, the Vatican declared its support for women's suffrage, which spurred the creation of several Catholic women's suffrage organizations and led the LPDF and LFF to change their platforms and support the vote.[70] The two groups merged in 1933 at the request of the pope, forming the two million–strong Ligue Féminine d'Action Catholique Française (LFACF). While the LFACF supported suffrage its members did not engage in advocacy on the issue. Instead, their top priority was to rechristianize France through the family. Emphasizing women's domestic and maternal nature, the group's supporters engaged in the types of social action that Catholic women had done for generations: providing welfare and health services, creating youth clubs and leisure activities, organizing catechisms and pilgrimages, and facilitating liaisons between churches and civil groups.[71] Conservative Catholics who wanted to engage directly in politics by advocating for suffrage created two new groups. Established in 1920, the Union Nationale pour le Vote des Femmes (UNVF) worked to win women suffrage rights and promoted women's right to work. A more conservative group, the Union Féminine Civique et Social (UFCS), also supported suffrage but questioned married women's right to work and perpetuated a hierarchical view of the wife and husband within the family.[72] In this way, by the interwar period some Catholics were reconciled to the Republic, others remained hostile to it, and women's social action had made significant contributions to civil society.

While in terms of numbers Catholic women's social action outstripped feminist organizing, the latter was still a critical arena of women's activism.[73] The 1860s were a turning point for feminists, as republican opponents of Napoleon's III's Second Empire created organizations that would "outlive their founders."[74] By 1900 suffrage campaigns were "well-established" in feminist circles.[75] In addition to suffrage, many feminists sought to improve the lives of mothers and children by demanding social interventions such as state-supported maternity leave, state-mandated insurance programs, and improvements in women's working conditions.[76] These concerns aligned with those of socialists and conservative Catholics, which resulted in a strong push for social and civic rights, or what several historians have noted was a clear articulation of social citizenship.[77] However, state-sponsored welfare was a double-edged sword for feminists, as the republican state regularly attempted to regulate motherhood. In response to high rates of infant mortality and other reproductive issues, the legislature passed laws restricting women's right to work. Although women were not compensated for lost wages, their work day was limited to ten hours, they were banned from working at night, and girls were prohibited from working in mines, pits, and quarries.[78] For these reasons, women's right to work would be a major concern for the women's movement well into the twentieth century.

By the interwar period, women activists thought of themselves in several ways; some identified as feminists, while many Catholics rejected the feminist label yet sought to expand women's role and influence in French society. Around a dozen major organizations demanded the attention of policy makers.[79] Of these, five groups were secular feminists who had two major priorities: winning suffrage rights and reforming the Civil Code.[80] While some feminists claimed equal rights on the basis of classic liberalism, others promoted women's rights by emphasizing the unique contributions that women made to society based upon their biological differences with men.[81] Whatever the rationale, secular feminist groups drew a membership of nearly 200,000 and pushed feminism into the mainstream. However, to the dismay of activists pressing for suffrage rights, the Senate refused to pass legislation that would have granted women the vote in 1922. The persistence of a rigid conception of the ideology of separate spheres among Radical politicians played a key role. Many of them cited women's supposedly domestic nature, aptitude for social action, and tendency toward higher rates of religious belief than men, as key factors for their vote against women's suffrage. The fact that major Catholic women's groups rallied to the cause of suffrage and became politicized magnified fears among Radicals that women's suffrage would provide an entrée for the Church to return to politics.[82] Despite these setbacks, feminist efforts were rewarded when the government established a commission in 1925 to address a long-standing feminist initiative: overhauling the Civil Code to redress women's subordination in marriage. While the commission initially produced a series of egalitarian proposals, the process was so contentious that when the reforms passed through the legislature in 1938, feminists had to accept that men were the *chef de famille* in order to win civil capacity.[83] Championing a hierarchical conception of the family was the position promoted by Catholic women's groups, which forced feminists to accept a compromise that many disdained.

A fundamental distinction between feminists and the wider women's movement thus emerged during the interwar period. Feminists believed in equality between the spouses while Catholic groups argued for women's civil capacity within the framework of the patriarchal family. Such challenges led to significant divisions between feminist groups over which reforms should be priorities and which strategies were effective. The most challenging question for secular feminists was the most pressing political question of the interwar period: whether to push for parliamentary reform or accept the republican status quo.[84] In concrete terms, feminists had to decide whether to support the Radicals, who repeatedly voted against women's suffrage bills in the Senate, or align with conservatives who supported suffrage but not because they believed that women were entitled to the same rights as men. For example, Cécile Brunschvicg, the leader of France's largest feminist organization, the 100,000-strong Union Française pour le Suffrage des Femmes (UFSF), worked tirelessly to promote suffrage and reform the Civil Code. She was willing to work with Radical politicians to do so, but refused to work with conservative leaders like Louis Marin, who was a leading supporter of women's suffrage as the head of the conservative Fédération Républicaine. One of the leading equal rights feminists of the period, Maria Vérone of France's second largest feminist organization, the Ligue Française pour le Droit des Femmes (LFDF, 25,000 members), assailed Brunschvicg for supporting the party that consistently blocked suffrage. Instead, Vérone welcomed any politician who supported suffrage rights, including Marin.

This was the dilemma that French feminists faced. Marin was a powerful conservative and supporter of the Republic; he headed the ethnographic museum and played a leading role in asserting an essentialist conception of French national identity that was traditional, provincial, Catholic, and imperial.[85] While Brunschvicg's secular republicanism exacerbated her hostility to Catholic politicians like Marin, Vérone pointed to Marin's tireless support for women's suffrage and promotion of legislation that held fathers accountable for their children.[86] Seeking to break from such dichotomies, some feminists favored the direct action tactics of British and American feminists. The most influential was Louise Weiss, who created the Femme Nouvelle in 1934 to engage in direct action on the issue that mattered most to her—suffrage. Weiss insisted that until the government answered to women, feminists would always have to face the difficult choices that divided Vérone and Brunschvicg.

Despite differences over strategy, Brunschvicg's UFSF and Vérone's LFDF worked together in the federation that united secular feminists. The Conseil National des Femmes Françaises (CNFF) fought one of the most daunting challenges that feminists faced: a strident pronatalist movement. Since 1870 pronatalists had identified France's declining birthrate as an impending disaster and blamed women for shirking their patriotic duty by refusing to have children.[87] Citing the supposed demographic catastrophe of the Great War, the legislature passed one of the most restrictive laws on contraception in Europe, which made it illegal to advertise or sell devices related to female contraception and instituted harsh penalties for abortion providers.[88]

Pronatalists next set their sights on the "problem" of working mothers and initiated programs and legislation to strip women's right to work. The Catholic Church joined forces with the pronatalists in 1931 when Pope Pius XI issued *Quadragesimo*

Anno, which reaffirmed and expanded upon the doctrine of social Catholicism. The encyclical called for a "just salary" for workers—but only the husband—by locating the basic cell of society with the family and assigning breadwinner status to the husband, leaving the wife to domestic duties.[89] Pius stated that the "natural function" of women was to have children, a claim that found ready acceptance in pronatalist circles. Galvanized by the notion that married women's work was "against nature," pronatalists and Catholics campaigned to "return women to the home," which culminated in demands by a leading pronatalist, Charles Richet, to make women's work illegal.[90] In 1935 the Laval government fired women in public service who were married to functionaries.[91] The maternalism that feminist groups had used before the Great War to expand women's social rights had restricted to a rigid view of the ideology of separate spheres that reduced femininity to a domestically contained motherhood and masculinity to a public breadwinner status.[92] These conditions forced the CNFF to make the defense of married women's right to work its main focus in 1931.

The onset of the Great Depression in 1931 made this regressive time period for women even worse by exacerbating hostility to women's work. Unemployment and financial hardships hit the working classes especially hard.[93] Workers had to spend as much as 60 percent of their income on food, which made soup kitchens and clothing depots a key source of subsistence for many.[94] Crowded housing conditions brought about by a "rural exodus" during the 1920s caused Paris to have the highest rate of tuberculosis in Europe, and the majority of Parisians were classified as poor and indigent.[95] The government responded to the economic crisis in several ways, in particular with the policy of deflation, which included raising funds by lowering the salaries of civil servants and cutting the pensions of war veterans.[96] The government also passed welfare legislation in 1932, which expanded social insurance laws, mandated that all employers pay family allowances, and promoted natality by seeking to return women to the home.[97]

While feminists and the broader women's movement focused on winning suffrage rights, reforming the civil code, and protecting women's right to work, women who joined the secular far Right focused on a different set of issues based upon their participation in mixed-sex ultranationalist organizations that sought mass appeal. Gender ideology was central to the extraparliamentary organizations, known as "leagues," and similar to that of conservative Catholics, pronatalists, and conservative republicans.[98] They all emphasized anti-individualism and an organicist view of the national community. The basic cell of French society, they believed, was the family, which was hierarchically divided between the spouses. It was preferable for married women to remain in the home and raise children, although it was permissible for women to demonstrate their nurturing nature through social action in public space. Men were to act as breadwinners in the family and engage in political action. In contrast, feminists such as Brunschvicg, Vérone, and Weiss acknowledged the importance of the family, yet they contested the conservative gendered hierarchy by maintaining that equality-based marriages were an important—though not a primordial—form of social organization.[99]

Aside from similarities in the gender ideology of the leagues, there were important differences in the extent to which they mobilized women. The conservative Jeunesses Patriotes was created in 1924 in response to the election of the Cartel des Gauches (a partnership of Radical Republicans and Socialists).[100] The league established its Women's Section the same year, which, as Kevin Passmore has noted, was the first one since the LPDF broke with the ALP in 1906.[101] Following suit, the self-described fascist group, the Faisceau, established its Women's Section shortly after it was founded in 1925, a pattern that was replicated in the Christian democratic Parti Démocrate Populaire (created in 1924) and in several fascist groups of the 1930s.[102] Despite the existence of these Women's Sections, women's integration into the organizations' most important activities varied greatly. The three most prominent fascist leagues never effectively mobilized women nor did they have the will to do so.[103] In contrast, as Magali Della Sudda explains, the Jeunesses Patriotes espoused a "conservative model of a sexual division of militant activities instituted within conservative groupings since the beginning of the last century."[104] While women's activities centered on social action, suffrage was often on the agenda at league meetings, which reflected the high degree of status held by its Women's Section leader, the prominent lawyer, Marie-Thérèse Moreau.[105] Moreau was a well-known activist, and like several other high-profile women in the league, was also in the leadership circle of the UNVF, which meant that she supported suffrage and the *chef de famille* clause in the 1938 revision of the civil code.

In contrast to the conservatism of Jeunesses Patriotes and the UNVF, the hypermasculinity of the fascist leagues was reflected in the subordination of women in each group's organizational structures and their limited attention to advancing women's suffrage and reforming the civil code. For example, women could only join the civic section of the Faisceau, and its activities were not respected by men. Women lacked authority in the league and few of them attended its general meetings.[106] Reflecting the influence of pronatalism and Faisceau leaders' patri-archal view of the family, the organization proposed replacing the parliamentary system with assemblies that would be headed by soldiers, producers, and heads of families.[107] Solidarité Française and the Parti Populaire Française (PPF) also created Women's Sections with a similar division of labor and subordination of women. Women's influence in the Solidarité Française served both to dilute and legitimate the racist language that was common in its newspaper by including "feminine touches" such as recipes and emphasizing family life.[108] In the PPF, Women's Section leaders stated that communism would be uprooted by "hus-bands," not women, although women could contribute to alleviating the social conditions that allowed communism to prosper.[109] While women had influence in these hypermasculine groups, they remained unable to break through to positions of leadership and influence policy in ways similar to the Jeunesses Patriotes, and more significantly, the Croix de Feu/PSF.

HISTORIOGRAPHICAL CONTEXT: THE CROIX DE FEU/PSF IN FRENCH POLITICAL CULTURE

Reflecting the broad nature of women's conceptions of their own activism, histori-ans of feminism have proposed definitions of feminism that include pro-suffrage Catholic groups.[110] In contrast, historians of the Right have drawn distinctions between women's activism and feminism.[111] Passmore, for example, argues that the Catholic women who joined the LPDF espoused antifeminist arguments because they rejected feminist claims that women and men were equal.[112] For Passmore, this antifeminist tradition included Catholics like Moreau who, despite her role in the pro-suffrage UNVF, perpetuated a gender-based hierarchy by ad-vocating for a "masculine style of politics" and arguing that women would find their ultimate fulfillment as "the smiling queens of the home."[113] Conservative Catholics' perpetuation of gender hierarchies through the family, and thus politics, have led Della Sudda to distinguish between feminists who fought for suffrage rights as an *end* in itself (the demonstration of women and men's equality) and Catholics who demanded suffrage as a *means* "to establish laws that conformed to Christian principles."[114] Anne Cova shares the skepticism of Passmore and Della Sudda in conflating suffrage activism with feminism. In studying the LPDF and its successor, the LFACF, she explains, "Distinguishing between the opinions of

Catholic women and those of feminists is not always easy but nor is it possible to combine, for example, the LPDF, a conservative league, with feminist groups under the pretext that it demanded the right to vote for women."[115] Because the LPDF/LFACF emphasized duty rather than rights, the millions of women who supported the league saw no contradiction between following the pope's dictates by demanding suffrage and accepting women's subordination in marriage.

There remains a gap in this vibrant scholarship on the role of women and gender in the Third Republic and Vichy period: assessing the influence of the some 300,000 women who joined the Croix de Feu/PSF.[116] In terms of numbers, women's participation in the Croix de Feu/PSF remains unprecedented for a mixed-sex political movement, and therefore much remains to be learned about their impact on the group and its efforts to transform Greater France.[117] Moreover, some of the literature is less than accurate, which derives from the specific challenges that scholars face when working with sources on conservative women. Methodologically, historians of conservative women must use sources differently than historians of feminism.[118] Because feminists engaged directly in politics, they published newspapers, made public speeches, and distributed tracts and pamphlets that clearly articulated their positions on major issues. While conservative organizations had a lively press as well, the disjuncture between rhetoric and practice was greater in the Croix de Feu/PSF because of its tendency to essentialize gender through a binary and hierarchical sense of public and private. In the case of the Croix de Feu/PSF, the empirical story that archives reveal about conservative women differed greatly from materials published for consumption by readers who assumed patriarchal views of the family and public action.

The complex nature of sources is a key reason why historians have varied wildly in their assessments of the role of women in the Croix de Feu/PSF. The first position was established in two articles by Mary Jean Green, who relied on newspapers and literature to argue that while many women joined the Croix de Feu/PSF, they were marginalized as the movement sought its electoral breakthrough.[119] Kalman expanded upon Green's analysis by pointing to the most regressive aspects of the Croix de Feu/PSF's doctrine, specifically its pronatalism, which emphasized women's duty as housewife and mother.[120] In the only full-length monograph in English on the Croix de Feu/PSF, Sean Kennedy focuses on the movement's associational life to argue that leaders envisioned women's role in France as strengthening the nation's moral values through their place in the family, which conflated womanhood with domesticity.[121] All three scholars agree that women were marginalized and unable to significantly influence the movement's ideology, strategies, and tactics. In contrast, a second position has been developed by Passmore and Laura Lee Downs, who have applied the methods of women's and gender history to intensive archival study of women's activities in the Croix de Feu/PSF.[122] Their articles have demonstrated that women, while remaining at a disadvantage in a patriarchal movement, effectively expanded their sphere of influence by using social action to make "social politics" central to the Croix de Feu/PSF's most important activities.

As the first full-length study of women's role in the French far Right in the age of fascism, this book seeks to extend and qualify the second position through comparison with North Africa by arguing that women's transformation of the Croix de Feu/PSF required the support of male leadership and the structural advantages of metropolitan-style republican civil society. While the Croix de Feu began in a manner similar to other leagues—a hypermasculine organization for veterans that used paramilitarism to fight "threats" to Greater France—it experienced a critical turning point in March 1934. The creation of the league's Women's Section allowed it to initiate a unique path toward transforming French political culture. The most powerful woman in the Croix de Feu/PSF, Antoinette de Préval, led the Women's Section, which under her direction created a massive network of social services. These services comprised the Croix de Feu/PSF's "social action" and enabled the movement to intervene in French *culture* as much as French society. Indeed, it would be accurate to call its social action "sociocultural" action. Encouraged by its increasing membership and the popularity of its social services, Croix de Feu/PSF propagandists unveiled the new "Social First!" slogan in late 1935, which revealed the top priority that social action played in remaking France and taking power. The Croix de Feu/PSF's Social First! mission, combined with the formation of the Popular Front, led many women and men to flock to the movement in the mid-1930s.

The innovative nature of the Croix de Feu/PSF's sociocultural action was based upon a distinct gender ideology and played a critical role in the movement's rise to prominence. Women broadened the movement's gender ideology beyond maternalism and domesticity to argue that they were soldiers who would save France through social action in public spaces. This language of war had particular resonance given the movement's veteran origins as well as the fact that some women had participated in the Great War and most had family connections to soldiers. In casting women as foot soldiers operating in civic space, the Croix de

Feu/PSF subverted the women in the home movement and thus undermined the
dominance of the UFCS and LFACF among conservatives. The movement further
differentiated itself from the LFACF by not requiring members to be Catholic.
Yet such ecumenicalism only went so far. Croix de Feu/PSF ethnoreligious nationalism was reflected in supporters' hostility toward secular feminism; many
women and some men used the movement to promote rechristianization, which
revealed the porous boundaries between Catholic Action and the Croix de Feu/
PSF. Structurally, unlike in the leagues and parliamentary parties, Croix de Feu/
PSF women moved from being auxiliaries in separate sections to heading several
of the movement's most important social and cultural associations. Antoinette
de Préval was on the movement's central leadership council, and several other
women held leadership posts that gave them decision-making authority over male
leaders. None of the organizations mentioned thus far were structured in this
way. Moreover, unlike the Jeunesses Patriotes, the Croix de Feu/PSF believed that
women were on the front lines of fighting communism. Unlike secular feminists,
Croix de Feu/PSF members believed that activism was best done in the streets
through social programs, not at the ballot box. Finally, one of the Croix de Feu/
PSF's most distinctive aspects was the ways in which the movement drew men
into social action. By 1940 Croix de Feu/PSF social action was not relegated to a
secondary feminized sphere but was a critical strategy that required the participation of women and men working together to "save" France.

Despite the empowering aspects of the Croix de Feu/PSF's gender ideology, the
movement nevertheless developed strategies to delay critical reforms that would
have broadened politically marginalized groups' access to full citizenship. While
the movement's "adapt and assimilate" policy served to delay colonial subjects'
demands for reform, the movement created a key subgroup in 1936 (Civic Action)
that was based upon the idea that women needed a proper education before earning the right to vote. In both cases, the argument was the same: neither women
nor colonial subjects could earn full citizenship without a proper education. Additionally, the Croix de Feu/PSF supported the family vote, which was a measure
that pronatalists proposed to privilege large families at the expense of small ones
and single people by allowing parents to vote for their children (proposals varied
over which parent might control the votes). The family vote was yet another challenge to feminists who argued for suffrage as an individual right that recognized
equality between the sexes. Many Croix de Feu/PSF women, however, ignored the
question of voting rights. Préval, for one, believed that suffrage activism consti-

tuted political engagement—a useless endeavor characterized by feminism. For Préval, politics were petty and best transcended through social action. In these ways, the movement clearly reflected a long tradition of conservative activism whereby leaders sought to mobilize elite women and men to control the masses.[123] Social and cultural action was the path to earning elite status for those who were ethnoreligiously suitable, which was an idea that propelled the Croix de Feu/PSF to lead conservative resistance to reforms that would undermine the gendered and ethnoreligious hierarchies of the French imperial nation-state.

In championing social action, and in the case of the PSF running candidates in elections, the movement drove the declining support for democratic principles during the late 1930s.[124] It was likely that if the 1940 elections had taken place, the PSF would have gained the plurality of seats.[125] Politically, the Third Republic was increasingly authoritarian in using decree powers in the late 1930s to marginalize a gridlocked parliament. While the Vichy regime appropriated one of the Croix de Feu/PSF's most used slogans, *"Travail, Famille, Patrie,"* to illustrate its authoritarian nationalism, in the late 1930s, the Radicals took another of the Croix de Feu/PSF's slogans, "National Reconciliation," to align the party with the people rather than a dysfunctional parliament.[126] Culturally, the Croix de Feu/PSF's ethnoreligious nationalism bolstered the rationale behind a November 1938 decree that announced the creation of camps for "undesirables" and broadened the types of offences that allowed the government to deport foreigners.[127] In North Africa, while Vichy continued the late Third Republic's policies of persecuting anticolonial nationalists through a variety of restrictions, imprisonment, and exile, it went a step further in 1940 when it revoked the citizenship of 110,000 Algerian Jews.[128]

Despite these continuities, the late Third Republic and Vichy regime diverged from the most distinctive feature of the Croix de Feu/PSF: its mobilization of women and men for social action. Many Vichyites believed that rejuvenating France rested upon the traditional patriarchal family whereby women would remain at home and men would act as the breadwinners.[129] Indeed, the regime sought to prohibit women from divorcing and having abortions, limit their access to work and education, and channel their bodies for the sole use of maternity, all of which echoed the principles of the UFCS, LFACF, and Jeunesses Patriotes, but did align strongly with what Croix de Feu/PSF supporters believed was most important.[130] The fact that gender was one of the only portions of the Croix de Feu/PSF's ideology and practice that Vichy did not adopt reveals the powerfully entrenched patriarchal modes of thinking of 1930s and 1940s France.

* * *

The following chapters explore how Croix de Feu/PSF women made the metropolitan movement an innovative force by creating a sociocultural program that became central to its political strategy of garnering popular support and taking power. Capitalizing upon a metropolitan civil society that was shaped by women's social action, Croix de Feu/PSF women designed and implemented welfare services such as soup kitchens, clothing depots, and health clinics. Their cultural activities comprised physical education programs, social centers, summer camps, and entertainment such as travel, sophisticated charity bazaars, and shows at exhibitions like the 1937 World's Fair. In contrast to this vibrant metropolitan enterprise, in the Maghreb, women were only able to organize soup kitchens, clothing depots, and rudimentary medical provisions. While the North African Croix de Feu/PSF claimed a Social First! strategy for taking power, its male leaders limited severely women's ability to create a sociocultural program similar to the one in metropolitan France. It was not simply that Social First! was expressed differently in North Africa, but that women's transformation of the metropolitan Croix de Feu/PSF enabled the movement's North African branches to use the new Social First! language to defend old ideas, namely, that practicing Muslims could not be French. The Croix de Feu/PSF's Social First! mission, and the "adapt and assimilate" policy at the heart of it, helped galvanize settlers in the Maghreb to reject reforms initiated by indigenous groups and the Popular Front, which played a key role in driving Arab and Berber activists towards anticolonialism. Women's marginalization in settler politics thus illustrated the hypermasculine and authoritarian political cultures of Algeria, Morocco, and Tunisia and the Croix de Feu/PSF's role in preserving them. Consequently, while the metropolitan movement moderated strategically but not ideologically, its branches in the Maghreb remained violently racist, misogynistic, and hostile to reform. The actions of the Croix de Feu/PSF in the French imperial nation-state reveal the ways in which the movement's Social First! mission and ethnoreligious nationalism were appropriated according to local cultural norms. The divergent practices that resulted—of which gender was the most important marker of difference—illustrate that the borders between authoritarianism and fascism were porous and shifted according to the attitudes of people who believed in a hierarchical organization of human society.

1

THE CULTURE OF WAR AND THE MASCULINE WORLD OF THE EARLY CROIX DE FEU, 1927–1934

In his 1862 masterpiece, *Les Miserables,* Victor Hugo used the 1815 Battle of Waterloo that ended the Napoleonic Wars to describe the relentless threat of death that soldiers faced during war. He wrote: "The colossal death's head, which the heroes saw constantly through the smoke in the heat of battle, advanced towards them and gazed at them."[1] In this passage, Hugo depicted soldiers who were duty-bound, fought with honor, and were willing to sacrifice their lives. In capturing the experiences of war Hugo appealed to generations of soldiers. A total war a century later—World War I—once again shook the foundations of European society and threatened the existence of the French nation. Once again soldiers stepped forward despite the constant gaze of the "colossal death's head" to save France. This narrative of bravery and sacrifice was one that many veterans told themselves and became dominant in French society after the war.[2]

The powerful images that Hugo conjured were central to the Croix de Feu. Upon its creation as a veterans' league, Croix de Feu leaders appropriated a variety of militaristic images to represent their organization, including those created by Hugo. League leaders took the long-standing military symbol of the death's head and superimposed it on the *Croix de Guerre* to create their infamous logo. Hugo's "death's head" passage from *Les Miserables* appeared often in its published press and propaganda. The Croix de Feu's name itself captured the fires of the trenches and the religiously understood redemption that soldiers might find there. This homage to the military experiences of soldiers defined the early Croix de Feu and contributed to its influence. Indeed, other large political formations would look to the Croix de Feu as a movement par excellence and seek to emulate its explosive growth and dynamism.[3]

An examination of the Croix de Feu reveals that it perpetuated what historians have termed the "culture of war."[4] Rooted in studies of the Great War, the "culture of war" thesis has focused on the links between war and civil society, the ways in which civilians and soldiers experienced war, and war's impact on political culture. Proponents of this thesis contend that civilians gave and maintained their support for the war despite the horrid destruction and loss of life.[5] Likewise, soldiers fought willingly because many believed that the war was ultimately a battle between civilization and barbarity.[6] In this way, the French were not coerced but consented to war; the wartime culture that developed gave meaning to war and its sacrifices—the French fought to defeat a barbaric enemy, save their families, and liberate their country.[7] The culture of war had a key racialized component as well. Atrocity stories depicted barbaric Germans pitted against the civilized French.[8] In sum, the culture of war thesis helps to explain why the French prevailed in a horrific war: many soldiers and civilians believed in the justness of the French cause and were willing to endure great sacrifice to see it through.

While the Great War has dominated studies of the culture of war, scholars have begun to explore its prewar roots and its postwar effects.[9] Elements of the culture of war that characterized French society from 1914 to 1918 were first established after the debacle of the Franco-Prussian War of 1870–1871. This defeat was so jarring that many French, once they recovered from war's immediate aftermath, used peacetime to prepare for future conflict by forming a variety of associations that remade civil society. As historian Rachel Chrastil has demonstrated, mutual aid societies, commemorative associations, and gymnastics and shooting clubs were all examples of how men, women, and youth from various class backgrounds "fostered a culture that largely consented to war when it came."[10] This preparation was effective in the sense that, compared with Russian and German society, French society did not break down during the war despite the strikes and mutinies that threatened its social and political stability in 1917.

By the interwar period, many French had become acculturated to the looming threat of war and to war itself, which was a key reason why some of them found the Croix de Feu appealing. Indeed, aspects of the culture of war persisted into the interwar period and were embedded in Croix de Feu discourse and practice, especially in its gender ideology.[11] Many former soldiers who joined the Croix de Feu did not want to forget their wartime experiences as they integrated into civilian life. They still saw themselves as heroic patriots whose first duty was to defend the French nation and their families against a vicious enemy. The Germans were still dangerous, but the greater threat among a growing pantheon of "anti-French" forces during the early 1930s were Communists and pacifists. Many ultranationalists believed that the former represented atheistic materialism and a class-based worldview, while the latter were selfish cowards who eschewed national duty.

While some veterans joined antiwar associations, ex-servicemen who believed that pacifists and Communists threatened France's Christian precepts were drawn to the Croix de Feu. Croix de Feu veterans claimed that it was their duty to protect and strengthen the French nation by way of spiritual rejuvenation. They did so through a heavy emphasis on Catholic traditions and rituals. This chapter seeks to show that the early Croix de Feu developed a masculine brand of Catholicism—not merely as a cultural practice but as a spiritually meaningful endeavor—which reveals that male ultranationalists played a key role in strengthening religious values in French society. Masculine Catholicism and organic nationalism contributed to the ways in which Croix de Feu leaders distinguished the league from other veterans' groups, all of whom sought to capitalize on the "mystique" they had earned from their sacrifices during the Great War.[12] In tracing the Croix de Feu's perpetuation of the culture of war from 1927 to 1934, this chapter argues that supporters used the "veteran's mystique" to cast ex-servicemen as the purest defenders of a hierarchically conceived *patrie*. Such purity was central to the league's gender ideology, which leaders used to justify the violence and intimidation of the league's early years. Moreover, the masculine world of the early Croix de Feu marginalized women and essentialized womanhood either as passive ideal or support function of men, thus revealing the antifeminism of the early Croix de Feu.

A HIERARCHY TO SAVE FRANCE: THE PRIMACY OF THE VETERAN, THE PROMISE OF YOUTH, AND THE SUBORDINATION OF NONCOMBATANTS

Multiple veterans' associations comprising some three million ex-servicemen were created throughout the 1920s, most of which advocated for welfare benefits for veterans and their families and vied for veterans to have a wider influence in French sociopolitics.[13] With regard to the latter, they did so by emphasizing the "veteran's mystique," which was based upon the notion that veterans had been willing to sacrifice their lives for France and were therefore the most virtuous and selfless representatives of the French people and the nation itself.[14] Alongside the veterans' associations, the paramilitary leagues railed against the democratic republic by seeking to rejuvenate France along authoritarian and ethnoreligiously exclusive lines. French political culture was thus saturated with organizations that ranged from conservative to fascist, which raises the question of why several right-wing veterans and financiers created the Croix de Feu in 1927. A specific impetus was the government's creation of the *carte du combattant* in 1927, which was for men who had served at least three months at the front and entitled veterans to benefits such as a livable pension. The carte symbolized the government's recognition of veterans' bodily and psychological sacrifices and reflected a generational bond among veterans who described themselves as the "generation of fire."[15] Hence the naming of the Croix de Feu and its death's head emblem, which infused this sense of generational identity with religious and militaristic significance. Such generational commonality was a key reason why veterans' organizations claimed to seek reform outside of politics, which was inherently divisive, engaging instead in what they called "civic action."[16] The leagues, on the other hand, were created for political action outside of the governmental apparatus and were therefore not subject to the same laws that regulated associations and political parties.[17] For this reason, paramilitarism was central to the leagues. The populism inherent in paramilitarism galvanized the leaders of all the leagues to create ancillary groups for women and youth.[18]

The Croix de Feu was a hybrid organization that fused the veteran's mystique of the veterans' associations with the paramilitarism and populism of the extra-parliamentary leagues. Like other veterans' groups, the Croix de Feu sought to rejuvenate French society by transposing the fraternity of the trenches onto civil society. Facilitating sociability was a key method employed by Croix de Feu leaders to make this ideological goal a reality. As in most political organizations, league leaders divided the membership into neighborhood sections that held regular meetings. Sections sprouted up throughout Greater France, which spurred leaders in Paris to create a monthly newspaper, *Le Flambeau* (the Torch), in late 1929. Typical of interwar newspapers, *Le Flambeau* was overtly partisan and its sellers competed with those on the extreme Right and the far Left, especially the French Communist (PCF) and Socialist Parties (SFIO).[19] *Le Flambeau* criticized "inept" politicians, advocated for veterans' pensions, emphasized the central role that veterans played in French society, and publicized local sections' events and activities. Indeed, military values of camaraderie and an esprit du corps dominated the section life. A 1930 circular aimed at the league's membership maintained: "We are all veterans and members of the Croix de Feu without any distinction of ideas or opinions."[20]

Colonel François de La Rocque initiated the first of several transformative steps for the Croix de Feu when he became the league's president in 1931. As a man of military discipline whose politics were authoritarian, he believed that the Third Republic's parliamentary system was chaotic. He had grand visions of using the Croix de Feu to remake France along militaristic lines of discipline and Catholic conceptions of hierarchy. Coupled with La Rocque's ultranationalism, the Croix de Feu quickly set itself apart from other groups that attracted conservative and right-wing veterans by becoming a mass movement. Following the lead of other veterans' organizations, the first ancillary group the Croix de Feu created was for male and female children. The youth group, along with the Croix de Feu's paramilitary formations, provided the organizational structure that absorbed the movement's first notable spike in membership, which occurred after the election of the second *Cartel des Gauches* in 1932. While the advent of the leftist coalition led to an increase in the membership of all the ultranationalist leagues, the Croix de Feu's populism made it especially attractive to the thousands who were alarmed that the Left was uniting to transform France through class warfare.

The Croix de Feu's youth group, the Fils et Filles des Croix de Feu (FFCF, Sons and Daughters of the Croix de Feu) not only benefited from the backlash against the cartel but revealed the deeply gendered nature of the league's ideology and practice. The FFCF was created in 1931 and open to both boys and girls, although the league devoted more resources and attention to the "sons" because leaders believed that they would become the future leaders of France. Gender structured virtually all of the FFCF's activities, as its ideology replicated the conservative gender norms that dominated French society in the 1930s. The girls prepared for domestic and familial duties by learning how to sew and knit while boys prepared for public service through field trips to battlefields, outdoor physical activities, and sporting events. Despite claims by league leaders that they sought to mobilize both boys and girls, evidence of the uneven gender status of youth was everywhere. For instance, activities of the boys merited its own section in *Le Flambeau* at the expense of the girls, who received limited attention. Boys but not girls were invited to attend the league's first summer camp in 1932. Even the word "daughters" occasionally disappeared from the FFCF as leaders called the organization the FCF (Sons of the Croix de Feu).[21] When leaders did acknowledge girls, they parroted pronatalist and Catholic rhetoric. A typical example was from a summer 1933 meeting when the FFCF leader, Pozzo di Borgo, told girls, "[You] must not take on a combative role, but maintain the home, comfort, dress physical and moral wounds, and above all, teach children to love their country."[22]

La Rocque was encouraged by the Croix de Feu's growth after the cartel's election and the prospect of attracting the energy and idealism of youth. "The blossoming of the FFCF in 1932–33 ranks among one of the most significant omens of the Croix de Feu mission in the quasi-miraculous history of our associations," he wrote to the readers of *Le Flambeau*.[23] Indeed, the league's membership more than doubled in a year and a half, from 22,644 in January 1932 to 49,000 in July 1933.[24] At the same time, only 120 women were either Croix de Feu or Briscards in July 1933, which La Rocque believed was unacceptable if the Croix de Feu was to become a mass movement.[25] While theoretically women holding the *carte du combattant* shared the same status as male cardholders, in practice the veteran's mystique was coded as male, leaving women to lack access to positions of influence in the league.[26] Moreover, several league leaders believed that young male adults were ineffectively mobilized as well. As Table 1 shows, for these reasons, they created two new groups for noncombatants in 1933. Aimed at nonveteran women and men, the Regroupement National autour des Croix de Feu (RNCF) was created in September, and a group for men too young to have fought in the Great War, the Volontaires Nationaux (VN), the following November. The VN sought to galvanize young men from the ages of sixteen to thirty by graduating them from the FFCF into what became one of the league's most dynamic groups. Lacking the same energy, the RNCF was for nonveterans of both sexes.

TABLE 1. Croix de Feu Ancillary Groups, 1927–1933

Croix de Feu	Briscards	Fils et Filles des Croix de Feu (FFCF)	Regroupement National autour des Croix de Feu (RNCF)	Volontaires Nationaux (VN)
YEAR THAT ELIGIBLE INDIVIDUALS COULD JOIN				
1927	1929	1931	1933	1933
MEMBERSHIP				
Decorated veterans	Veterans who fought at least six months	Children of Croix de Feu members and supporters	Noncombatant men and women	Men over sixteen who were too young to have fought in the Great War

While virtually all veterans' associations, political parties, and ultranation-alist leagues created ancillary groups for youth and women along these lines, the ways in which each subgroup influenced the wider political formation itself varied.[27] In the early Croix de Feu a hierarchy developed between those who fought, those who could do so in the future, and those who did not fight. As former and future combatants, the Croix de Feu and VN enjoyed a high degree of status and autonomy in comparison to the RNCF, which never received that same allocation of resources or level of respect. While the RNCF offered women the first opportunity to join the Croix de Feu, it limited their access to the league's most important activities. La Rocque maintained that those who joined the VN possessed the qualities of a *combattant:* self-control, decisiveness, and a sense of responsibility.[28] For this reason, Croix de Feu leaders envisioned the VN as the training ground for future leaders and superior to the RNCF, which was intended to facilitate among its members a peaceful and familial nature. As the RNCF's statutes put it, the purpose of the group was to "restore order in our home we call France and to ensure exterior and interior peace."[29] In this way, the VN promoted an aggressive yet controlled conception of masculinity that was based upon national defense. The RNCF emphasized peace and familialism for women and the emasculated nonveteran men who were eligible for the group. It was no surprise that male RNCF members were rare even though the Croix de Feu claimed that they were welcome in the league.

In many ways, the masculine ideal embodied by Croix de Feu veterans was one that had dominated the French Right since the Dreyfus Affair. Proper men were men of action (not thought), were physically strong and virile (not flabby and impotent), and enjoyed unquestionable personal credibility.[30] Of all men, soldiers best embodied this masculine ideal and were thus celebrated by right-wing Catholic antidreyfusards and the groups that emerged in the Affair's after-math.[31] In the case of the Croix de Feu, league leaders believed that they could bring about national rejuvenation by restructuring French society along the same lines as the Croix de Feu itself. The subordinate status of noncombatants was the best example of the league's authoritarian hierarchy and was reified in the distinctions between the Croix de Feu and the RNCF. RNCF statutes reminded members that they were to "provide to everyone the moral values that form the very soul of the *patrie—the head* of which are the veterans of fire and the national army"; the RNCF meanwhile comprised "the *mass* of citizens of all ages, of all conditions, of all origins."[32] The RNCF were thus true auxiliaries. To further enshrine this hierarchy, members of the RNCF were forbidden from attending the same meetings as the Croix de Feu or the VN.[33]

In casting distinctions between the veterans, future soldiers, and the amorphous feminized mass, league leaders believed that they were preserving traditional French conceptions of authority. This hierarchical structure attracted veterans because it affirmed their status as defenders of France and appealed to noncombatants who trusted the veterans to preserve social order and political stability. These precepts dominated much of the early Croix de Feu's propaganda, especially posters, which were central to an intensive recruiting campaign. La Rocque emphasized the significance of hierarchy to the artist who created several of the league's most ubiquitous posters, Hermann-Paul. The colonel wrote:

> We thought that a veteran with his decorations and the tricolored armband of our association could be in the foreground of the poster.... This veteran should push to the front a young man with an attitude of resolve, symbolizing the VN. Behind them, the amorphous beginnings of a crowd, and lightly sketched, a mother evoking the family home, which we reserve a prominent place in our propaganda. This scene would powerfully illustrate that members of the RNCF must now evolve under the energetic impulses of the Croix de Feu.[34]

Composing the poster in this way encapsulated the social hierarchy that the Croix de Feu believed was necessary to regenerate French society (Figure 1). The veteran was a symbol of unity and reconciliation, which as the poster put it, was the only way to "save the country." This type of propaganda effectively recruited men who were looking for a dynamic organization that could not only counter the energized Left but one that disdained the chronic instability of the Third Republic's interwar governments and its inability to grapple with a looming economic crisis.

THE CULTURE OF WAR: PARAMILITARY VIOLENCE AND SHAPING THE VETERAN'S MYSTIQUE

Although the early Croix de Feu lacked the misogyny that characterized the Italian *squadristi* and the German *freicorps,* it was nevertheless antifeminist in its hierarchical conception of the social order. Women and men were to maintain separate spheres based upon their allegedly distinct natural instincts. The discipline inherent in being a veteran supposedly enabled a man to develop and control his natural inclination toward aggression. The Croix de Feu thus asserted its own version of the veteran's mystique in developing its paramilitary wing and legitimizing the intimidation and violence inherent in paramilitarism.[35] The Croix de Feu's conception of the veteran's mystique was a key reason why veterans, including those with membership in other organizations, were drawn to the Croix de Feu. For the Croix de Feu, the veteran's mystique underpinned the claims of ex-servicemen that they constituted societal elites, which entitled them to the status and recognition. Indeed, this was a fight for the politics of the veteran itself. Antoine Prost has demonstrated that hundreds of thousands of veterans joined antiwar and pacifist organizations that, in the spirit of Briandism, rejected war.[36] In contrast, Croix de Feu supporters cast themselves as defenders of peace and order who were reluctantly willing to use intimidation and violence, which, if employed with control, discipline, and the spirit of civic virtue, could be righteous.

The paramilitarism of the leagues was at the root of political violence that occurred during the interwar period.[37] Combined with mass mobilizations, Croix de Feu paramilitarism garnered the league its first publicity and subjected it to both accolades and scorn.[38] One of the priorities for Croix de Feu leaders was to organize a paramilitary wing to defend the league's nationalistic interests and remind the public that the veterans were the premier force for order in French society. To this end, the league's shock troops, the *disponsables (dispos),* were created in 1931 by one of its early leaders, Paul Chopine, who had spent 1928–1929 organizing sections in Algeria.[39] Chopine organized the *dispos* into groups of five, which operated with two other groups of five at any given time, each of which had a direct superior who answered to a chain of command that began with La Rocque. This organization enabled the Croix de Feu to mobilize at a moment's notice. In preparing for one such mobilization, a 1930 circular urged supporters to be mindful that they had an opportunity "to show Parisians and public authorities the formidable development of our association.... If we want to be influential, we must, above all else, demonstrate our strength and cohesion."[40]

One of the first times the Croix de Feu used the *dispos* was when the league attacked a pacifist congress held in Paris at the Trocadero in 1931. The Croix de Feu organized as many as fifteen hundred protestors and joined the Action Française and Jeunesses Patriotes in storming the congress. La Rocque commandeered the microphone, the audience was forced to scatter, and the police were called in. The Croix de Feu intended to show the French public that pacifists were not proper men and therefore were unfit to sit atop the hierarchy upon which the *patrie* was built. In Chopine's words, pacifists were "traitors."[41] He believed that pacifist veterans were the worst because they rejected war and betrayed the sacrifices that soldiers had made. The Croix de Feu thus attacked several more pacifist meetings.

Encouraged by the press generated by such demonstrations, Chopine continued to make the *dispos* highly visible in public spaces under the guise of preserving public order.[42] Characteristic of paramilitary action across Europe, Croix de Feu supporters claimed that the league's paramilitarism was defensive. In practice, however, it often provoked outbreaks of physical political violence.[43] Indeed, La Rocque and other supporters regularly used a maxim that Marshal Louis-Hubert Lyautey made famous: "We show force so that we don't have to use it."[44] Epitomizing self-control, not only did Lyautey use this principle to keep colonial subjects from rising up against French rule, but the Croix de Feu employed it to justify paramilitary action in the face of vaguely defined threats to the *patrie*. To meet anti-French threats, Chopine stationed the *dispos* at the most conspicuous places—metro entrances, parks, busy streets, café entrances, and public ceremonies—under the pretense of providing protection from the aggressive tactics of the Left. The shock troops also provided "security" for Croix de Feu meetings, yet the police regularly reported that it was the *dispos* who harassed attendees at the meetings of Communists and Socialists. During the league's early years, this street presence and the notoriety that resulted from the publicity was how league leaders defined success. They subsequently emphasized paramilitary mobilization throughout the early 1930s, "perfecting" the tactic by mid-1934.[45]

Most ominously for supporters of democratic processes and the rule of law, Croix de Feu section leaders regularly declared at weekly meetings that their troops were ready to mobilize at a moment's notice—called "J-Day" and "H-Hour"—to seize power in a time of national emergency. While veterans groups and the leagues often proclaimed that H-Hour was close at hand, police regarded the Croix de Feu as one of the most dangerous organizations due to its growing numbers and demonstrated ability to provoke disorder. Indeed, events in Germany in 1933 reminded many of the Fascists' March on Rome in 1922. In both cases, the paramilitary arm of fascist groups played central roles in their ascension to power; both Hitler and Mussolini claimed that Germany and Italy respectively faced national emergencies that necessitated a suspension of the democratic governments. Croix de Feu section leaders regularly issued similar threats although they cloaked them in the language of order. The head of one of the league's Parisian sections put it this way: "The veterans are partisans of order and plan to eventually place at the head of the Government, one of [our] leaders, who are not *corrupt and rotten* politicians, but *proper men,* already having once already sacrificed their life for the country."[46] Here, the dichotomous nature of the Croix de Feu's masculine gender ideology was clear; there were "proper" men and those who were "rotten" and "corrupt." The choice the league presented to the public was stark: the *patrie* could crumble and decay or it could be saved by the veterans.

The intimidation and violence that were central to Croix de Feu paramilitarism contributed to increasing tensions in French society and often resulted in quotidian violence at the individual level. Violent encounters ranging from fist fights to shootings were regular occurrences as those on the Left and Right attacked each other upon identification and the police responded with force. Many political activists used weapons such as canes, whips, and bricks, which were nonlethal yet readily available and could cause serious injury; firearms were severely restricted by the state but were used on rare occasions.[47] Identification symbols played a crucial role in efforts by left-wing and right-wing groups to intimidate their opponents and gain the upper hand in the streets. Croix de Feu leaders understood that visual culture was important and league statutes not only required members to wear the death's head insignia at all times but encouraged supporters to memorize the insignia of their "enemies."[48] Police reported that Communists were in the practice of buying Croix de Feu insignia and membership cards to infiltrate league meetings.[49] Consequently, regular fights occurred at the lighting of the flame at the tomb of the Unknown Soldier in Paris, at wreath-laying ceremonies, and between rival newspaper sellers and propagandists hanging posters.[50] By 1934 rhetoric was so heated and fights so common that police in Paris, Lille, and Lyon reported that the extreme Right and Left had poisoned the political environment; police in Lyon, for example, stopped reporting street fights unless one of the fighters was hospitalized.[51]

THE VETERAN'S PURITY, POPULAR CULTURE, AND ENGENDERING NATIONAL IDENTITY

The veteran leaders of the early Croix de Feu sought to infuse the league's ideology with their conception of the veteran's mystique and rejuvenate the *patrie* by transmitting that mystique into French culture. To this end, the Croix de Feu sought to remake sites central to French national identity along the league's own militaristic, ultranationalistic, and Catholic lines. In this sense, the Croix de Feu was one of many groups competing to capture the essence of "true France" by using public space to shape the nation's political culture. This competition pushed France to become a European leader in terms of memory building: no other country had as many state funerals, the 38,000 war memorials that sprung up during the interwar period ranked among the most on the continent, and national symbols such as Joan of Arc were subject to a dazzling profusion of images and texts.[52] As Pierre Nora's landmark study on the development of French national memory demonstrates, groups across the political spectrum worked inside and outside of the government to assert their vision of national identity through a contested use of symbols, sites, rituals, and traditions. The Croix de Feu sought to form a collective memory among the citizenry and create an underlying social consensus that society's proper men—the veterans—were best suited to lead an authoritarian version of republican France. To this end, the league sought control over sites that dotted the French cultural landscape. It created its own song and sang "La Marseillaise" in public spaces; it held religious ceremonies in cathedrals; supporters organized and participated in numerous commemorations and memorial building; and men and women took youth on pilgrimages to important battlefields such as Verdun. Each of these activities reified the veteran's mystique by emphasizing the male nature of war and coding national honor as masculine.[53]

The early Croix de Feu thus developed a gender ideology that was relatively unique for the interwar period: veterans epitomized civic virtue through the *purity* of their spirit and deed.[54] Integrity, honor, decency, and personal credibility all comprised the league's conception of purity.[55] Croix de Feu propagandists claimed that these traits were easily knowable because of the relationships among fellow soldiers who depended upon one another for life and death. One soldier could vouch for another in terms of describing the horrors of war and what it took to survive. The Croix de Feu's emphasis on esprit de corps and the purity of the soldier led some ex-servicemen to overlook the league's strident Catholicism, which was a key reason that several Jewish, Muslim, and Protestant veterans joined the league in its early years. Indeed, the early Croix de Feu held ceremonies in synagogues and welcomed Muslim veterans into its ranks so long as they recognized the Christian roots of French civilization. In select cases, it was possible for "cowardly" pacifists to constitute more of an Other than ethnoreligious minorities. This is not to say that the ethnoreligious diversity of interwar France was reflected in the Croix de Feu but to note that during its early years, the league practiced a degree of inclusivity that would dwindle as the decade progressed and veterans lost their primacy.

The purity of Croix de Feu veterans was best revealed by the "Song of the Croix de Feu," which league members sung at meetings, parades, and commemoration ceremonies. The song grew so popular that in 1935 its leaders made it into a record that was sold at the league's charity bazaars.[56] The "Song of the Croix de Feu" borrowed from the militaristic sentiment and pastoral imagery of "La Marseillaise," which the extreme Right co-opted during the interwar period for its own nationalistic purposes to celebrate the permanence and glory of the French nation. Communists and Socialists countered by singing the "Internationale," a song of protest that captured the transnational struggles of the working classes and promised revolution.[57] These singing duals were part of a vibrant aural culture in which many groups developed their own songs as a way to transmit their values to the public. The lyrics of the "Song of the Croix de Feu" *repeatedly* used the word "pure" to describe veterans who ended suffering and brought hope, honor, and pride back to the French nation by leading a vanguard of youth. The song's third verse was typical: "The Croix de Feu has a pure soul; and the Volontaire (VN) a pure heart; Paladins of France, stand up! Raise the dead from the fields! The Croix de Feu are in front of you, France is reborn by them."[58] Propagandists cast current and future veterans as pure to reveal the redemptive nature of any action that the Croix de Feu chose to take. The idea of purity also countered the Croix de Feu's numerous detractors who sought to undermine the league by calling it fascist. If the veterans were exemplars of purity, then any violence in which they engaged could be justified as redemptive and therefore legitimate.

Purity was thus at the heart of the league's many public activities, including one of the most important of its mass mobilizations, the Mass of the Marshals. Created and organized by Croix de Feu supporters, the Mass of the Marshals fused Catholic religious practice with the most distinguished symbols of French military leadership. The league organized the Mass to honor men of extraordinary military achievement (only eight marshals were named during the Third Republic) and celebrate the memory of those who died in war. Held from 1932 to 1936, organizers used the Mass to emphasize national unity by inviting anybody with a degree of social, cultural, or political clout: representatives of the Republic such as the president and leaders in the Senate, Catholic clergy like the archbishop of Paris and the bishop of Nice, the entire foreign diplomatic corps, foreign royalty, celebrities like Colette Yver and Madeleine Grey, right-wing cultural icons like

Drieu la Rochelle, the heads of the Yacht and Automobile Clubs of Paris, and of course, the marshals and their families.[59] Acceptance rates were spotty due to the Croix de Feu's violent reputation. Every year, for example, Cardinal Verdier of Paris was invited and declined. More hard-line clerics, on the other hand, did attend. While some foreign diplomats attended the service in 1933, none did so in 1936, which reflected the Croix de Feu's growing international notoriety. Despite this infamy, the Croix de Feu's status as France's premier ultranationalist league in France was growing—attendance at the Mass increased steadily; police reported that the one in 1935 drew six thousand.[60]

The Mass of the Marshals ceremonies were rife with nationalism, religion, and militarism, three themes that demonstrated the persistence of the culture of war in the Croix de Feu. The league held the Mass at Notre Dame Cathedral in Paris as a testament to the fortitude and exceptionalism of the French "race." In this case, the Croix de Feu's agenda aligned with that of the state, as there had been a growing interest in what cathedrals meant to the French nation. Since the creation of the Third Republic, the state had been working with municipal authorities to restore the many cathedrals that had fallen into disrepair after the 1789 revolution.[61] For republican officials, the value of the cathedrals was in their historical rather than religious significance. The Croix de Feu agreed about the former in the sense that cathedrals demonstrated French racial exceptionalism. In the sermon at the 1933 mass, the priest performing the ceremony, R. P. Vauplane, explained it this way: "Our land of France, which we love passionately, is a land whose innumerable monuments attest to the incomparable genius of our race: grandiose cathedrals—such as the one that we are in now—and humble churches in such perfect harmony with the country's enchanting landscapes."[62]

In other regards the Croix de Feu used the Mass of the Marshals to contest republican anticlericalism by claiming national patrimony as Catholic, and in doing so, infuse religiosity into national identity. Indeed, Vauplane personified the French nation in an effort to conflate the *patrie*'s future with the rejuvenation of its Catholic soul. He proclaimed, "This land bears a great wound on its flank due to the marches from the East; a gaping wound from where the best of our blood has flown.... We prayed that all that was Catholic in the French soul awaken. We prayed and we asked God to assure us Victory."[63] In this way, the Croix de Feu proposed that France's national destiny and divine intervention were intertwined.

The Catholic dimension of the Mass of the Marshals was one of its most salient features and demonstrated the central role that religion played in the league's efforts to raise its public profile. Indeed, it regularly participated in an array of ceremonies that were organized by any group who shared its principles. On a weekly basis, the league's sections across Greater France attended ceremonies at the tombs of unknown soldiers, made pilgrimages to battlefield sites, celebrated the erection of statues to important military figures, and marked important days as sacred. Celebrating the armistice that ended the Great War on November 11 was a particularly solemn affair, as were pilgrimages to the most bloody of battlefields, Verdun, where nearly every ex-serviceman had fought because of how the high command rotated troops. As Antoine Prost notes, veterans sought to remind the French public of their pain and suffering.[64] Yet conflicts between veterans of the Left and Right at the memorials were regular occurrences, which suggests that interwar memorialization never shifted from mourning to celebration as it had in the years between the Franco-Prussian War and the Great War.[65] In this sense, interwar monuments were sites of conflict over the politics of veterans as often as they were sites of consensus.[66] The Croix de Feu had its own unique purposes beyond the democratizing intent behind the memorials discussed by Prost. By gathering in public spaces wearing their insignia, holding the Croix de Feu flag, and singing the Croix de Feu song, league supporters sought to shape the meaning of the event. The league's actions also demonstrated the sacrifice and virtue of the veterans, which was a call to *future* action, not simply remembrance of the past. The league's propaganda bureau called the veterans "missionaries, having made an act of faith," and reminded members that it was their duty to use "incessant repetition" to achieve the "spiritual formation of a group and the creation of a mystique of ideas."[67]

Perhaps the only event to eclipse commemorations such as the Mass of the Marshals in terms of significance and rates of attendance was the Croix de Feu's annual participation in the national fête that celebrated Joan of Arc. Like cathedrals, Joan of Arc as a symbol had fallen into relative obscurity for centuries but was resuscitated by the Third Republic as officials sought to find nationalistic symbols that could unite all French men and women.[68] Despite efforts by the state to depoliticize Joan of Arc, she became an icon to the ultranationalist Right. Antidreyfusards emphasized her military heroism, sense of sacrifice and duty, and devotion to the *patrie*. Thereafter, she remained a rallying point for right-wing nationalist and Catholic groups until her canonization in 1919.[69]

Seeking to wrestle the meaning of Joan of Arc away from the extreme Right, the state created a national Joan of Arc holiday and organized parades and celebrations that took place every May throughout Greater France. The government claimed that the purity of Joan of Arc was rooted in military victory and nationalist glory, which made her a unifying figure and a rallying point for French across the political spectrum. Yet the government's attempts to overcome the extreme Right's stranglehold over the symbol of Joan of Arc were ineffective. Throughout the 1920s the Left's hostility to the fête was constant and sometimes violent; the police kept a close watch on the marchers and at time restricted participants.[70] The Communist Party, for example, took the fête's occasion to mock its participants: "Just like every year, the pseudo 'national celebration' of Joan of Arc was a shameful exhibition of all the fascist scum, who marched in a ridiculous procession from Saint-Augustin to the Rue de Rivoli."[71] The Communists were right to be skeptical of the government's assertion that the national fête belonged to all French, as it was only Catholic and extreme Right groups who routinely participated (Table 2).[72] Indeed, the Croix de Feu had not only displaced the Action Française as the numerically superior group by the 1930s, but achieved unprecedented participatory numbers by 1935.

The Croix de Feu's participation in the Joan of Arc parade revealed a great deal about how league leaders and supporters envisioned national rejuvenation. The

TABLE 2. Participants in the Joan of Arc Celebration, 1927–1935

Year	Catholic Groups and Scouts	Jeunesses Patriotes	Ligue des Patriotes	*Croix de Feu*	Action Française, Grandes Ecoles	Notes	Total Participants
1927	11,150	2,800	350	0	7,700		21,700
1928	12,000	3,000	450	0	8,000		23,560
1929	11,760	3,000	100	1,250	5,790		26,055
1930	13,250	2,740	200	1,500	5,220		23,055
1931	13,285	2,000	300	2,100	4,680		22,480
1932	Canceled due to day of mourning	540	120	1,050	4,120	150 Fils de CF	5,830
1933	12,280	1,725	150	2,000	4,010	250 Fils de CF	20,250
1934	12,400	2,980	205	6,300	6,985	500 Fils de CF; 1,000 VN	30,200
1935	NA	NA	NA	14,000	NA	NA	NA

Source information given in Chapter 1, Note 72.

parade itself began in the center of the city and moved down the Rue de Rivoli toward the Place des Pyramids, where marchers laid a wreath at the base of the Joan of Arc statue that towered over the square. The Croix de Feu marched in military formation during the procession so as to appear as a force for order and discipline. Marchers responded only to orders from the league's superiors and not hecklers or provocations from rival groups. The formation itself reflected the hierarchies along which the Croix de Feu sought to rejuvenate French society: the veterans took the lead, followed by the young men of the VN and FFCF—but not the daughters—while the RNCF and children took up the rear.[73]

The parade was of special significance to the Croix de Feu because of Joan of Arc's central role in its iconography, which was in many ways typical of the extreme Right's long-standing emphasis on nationalism and martyrdom. Indeed, Joan of Arc lore, as it developed throughout the first decades of the twentieth century, reflected ultranationalists' most cherished historical narratives: the young virginal peasant girl exhibited selflessness in leading French troops against the invading English; inspired by God, she rose up bravely and led the army to a military victory that saved France, and ultimately died as a martyr for the *patrie*. For the Croix de Feu, one of the most important aspects of Joan of Arc was her purity, which embodied her innocence and ability to commune with God. *Le Flambeau* proclaimed that Joan of Arc was "the strong virgin, who by her heroism saved France and liberated it from foreign occupation."[74] In this way, the similarities between the veteran and Joan of Arc were many. The purity of both underlined their selflessness, self-control, and credibility. They both believed in a cause greater than their individual interest: saving the *patrie* from destruction and preserving the purity of France itself.

On rare occasions the Croix de Feu sought to shape the mythology surrounding Joan of Arc by framing her as an empowering model for ideal womanhood. One of the only articles about a real woman that appeared in the first few years of *Le Flambeau*'s existence compared the actions of Mademoiselle Carlier to Joan of Arc. Carlier had left France for Russia in 1900 and was living as a professor in Moscow at the time of the Bolshevik Revolution in October 1917. A staunch anticommunist, Carlier provided aid to enemies of the Bolsheviks and to French citizens trapped in the chaos. For this the Bolsheviks imprisoned her for sixteen months, nine of which she served in solitary confinement, before she returned to France in weakened health in 1922. Carlier used her own story to highlight the similarities between herself and Joan of Arc by stating that she was inspired by

Joan's sense of earthly transcendence and divine guidance. She explained, "The land of France was reconquered by a peasant... she saw the necessity of her work and her sacrifice. She had confidence in the eternal destinies of France."[75] For his part, La Rocque believed that Carlier was a righteous warrior who exhibited the same bravery as Joan of Arc in fighting the atheistic Communists. She was, according to La Rocque, "a real-life Joan of Arc" who offered "the most magnificent model of the soul of a leader."[76]

More typically, Croix de Feu propagandists depicted Joan of Arc as an allegory of a dependent France rather than a symbol for women's emulation of the pure and able veteran. In this vein of idealized femininity, Joan of Arc represented the nation, albeit in a weak and helpless manner. She needed the veteran to save her. As this 1931 cartoon revealed, she was shown as the classic damsel in distress (Figure 2). The pyre upon which she was placed appeared in the shape of France. Joan herself was the hapless feminine symbol of France, waiting to be rescued by the masculine veterans rushing below her as they held the Croix de Feu flag emblazoned with the death's head emblem. The flames behind Joan formed a subtle outline of the *Croix de Guerre,* which not only referenced the Croix de Feu's name but suggested that Croix de Feu veterans believed that they protected the memory of Joan's sacrifice. Joan of Arc's purity—indeed her very life—were threatened, yet the viewer could be assured that the veterans would not let either die. The individual veterans were not shown but represented only by the Croix de Feu flag, their individuality subsumed into the collective. In this way, Joan of Arc's lack of autonomy reflected the primacy of the veteran's mystique and the concomitant passive status of women in national rejuvenation.

Occasionally as a symbol of women's empowerment but more often as one of dependency, the Croix de Feu's emphasis on Joan of Arc's sexuality was emblematic of wider discourses across French society. When empowered, Joan's purity, which was expressed sexually in terms of her virginity, enabled her to act as a soldier for France. The veteran's purity on the other hand was not expressed sexually but in terms of character and embodied in his civic virtue. It was common for the French to allow maidens to participate in traditional men's work, particularly combat, while mothers (life givers) were barred from fighting, which was synonymous with killing.[77] As a woman without children, Carlier was eligible for some of the freedoms allotted to men, in this case, that of leadership. However, during a time when the vast majority of French women were married and had children, this rigid conception of gender was not an option for women who wanted to participate in conservative movements.

The Croix de Feu's inconsistent portrayal of Joan of Arc depicted women in a more empowering manner relative to the regressive representation of the only other female symbol that appeared in the league's early years: the bourgeois homemaker. The latter was featured in an irregular column that appeared in *Le Flambeau* called "What a Woman Should Know," which mirrored a column aimed at men called "What's Necessary to Know." First appearing in June 1931 and disappearing after the league created its Women's Section in 1934, the women's column was included in only ten issues and usually off to the side of a back page, whereas the men's column first appeared in April 1930 and was featured prominently in virtually every issue until 1935. Emphasizing the public life expected of a male citizen, the men's column featured information on community affairs of interest to veterans, the dates and locations of neighborhood commemoration ceremonies, local section events, and suggestions for how to increase one's involvement in the Croix de Feu. In contrast, "What a Woman Should Know" reflected the early Croix de Feu's conflation of femininity and domesticity by including tips on cooking, knitting, interior home decoration, housework, classic French recipes, and beauty tips. One column, for instance, instructed a woman on the best ways to remove unsightly warts to increase her beauty.[78] Another entitled "For Her" showed women how to make their own shampoo and have beautiful flowing hair: "Your hair will be soft, flowing, and thick—for your husband."[79]

Discursively, the early Croix de Feu paid little attention to femininity, and when it did, conceptualized womanhood in a bifurcated manner in the same way as the league's propagandists contrasted the pure Croix de Feu veteran with the cowardly pacifist and unmanly politician. Once women were mobilized in the Women's Section, the bifurcation fissured and women used Joan of Arc as a symbol to negotiate larger spaces for women's empowerment in the movement. Before this shift, however, the discursive spaces were more limited. In the early Croix de Feu, if a woman was not going to emulate Joan of Arc—and no married woman or mother could—then she belonged in the home and was to look classically feminine. Indeed, before the Croix de Feu's Social First! strategy came about, the movement embodied conservative attitudes towards proper womanhood, which reflected the backlash against the rise of the "modern woman" of the 1920s who wore her hair short, was single, and flouted motherhood.[80] Conservative social commentators bemoaned the fact that the modern woman epitomized France's civilizational crisis. Fascists like Drieu la Rochelle claimed that the modern woman followed her own selfish desires instead of sacrificing for the needs of a country that had just experienced the trauma of total war. For the early Croix de Feu the modern woman was especially unsettling when contrasted with the pure selflessness of the Croix de Feu veteran.

It was thus not coincidental that one of the leading interwar antifeminists, Colette Yver, became the early Croix de Feu's spokeswoman for its campaign to mobilize women through the RNCF. Yver, a famous Catholic writer and one of the first women to join the RNCF, spoke regularly at the league's section meetings and was often featured in *Le Flambeau*. At an important November 1933 meeting that highlighted the league's mass mobilization campaign and drew ten thousand men, Yver spoke of the significance of the RNCF and opined on women's political capabilities. She informed the audience that she was "seduced" by the RNCF and its emphasis on a highly structured social order. The league's structure was perfect for both sexes because, as Yver put it, "women, sirs, don't like politics. They only want a government. The histories of parties and partisans confuse them."[81]

Yver's beliefs reflected the early Croix de Feu's gender ideology—in French culture and politics, women were to provide merely an auxiliary role to that of men. Even social activities, which women would come to dominate after 1934, were often done by men. The league's first Parisian social service, for example, was a clothing depot created by two men in January 1930. One of the first activities that Chopine assigned to his *dispos* in Algeria in the late 1920s was to create neighborhood soup kitchens.[82] While soup kitchens would come to be a primary Croix de Feu activity as the Great Depression worsened, in 1932 the league did not have a program to organize food distributions, which left social services subject to individual initiative.[83] This was one of the few entrées available to women in the early Croix de Feu. For instance, Madame Marie Thérèse Hidieu organized a soup kitchen in Paris's fifth arrondissement, which served one hundred meals daily at the local brasserie owned by a Croix de Feu member.[84] As a holder of the *carte du combattant,* Hidieu was one of the few women who was an official member of the Croix de Feu. She advertised the soup kitchen by hanging posters in churches and cinemas and funded it by asking for collections at the same places.[85]

Hidieu's actions reflected women's participation in the league's early years. It was up to her own initiative and energy to find the location for the soup kitchen, ensure that it operated legally, and publicize it at the neighborhood level. She could then call it a "Croix de Feu Soup Kitchen" and the movement's propaganda emphasized it as such, but the responsibility to establish, sustain, and publicize its services fell on Hidieu. While men were willing to provide social services, the early Croix de Feu's emphasis on paramilitarism and mass mobilizations showed that league leaders and supporters placed greater significance on actions that they associated with traditional masculine power. Women's visibility in the league coincided with their membership status, primarily because a structure to organize their activities did not exist. Consequently, women's activities were carried out on an ad hoc basis and antifeminists like Yver were prominent.

CONCLUSION: MISOGYNY AND ANTIFEMINISM

In the masculine world of the early Croix de Feu, leaders and supporters prized the wartime experiences of the veteran and heralded his selfless purity in defending the *patrie*. This soldierly expression of civic virtue motivated many of the men who joined the league and participated in mass mobilizations and paramilitary action. Women were not only marginalized in the league's perpetuation of the culture of war in terms of real numbers, but their lack of status limited their sociopolitical clout. In this context, the distinction between antifeminism and misogyny is important. While the gender ideology of the early Croix de Feu limited women's ability to expand their spheres of influence, it did not, in the words of Christine Bard, "express hatred for women's regard."[86] The early Croix de Feu may have been antifeminist but it was not generally misogynistic. While La Rocque did not believe that men and women were political equals, he never echoed Hitler's position that women, like the masses, wanted to be dominated.[87] The majority of *dispos* did not follow the extremes of the *freicorps* in stereotyping women as either a virgin or a dirty whore with the potential to destroy a man's body and soul.[88] Top Croix de Feu leaders avoided using sexualized language in the manner of the French fascist intellectual Robert Brasillach, who declared that the Third Republic was "wrinkled and decrepit... a syphilitic strumpet, smelling of cheap perfume and vaginal discharge."[89]

While women in the early Croix de Feu lacked authority and discursively they alternated between the virgin soldier and bourgeois homemaker, these practices were a function of the league's formation as a veteran's association and not an intentional move to marginalize women within the organization and society at large. Extolling the primacy of the veteran rendered women politically marginal, which was a key reason that antifeminists like Yver were initially drawn to the league. Yet once Croix de Feu leaders sought to turn the league into a mass movement they reconsidered the best way to galvanize the entire population. The leadership thus shifted from not thinking about women at all (1927–1931), to halfheartedly seeking to mobilize girls and women and essentialize them as they did so (the FFCF and the RNCF, 1931–1933), to eventually making women's mobilization a top priority after 1934. Women's increasing importance in the Croix de Feu becomes clearer when comparing the movement's metropolitan and North African sections. As we shall see in Chapter 6, the antifeminism of the early metropolitan Croix de Feu was different in form and function from that of the North African Croix de Feu. The metropolitan Croix de Feu's celebration of purity and civic virtue, its insistence on authoritarian hierarchies, and the ease with which it referenced France's Christian heritage, contrasted with the ideological and strategic options available to the North African Croix de Feu, which sought to preserve French control over a Muslim majority in spaces that were influenced strongly by Islam.

2

BUILDING A SOCIAL ACTION MOVEMENT

WOMEN, CATHOLICISM, AND THE CROIX DE FEU/PSF'S

SOCIAL FIRST! STRATEGY, 1934-1939

Women first entered the Croix de Feu en masse in March 1934 and thereafter played a crucial role in driving a profound strategic shift that was not merely a tactical change but a fundamental redefinition of the movement's path to power. In doing so, the woman who led this transformation, Antoinette de Préval, became highly influential. Mademoiselle de Préval was born in 1892 in Béziers and volunteered as a nurse during the Great War, where she was wounded and received the *Croix de Guerre* for her bravery. The military defined many of her closest personal connections. Her father had been a general and she had a kinship connection to François de La Rocque, who had devoted his life to the military before becoming the Croix de Feu's president. Préval was a tall, slightly heavyset woman of forty-four years who preferred working behind the scenes, rather than giving bombastic speeches, when she led the creation of the Croix de Feu's Women's Section.[1]

As a conservative bourgeois Catholic whose faith was central to everything she did, Préval had long believed that France needed women and men of integrity who would sacrifice their individual needs for those of the nation. These ties between military and Catholic values had emboldened the French Right since the Dreyfus Affair and informed Préval and La Rocque's strategy to make the Croix de Feu into a mass movement. Préval appointed two of her friends, Marie-Claire de Gérus, who had also been a war nurse and was married to a general, and Germaine Féraud, who was the daughter of a general, to run the new Women's Section. While the Women's Section would eventually evolve into five different organizations run by professionals and volunteers, its military origins were critical. Like the male veterans who joined the Croix de Feu, Préval, Gérus, and Féraud applied the principles of the culture of war to peacetime. France, they believed, was in an existential battle between those who defended its heritage as a Christian civilization and those who sought to destroy the nation's spiritual underpinning by championing secularism and recognizing ethnoreligious particularism.

La Rocque and Préval worked together to conceptualize the Croix de Feu/PSF's unique approach to saving France, which centered around empowering women as agents of social action. Indeed, from 1934 on, virtually all of Préval's actions centered around expanding opportunities to women of various backgrounds so long as they sought to save France by invigorating its Christian roots. By 1935 roughly one out of every three members was a veteran, which was a remarkable change in a short period of time.[2] The influx of new members altered irrevocably the primacy of the veteran's mystique as a code for male hegemony as noncombatants joined and appropriated the principles of the culture of war for their own ends. Capitalizing upon the civil society of French republicanism, the women who flocked to the Croix de Feu/PSF mobilized themselves in what they called "civic space," which was the public arena where women could express their nurturing nature through social action and men could continue to promote civic virtue. On one hand, the Croix de Feu/PSF's emphasis on women's social role in civic space perpetuated stereotypes of women as natural caregivers. By not contesting the social/political dichotomy between women and men, the Croix de Feu/PSF helped ensure that women's political rights remained suppressed throughout the 1930s. On the other hand, Croix de Feu/PSF women transgressed the "women in the home" movement by using the culture of war to transpose traditional notions of women's nature to metropolitan civic space, which created a distinct public arena for nationalistic women's activism.

While historians have emphasized La Rocque's leadership in directing the Croix de Feu's increasing emphasis on social action—what several scholars have called the movement's "social turn"—this chapter demonstrates that the movement's transformation stemmed from the organizational effectiveness of the Women's Section and the exhaustive efforts of Préval and her adjutants.[3] This is not to diminish La Rocque's role, but to emphasize that of Préval, who, as the architect of the Croix de Feu/PSF social program, worked diligently to foster the conditions and build the organizational structures for women's activities to flourish. Led by Préval, women built the Croix de Feu/PSF's social program during the years of the movement's most explosive growth (1934–1936), thus making themselves indispensable transmitters of ultranationalism and central to the movement's impact on political culture. Indeed, women formulated and implemented the movement's social program by creating local sections in over 90 percent of France's departments by 1936. From then on, these sections became crucial sites for women to create programs that promoted ethnoreligious nationalism and fundamentally altered support for the parliamentary republic.

TRANSGRESSING WOMEN'S "MATERNAL MISSION":
THE INAUGURATION OF THE WOMEN'S SECTION AND
ETHNORELIGIOUS INTEGRATION

From 1860 to 1914 the French state initiated a systematic campaign to minimize religious influences in French society.[4] Social Catholicism played a key role in Catholics' response. The doctrine influenced the Croix de Feu's view of women as social actors and the social services developed by the Women's Section. However, the movement's gender ideology diverged from what the Church called women's "maternal mission." As a political organization rooted in the veterans' movements of the 1920s, the Croix de Feu was not bound to official Church precepts to the same extent as groups like LFACF, UNVF, and UFCS, which fostered relative independence for Croix de Feu leaders in crafting their authoritarian agenda. These comparatively more secular origins meant that the women who joined the league in 1934 entered into a militaristic environment that prized duty and nationalism, values that led the Croix de Feu/PSF to pursue a nominally ecumenical agenda. While membership in the LFACF required one to be a woman and a Catholic, identity issues in the Croix de Feu were more complex. Croix de Feu statutes stated that individuals of all ethnoreligious origins were welcomed to join, although in practice, the vast majority of its supporters were conservative and reactionary Catholics. Despite the Catholic background of most Croix de Feu members, the movement's veteran roots led its leaders to claim that they could transcend sectarian interests by regenerating the *union sacrée,* thereby subsuming individual interests into those of the nation.

A major turning point in the history of the late Third Republic was the massive street riots of February 6, 1934, which brought down the government and nearly caused the Third Republic itself to collapse. Throughout January, veterans' groups and extreme Right leagues demonstrated against the left-leaning government of Edouard Daladier.[5] A series of scandals led supporters to protest what they saw as the corruption, individualism, and materialism that was endemic among government politicians. The demonstrations culminated in a riot on the night of February 6, which not only killed over a dozen and injured over one thousand but spurred a week of rioting across France that ultimately killed around thir- ty-five.[6] In the aftermath of the riots, right-wing paramilitary and veterans' groups honed violent tactics that they used to destabilize public order by threatening the government, Communists, and Socialists. The Left banded together to fight the so-called fascist threat in what became the Popular Front. Top Communist leaders pointed to the growing power of the Croix de Feu as a key reason why they joined the Popular Front.[7] In this polemical environment, Croix de Feu women and men debated strategies to address the shortcomings of republicanism and the divisiveness they believed it engendered. While the riots led the Croix de Feu to radicalize, they also hastened women's mobilization.

The approach to political renovation held by top Croix de Feu women was perhaps best articulated by François de La Rocque's daughter, Nadine. Nadine's influence was short-lived, as she died from typhus at the age of twenty in the summer of 1934. While Croix de Feu propagandists portrayed her as a dutiful daughter constantly at her father's side, Nadine was keenly interested in the type of government that would best serve the French people. Indeed, Nadine's approach to politics represented the complexities of French republicanism; while republicanism denied women status as political citizens it created space for them as civic actors.[8] For this reason, Nadine refused to condemn republicanism outright. Providing lukewarm support to the state of the Republic in the 1930s, Nadine argued that it was possible for republicanism to be a good form of gov- ernment. She acknowledged, "The Republic is *perhaps* a good government—it's not one currently, but that doesn't destroy its chances of being one someday."[9] Following Rousseau, Nadine argued that sovereignty was rooted in the general will of the people. This general will was crystallized during the French Revolution, which Nadine believed was a moment of progress because it enabled individuals to overthrow the monarchy and band together as one: "A race arrives at a certain point in its evolution when it can no longer support an absolutist regime . . . the Revolution was beneficial because it permitted the development and blossoming of a collective soul . . . these are the mark of a people's vitality and ideas upon which the republic was founded: *liberté, égalité, fraternité.*"[10] Nadine's "republic" was not one that encompassed the autonomous citizen, but one in which the individual was subsumed into the collective.

Shortly after the riots François de La Rocque published his first political treatise, *Service Public,* which echoed Nadine's critiques of the Republic, and proposed a range of solutions that became embedded in Croix de Feu ideology. *Service Public* revealed La Rocque's ethnoreligious nationalism and hostility to parliamentary politics. Moreover, the colonel respected strong women like Nadine and Préval, which contributed to his belief that social action was a path to power. In *Service Public* he argued that mass mobilization and women's role in national rejuvenation were interconnected: "Since 1914 . . . the social and professional role of women has developed considerably. Her familial mission is not diminished, to the contrary. . . . The manner in which women are *reduced* to the role of mothers, wives and guardians of the home, is altogether too easy a way of dealing with the question."[11] Directly challenging discourses concerning women's "maternal mission," La Rocque had a complex view of women's role in French society and believed that substantive reform depended on women's action: "The use of women's inherent virtues and qualities in our 'social lives' has enabled a real acceleration to take place in human and civic progress. . . . Irrespective of the State, and in spite of the State, many of our social institutions and institutes of public health owe their inception to the magnificent enterprise of our women . . . France needs men and women of action."[12] In the tradition of social Catholicism that prized local control, La Rocque believed that the corporatist version of social reform was preferable to the trend of state intervention in social policy that had characterized the interwar years.[13] In this vein *Service Public* outlined one of the Croix de Feu's major ideological presuppositions: the republican state was the problem, not the solution. Since women were responsible for some of France's most important social advances, La Rocque insisted that they work outside of the state apparatus to drive the reform so crucial to France's fate.

While Nadine's and François de La Rocque's critiques of the Republic created conditions favorable for women's mass mobilization, it was Antoinette de Préval who designed the structures necessary to bring about national rejuvenation. Frustrated with the RNCF's ineffectiveness and the Croix de Feu's inability to capitalize on women's moral and spiritual authority, Préval sought to elevate women's status in the league. While chance played a role in Préval's position as a top Croix de Feu/PSF leader because kinship granted her close proximity to La Rocque, her savvy leadership style and astute eye for women's leadership potential and grassroots activism was equally important. As Chopine observed: "Two people above all have a great influence on [La Rocque] and it is not an exaggeration to say that they have completely inspired him for the past several years. His first advisor is his cousin, Mlle de Préval, who goes to all the demonstrations, is passionate about the movement, and most certainly gives him suggestions. She has even written his articles, corrected *Le Flambeau,* and without doubt, inspired his speeches. She has a huge influence on him and seems very ambitious."[14]

In organizing the leadership of the Women's Section, Préval promoted two women she called her "spiritual sisters," Gérus and Féraud, from their positions in the FFCF to travel throughout metropolitan France and oversee the creation of Women's Sections in Paris and the provinces.[15] Préval described herself with characteristic modesty as merely the "coordinator" of the Women's Section, but her colleagues recognized her critical role as the true "architect" of women's mobilization.[16] Préval's preference for working behind the scenes has diminished her historical significance, as press outlets often credited La Rocque with creating and directing the Women's Section. Despite her central role in the Women's Section, Préval stated that she could not serve as its official leader because poor health occasionally forced her to work from home. Explaining her preference for working in the background, Préval maintained, "The issue was giving Gérus and Féraud their just place in the sun, leaving me to my laboratory for preparation and studies."[17]

The creation of the Women's Section six weeks after the February riots was a turning point in the Croix de Feu's transformation from a league to a mass movement. The public ceremony on March 19 was celebrated with fanfare; it was led by La Rocque, featured multiple speakers, and covered by *Le Flambeau.* While some scholars have contended that the inauguration embodied the Croix de Feu's regressive view of a domestically oriented womanhood, the gendered dynamics of the ceremony were more complex.[18] A close examination of this formative event reveals that the Croix de Feu's gender ideology challenged the "women in the home" movement by championing women's public mobilization in civil society.[19] As the inauguration ceremony revealed, the Croix de Feu's conception of civic space centered around transposing women's spiritual and nurturing abilities to the public sphere where they would fight national decline through a spiritually conceived national rejuvenation. This conception of civic space as a site for women's activism was remarkably similar to republican conceptions of civil society that had developed in metropolitan France—but not the colonies—since the Revolution.

The inaugural ceremony itself followed the limited ecumenicalism of the veteran's mystique that downplayed ethnoreligious difference among certain groups. This selective ecumenicalism was demonstrated in the early Croix de Feu's recruiting materials. One widely distributed tract, for instance, asked "Which men?" might join the Croix de Feu. The answer was "All those of [similar] ideas, sentiments, and faith in action and sacrifice... Catholics, Protestants, Freethinkers, good Jews!"[20] In this way, the Croix de Feu contested the integral nationalism of the Action Français, which conceived of four domestic threats, or "alien elements": Jews, Protestants, Freethinkers, and foreigners.[21] Coded white, the Croix de Feu maintained that these ethnoreligious groups were legitimately "French" because they had lived on French soil for centuries and won citizenship during the Revolution.[22] However, not all veterans were eligible for membership in the national community. Black Africans and North African Muslims were notably absent from this list even though La Rocque himself had commanded Muslim troops during the conquest of Morocco and spoke Arabic. "Good" Jews were those who had integrated into French culture as opposed to Jewish immigrants from Eastern Europe. Croix de Feu xenophobia and its refusal to consider colonial subjects as French revealed how the movement perpetuated ethnoreligious hierarchies that could expand and contract according to time and place.

The Croix de Feu thus sought to transcend sectarianism, but only to a certain extent, which was revealed by the speakers that Préval invited to officiate the inauguration of the Women's Section. The evening featured speeches on women's domestic, public, and national duties: Pastor Durleman spoke on "Women in the Home," Rabbi Kaplan discussed "Women in Civil Society," and Father Dieux focused on "Women in the Nation." These speeches were bookended by those given by Gérus and Féraud, who explained the Women's Section's doctrine and organization, respectively. While the diversity of religious speakers reflected Préval's desire to move beyond sectarian interests by showing that individuals of diverse backgrounds could integrate into a national tradition, each religious leader ignored the particularistic aspects of his religious tradition in order to do so.

The evening's first speaker, Gérus, not only defined the doctrine of the Women's Section to the large mixed-sex audience, but she also represented one model of feminine sociopolitical action. In introducing her, La Rocque stated, "as a former war nurse and mother, she is particularly qualified to direct our sections."[23] Gérus's national service and her status as a mother were equally important; one was not tied to the other, nor did her motherhood preclude her from public action. Indeed, Préval and La Rocque believed that women like Gérus did not belong in the home but were needed to help mobilize nationalistic women in civil society.

For her part, Gérus defined the doctrine of the Women's Section by using scientific language to call for ultranationalistic unity. "The scandals and the assassinations have shaken our confidence with regards to mastering our destiny," she declared, "the press and the cinema show us distressing news ... the daily bread that is brought to us represents ... poisoned food."[24] For this reason, Gérus argued that the Croix de Feu's mission was to bring about the "public purification" necessary to fight the "ferments of moral decomposition."[25] The means to accomplish this, she argued, was for the Croix de Feu to lead a renewal of the *union sacrée:* "A grand reconciliation has announced itself; this evening's event is brilliant proof of it. The social, political, and confessional barriers fall, just as they did in 1914."[26]

The three clerics who followed Gérus all echoed her argument that the Croix de Feu would lead a national renewal. In his speech, "Women in the Home," Pastor Durleman continued the evening's palingenetic tone as he spoke of the moral, religious, and spiritual forces that needed to be, as he repeatedly put it, "resurrected."[27] A crucial component of this resurrection, Durleman maintained, was a woman's love of her home, which reflected her love of France. Of the speakers, only Durleman integrated pronatalist language into his speech, as he decried the paucity of births in France in comparison to Germany, England, and Italy. He asked women to show their devotion to France by populating the home, yet he devoted more of his speech to unmarried women, suggesting they become "indirect" mothers through adoption. Indeed, Durleman's speech contained several contradictory messages. He not only hailed the nuclear family while providing a rationale for women to avoid marriage, but urged women not to consider their domestic duties as the panacea for all social ills. He cautioned women to be equally concerned with fulfilling their civic duties, stating, "I have asked you to not underestimate the home. Permit me now to ask you to not *overestimate* it."[28]

Durleman's speech urging women not to overestimate the power of the home was a bridge between Gérus's call for public purification and Rabbi Kaplan's talk entitled "Women in Civil Society." Perpetuating the inauguration's ultranationalism, Kaplan maintained that the ceremony was evidence that "representatives from France's spiritual families"—Catholics, Protestants, and assimilated Jews—could once again come together and save France, just as they had during the Great War.[29] Drawing distinctions between talk and action, Kaplan contended, "the women organizers of this inauguration are women of great heart who have taken the initiative and decided that it doesn't suffice to say to corruption 'Halt!' ... [but that] it is necessary to drive immorality out from the positions in which it is entrenched."[30] In this way, Kaplan reminded women that their social role was the key to reinfusing French national identity with spirituality, or as he put it, "to rectify the spiritual order that brings France its brilliant worldwide moral prestige."[31]

It was paradoxical that a militaristic league only six weeks removed from the February 6 riots would espouse a commitment to peace, yet the intersection between feminized civic space and peace was an important theme at the inauguration. Evidenced by her invitations to the three religious leaders, Préval believed that religion and women's activism were critical ingredients to regenerate civil society. To this end, the night's fourth speaker, Father Dieux, expressed particular concern with the Third Republic's assault on religion. He implored the audience, "Look around you! You see what is happening . . . you see atheistic positivism, atheistic capitalism, atheistic Marxism, atheistic science," which, Dieux cautioned, were the direct causes of "all the crime, all the theft, and all the assassinations" ruining the national body.[32] Like Gérus, Durleman, and Kaplan before him, Dieux contended that women would play a key role in saving France from the violence that was corrupting the French nation: "Religions accomplish nothing without women. . . . If I could open [history] I could make you see how many wives and daughters of Roman emperors, how many wives and daughters of kings of France have worked effectively to *soften the violence* of men and institutions. If the women of France join the Croix de Feu in the same spirit, with the same will . . . victory will be assured. What woman wants, God wants."[33] For Dieux, women's civic activism offered the French public a corrective contrast to the paramilitaristic violence for which the Croix de Feu was notorious.

The evening's final speaker, Mademoiselle Féraud, moved from discussions of spirituality and national renaissance to explaining how the Women's Section was set to mobilize nationalistic women. Signaling that they were ready to begin the heavy lifting necessary to rejuvenate the French nation, she declared, "We are ready for individual and collective propaganda . . . we want as many adherents as possible in the countryside and the cities."[34] Féraud then asked audience members to help her publicize the Women's Section by telling women they knew who worked in social centers, study circles, workshops, and factories to go to their local Croix de Feu office so that they could gauge the level of interest in creating a Women's Section. Indeed, it was Féraud who best understood the challenges facing her new organization: "The realities [we create] must be better than the promises."[35]

SOCIAL ACTION AND THE EXTRAORDINARY GROWTH OF THE WOMEN'S SECTION AT THE NATIONAL AND LOCAL LEVELS, 1934–1936

By early 1934 many in the Croix de Feu believed that mass mobilization would lend legitimacy to the league's claim that it alone represented the nation's general will. The Croix de Feu's conception of civic space and its creation of structures that facilitated effective organizing were two important factors in its remarkable mobilization of women. Other interwar ultranationalist groups were either smaller, shorter-lived, or losing influence; the Jeunesses Patriotes and Françisme were smaller than the Croix de Feu, Solidarité Française existed only from 1933 to 1936, and the Action Française struggled to maintain its influence after the 1926 papal condemnation. While each of these ultranationalist leagues organized Women's Sections and discursively made women central to their vision of France by considering the family as the basic cell of the nation, they lacked the leadership, organizational skills, and will to mobilize women on a par with the Croix de Feu. Féraud best articulated the reasons behind the Croix de Feu's success, arguing that it was rooted less in its ability to create new ideas and more in the skillful organization of its membership to provide services. "The originality of the Croix de Feu movement is not to make anything new. We invent nothing, but have immediately created, brought to life, and coordinated an ensemble of works," she proudly told the audience at the first Women's Section Congress in late 1935.[36] Through effective leadership and structure, the Croix de Feu's Women's Section not only flourished, but spawned a variety of affiliated organizations, all of which were imbued with ethnoreligious nationalism and a social reform mission.

Creating a grassroots organization required Préval, Gérus, Féraud, and many other activists to embark upon a massive drive to recruit women for new local sections of the Women's Section. Préval appointed Féraud to take charge of the Parisian Left Bank sections, Gérus to run the Right Bank sections. She also instructed both of them to travel throughout metropolitan France to help local leaders get their sections up and running. Beginning in March 1934, Women's Section leaders called their recruiting activities "individual propaganda [which was] necessary to obtain a mass sufficient for groups to function efficiently."[37] The "individual propaganda" campaign had several main features. Since each Women's Section was attached to a Men's Section, section leaders asked men to encourage their wives, sisters, mothers, and daughters to join. In addition to these family networks, the Croix de Feu expected its recruiters to act with missionary zeal in hanging posters, distributing tracts, and circulating *Le Flambeau* in their local neighborhoods. One widely disseminated tract, for example, framed women's role in national rejuvenation not in maternalist, familialist, or pronatalist but nationalistic terms: "French Women—for those of you who are devoted to the social and civic works that make national recovery possible, for those of you who want to combine all the generous and charitable initiatives into a joint effort . . . join our Women's Section to show the commitment of your devotion, your love of the people, and your adoration of the tricolor flag."[38] To this end, recruiters focused on informal social networks of family, friends, and church parishioners. For example, each Women's Section gave newcomers a form and asked them to provide information about friends, family, and business associates.[39] Section members then used "sympathizer files" created from these forms to mail propaganda tracts and meeting invitations to potential recruits. If the individual was not receptive to these overtures, he or she received a visit from a recruiter, although at times, novice and overzealous recruiters caused problems by showing up accidentally at the homes of Communists and lecturing them.[40]

One of the top priorities for Préval, Gérus, and Féraud in building the Women's Section was to fill the leadership positions within local sections. Either Gérus or Féraud worked with the male section chief to which the Women's Section was attached to nominate the section's leader; the nomination was passed on for La Rocque's ultimate approval.[41] The female section leader had the authority to appoint women to seven posts, which reflected each section's social and youth services. Delegates in charge of the sewing room, clothing depot, visiting nurses, and social assistance, ran each section's social services, while two delegates organized programs for boys and girls under thirteen years of age and girls over the age of thirteen. The only man in this leadership circle was the delegate assigned to boys under sixteen, who was required to join the Croix de Feu or VN.[42]

Most Women's Sections had filled their leadership positions when the Popular Front dissolved the Croix de Feu in June 1936. From April 1934 to the first Women's Section Congress in October 1935, Gérus and Féraud nominated approximately 363 women to section leadership positions, of whom 78 percent were married (Figure 3).[43] If a woman showed the proper "order, discipline, and devotion," Women's Section leaders and the male section chief promoted her to the highest rank available to women in the Croix de Feu, that of general secretary.[44] Of the nineteen women who advanced to this demanding position, thirteen were married (68 percent). While married women dominated the regional and voluntary positions, unmarried women were more prevalent in the league's centralized leadership in Paris, and as Kevin Passmore has shown for the PSF, employed among the party's professional social workers and nurses.[45] As these statistics demonstrate, the Croix de Feu/PSF's reliance on married women for the general secretary position and the lack of evidence of conflict between single and married supporters confirmed the path to national rejuvenation established at the March 1934 inauguration: married women should not overestimate the power of the home and were more than qualified for leadership positions. This mobilization of married women in civic space as elite nationalists reflected the manner in which Croix de Feu/PSF women contested the narrow conception of womanhood that epitomized the "women in the home" movement.

The exhaustive efforts of Préval, Gérus, Féraud, and local activists increased dramatically the number of Women's Sections in metropolitan France. By June 1936 the Women's Section had approximately 315 new sections, of which 96 were in Paris and its suburbs, 187 in the provinces, and 32 in the Maghreb (Figure 4).[46] While a section was considered to be constituted once fifty women registered, it was not unusual for sections to have hundreds of members.[47] The Paris sections were organized by arrondissement and grew quickly. By June 1936 organizers subdivided the hundreds of women in each section into quarters of thirty members, then again into "cells" of a dozen.[48] Membership totals for provincial sections are fragmentary, although they regularly reported hundreds of members. While the growth rate of the Women's Sections lagged behind that of the Men's Sections, it was still impressive. In Normandy, for example, between the February riots and January 1935, activists created twenty-seven new Women's Sections in comparison to forty new Men's Sections.[49] Moreover, the growth of the Women's Section accelerated after the Croix de Feu transformed into the PSF. The Women's Section in southwest France, for instance, grew from seven to twenty-one sections by the end of 1937.[50] By 1939 the Women's Section was active in well over 90 percent of the departments, and local sections reported on their social services in over sixty regional newspapers.[51]

The geographical distribution of the Women's Section demonstrates that women's recruiting efforts were most effective in urban bourgeois districts of large cities (Figure 5). These were areas where Men's Sections were already established, and for this reason, the density of Women's Sections followed that of the movement as a whole. Additionally, it appears that the Women's Section was the most active in locales where nationalist groups and Popular Front parties engaged in fierce competition for supporters. In the eight departments where the Women's Section was most active, Popular Front parties averaged 45 percent of the vote.[52] This lack of dominance indicates that both groups were battling for support. Additionally, the Women's Section was weak in working-class and rural areas where the Popular Front parties were either very strong or very weak. For example, the Women's Section was less active in 72 percent of the departments where the parties of the Popular Front were very strong, notably in the underpopulated and rural areas of the South.[53] It was less active in 70 percent of the departments where Popular Front parties were also weak.[54]

While the Women's Section grew quickly in politicized urban districts, areas where bourgeois women themselves were more politicized may have been another factor in its growth. There appears to be a correlation between the strength of feminist organizing and rates of women's participation in the Croix de Feu. Between March 1934 and June 1936, Croix de Feu women established a relatively strong foothold in 64 percent of the departments in which Steven Hause maintained that the activities of feminist organizations were "frequent."[55] The evidence is fragmentary, but it is possible that fears over feminist activities may have driven women concerned with nationalist issues toward the Croix de Feu/PSF. At a conference in Montpellier, for instance, section leader Madame Merle warned women that, "a number of French cities already have municipal councilors who have been the choice of feminist groups, which is proof of their civic action, and, of the necessity for PSF women to do as much [as the feminist groups] if our ideas are to take power."[56]

The Croix de Feu's efforts at mass mobilization paid big dividends, as its membership dwarfed its competitors on the ultranationalist Right and secular Left and rivaled the Catholic Right. By mid-1935 police estimated that 70,000 of the Croix de Feu's 240,000 members were women.[57] Moreover, the Croix de Feu's general membership far surpassed that of other ultranationalist leagues. Police, for instance, reported that the Action Française claimed 1,600 women out of 70,000 members and that the Jeunesses Patriotes had 500 women out of 100,000.[58] As for the Left, the Communists and Socialists claimed a combined total of 248,000 members in 1935, but neither group organized women as effectively as the Croix de Feu.[59] Women attempted to convince Socialist Party leaders to recognize an official women's group with the party's founding in 1905, although this did not happen until 1931, and once established, it was unable to attract women in large numbers.[60] The Communist Party had established a Women's Section in 1921 as a recruiting mechanism but was unable to entice women to join in large numbers. In 1936 the party congress passed a resolution against creating women's groups as part of its stance that women's emancipation was based upon dismantling existing class structures, although it did create a youth group that attracted young women but in fewer numbers than the Croix de Feu.[61] The only group that outstripped Croix de Feu/PSF women's membership was the LFACF, which, according to its own self-reported figures, claimed two million members in eighty departments in 1937.[62]

The services provided by a growing number of Women's Section grassroots supporters fundamentally changed the scope of the Croix de Feu social program and permitted the league to reach thousands at a time of economic depression. The structure of the Women's Section enabled supporters to replace piecemeal services with a systematic program that facilitated the movement's ability to move from aiding dozens to tens of thousands (Table 3).[63]

At the most rudimentary level, local sections established a clothing depot, sewing room, and soup kitchen. As sections grew in size, so did the scope of their services. The largest sections developed youth initiatives such as social centers (the French version of settlement houses in the United States and Great Britain, the most famous of which was Jane Addams's Hull House), summer camps, physical education services, and programs that sent social workers and nurses to the homes of the needy. Explaining why women's social action enabled them to be better agents of nationalism than men, Madame Buisset, the section head in Charleville, told a mixed-sex general assembly meeting, "I'm asking women to penetrate wherever men cannot go in order to find misery and relieve it."[64]

The growth of Croix de Feu social action enabled top leaders to emphasize the relationship between social regeneration, mass mobilization, and national unity. Writing in *Le Flambeau,* for instance, La Rocque declared, "Men and women of good will whose *mass* will give the Croix de Feu movement its definitive scope must be social. If not, they have no place among us."[65] As 1935 progressed La Rocque became convinced that Croix de Feu social programs were a viable means to win the support of large segments of the French public. The police recognized this shift but ignored women's role in it: "La Rocque is striving to reorient his movement in a more social direction. With this goal in mind, over the last few months, Croix de Feu propaganda has above all emphasized the creation and maintenance of social work: health clinics, soup kitchens, clothing depots, and summer camps."[66]

TABLE 3. Growth of the Croix de Feu Social Program, 1927–1936

	CROIX DE FEU SERVICES (1927–1934)		THE WOMEN'S SECTION SERVICES (APRIL 1934 TO JUNE 1936)	
	Location/Scope	*Activities*	*Location/Scope*	*Activities*
Clothing Depots	One in Paris (1930)	No records	Hundreds attached to local women's section	Distributed 87,000 pieces of clothing
Sewing Rooms	None	None		Made 2,500 undergarments
Soup Kitchens	Several in Paris	No records	Eight in Paris; dozens in the provinces	Paris: 192,000 meals; provinces: 500,000 meals
Medical Center	None	None	Parisian clinic opened in 1934	4,292 office visits
Summer Camps	One in Vosges, summer 1931	Twenty boys attended in 1932	Thirteen camps across France	4,487 children attended in 1935
Social Centers	None	None	Five in Paris; several in the provinces	Food/clothing distribution, leisure activities
University Center	None	None	Women's Center in Paris (1935)	Study/socializing; 180 women joined
Physical Education Centers	None	None	Four in Paris; eleven in the provinces	Paris: 1,200 children; provinces: hundreds joined

Source information given in Chapter 2, Note 63.

The Croix de Feu's growing emphasis on social action was reflected by a step of symbolic significance when La Rocque renamed the organization the Mouvement Social Français des Croix de Feu (MSF des CF, or simply, MSF) in November 1935. The MSF was the umbrella organization for the Croix de Feu, VN, and Women's Section, which was now led by a new general secretary, Mademoiselle Simone Marochetti. Working with Préval, Marochetti oversaw two branches: one devoted to social action and the other devoted to civic action. La Rocque explained the purpose of the MSF in a circular distributed to all Croix de Feu leaders, "Our social works situate the MSF at the antipodes of party politicians. . . . By way of Croix de Feu sections we are reaching the generation of fire; by way of VN sections, generations born after the war; by the MSF training, we must reach all the other French and give to the Movement its character of universality."[67]

In this way, the hierarchy that the early Croix de Feu sought to impose on French society as the vehicle for national rejuvenation was shifting. Veterans were losing their universalist claims to represent all French, and women were no longer the "amorphous mass." Rather, through social action, women had the capacity to join veterans as elites. Reflecting this shift, Croix de Feu leaders announced that women engaged in social action would no longer march behind Croix de Feu veterans at the 1936 Joan of Arc parade, but alongside them.[68]

Croix de Feu social services became the movement's primary entrée into neighborhoods that were political battlegrounds between ultranationalists and the Popular Front. These battles centered around persuasion more than physical confrontation. The case of Paris's ethnically diverse fifteenth arrondissement was a typical example of the ways in which the movement's social action functioned at the grassroots level. In December 1934 fifty women living in the fifteenth wanted to join the Croix de Feu, which was enough to constitute a section. By the spring of 1936, the section had grown to establish a central office, soup kitchen, clothing depot, sewing room, and youth program.[69] The fifteenth was densely populated and home to several vibrant immigrant communities, including Russians, a large number of immigrants from the Antilles, and most importantly in this case, Muslim workers from Algeria. The Algerian Muslim community was centered around Algerian-owned small hotels with attached cafes, which were culturally significant community centers. Knowing that Algerians congregated at these hotel-cafes, Croix de Feu men and women ramped up their recruiting efforts. Croix de Feu men entered the cafes and directed the men to the movement's free welfare and social services.[70] Assuming the Algerians were anti-Semitic—which was often not the case—Croix de Feu recruiters told them that the league was the adversary of the Jews and the Jews' Marxist allies.[71] Police reported that league recruiters promised the café-goers that if put into power, the Croix de Feu would grant them the same citizenship rights that Algerian Jews enjoyed under the conditions of the Crémieux decree.[72] Croix de Feu men thus deployed these two tactics in the hotel-cafes throughout the fifteenth: they dangled the promise of welfare and sought to provoke anti-Semitic sentiments within the Algerian community in order to draw them into the movement.

While the Croix de Feu attracted a small number of Algerian supporters, their overtures were generally not welcomed due to the activities of the Etoile Nord-Africaine (ENA), which was well entrenched in the fifteenth. Founded in 1926 in Paris, the ENA advocated for Algerian independence and was one of the leading rights groups for Algerians in Paris. ENA leaders had made it their mission to warn Algerians against what ENA leaders called "fascist propaganda" and "false promises."[73] ENA actions only accelerated Croix de Feu propagandizing and offers of material aid. This battle for support between the ENA and the Croix de Feu not only reveals the ways in which the far Right sought to drive a wedge between the Communists, the ENA, and Algerians, but the ethnoreligiously divisive impact of its social action.

THE PATH TO POWER: NATIONAL RECONCILIATION, SOCIAL FIRST!, AND CATHOLIC NATIONALISM

Women's success in broadening the Croix de Feu's use of social action drove a major announcement that revealed a definition of the movement's path to power. On December 6, Jean Ybarnegaray, a representative in the Chamber of Deputies and member of the Croix de Feu's leadership council, issued a call for "national reconciliation" on the floor of the Chamber. This call for unity required a disarmament on the part of the nationalist leagues and the Left.[74] Indeed, it was a direct challenge to the Popular Front and its coalition of support that centered around the working classes and those concerned about the Croix de Feu's ultranationalism. Subsequent issues of *Le Flambeau* ran banner headlines emphasizing "Reconciliation," and the movement's leadership initiated a campaign to convince the public that France could be saved through unity brought about by social action. At the heart of national reconciliation was the Croix de Feu's strategy to galvanize Catholics to fight what many believed to be a civilizational crisis. Women were at the front lines of this battle. Charles Vallin, the PSF's chief propagandist, explained, "We won't save France without women because we won't save France unless we create first a moral climate.... It's women who create this climate, especially in a Christian civilization like ours."[75] La Rocque echoed this sentiment in addressing the movement's social action activists: "You will serve our Work, our *Patrie,* and Christian civilization, which must be restored in order to rediscover its spiritual essence."[76]

The Croix de Feu's campaign to save France through social action was sophisticated and ambitious. It included top Croix de Feu leaders seeking the support of the Catholic hierarchy, interviews with the Catholic press, efforts by the leadership to recruit social work professionals, and grassroots organizing that aligned Croix de Feu social services with those of local parishes. This shift in strategy was critical for several reasons. First, the Croix de Feu/PSF's tactics moderated over the remainder of the decade as its leadership decreased paramilitary mobilizations in favor of social action. Second, while the Croix de Feu moderated tactically, it grew ideologically strident as its hard-line Catholicism became increasingly apparent. Indeed, through social action, Croix de Feu/PSF supporters used the movement as a vehicle to intermix hard-line Catholicism and politics, which played a key role in the conservative shift in the political culture of the late Third Republic.

While the Croix de Feu had obtained the support of far Right clergy, as demonstrated by Vauplane's officiating of the Mass of the Marshals and Dieux's participation in the inauguration, the leadership also sought the support of mainstream clergy. In doing so, the Croix de Feu walked a fine line between breaking the Church's rapprochement with the Republic and offering the Church an opportunity to align itself with a political group that sought to bolster Catholic Action. At the back of La Rocque's and Préval's minds was the fate of the Action Française, which saw its numbers decline after a 1926 papal condemnation brought about by its violence, overt political activity, and Charles Maurras's atheism. The condemnation devastated the group's already weak Women's Section.[77] Capitalizing upon the prominence of the Action Français's "Politics First!" slogan and seeking to differentiate the Croix de Feu from a group that many considered more intellectual, Croix de Feu propagandists created a new slogan, "Social First!," and made it ubiquitous in the movement's media outlets. As Préval explained to an audience of women leaders in 1936: "My fellow women, when someone comes to you and says, politics first, followed by the social, you should respond like true French women: the social *first!*"[78] In this way, the call for national reconciliation and the use of social action as the means to accomplish it invigorated activists' ability to lobby Church officials to support the league. The initial results of this new strategy were successful; police noted that growing numbers of priests attended Croix de Feu meetings, health clinics, and youth clubs.[79]

Of all the Catholic clergy, Croix de Feu leaders most wanted the support of Cardinal Verdier of Paris. One of the most powerful clerics in France, Verdier had consistently declined the movement's invitations to the Mass of the Marshals while attending events for officially sanctioned groups like the LFACF and the Jeunesse Ouvrière Chrétienne (JOC), a group for working-class youth whose purpose was to promote class fusion and rechristianize French society.[80] La Rocque knew that obtaining the cardinal's endorsement would help legitimize the Croix de Feu in the eyes of the Catholic faithful. In corresponding with him, La Rocque argued that December 6 was a turning point in the history of France because that was the moment when the Croix de Feu formulated its mission to bring about a permanent *union sacrée*. La Rocque explained the movement's mission to Verdier in this way: "[Our] general goal is civic reconciliation, then to build a great moral force throughout the country capable of crystallizing this reconciliation. We would not know how to obtain such a result outside of social reform. . . . The Croix de Feu represents a *model* of what we would like to make the France of tomorrow."[81] La Rocque informed the cardinal that the "model" of this new France was centered around five types of social action: services aimed at children, unemployment placement aid, medical and social assistance, services for nonmembers, and university circles.

While La Rocque suggested to Verdier that Croix de Feu social action was ecumenical, in practice, its ideology and activities exacerbated sectarianism. Indeed, the movement's social action was based upon a universalism that was cast in religious rather than secular terms. La Rocque explained to the cardinal: "The religious question is above all restricted; this is necessary to make sure that our associations receive adherents from all origins. But the instruction is applied strictly to *establish a census* of confessional membership and to enter in immediately with church authorities in order to *compel* the children to renew or maintain their religious practice."[82] In this way, the Croix de Feu catalogued the religious affiliation of youth and adults in the movement's social programs. Moreover, La Rocque informed Verdier that the movement's emphasis on compulsory religious practice promoted rechristianization because Croix de Feu women stepped in for nonpracticing parents by driving children who had been baptized and taken their first communion to the local parish so that they could reengage in religious practice.[83] La Rocque believed that Croix de Feu/PSF social action was literally saving the souls of those in their programs. While Verdier never gave La Rocque the public support the colonel sought, the cardinal did send his coadjutor to several Croix de Feu events, including the funeral of a prominent member.[84]

A key component of the Croix de Feu's campaign to engage Catholics was interviews that La Rocque conducted with Catholic journals to explain the movement's social mission. One of the most prominent intellectuals drawn to the Croix de Feu was the hard-liner Jean Daujat, who founded the Center for Religious Studies in Paris and began teaching there in 1931.[85] Luminaries such as Jacques Maritain and Maurice Merleau-Ponty contributed to the center and wrote for his magazine. After talking with La Rocque, Daujat declared that the Croix de Feu was promising because "it conforms to Christian conceptions of politics and its principal leaders are nearly all fervent Christians in their personal lives."[86] Moreover, La Rocque convinced Daujat that the Croix de Feu was France's premier defender of Christian heritage amidst a civilizational crisis. Daujat stated: "We have said that France was the first-born of the Christian nations when the Roman Empire fell due to invasion and decay as a result of internal corruption. . . . France, the eldest sister of European civilization found its origins in human and Christian principles."[87] France's Christian origins put the nation on the front lines of fighting for European supremacy. Daujat claimed that not only was European civilization "divided, ruined, and exhausted," but that it was threatened by the "double paganism" of a class-based communism and race-based Nazism.[88] Hope for the future of Europe, he proclaimed, was in the Croix de Feu. Daujat explained it this way: "France, and France alone, can be the source for a new order founded on the true human and Christian principles on which the salvation, the future, the renaissance of Europe depends . . . this resurrection of France is the mission of the Croix de Feu/PSF."[89]

The Croix de Feu also sought the support of Catholics who were more progressive than Daujat, although La Rocque refused to temper the movement's ethnoreligious nationalism. For example, La Rocque interviewed with the moderate Dominican weekly *Sept,* which was established in 1934 to further Pius XI's attempt to break French Catholicism from the extreme Right.[90] La Rocque believed that he could convince *Sept* readers of the Croix de Feu's religiously based universalism. "It is necessary to understand that the Occidental civilization—ours—is a Christian civilization," he informed a *Sept* journalist, adding that all Croix de Feu/ PSF adherents, "whatever their level of belief or unbelief may be," accepted the movement's criterion that France was a Christian nation.[91] While *Sept* published interviews with hard-liners such as La Rocque, the journal could not withstand the conservatism of Church officials. When *Sept* refused to support Franco's efforts against Spanish Republicans, demonstrated tacit support for the Popular Front's social reforms, and finally, published an interview with Leon Blum in 1937, the Vatican responded by banning the journal.[92]

While the Croix de Feu's efforts to draw the support of the clergy and publicize its activities in certain Catholic journals were important, Préval's recruiting of social work professionals had the most profound effect on the movement's grassroots organizing capabilities. Préval sought to create an army of social service providers led by social workers who would be supplemented by auxiliaries. Such action was the best way to remake the basic cell of French society: the family. She explained this plan at a major conference in October 1936: "Remember that the Communists want to have a social worker in each district. A social worker is better than a teacher because she looks after not only the child but the entire family."[93]

The Social Action Mindset, Will, and Disability in Greater France

One of the first professional social workers that Préval recruited was Suzanne Fouché, who came to the Croix de Feu in late 1935 to create courses for young women who wanted to be auxiliaries to social service professionals.[94] Fouché was well known in social Catholic circles that included the likes of Cardinal Verdier and François Mauriac.[95] Before supporting the Croix de Feu, Fouché gained prominence for her leadership in promoting social causes and advocacy for the disabled. She was a *professeur d'assistance sociale* in Paris and had founded the Ligue pour l'adaptation du diminué physique au travail (LADAPT, League for the Adaptation of the Physically Impaired to Work) along with another Croix de Feu supporter, Simone Gouin, in 1929. The LADAPT was one of the first leagues in France to advocate for those who were physically disabled. In addition to Fouché's teaching and civic work, she was the author of several books that explored philosophical approaches to social action, the most famous of which was *Suffrance, école de vie*, which was in the libraries of most Croix de Feu/PSF social centers. The prominent hard-line Catholic, Académie Francaise member, and future Nobel Prize winner François Mauriac wrote the book's preface, praising Fouché for her allegiance to Christ's principles of sacrifice and disdain of worldly pursuits.[96] While Mauriac's views would shift to the left after the Second World War, during the 1930s his fears of Bolshevism led him to express sympathy for Mussolini and support for the French extreme Right after the February 1934 riots.[97] Moreover, as Frantz Fanon pointed out, Mauriac epitomized French racial thinking by worrying that "black, brown, and yellow hordes" were poised to invade France's shores.[98] In these ways, Mauriac's endorsement of Fouché's work was representative of many conservatives whose worries over the ethnoreligious character of the French nation were at the forefront of their minds.

Fouché's prominence as a Catholic intellectual was representative of the ways in which Croix de Feu leaders attempted to appeal to the French public. She wrote in her memoir that she found in the Croix de Feu a movement that could "rechristianize" France by imparting a sense of social solidarity that would make society more humane.[99] Fouché's interest in humane action was rooted in her own personal suffering, which stemmed from contracting bone tuberculosis at the age of sixteen. This experience with disability was a key reason why she cofounded LADAPT, which was recognized by the Ministry for Public Health in 1934 as an important provider of social services and thus eligible for state subsidies.[100] Perhaps the determinant factor in convincing Fouché to work with the Croix de Feu was that La Rocque promised her complete autonomy in training social auxiliaries, including freedom from section presidents.[101]

Fouché's social auxiliary courses for young women were so effective that Croix de Feu leaders asked her to broaden her message by instituting a series of public conferences, which took place in metropolitan France and North Africa.[102] Fouché believed that she could use the Croix de Feu to change the "collective mentality" of the French people by instilling in them what she called the "social sense."[103] She thus spent significant portions of time in the mid- to late 1930s on the road, conducting her "social sense" conferences to form a new generation of social cadres (Figure 6). Insisting that human consciousness was more sophisticated than many typically understood, Fouché taught that in addition to the five human senses, there was a sixth sense—the social sense. She explained that the five senses put humans into contact with the world around them, which left the individual walled-up and isolated, trapped in one's own superficial perceptions of the external world. In contrast, the "sixth sense" enabled human beings to develop a deeper understanding of the world, or as Fouché put it, "the *sentiment* of our inter-dependence."[104] Impressed by Fouché's conference in Tunis, the leader of the Tunisian Croix de Feu, Dr. Minguet, a notorious racist and anti-Semite, wrote, "Mlle Fouché showed us that . . . just as the senses are how we communicate with the exterior world—they are the open windows that surround us—the social sense binds us to each other."[105] For Fouché, human beings lived in two realms: a physical or material realm, and a moral or spiritual realm. To truly develop human appreciation for the realm of sentiment, spirituality, and morality, Fouché argued that human beings needed to be reminded that they possessed such innate capabilities.

The social sense was the key to organizing human society not around individuals and their rights but the needs of a human collective, or what Fouché referred to as "the grand body."[106] It was the social sense, she said, that formed "the base of French reconstruction."[107] As one of the leaders of an Algerian Women's

Section, Madame d'Arras, noted, "The social sense helps relationships in human lives. It enables and sheds light on this solidarity, [which is] necessary for mass harmony."[108] Reminding the audience that "each human being is a *living cell...* part of a whole, members of a large body," d'Arras reported that Fouché believed that some people had forgotten about their collective duties.[109] Fouché rejected excessive egalitarianism and the communalism of Marxism. However, reining in individual liberty was not negative. As Minguet explained, "We aren't free because we aren't alone. This interdependence must not be constrained; it must exist in joy."[110] D'Arras too emphasized the joy inherent in blending into an orderly collective: "Scatter this interior joy which supports [our ability] to reestablish this moral order, which is necessary for a lasting harmony."[111] In this way, blending into the collective was the duty of all inhabitants of the *patrie,* whether one was a French citizen or colonial subject.

The notion that social reconstruction began by developing a joyful sentiment of collectivity and a hierarchy of values was a rigid path toward national rejuvenation, premised upon the complete assimilation of difference. Not only were the ideas that Fouché promoted in North Africa the same as those she presented across metropolitan France, but she interacted only with settlers. As Fouché explained at one of her conferences in the Gironde, "In Bordeaux, as in Paris, as in Algiers, as in everywhere, I've been supported by the kindness and sympathy of my students."[112] In seeking to reach her students, it was the uniformity of experience that struck Fouché. In the case of the Maghrebian conferences, Fouché's ethnoreligious view of Frenchness precluded her from altering her agenda to grapple with the minority status of French settlers and appealing to indigenous women and men. Ignoring the ethnoreligious division that colonial rule engendered, she assumed the privileged status that her ethnoreligious background granted her. While some social reformers still bought into the notion of the civilizing mission, for Fouché colonial subjects were invisible, which reflected the associationist stance of Croix de Feu settlers. Republican social reformers of the Musée social, for example, believed that social services could "civilize" Muslims and assimilate them into Greater France.[113] Many of these social reformers used social services to enter into Muslim homes, which not only remained off-limits to the state but enabled them to interact with Muslim women in a way that others could not, albeit usually in paternalistic and demeaning terms. However, Fouché's actions revealed the ways in which the Croix de Feu/PSF's Catholicism drove a wedge between Catholics and Muslims.

Fouché's emphasis on suffering reflected a twentieth-century trend in Catholic revivalism that emphasized suffering as the key to overcoming humanity's bodily shortcomings and finding spiritual redemption.[114] She stated that her experience with disability enabled her to transcend physicality and find empowerment in spirituality. While a body might be racked with pain, a person's character was revealed by her or his worldly interactions. Fouché explained, "My suffering is a divine currency, confided to my poverty in order to be, by my acquiescence, transformed into a treasure that is redeemed."[115] Dividing sickness and suffering into three categories, physical, intellectual, and spiritual, Fouché explained that the physical aspect of pain was the most salient because it drove the latter two. D'Arras reported that Fouché maintained that "The physical shock of sickness is cruel, exhausting in its continuous pain… the moanings of acute pain are outlets of such pain."[116] For Fouché, experiencing life in this way made her more attuned to the intellectual component of illness since the sick often asked why suffering was necessary. As d'Arras explained, "Mlle Fouché shows us that suffering is like a means of action, like a marvelous radiance. The interior life grows while the exterior life dwindles; there's splendid enrichment for those who find God there… be joyful in communicating serene peace."[117]

For the Croix de Feu, Fouché's success showed that issues surrounding disability were best left to private religious work and individual initiative rather than state intervention.[118] Fouché believed that private work was the most effective way to contest the "rhetoric of pity" that sometimes characterized interwar discourses concerning disability.[119] Indeed, LADAPT was one of several disability rights groups that arose across Europe and the United States during the interwar period, many of which advocated for disabled veterans, the blind, and the deaf.[120] However, LADAPT struggled to garner the funding necessary to engage in the advocacy that Fouché envisioned. Fouché stated she joined with the Croix de Feu/PSF in part because state subsidies were not enough and she had exhausted her personal resources in covering LADAPT's continual budget shortfalls; the Croix de Feu/PSF not only paid her six hundred francs a month but funded her initiatives.[121]

The relationship between Fouché's social sense conferences and Croix de Feu social action raises the question of what Fouché's disability rights activism reveals about the Croix de Feu/PSF. "Disability," writes Catherine Kudlick, "is crucial for understanding how Western cultures determine hierarchies and maintain social order as well as how they define progress."[122] As we shall see, Croix de Feu/PSF physical education programs were obsessed with ugliness and beauty; its physical culture theorists believed that ugliness revealed a weakness in character. Yet the Croix de Feu/PSF also emphasized health and positive eugenics, which left narrow space for those who were sick or weak to improve their bodily strength and level of wellness. Thus, in terms of physicality, "difference" was recognized *if* the individual displayed the work ethic necessary to overcome it. The Croix de Feu/PSF maintained that Fouché's life revealed that a disabled person imbued with the social sense was richer than an able-bodied person whose inner life was empty and stale. Indeed, Fouché was held up as a symbol of the power of *will:* she did not complain about her disability but used it to her advantage.

CONTESTING THE REPUBLICAN SOCIAL MODEL: THE ADVENT OF THE PSF

Fouché's conferences not only revealed the intersections between Catholic revivalism, political rejuvenation, and national reconciliation, but the ways in which the Croix de Feu/PSF sought to create an alternate social model to the secular one that emerged in the late Third Republic. The Croix de Feu/PSF social model emphasized privately provided services and a spiritual conception of French heritage. It sought to invigorate lingering prewar localist sentiment that rejected republican reformers' emphasis on state intervention into social protections in favor of parish-based charity.[123] This localism was diminished by the devastation of the Great War, which spurred many social Catholics to work with republican officials in providing desperately needed services at the municipal level.[124] The interwar years were a triumph for republican reformers, as policy makers used social initiatives to bring together mutual-aid societies, social Catholic charities, and employers to ensure basic social protections.[125] These services promoted a secular national consensus, or what Laura Levine Frader argues was the emergence of the French social model.[126] While various sectors of French society and the Church hierarchy had officially reconciled themselves to the Republic, the actions of Croix de Feu supporters demonstrated that many remained hostile to it. For disaffected Catholics, and a scant minority of Jews and Protestants, the Croix de Feu provided an opportunity for ultranationalists to hold on to their vision of French heritage and contest the republican social model.

In championing private and religiously motivated aid, the lines were drawn between the Right, led by the Croix de Feu, and the Popular Front, which put social concerns and governmental aid to the working classes at the forefront of its agenda. For this reason, some Popular Front supporters believed that Croix de Feu social action was the top threat to state-sponsored public assistance. Led in part by prominent Socialist Paul Rivet, the Comité de Vigilance des Intellectuels Antifascistes (CVIA) was created in the wake of the February 6 riots and played a critical role in forming the Popular Front. Alarmed by the Croix de Feu, the CVIA catalogued the movement's medical centers, soup kitchens, and clothing depots. Believing that it was their duty to defend the emerging French welfare state, the CVIA alerted the public about Croix de Feu corporatism: "The Croix de Feu are trying to avoid admitting that in their system of government this charity will be called upon to replace all national welfare."[127] The battle between the Popular Front and Croix de Feu over the role of government was the defining issue of the historic May 1936 elections. Not only had the Popular Front campaigned on expanding the social rights of workers but it had promised to dissolve what it called the "fascist" leagues. Despite the Croix de Feu's call for reconciliation and its increasing use of social action, it was difficult for the movement to divorce itself from its paramilitary origins. The Popular Front constantly labeled the Croix de Feu as fascist, which was a key reason that the leftist coalition was able to win the elections. It fulfilled its campaign promise and dissolved all paramilitary leagues, including the Croix de Feu.

Unfortunately for the Popular Front, its leaders underestimated women's strong influence in the Croix de Feu and the movement's concomitant emphasis on social action. While the dissolution completely undermined the other leagues, the Croix de Feu emerged relatively unscathed. In keeping with the Social First! strategy of national reconciliation, La Rocque simply renamed the group the Parti Social Français and received an exemption from the interior ministry not to dissolve the MSF so that it could continue providing social services.[128] While Men's Sections reoriented themselves to run in elections, the Women's Section continued to function in a bifurcated manner. Moreover, several of the associations that Women's Section leaders had established to better organize their services were undeterred. Seeking to cure diseased bodies, Women's Section leaders created the Association Médico-Sociale Jeanne d'Arc (AMSJA) in early 1936 to organize health clinics, visiting nurse programs, insurance aid to the indigent, and a convalescent home in Pau.[129] Forming healthy bodies was equally important, and to this end, the Société de Préparation et d'Éducation Sportive (SPES) was established at the same time to regenerate the so-called "French Race." With the advent of the PSF, the Women's

Section changed its name to reflect the nature of its operations. Préval channeled the energy and enthusiasm of her most passionate supporters by creating an elite group that organized the movement's social services called Social Action (Section Féminine d'Action Sociale), which differed from a new organization dedicated to propaganda and recruiting, Civic Action (Action Civique). Whereas Civic Action sometimes struggled to define its mission and galvanize members, Social Action operated with a great degree of autonomy and professionalism and grew rapidly. While national figures are fragmentary, 117 social action sections operated in the Nord alone by 1938.[130]

Préval was now the only woman on the PSF's executive committee, and while the new organizations that grew out of the Women's Section had titular leaders, she also sat on the leadership council of each and worked with Marochetti to formulate their programs, assign staff, and organize activities.[131] Moreover, for the first time, Préval took on a public leadership position in what became one of the PSF's most important affiliated groups, Travail et loisirs (Work and Leisure). Created soon after the Croix de Feu's dissolution, this new association was a cultural organization that organized youth and leisure activities for working-class families, especially those living in urban areas throughout Greater France. Travail et loisirs took over many of the activities that the Women's Section had created, including summer camps, social centers, and entertainment activities.[132] While Travail et loisirs, AMSJA, SPES, and Social Action were nominally independent, in practice they coordinated activities and staff. For instance, Marochetti was one of several high-ranking women to conduct inspections and evaluate the staff at social centers and summer camps.

To administer the coordination of services and manage the movement's growing social action bureaucracy, La Rocque and Préval created a Social Studies Bureau, which was led by a respected social service professional, Jeanne Garrigoux. As the movement's new expert on social policy, Garrigoux wielded a great deal of authority over many PSF men. La Rocque called the Bureau "the organizer and controller of the sum of our action," and attached it to his cabinet, which granted Garrigoux proximity to the colonel and a high degree of influence.[133] For instance, the male heads of PSF sections, committees, and federations received instructions from the Bureau in how to implement local social and cultural initiatives. The Bureau also supervised home visits made by social workers and nurses and oversaw inspections made by women and men at social and physical education centers, summer camps, and health facilities.[134] One of Garrigoux's most important duties was to determine the ways in which the politics of a municipality (specifically the affiliation of the mayor) would affect the implementation of the PSF's social services. For example, when PSF supporters wanted to set up a Travail et loisirs social center in Compiègne (Oise) in fall 1937, Garrigoux met with the PSF federation president and Social Action delegate to determine if cooperation with municipal authorities was possible.[135] After finding a benefactor who had a good relationship with the mayor and seeing the need among synthetic leather workers subjected to a lack of services and frequent accidents at their factory, Garrigoux approved the project. In contrast, in Antony, a commune south of Paris, Garrigoux determined that local hostilities were too tense for Travail et loisirs to establish a social center there.[136]

The advent of the PSF, the evolution of the Women's Section into five different organizations, and the creation of the Social Studies Bureau enabled the movement to use its social program as the basis of national rejuvenation. At the PSF's First Social Congress in 1939, Suzanne Fouché excitedly proclaimed: "Joan of Arc was alone in believing in her mission and she remade France. We are in the millions! Why can't we?"[137] In seeking to remake the social politics of Greater France, PSF women used the movement's social program to attract individuals, overcome class divisions, and integrate the working classes and colonial subjects into the movement's vision of Greater France.[138] While some of the movement's more radical members left out of disgust because La Rocque accepted the league's dissolution peacefully and did not attempt a coup, the PSF increased its membership and garnered more support precisely because it had become more palatable to the French public. Indeed, the movement's social programs developed within the tradition of welfare reform that sought to pacify the working classes and integrate them into the national community.[139] Many French were attracted to the PSF out of fear that workers were overly influenced by a Marxist worldview, which inflamed social discord. The police acknowledged this, noting, "The philanthropic works hold an important place in the association, which sees in them an excellent means to win over the people and the working masses."[140]

With professionals such as Fouché and Garrigoux joining La Rocque and Préval, the PSF built a formidable social action apparatus, which facilitated the movement's grassroots implementation of its social programs. However, La Rocque and Préval became concerned that the movement's services might inadvertently undermine Catholic Action. To this end, La Rocque established a policy that depended upon elite women and men working together. The colonel stated in a circular that was distributed in April 1937 to leaders at all levels of the party's bureaucracy, "I insist upon a relationship with religious organizations operating in our districts and in the areas surrounding our sections."[141] La Rocque reiterated what he had explained to Cardinal Verdier—that the movement sought to align its works with other groups that shared its social Catholic precepts. "It will be necessary for our social delegates and our section presidents to personally visit parish priests, not to coordinate our efforts but to remain independent," La Rocque instructed his adjutants of both sexes, adding that they needed to check the hours that parish youth groups operated to avoid conflicts with PSF hours of operation.[142] Maintaining these lines of communication would ensure that PSF and parish services complemented one another. Moreover, La Rocque explained that the PSF would not promote its own services if they were already offered by a parish. If a parish had a vibrant Catholic scouting group, for example, the PSF would reorient its own youth development activities to avoid redundant activities. "We must not divert any spiritual activity," he wrote; "in the case where local works exist that deal with the same questions that we do and are *emancipated from the influence of the Popular Front* we must not double them."[143]

While La Rocque established this coordination policy, it was Préval who organized its implementation. Communication with regional leaders was critical in this regard, which again reflected the ways in which women and men worked together in organizing the movement's social services. Of specific concern was the relationship between the PSF, local parishes, and organizations that were officially sanctioned by the Vatican. For instance, at the behest of Paris, the Lyon PSF sought to expand its social action by implementing fully the activities of Travail et loisirs. Préval announced that she would visit Lyon and work with the PSF head there, J. Bruyas, for an on-site inspection of all social activities. Cognizant of the PSF's constant evaluation of its relationship with the Church, Bruyas warned Préval that parishes in Lyon exhibited more hostility than support toward PSF activity. He asked if such hostility meant that the PSF should seek more collaboration with the JOC.[144] Préval replied that PSF delegates needed to consistently visit the parishes, explain to the priests that children would be welcome in PSF social centers, and reiterate that Travail et loisirs sought to complement—not compete with—parish services. As for the JOC, Préval suggested similar visits to JOC sections but not constant cooperation. "We serve the Church; we are not dependent on its affiliates," she wrote Bruyas.[145] Further clarifying the distinction between PSF services and those of parishes, Préval explained that social centers were "the opposite" of a parish because centers provided technical services that parishes lacked. She explained: "Physical education, for example, is deplorable in all French parishes. International competitions have proved our inferiority."[146]

In this way, Préval led the coordination of PSF social action with Catholic Action. Indeed, she regularly instructed her adjutants, including those who were not Catholic, to buy children their first communion robes and drive them to local churches.[147] For instance, in a private letter to a friend, Préval praised the work of Madame Javal, one of the few Jewish women in the movement. Javal sat on the leadership councils of AMSJA and Travail et loisirs, a position that made her one of Préval's most trusted adjutants. One of Javal's primary duties was to inspect the movement's social centers, summer camps, and its convalescent home in Pau. In preparing for one such visit, Préval felt the need to warn her friend of Javal's Jewishness and instructed her to keep this highly sensitive information to herself; "confide this to nobody," Préval wrote. She added, "Madame Javal's a Jew who has done a lot for our movement in the hours of fear and unforgettable sacrifices . . . Madame Javal has paid for several first communion dresses and a trip to the Catholic [pilgrimage site] at Lourdes. These are details which will show you that sectarianism has no hold on some souls."[148] Here, Préval lauded Javal for participating in Catholic ritual while claiming that Javal's willingness to conform to such ritual was confirmation of the movement's integralist principles. As a Jew, Javal was not free to publicly practice her religion and be a trusted member of the PSF, yet she remained one of Préval's more important lieutenants.

Emphasizing ethnoreligious and class integration into the Catholic national community was a key component of Travail et loisirs. As its statutes put it, the association's goal was to bring together people from "different social and intellectual categories into one collective soul . . . a fusion of the classes."[149] In traveling around metropolitan France and speaking at conferences attended by PSF supporters, Préval repeatedly stated that the movement's social action had a pacifying influence on the working classes. A favorite story of hers told of how three Paris police officers thanked her for opening a social center in their district because it led to a decrease in children playing in the streets with knives.[150] In another case, a young man reportedly said to Préval, "Now that I am no longer in the streets it's easy to be honest. Look after me!"[151] Privately, Préval was encouraged by the progress that the PSF was making in working-class communities. As she wrote to a social action colleague in mid-1937, "We must redouble our caution, our diplomacy . . . these children are still very frustrated, very savage, but profoundly endearing and loyal. They no longer sing the Internationale thanks to the pacifying influence of my admirable colleagues. These little ones now know the entire Marseillaise and understand friendship and warmth; they have abandoned the spirit of hatred and of 'clan,' they are beginning to understand the spirit of solidarity and of team[work]."[152]

While Préval genuinely wanted working-class French to understand that they would be welcomed in the PSF, she did not believe that the movement's efforts to "pacify savages" were demeaning to many of the people they sought to attract. This incongruence caused irrevocable contradictions over dispensing aid at a time of limited resources. For instance, the Lyon section leader, Bruyas, asked Préval, "Can naturalized children of non-naturalized parents participate in our courses equally to the French," to which Préval replied, "Help the French first, but I have never refused to help a child who may need it. It's a question of morality, of humanity."[153] In this way Préval rationalized constructing a hierarchy of who was worthy of aid while simultaneously applauding her own humane work. Likewise, Préval wrote another social service provider, "help the French families first and avoid [aiding] the 'pure hooligans' because if, like in the gospels, one can save one lost sheep of one hundred, it's beautiful and useful."[154] In this way, not only did Préval's hierarchical outlook preclude her from dispensing aid on an equal basis or according to need, but she was unable to comprehend the discriminatory aspects of such a hierarchical policy.

While most PSF supporters would have denied any disparity between their vision of a unified France and their divisive practices, the Popular Front sought to undermine the PSF's growing influence by exposing the PSF's opportunism. The Popular Front's concern with PSF social action was especially important because, as Laura Downs has pointed out, the PSF's social centers were not typically located in Communist or Socialist municipalities, but in shanty towns such as Paris's "zone" that lacked proper administration and access to services.[155] Seeing the zones as entrées into areas controlled by the Popular Front, the PSF used subterfuge to make its services appear apolitical. One propagandist put it this way: "the best propaganda is discrete."[156] A section president explained that social action served "to inculcate the PSF spirit, but without the label."[157] PSF efforts to mask its services put Popular Front supporters on alert. In response to a new PSF social center in Aubervilliers, Communist propagandists attacked the center's director, Madame Déléchant, who had left the Communist Party to join the PSF. "She's in charge of your children!" the PCF exclaimed, adding that the

PSF's real goal was to "exploit the misery or the naivety of people for political ends."[158] Another social center, Préval proudly explained, was located in what she called "a terrible area ... home to the aristocracy of the revolutionary worker," and added that Travail et loisirs was bringing "morality and necessary hygiene" to the entire neighborhood.[159] Another center was in what Préval called a "very hostile" area, and yet another dealt regularly with break-ins and vandalism.[160] In some of these instances, Préval was forced to request security from local officials to protect property, participants, and staff.[161]

Violence against property sometimes spilled over into physical violence that at times resulted in death. One of the most infamous cases was the March 1937 Clichy riots that left six dead and hundreds injured. Following the movement's social action strategy of infiltrating working-class areas, the riots were precipitated by Travail et loisirs's decision to show a movie based upon Claude Farrère's *Bataille* in the working-class Parisian suburb of Clichy. Tensions between the PSF and Popular Front were already high because a PSF employer had shot to death one of his Algerian workers.[162] Popular Front supporters thus planned a demonstration against what they believed was a PSF provocation by marching on the town hall to avoid the cinema and the potential for violence. Unfortunately, the town hall was near the cinema, and a small number of the 6,000–10,000 Popular Front supporters who had gathered clashed with police.[163] While technically the PSF was not involved in the violence because the cinema was evacuated before the worst of the violence began, municipal authorities feared further provocations and banned several Travail et loisirs meetings to avoid repeated incidents.[164] This municipal action infuriated PSF supporters and further alienated them from public authorities. Préval bristled that the authorities had blamed Travail et loisirs for the violence, while, she insisted, culpability rested solely with Communists.

Smaller incidents of violence, centered around PSF social action, occurred in addition to the spectacular events such as the Clichy riots that have drawn the attention of historians. An especially tragic case occurred in a Parisian working-class neighborhood when the nine-year-old son of a PSF member who was selling raffle tickets for a Catholic charity was killed.[165] The PSF press framed the death by stating that he was killed by several Communist youth who were driven toward hatred by their parents and the Popular Front.[166] For PSF supporters, this incident testified to the urgency with which they worked, and it reflected why Préval regularly referred to Communists as savages. Indeed, while PSF leaders claimed that their work was peaceful, the movement's supporters' singular conception of

French national identity as Christian was at the root of violence that continued despite the movement's emphasis on social action. Indeed, the culture of war persisted as the influx of more Catholics exacerbated supporters' tendencies to believe that they were in a battle for Christian civilization.

CROIX DE FEU/PSF MASCULINITY: EMBRACING SOCIAL ACTION

As social action garnered the Croix de Feu/PSF high levels of support among bourgeois Catholics and enabled it to make inroads in working-class neighborhoods, increasing numbers of men believed that social action could remake French society. Indeed, whereas women appropriated the culture of war to legitimate their role in the movement, men's view of their role in the national community broadened to include social action. Perhaps the best example of the movement's attempts to mobilize men for social action was the case of male university students. Croix de Feu/PSF leaders sought to convince French youth that a new order, built upon peaceful means of social change, was essential to a stable and powerful France. To distance itself from its violent past, including the radical elements of the VN and *dispos,* the PSF program for male youth specifically forbade violence. It instructed that a student's political action should be done "without agitation and brutality" and that young men should "act as shining examples."[167] Discipline was still at the movement's ideological core, as its leaders preached that young men needed to respect their elders and act in a controlled and dignified manner. In this way, the purity that had been central to the veteran's mystique was transferred to the social action of male youth.

At the heart of the Croix de Feu/PSF's mobilization of young men was the creation of university centers across Greater France. The movement's leaders of both sexes repeatedly stated that youth possessed boundless physical and intellectual energy that needed to be channeled for purposeful ends. It is difficult to determine the exact numbers of students that the PSF eventually attracted; one PSF leader claimed in 1938 that 12 percent, or roughly eight thousand French students, supported the PSF.[168] By June 1939 subscriptions to the obligatory student journal, *L'Etudiant Social,* totaled 26,827.[169] The centers themselves were not associated with local universities, but were independently located, subsidized, and run by the PSF. Membership in a center required an application, PSF membership, and a subscription to *L'Etudiant Social.* Student leaders and PSF administrators oversaw the centers, designed to facilitate sociability, and organized conferences, speakers, and meetings as well as creating spaces for restaurants and libraries.

Preparing young men to become France's next generation of leaders was one of the primary purposes of the university centers. In this regard socializing the students according to Croix de Feu/PSF precepts was critical and reflected a shift in the movement's conceptions of ideal masculinity. As the Social First! strategy developed, the archetypal model for Croix de Feu/PSF masculinity in the university centers shifted from the veteran, and his experience in war, to social action heralded by the famous French aviator Jean Mermoz. In France, Mermoz's fame paralleled that of Charles Lindbergh's in the United States and reached its height in 1936. Indeed, he was the second most recognizable face in the movement behind La Rocque.[170] Mermoz joined the Croix de Feu in 1934 as it shifted toward social action and became a member of its leadership council shortly thereafter. Jean Bernard, the general secretary of the Parisian university center, explained Mermoz's entry into the movement in *L'Etudiant Social:* "Jean Mermoz came to the Croix de Feu because he despised politics. Only social questions impassioned him.... In his eyes, France would only be saved by men who would tirelessly strive towards social action, and, without ceasing, sacrifice himself for children and youth."[171] In this way, the league's propagandists used Mermoz's celebrity status to attract new members by casting the aviator as an agent of moderation and paternal devotion.

In December 1936 Mermoz left France on a trans-Atlantic flight from which he never returned. Croix de Feu propagandists, while surely in mourning, nevertheless saw an opportunity to elevate Mermoz's already sterling reputation by casting him as a Croix de Feu martyr. His commitment to youth development and spiritual devotion to flying made him a powerful symbol of national reconciliation. After his death the movement's press outlets quoted Mermoz as saying, "I've often wondered how someone can live without enthusiasm or passion ... you must SERVE, serve your country, the community, and human progress."[172] In death, Mermoz became a symbol of spiritual renewal and social action. In the university centers, Mermoz was celebrated because his dedication to social issues allegedly drove his action, including his work with children and youth. The movement paid homage to his memory by naming a library, social center, and flying club after him.

The emphasis on Mermoz as an archetype for male action and the university centers' focus on social issues reflected the principles behind the movement's social action. One of the leaders, Pierre Suire, echoed these ideas, writing that each center's purpose was to "fully develop social activity among the students within and outside of the University Center, and prioritize it over politics. Politics has no reason for being unless it allows the development of the Social.... The spiritual leads to the social and the social is the expression of life.... without Social Action, the University Center would have no reason to exist."[173]

Reflecting wider PSF discourses about the necessity of the social, Suire dismissed politics as a subset of social action. It was through social action—not political action—that young men would find the most spiritual fulfillment. In January 1938 the PSF held the First National Congress of PSF students, and the theme of social action was central once again. In a speech Suire asked, "To the question 'Politics or Economics first,' we substitute the formula 'the Social first.' Social Action is more necessary to the student than to any other French citizen."[174] Suire offered young men an alternative to the male militarism of the movement's early years. For Suire, moral conviction and devotion to France was not expressed in militaristic terms, but through commitment to social reform.

Young men thus became increasingly involved in the practice of a masculinized brand of social action. PSF leaders, including Préval, encouraged male students to become counselors for young children at PSF social centers and summer camps. As *L'Etudiant Social* put it, Préval used her oratorical skills of "warmth" and "persuasion" to invite male students to become youth counselors to fulfill their "social duty."[175] The social services that men provided were both similar to and different from women's social action. Male students at elite institutions tutored their classmates who experienced academic difficulties. Professionals such as doctors, dentists, veterinarians, and pharmacists affiliated with the PSF offered temporary employment to students seeking work experience. Medical students made house calls to ill PSF members and volunteered at PSF social and medical centers. In other cases, women and men worked together in a multitude of programs. As we shall see, young men were central to the PSF's physical education programs, summer camps, social centers, and entertainment.

CONCLUSION

Women's entry into the Croix de Feu in early 1934 not only transformed the movement's gender ideology but changed how many French women and men influenced France's political culture. Women, disillusioned from being essentialized by the "women in the home" movement, found in the Croix de Feu a sociopolitical movement that valued their contributions and needed their activism. Indeed, women played the determining role in expanding the movement's gender ideology beyond maternalism and domesticity by using the language of the culture of war to argue that women from a variety of backgrounds could use social action to save France. In doing so, they broadened the movement's conceptions of masculinity by urging men to work alongside women in pursuing social reform. In this way, the Croix de Feu/PSF shifted from a hypermasculine organization that used violence and intimidation to one that put women on the front lines of social action to remind people that the Croix de Feu protected the mystique of France's Christian heritage.

Paradoxically, while women played a key role in broadening the Croix de Feu/PSF's gender ideology, their action led directly to the movement's increasingly exclusionary ethnoreligious nationalism. The movement's soaring universalist rhetoric at events such as the inauguration of the Women's Section was not matched in practice by its recruiting strategies, the composition of its membership, or its approach to dispensing aid. Moreover, the movement's attempts to transcend sectarianism were belied by the actions of its supporters, who conflated French identity with Catholicism, seeking to align their work with Catholic Action and to use religion as a method of census-taking and working-class coercion. Moreover, in North Africa, women's marginalization limited the movement's ability to support the Catholic Church (and vice versa). Despite decades of republican anticlericalism, Catholicism remained culturally embedded in metropolitan life in ways that were absent in the Maghreb. The sheer demographics of North African societies meant that Catholics could never rival Muslims in terms of the latter's ability to promote grassroots activism. The JOC, for instance, was not a viable alternative to the Croix de Feu/PSF for settlers and Catholic converts in the same way that it was for metropolitan workers. It was relatively simple for parishes in Lyon to reject aligning with the Croix de Feu/PSF because priests could throw their support behind a variety of political groups that were sympathetic to the Church. Young male settlers did not have the option of joining a PSF University Center that was oriented toward social action, which spurred them to look elsewhere to express their nationalism and explains, in part, why they were behind some of the worst political violence in North Africa. The North African Croix de Feu/PSF's comparative lack of interest in aligning with the Catholic Church was best revealed in *La Flamme*'s coverage of Fouché's conferences. While regional metropolitan newspapers recognized the key role that Catholicism played in Fouché's activism, *La Flamme* instead reported on her conceptions of collectivity, solidarity, and harmony. Such reports reflected the interests of the North African Croix de Feu, which were centered around undermining anticolonialism rather than the metropolitan emphasis on garnering mass support and taking power.

3

CHALLENGES TO WOMEN'S
AUTONOMY AND AUTHORITY

HEALTH, FINANCING, AND CIVIC ACTION, 1934–1939

The Croix de Feu/PSF's huge growth and influence led other groups to emulate what they believed were reasons behind the movement's success. Its most viable ultranationalist challenger of the late 1930s, the PPF, borrowed from the Croix de Feu's ideology by diagnosing France's problems as social. It explained it this way in a widely distributed brochure: "How to fix the social problem? ... substitute the doctrine of class struggle with the doctrine of the collaboration of men."[1] Despite its social emphasis, PPF leaders refused to let women formulate ideology and implement policy in the same manner as the Croix de Feu. Nor did it empower women's groups to the same extent or encourage women and men to work together.[2] The largest veteran's group in France, the Union Nationale des Combattants (UNC), also sought to emulate the Croix de Feu's explosion in membership but misread how it achieved mass support. The UNC's leader, Jean Goy, asked, "Where does their success come from?" Ignoring gender, the answer, he claimed, was from the Croix de Feu's propaganda aimed at youth and noncombatants, its large assemblies and meetings, its discipline, and the charisma of La Rocque.[3] Neither the PPF nor the UNC recognized that the Croix de Feu/PSF's mobilization of women as agents of social action was at the heart of its transformation.

Feminist groups, on the other hand, watched with interest as women flocked to the Croix de Feu/PSF. Seeking to capitalize on the movement's momentum and hopeful that some of its supporters might engage in the major women's issues of the day, Louise Weiss, the most prominent French suffragist at the time, invited the Nord PSF to a feminist conference in Lille in October 1937. The conference focused on four major issues concerning women's role in French society and politics: suffrage rights, enshrining married women's civil capacity into law, achieving equitable access to public office, and ensuring equal salary for equal work.[4] The PSF's social action was strong in the Nord, and Weiss, while aware that PSF women were not feminists, nevertheless hoped that their Catholicism would inspire them to follow Catholic women's groups like the UFCS and UNVF and declare their support for suffrage. However, the male leadership of the Lille PSF denied a PSF *oratrice* from speaking at the conference and used its local newspaper to lecture Weiss, claiming that she was too radical and divisive.[5] As a feminist who argued that women and men were equal, protested in the streets, organized leaflet drops from planes, and chained herself to public buildings, Weiss embodied what many PSF supporters despised: a confrontational woman who made public demands of an explicitly political and secular nature. In demeaning Weiss, her direct action politics, and her conference, the Lille PSF maintained that feminism was outdated and insisted that women would enjoy true equality as soon as French society exhibited the same degree of respect toward women that they experienced in the PSF.

The differences between the Croix de Feu/PSF, PPF, UNC, feminist groups, and Catholic women's groups, revealed the distinct space that the Croix de Feu/PSF carved out during the 1930s. While Croix de Feu/PSF women earned a high degree of autonomy and authority, the issues they cared about centered around rejuvenating France's status as the premier Christian civilization and respect for social action, rather than women's individual rights, which left them at a disadvantage in comparison with men. Employing the language of the culture of war was empowering to a certain extent, but the soldier was ultimately coded as male. Some men may have respected and admired women's sacrifices and willingness to fight for ultranationalism, and at the same time, not considered women as equals. The Lille PSF's refusal to grant women permission to participate in Weiss's conference revealed that at times, women's lack of equal status directly influenced their inability to make autonomous decisions. In these ways, women's unceasing focus on social action limited their ability to engage in pressing political issues. While Downs has accurately described the borders between the Croix de Feu/PSF's political and social action as "porous," women's refusal to cast their actions as political limited their ability to claim authority on a par with men.[6] Moreover, many women's focus on the social realm was the rationale they used to explain their rejection of political engagement, which they maintained distinguished their action from that of feminists. Because most Croix de Feu/PSF supporters conflated feminist activism with the direct action tactics of Weiss, they believed that feminism was divisive at the precise moment that France needed to be unified.

This chapter explores the distinct set of challenges that metropolitan Croix de Feu/PSF women faced in implementing effective programs and that made their work difficult and exhausting. The challenges were threefold, the first of which was not unique to the Croix de Feu/PSF while the latter two were rooted in the movement's authoritarian conservatism. First, long-standing social barriers limited women's access to professional opportunities, which leaders like Préval felt acutely in organizing social services that depended on medical professionals. Second, if budgets reflected values, then the Croix de Feu/PSF's funding of its social action revealed women's lower status relative to that of men. While the movement sought to accomplish national reconciliation through social action, its leaders were not willing to fund women's activities properly, which left women leaders facing challenges that undermined their authority and the general effectiveness of some of the movement's social programs. Third, Préval and her adjutants were unable to eradicate completely the antifeminism of the early Croix de Feu. Hostility toward women's empowerment lingered and was reified when the PSF created a new women's group, Civic Action, which held that women were not yet ready for suffrage and was subordinated to Men's Sections.

THE LACK OF QUALIFIED STAFF AND INFIGHTING IN THE ASSOCIATION MÉDICO-SOCIALE JEANNE D'ARC

Some of the most daunting issues facing France during the Great Depression centered around health, from the tuberculosis epidemic that hit working-class communities especially hard, to high rates of indigence in the general population. The Croix de Feu responded by making health care one of its top priorities and set out to organize a health program in late 1934. To this end, at the Women's Section's first national congress in 1935 the leadership proudly highlighted one of their newest social initiatives, the Croix de Feu health clinic, which had opened in Paris in December 1934. Its director was Madeleine Ducrocq, whose father was a veteran and whose brother died in the Great War. Mademoiselle Ducrocq enjoyed the trust of Préval due to her family's military background and the fact that she had earned the highest nursing degree available, the *infirmière diplômée d'Etat*.

Despite having no titular or official position associated with the clinic, Préval worked closely with Ducrocq to run it and coordinate its services with the movement's other social programs. While Ducrocq's expertise was on the medical end, Préval's talent was gathering qualified personnel. During the clinic's first year, Préval focused on appealing to Croix de Feu supporters' sense of duty by convincing them to donate their time to help the organization. In response to one of Préval's requests, for example, a Doctor Chiray told Préval that he would be willing to donate his time as long as he only helped Croix de Feu members and could choose his own hours.[7] As this case demonstrates, Préval did not dictate terms to her volunteers but was forced by circumstances to exhibit flexibility. Nevertheless, it was this type of lobbying that played a key role in convincing doctors to contribute to the league's social programs.

In terms of clientele, the clinic aided needy families who coped with deteriorating economic conditions brought about by the Depression, unemployment, and low wages. Aimed at Croix de Feu and VN members and their families, the clinic's doctors volunteered their time in the fields of pediatrics, gynecology, nutrition, dentistry, and general medicine. The clinic's day-to-day operations depended upon its paid nurses, who served clients and ran the visiting nurse program. In its first year, the clinic reportedly helped 4,292 individuals, which included free consultations, urinalyses, cleaning out ears, bandaging and disinfecting wounds, providing vaccinations, examining children in preparation for their participation in Croix de Feu summer camps, and sending nurses into the homes of the sick.[8]

Préval and Ducrocq were encouraged by the clinic's popularity and recognized they had an opportunity to provide care to large numbers of people. Always concerned with the big picture, Préval understood that providing health care that was infused with the movement's ultranationalist principles would improve its public image. Indeed, nurses who visited the homes of the sick were far less divisive than newspaper sellers who started fist fights in the streets. For these reasons, La Rocque and Préval established an association solely devoted to healing the sick, AMSJA, in late 1936. Affiliated with the Croix de Feu/PSF, the AMSJA's mission was to establish health clinics throughout Greater France, expand the visiting nurse program, and create a convalescent home in the southwestern city of Pau.[9] Serving as the model for AMSJA clinics, the Parisian clinic was reserved for the needy and those with access to insurance; doctors recommended indigent individuals for the convalescent home in Pau, called Les Allées. Clinic services offered by AMSJA's eleven doctors and nursing staff included consultations made by appointment, general medicine, surgery, gynecological care, dressing of wounds, home visits made by nurses and social workers, and a service that placed the needy in hospitals or other facilities.[10] The indigent, *les familles nombreuses,* and the unemployed were eligible for free or reduced dental and medical consultations.

Women comprised AMSJA's leadership and staff and had nearly complete control over its programs. As AMSJA's secretary general, Ducrocq oversaw the health clinics and Les Allées. She was responsible for five nurses at Les Allées and supervised inspection visits from Paris, which were conducted by the same women and men who inspected the services for Travail et loisirs, SPES, and Social Action. Seeking to strike a balance between retaining and delegating her authority, Préval wrote that her most important duty was "the centralization of the most important and multiple works," and that she sought to "avoid all detailed questions and let them [be] sorted out on location by those in charge."[11] Préval relied a great deal on Ducrocq, crediting her friend with formulating the "impetus and doctrine" of AMSJA, noting, "the actual social necessities never escape her."[12] While Préval attempted to delegate work, she was nevertheless intricately involved in many of AMSJA's details. For instance, she instructed her adjutants to submit to her their reports on Les Allées, and she wanted to be kept up to date on such minutiae as the weight of individual patients and how funds were spent.

Les Allées was for noncontagious women and their children deemed "weak" or "sick" and in need of recuperation and fresh air for an extended period of time. AMSJA leadership chose Pau, a city of 40,000 inhabitants, as the location for their convalescent home primarily for its "salubrious, calm, and warm" climate and proximity to outdoor activities. In more practical terms, the regional head of Social Action for the Pyrenees region was Madame Perrineau, who like Ducrocq had earned the highest nursing degree offered in France, was dedicated to the movement's ultranationalist principles, and was a friend of Préval's. While Perrineau was not directly in charge of Les Alleés, Préval hoped that her strong leadership would set an example for local supporters. Perhaps most exciting to the Catholic staff was the nearby pilgrimage site of Lourdes, site of a Marian apparition and home to a grotto that purportedly had healing powers, which had attracted millions of pilgrims going back to the mid-nineteenth century.[13]

Les Allées itself was a stately villa outside of town surrounded by trees and a park. It comprised two wards, both with central heating, and numerous rooms holding 150 beds, baths, and showers. AMSJA leaders designed Les Allées for individuals without the resources necessary to pay for their own health care, and therefore, their stays could be subsidized by a variety of sources.[14] Patients were admitted to Pau with permission of the PSF Federation president, and a doctor's certificate attesting that the individual was not contagious, that they had not been running a fever for eight days, and that their lungs had been clear for fifteen days.[15] The staff also supervised children who were either sick or had joined their sick mother. Children's services included a kindergarten, physical education, and activities modeled on the movement's youth program.[16]

Because AMSJA provided care to thousands of needy individuals at its clinics and Les Alleés, Croix de Feu/PSF public events championed its work. After a year of operation, La Rocque presided over an AMSJA general assembly meeting where the association's members rallied to celebrate their accomplishments. The treasurer stated that the association's total expenses were 602,592 francs, with roughly one-third going to Pau, making it one of the most expensive PSF endeavors.[17] Several nurses spoke, celebrating what one of them called their "Great work of French reconciliation."[18] Ducrocq reported that nearly four thousand families were registered with the health clinics and that they had sent nearly four hundred sick individuals to Pau. She ended her presentation by telling the audience, "I hope that in all the branches, AMSJA will develop and perfect the services rendered; this will be the best way to increasingly radiate the social and beneficial spirit each day."[19] La Rocque closed the evening by encouraging his activists, declaring that their work exemplified perfectly the "French social spirit."

There was a gap between the soaring rhetoric at the general assembly and the realities at the Parisian clinic and Les Allées. Indeed, Les Allées was plagued by incompetent staff and infighting that gave Préval, Ducrocq, and Perrineau endless headaches. They found it difficult to hire nurses and staff with proper credentials who also adhered to PSF ideology. For instance, they were hesitant about hiring one nurse because she was not a member of the PSF.[20] The steward at Les Allées, Mademoiselle Belloir, also presented a problem to the leadership because she was not "gentle" enough, nor did she display the "warmth" necessary toward those who were ill.[21] In a letter that she instructed Perrineau to destroy, Préval expressed concern about another staff member, writing, "There is in her a strange mix of the old maids of religion and bigotry. If religion is the best of goods, bigotry is the worst of evils."[22] Préval suggested that Perrineau monitor the nurse's daily behavior closely by encouraging her religious devotion but discouraging gossip. Whether Perrineau wanted to control the behavior of the staff to such an extent is unclear, but such suggestions reveal that Préval found it difficult to delegate.

Problems with both the staff and boarders at Les Allées threatened to compromise its overall mission by the summer of 1937. According to the home's director, Mademoiselle Vieira, one nurse was "inexact" in treating patients and "intemperate" with the boarders, another was "extremely lazy," and yet another was both lazy and "incapable."[23] Most upsetting to Vieira was that all three women worked with the gardener to facilitate "clandestine" meetings, among the boarders and outside visitors, which resulted in the dismissal of all four staff members from Les Allées and the revocation of their AMSJA membership. Clandestine meetings occurred more than once, as on another occasion Préval expressed dismay over a young woman and man who the staff had discovered were "meeting in secret."[24] Specifically noting their ages—between thirteen and twenty-one—Préval stated that they had "moral difficulties" that were characterized by a "physiological restlessness" that made the work of PSF women "necessary and delicate."[25] In this way, emphasizing sexual morality was central to how Préval dealt with youth. She underlined the significance to Perrineau by writing, "To be sheltered from all scandal, from all villainy, [we] cannot and must not ignore any difficulty. We have created our works not only to alleviate physical miseries, but also to familiarize ourselves with the moral troubles that families can have, and to spiritually educate in a social manner the youth confined to us."[26]

As Préval learned more about the "moral troubles" that families faced, she was increasingly concerned about fighting sexual "immorality" with a spiritual and social education. She demanded that the women supervisors be competent, firm, clear, and above all, concerned with children's moral development. While other PSF-affiliated associations strictly separated boys from girls, Préval counted on women's diligence to serve as a deterrent against what she believed were improper liaisons between young women and men. Moreover, she maintained that teaching youth in a "spiritual" manner would alleviate their physiological urges. "The PSF ... seeks reconciliation and wants to bring together lost brothers and healthy ideas; the PSF must have a convalescent home corresponding to this spiritual orientation," she wrote to Perrineau.[27] However, this ideal was difficult to meet in practice. One inspector noted, "It's not going well at Les Allées"; there was reportedly "lots of good will but not authority," and the atmosphere at Les Allées was characterized by "gossip, chatter, and pettiness, which cause harm."[28] Ultimately, the inspector told Préval, "the PSF spirit is absent from the house."[29]

Despite the best efforts of Préval and Ducrocq, problems persisted at Les Allées two and one-half years after its initial creation. The heating system was "defective" and would not work properly during winter, there were too few toilets, and the paintings and wallpaper adorning the walls were too damaged to provide the restorative ambiance AMSJA leaders wanted. Lice were endemic among the children as new arrivals continually infested the boarders.[30] In the summer of 1939, while the overall health and spirits of the children was reportedly good, the leadership bemoaned the fact that only fifty boarders and thirty-six children were at Les Allées.[31] To increase the number of boarders, one report recommended that Les Allées attempt to register with the state and private welfare services to better facilitate operations and increase recruitment. They also sought to increase publicity for Les Allées in the movement's newspaper, *Le Petit Journal* (which La Rocque bought in 1937), campaigned for doctors in the area to direct their patients toward the home, and obtained a list of PSF doctors who explained the benefits of the rest home to their patients. Attempting to address inspectors' reports of weak leadership, in 1939 Perrineau replaced one problem director with Madame Regnault, who had run one of the best Travail et loisirs social centers (Saint Ouen) from 1937 to 1939. While the change initially "purified the atmosphere," the mood soured only several months later, causing the September inspector to report that, "the PSF spirit does not reign in the personnel."[32] This inspector catalogued several deficiencies: the staff forgot to pick up children waiting at the train station, making them wait for two hours on the platform, and these same children were made to sleep without sheets on their beds. The two women charged with this error blamed a miscommunication over time and the inability to leave the home because it was understaffed.

Préval, Ducrocq, and Perrineau had great trouble combining PSF ideological goals with the everyday challenges of running a convalescent home, which included receiving patients for whom they could not provide proper care. The staff depended upon doctors at the association's clinics to perform thorough examinations to ensure that patients with communicable diseases did not arrive in Pau. They expressed frustration with doctors who sent them unsuitable patients. As Ducrocq wrote to one of her nurses, "For the past three months, we have been very surprised by all the diagnostic errors which have been made by very competent doctors who have filled out and signed the organization's medical records."[33]

Likewise, the staff was unprepared to grapple with the mental health issues brought on by patients' illnesses. One such patient, Madame Rey, suffered from outbreaks of tetanus that grew increasingly violent and "upsetting," which caused her adopted daughter to fall into "imitative cries" filled with increasing hysteria.[34] Préval recounted Rey's deteriorating condition to Ducrocq by explaining that Rey had made an unauthorized visit to Lourdes when she "escaped during Mass" in Pau and made her way to the pilgrimage site. Interpreting Rey's secretive actions as evidence of her lack of discipline and respect for authority, two nurses from Les Allées went to Lourdes, dragged the unwilling Rey out of the grotto, and returned her to Pau. Back at Les Allées against her will, Rey grew increasingly paranoid, and spoke "without ceasing of suicide," upsetting the other patients. Unequipped to provide proper care, the staff at Les Allées was forced to move Rey to a local hospital. For reasons such as this, the central leadership at AMSJA was concerned about the qualifications of their staff, and made compromises by hiring and keeping on women who may not have shared the "PSF spirit."

Staff infighting at the Parisian health clinic mirrored some of the problems in Pau, and threatened Ducrocq's ability to manage a well-run clinic. Despite Ducrocq's professional qualifications and support from Préval and La Rocque, she faced virulent personal attacks in attempting to exert her authority in supervising staff. For instance, morale at the Parisian health clinic took a severe blow when Ducrocq attempted to dismiss a reportedly unqualified and unpopular nurse, Mademoiselle Tempucci. Upon receiving word of her pending dismissal, Tempucci told Ducrocq that she was the victim of bullying from a clique led by the top nurse at the clinic, Madame Borel. In response to being fired, Tempucci told Ducrocq, "You don't know what's happening in your own clinic! You don't know the atmosphere there."[35] Ducrocq responded to Tempucci's claims of being out of touch by questioning all of the clinic's nurses. In referring to a recent illness that had struck Ducrocq, one nurse stated that her cohort wished that Ducrocq's poor health would have kept her away from the clinic; the nurse added that the staff regularly mocked Ducrocq and her new husband.[36] Ducrocq then called in Borel, who immediately denied the claims and accused Tempucci and the other nurse of lying. These conflicting stories led to difficulties in getting the situation resolved, and morale at the clinic was extremely low. Ducrocq noted that her friendship with Borel had been declining for the past year and expressed regret that it was affecting their work and the entire environment at the clinic. After conducting an investigation, Ducrocq sided against Tempucci, stated her desire to keep Borel, and defended the latter's actions by claiming that Borel's sarcastic and blunt nature offended women who were "shy" and that Borel's skill was of the utmost importance.[37] This entire episode reveals another case where AMSJA leaders put aside PSF ideals emphasizing joyous women in favor of keeping their qualified personnel on staff.

It is difficult to imagine one of La Rocque's (or any other male leader's) acting subordinates attacking him with the type of virulence that Ducrocq experienced. While male authority was sacrosanct in the Croix de Feu/PSF, the cult of the *chef* and militaristic adherence to hierarchy did not always translate to women in positions of authority. In this sense, it was more difficult for women to maintain their legitimacy as authority figures, which rendered them more vulnerable to draining experiences. Moreover, the lack of respect for Ducrocq's authority harmed the work environment at the clinic and the productivity of everyone involved, particularly Ducrocq herself. Like many other PSF women leaders, she was already overextended, and instead of addressing the legitimate problem of unqualified staff and doctors who were sending inappropriate patients to Les Allées, she was forced to quell tempers at the clinic. For her part, Préval believed that the attacks against Ducrocq were unfairly gendered, although she used her characteristically opaque manner of phrasing to express her concerns. In a private letter to Perrineau, she explained: "You know the evolution of ideas. You know the subtlety, the adaptation required by the modern foundations upon which we embark. Everything that reminds us of the most respected systems of the past must disappear: in a word, paternalism is totally erased. It's against that which Ducrocq has been struggling for two years."[38] In this way, the problems stemming from the lack of professional nurses available for Préval and Ducrocq to hire, reflected wider problems in France that were rooted in women's inequitable access to education, the undervaluing of their skills, and a lack of recognition that society as a whole needed their contributions. Consequently, the problems at AMSJA demonstrated that the demand for professional nurses outstripped the supply, which directly affected the movement's ability to provide health care in the competent and caring manner that its leaders envisioned.

LACK OF RESOURCES, EXHAUSTION, AND PROVINCIAL DISSENSION

As Préval's frustration in dealing with dysfunction at AMSJA reveals, participation in the PSF left some women overworked. Women's exhaustion was generally un-recognized and considered by many supporters to be the normal state of affairs. Men's dedication to the PSF was celebrated in the party's prescriptive literature and privileged in comparison to that of women's. Women in Civic Action, for instance, were instructed to act as "auxiliaries" to men, because as one regulation booklet put it, PSF men faced "crushing and overwhelming" tasks. Therefore, women's "duty" was to serve as men's secretaries and distribute *Le Petit Journal* for them.[39] While men surely worked hard as PSF participants, it was not unusual for women to suffer from their workload and the expectations that came with it. In 1938, for instance, Simone Marochetti wrote to one of her friends that Préval was "very ill" and that her doctor had recommended "complete rest," which she pointed out would be "very difficult for [Préval] to take."[40] Ducrocq fell ill in the summer of 1937, which played a key role in exacerbating problems at AMSJA. Préval wrote to one colleague that she was concerned about "the condition of our poor friend Ducrocq. I'm sorry that her fatigue has taken over in this way and that she is ill. For the past year, she has worked so much, that explains it: she's paying for it physically."[41] In another letter to Ducrocq, Préval mentioned that their work had been "heavy and laborious," and admitted, "we are a little exhausted from the effort provided."[42]

At the heart of Préval and Ducrocq's exhaustion was a persistent lack of monetary resources, which inhibited women's ability to implement the movement's ambitious social programs. While the summer camps were one of the most important and publicized of all PSF social activities, they were not properly funded. "We are terribly poor . . . sending hundreds of children to summer camps is terribly expensive," Préval confidentially wrote to one of her adjutants, describing what she called the "grave difficulties" of running the camps.[43] Even though all four PSF social organizations held fund-raisers, such activities did not provide enough money to ease the strain placed upon the women who organized the camps. The ways in which limited resources led to low attendance were direct. For instance, the cost for Tunisian Social Action to send children to French summer camps was exorbitant, which led local women to create their own camp. However, creating camps for boys and girls proved too costly, and they subsequently established one for boys and sent five girls to the Franciscan sisters.[44] While Garrigoux claimed that in 1937 over 15,000 children attended various camps, a report at an administrative council meeting of the same year noted that only 3,500 children had been sent to six PSF summer camps.[45] Low registration numbers in June 1937 suggested a lack of interest among the children and their parents, prompting Garrigoux to worry that registration for the camps "was not sufficient."[46] Consequently, she decided to "decentralize" them for the 1939 season.[47]

The pressures these budget problems exerted on Travail et loisirs women led to an irreparable schism between leaders of the PSF in the Isère and the central leadership in Paris. As Travail et loisirs struggled to fund its summer camps, local leaders were under pressure to find the funds necessary to keep their camp open. Such was the case with Suzanne Carpano, the head of the Women's Section in Pont-de-Beauvoisin (Isère). Madame Carpano's male and female colleagues described as her as being so "devoted" to the PSF that "her valor was rare."[48] In an effort to scrape together funds for the Pont de Beauvoisin summer camp held in neighboring Savoie, Carpano planned a charity bazaar at the camp's location, a factory run by a PSF supporter named Guinet. Having organized a similar bazaar the preceding year, Carpano understood all the time-consuming details that went into planning such an event, which included finding a suitable location, soliciting vendors, raising funds, and running publicity. Several days before the bazaar was to take place, Préval informed Carpano that it infringed upon a clause in the factory's lease and needed to be cancelled. Préval's letter canceling the bazaar enraged Carpano because she had repeatedly sent letters and telegrams to Préval asking for permission to move ahead with the sale. When Carpano's communications went unanswered, she had no option left but to obtain written permission from Guinet to use his factory, hoping that his authorization would be enough to meet the regulations governing charity bazaars that had been established by Paris.

Carpano's angry rebuke of Préval reveals tensions between Paris and the provinces and the extent to which Préval's overextension prevented her from defusing what became a major problem. Carpano complained that Préval was fifteen days late in responding to an "urgent request" and told her, "Your response lacks candor. I want absolutely to know the true reasons of your refusal, because I'm horrified by this lie. . . . I also want to alert you to a situation which will have a very bad effect in the country: many of us are unpaid, without any explanation or excuse. . . . Thanks to you, our bazaar will not take place, as a repercussion the needy will suffer, and our enemies will be delighted."[49]

Carpano was not exaggerating in warning about potential fallout. Both she and her husband were reportedly popular leaders, and many section members followed them in resigning from the party. The Isère PSF section chief, Lefevre, submitted his resignation to Préval and told her, "We don't deserve this affront, which is going to give joy to our adversaries, and will leave us without resources for our social works, when we have already committed heavy expenses so close to our goal."[50] A slew of letters, equally distraught, were sent to other PSF leaders, including La Rocque. One letter from Carpano's husband told La Rocque that his section felt "abandoned by him," and implored, "Do you give your acquiescence to this injustice? In the provinces, are we always the victims?"[51]

While La Rocque and Préval did not engage the Carpanos, one PSF leader was not only appalled at the couple's behavior, but chided Préval (but not La Rocque) for being "too kind and conciliatory in this circumstance," expressing dismay at the fact that she "wanted to forget the whole thing."[52] The PSF Federation president in Grenoble warned La Rocque that the affair had emboldened the Socialist mayor and empowered the Socialist Party, which dominated the area around Pont de Beauvoisin.[53] The mass of resignations did not help, and he begged La Rocque to make amends with Madame Carpano, calling her "one of the best PSF militants of Isère." He suggested that if she could be "rehabilitated," men and women would return to both Travail et loisirs and the PSF.[54] For an organization that hailed discipline and unity to such an extent as the Croix de Feu/PSF, the infighting brought about by the shortage of qualified personnel and underfunded programs undermined the movement's ability to transmit its ultranationalist messages despite the Social First! mission.

STRUCTURALLY SUBORDINATING WOMEN IN CIVIC ACTION

While women in Travail et loisirs, Social Action, SPES, and even the dysfunctional AMSJA enjoyed a great deal of autonomy and authority, one PSF group for women stands out. Created with the advent of the PSF in 1936 alongside Social Action, and replacing the Women's Section, Civic Action—the only group open to all women—was regressive in the sense that it fostered women's dependency on men and limited their participation in decision-making at the local level. The statutes of Civic Action explained the group's purpose in this way: "As long as women don't have the right to vote they cannot speak properly of politics. They will participate, however, in the life of the country and will be able to indirectly have a very large influence on politics through their civic action."[55] While in feminist and Catholic groups such recognition of women's lack of access to full citizenship was followed with demands for suffrage, similar activism was not the case with Civic Action. Instead, its statutes defined its purpose vaguely, noting that women needed to be properly educated before they could vote, which was an affirmation of their subordinate status and the same argument that the PSF used to deny colonial subjects citizenship. Indeed, while men allegedly possessed sufficient knowledge to intelligently discuss politics, women had no business doing so, and if they did, they would not be taken seriously. For this reason, the group's statutes stated: "The principal goal of Civic Action is the civic formation of women."[56] In this sense Civic Action simply replaced the Croix de Feu Women's Section, although women's influence diminished.

Unlike Civic Action, the Women's Section emphasized civic space, and its structures were not informed by specific references to the vote and politics. Indeed, the manner in which Civic Action denied women's political capabilities by championing their civic formation not only ignored the decades-long struggle by feminists for suffrage and the expansion of women's social and civic rights but ignored the sociopolitical work done by women in the Croix de Feu/PSF itself. Even La Rocque abandoned the pretense that women were not ready for political action in a circular he wrote to Social Action Delegates that explained their duties in the PSF: "We will only save France by fulfilling an elementary duty. In all fields of our political, social, and civic activity we must be simple people."[57] While La Rocque's point was to urge female delegates to act with humility, he inadvertently recognized that Social Action women were political actors because the party's various fields of action were intertwined.

The distinctions between Social Action and Civic Action not only reveal the way in which women's subordination in the Croix de Feu/PSF functioned but also the sometimes fraught relationship between men and women. Some male leaders were insecure about their dwindling authority over women. La Rocque responded to their fears by subordinating Civic Action to the authority of male PSF section presidents. Since all PSF sections had Social and Civic Action sections attached to them—just as Croix de Feu sections had a Women's Section attached—this structure had significant implications for the behavior of men and women who participated in the PSF. In a circular explaining the relationship between the women's groups and PSF sections, La Rocque maintained that the leader of each Civic Action section—the delegate—was to operate "in absolute dependence of the PSF section president for all the affairs of the civic order."[58] In this way, the top leader of Civic Action sections and her adjutants were unable to initiate and organize activities. There was a clear contrast between Civic Action's dependency and the responsibilities of the delegate that led Social Action groups, and in particular, the relationship between the Social Action delegate and the male PSF section president: La Rocque informed each section president that he could only intervene if the Social Action delegate requested his opinion or forgot some of the rules that governed her section.[59] The colonel insisted that the male leadership respect Social Action's autonomy and not meddle in its activities. Indeed, he instructed his section presidents that if they were to intervene, they were to "give your Social Action Delegate the very clear impression that you are neither looking to restrain nor bully her."[60]

Perhaps even more striking than Civic Action's mandated dependency upon male section presidents was the nullification of its authority in the decision-making processes of PSF sections. "Civic Action groups will not have the capacity to be involved in decisions of PSF sections," La Rocque wrote in a circular to male leaders, assuring them that their authority over Civic Action would remain intact.[61] Again, such subordination was in direct contrast to the high degree of authority that Social Action delegates enjoyed. Perhaps the best example of the elite status of Social Action delegates was in the crucial arena of budget allocations, which bridged the divide between PSF and Social Action sections. La Rocque informed the section presidents that they were to stay out of budget writing for social services. "You must exert no inquiry on the details of the distribution of expenditures," he told them.[62] In addition to expenditures, the section president was to work alongside the Social Action delegate in determining the budget for each section's social services. The delegate was to put together a budget proposal and then, as La Rocque explained, "reach an agreement" with the section president in determining allocations for children's education, interior party aid, and social assistance.[63] As the problems at Pont-de-Beauvoisin revealed, often there was not enough funding to go around, yet at this mid-level decision making, the Social Action delegate's authority was on par with that of the section president.

Civic Action's lack of autonomy and limited authority was furthered revealed in how the PSF's male leadership determined which women would lead Civic Action. While hostility to democratic principles was pervasive at all levels of the Croix de Feu/PSF, La Rocque lauded the fact that the delegate in charge of each Civic Action section was not appointed but elected by her group. The Civic Action delegate was one of the only leadership positions in the movement's entire bureaucracy that was determined by voting. However, the elections were something of a sham because the delegate's candidacy required the approval of the section's male leadership bureau and ratification by the male-dominated PSF federation to which sections belonged.[64] Again, the manner in which leadership selection in Civic Action contrasted with Social Action reveals the regressive nature of the former. The section president nominally appointed the Social Action delegate, *but only after* she had already been designated by the upper echelons of the movement's leadership.[65] Because women dominated the top ranks of all Croix de Feu/PSF social action, and were present in the leadership structure at the national level, women most likely determined the Social Action delegate.

Despite the fact that the purpose of Civic Action was at odds with much of what Croix de Feu/PSF women were doing in practice, the group's subordinate status stemmed in part from patriarchal attitudes that seeped into the rhetoric of some of the activists who helped formulate the transgressive aspects of the movement's programs. Indeed, women themselves lacked consistency in envisioning their own place within the movement and women's role in French society. Jeanne Garrigoux, for instance, often promoted an essentialized view of women's nature more common in the LFACF and UFCS rather than the Croix de Feu/PSF. Indeed, she employed language that Préval never used. In a published brochure on PSF social services, Garrigoux echoed the regressive maternalism that had characterized French sociopolitics throughout the 1930s, suggesting that since "the essential problem is a problem of social order . . . the mother must be encouraged and led back into the home."[66] At Social Action's 1939 congress, Garrigoux remarked, "If a young girl has been raised well, she will raise children who resemble her. The merit of a woman is to keep her home, to make her husband happy, and to raise her children."[67] As a social action activist, Garrigoux would have considered herself an elite whose calling was to guide the masses toward proper behavior, which in this case centered around the rigid maternalism of pronatalists and antifeminist social Catholics. Although Garrigoux's rhetoric differed from that of Préval, Gérus, Féraud, Fouché, Ducrocq, and other Croix de Feu leaders, her technical expertise, devotion to social action, and staunch Catholicism made her the type of elite member that prospered in the Croix de Feu/PSF.

While women in Civic Action groups lacked the status of women in the movement's other groups, some women nevertheless joined Civic Action to widen their sphere of influence and participate in national rejuvenation. In this way, Civic Action was similar to the Women's Sections of other ultranationalist leagues and parties. According to Civic Action's program, in promoting women's "civic formation," the PSF sought to help women develop a "deep and accurate" understanding of political, social, and economic problems so that they could form a "cultural elite" and pass on knowledge to others living in "different milieus."[68] In practical terms, Civic Action sections were to recruit enough women to support regular meetings, create a library and study group, and organize regular courses and conferences that could take place at a woman's foyer.

Civic Action's ability to meet these objectives varied. Sections in Nièvre, for example, reached 276 members (including 72 in Nevers), which constituted enough members to organize piecemeal activities.[69] Claiming 390 members in January 1939, Lyon's Civic Action was relatively effective in organizing their activities.[70] For example, leaders held monthly meetings for cadres on topics that ranged from reporting on the party's national congresses to exploring strategies on the best way to return the woman to the home. Other activities included general meetings that took place every two months, hygiene classes, art shows, and the management of a small library that had twelve regular attendees.[71] This modicum of success spurred the Lyon Civic Action to consider future initiatives, the most promising of which was a biannual celebration honoring mothers of large families.[72] Leaders planned to invite Men's Sections as a way to encourage men to become interested in Civic Action and make them aware that the group could help the PSF to increase its level of support.

While Lyon's Civic Action had enough support to accomplish its objectives, Civic Action in the Bouches-du-Rhone was not only a disaster but demonstrated that many sections lacked the resources and leadership to be effective. Civic Action's leader there, Madame Casanova, complained to Préval that the group's statutes ceded too much control to men; the effectiveness of each section depended upon its president and his appreciation of the group's purpose. Casanova noted that while a few section presidents were excellent, many others were incompetent. She contended that this lack of consistency was a key reason for why the general state of Civic Action in the Bouches-du-Rhone was "deplorable"; male section leaders had nearly "dictatorial control" over women.[73] Casanova was one of Civic Action's most dedicated activists, yet she was disheartened by the barriers she confronted in her attempts to mobilize women. For this reason, Casanova urged Préval to initiate a complete overhaul of Civic Action. Among Casanova's numerous suggestions, the most important included changing the group's statutes to allow delegates more autonomy, ending the democratic elections of the delegate, and most significantly, urging Paris to send more female inspectors to report on Civic Action sections in the Bouches-du-Rhone. These reforms, Casanova told Préval, would "bring the spirit of Paris to the provinces" and compel section presidents to exhibit more respect for women's potential as civic-political actors.[74] Casanova also argued that revamping the group's structure could invigorate its recruiting efforts, which were badly needed because attendance at section meetings was quite low. Casanova suggested that the PSF reorganize its recruiting by directing propaganda to women's homes and more clearly articulating the group's purpose. She explained that more publicity was essential and urged Préval to follow the actions of the PSF's many regional papers by including a section on Civic Action in every issue of *Le Petit Journal*.[75]

The problematic involvement of section presidents and concomitant low attendance at section meetings in the Bouches-du-Rhône was most likely not the exception but the rule. Perhaps the best example of such struggles outside Provence was when Garrigoux was called to inspect the PSF section in Péronne (Somme) after receiving reports of problems in the section there. Upon her arrival, she found only four audience members—all women—at a public PSF meeting, only one of whom, Madame Dauré, understood the mission of the PSF. After talking with Dauré, Garrigoux concluded: "it is impossible for us to fulfill our mission," because the male members did not want to be "bothered" with activities that they claimed were a "women's matter."[76]

Despite women's subordination in Civic Action, the group's recognition that women might one day be ready to be political actors led women with wildly differing agendas to join the PSF. Indeed, some seized the opportunity to exert political influence through civic action while others denied that women had a political nature at all. Civic Action thus became the site for an odd mix of feminist and antifeminist sentiment. The Civic Action delegate in Nancy, for example, emphasized to women that they could engage in political action. Writing in the PSF's local newspaper, Madame Desmons insisted, "In principle, nothing stands in the way of a woman participating in the political life of her country. Neither religion nor natural rights can restrict her from taking an interest in the well-being of the society in which she lives.... My fellow women, to help you rise to this challenge the PSF demands your political rights."[77] In other cases, sentiment challenging the "women in the home" movement found fertile ground in the movement's disdain for democracy. For instance, the Civic Action delegate for Deux-Sèvres, Madame Bernard, was hostile to universal suffrage and its claims that self-governance promoted liberty. She argued that the French people were not Marxists, yet they were subject to a Marxist government: the Popular Front. Women, she maintained, could play a key role in saving what she called "our decadent republic." Bernard argued, "In reality, it's opinion that governs us; and there, my fellow women, no law can prevent you from exercising your activity, which is an urgent duty.... This duty is your civic duty, to which you are subject to the same title as men. Those who want to keep the woman in her only role as the housewife are obsolete and useless champions of a revolutionary era."[78] In this way, Civic Action leaders were more than willing to demand changes to the status quo and berate those who stood in the way of advancing women's place in society.

While Civic Action attracted a minority of women who fought to expand their spheres of influence in French society, far more common were those content with the patriarchal social order and who held a deep-seated contempt for those who sought to change it. Croix de Feu/PSF supporters expressed the highest degree of scorn for suffragettes—a direct rebuke of the direct action tactics of Weiss's Femme Nouvelle. A Civic Action supporter in Provence explained it this way: "What is the goal of Civic Action?... It has never been the PSF's intention to throw our members into politics, to make politicians of them, or even worse, suffragettes."[79] A Civic Action leader in the Sarthe and Mayenne expressed similar sentiments toward progressive feminists by proclaiming, "We must be mindful of giving the impression of being suffragettes brandishing the tricolor flag on the street corners. Politics is not our affair!"[80] Indeed, the movement's antifeminism was best summed up by the vice president of a PSF section in Niort: "We are not feminists because feminism is an imbecility that is not in harmony with our realism. 'The woman is equal to the man'; that's the battle slogan? It's an absurd equation, which gives the impression that one protests against the other, that the woman must struggle against the man.... Your enemy, *mesdames,* is not the man but rather prejudices, unhinged morals, misery, and outdated institutions."[81] This sentiment characterized the vast majority of women in Civic Action. Even for women willing to push to broaden women's status in French society—such as the delegates in Nancy and Deux-Sèvres—they refused to identify with feminism and the divisiveness they believed it engendered.

CONCLUSION

The case of Civic Action reveals a demand in French society for a nominally secular conservative organization that did not identify itself as feminist, yet offered women opportunities for political and civic action. For this reason, energetic activists who were neither trained nor interested in providing social services—women like Casanova, Desmons, and Bernard—were attracted to the PSF. Indeed, Casanova was a dynamic activist who was unafraid to critique the patriarchal structures that blocked her attempts to mobilize conservative and reactionary women. Despite the promise of Civic Action, women who joined the group generally experienced more frustrations and failures than successes. Women who participated in Social Action were the ones who earned elite status and thus had the transformative effect on the PSF, rather than women who were interested in politics. If the PSF had its way, women may have had to wait longer than 1944 for political citizenship. Moreover, Casanova's argument that the structural barriers that women faced impeded the overall progress of the PSF applied to the movement's North African branches. While in metropolitan France, Civic Action was an exception as the only PSF group that officially subordinated women to men; in North Africa, such subordination was the norm. AMSJA, Travail et loisirs, and SPES were not active. As we shall see, Social Action was weak and structured differently, which inhibited its effectiveness in creating social centers, summer camps, and a full range of welfare services. These limits on women's action not only revealed the barriers that women faced in achieving legitimacy as political actors in metropolitan France, but the comparatively regressive effects of the hypermasculinity of settler political culture in the Maghreb.

4

TRANSFORMING FRENCH PHYSICAL CULTURE

SOCIAL DARWINISM, BODILY FITNESS,

AND GENDER, 1934-1939

While the degree of women's authority and autonomy in the Croix de Feu/PSF was uneven, the movement's Social First! strategy was characterized by a growing acceptance that women and men could work together. Indeed, the growth of the movement's social action enabled supporters to organize programs that broadened beyond those traditionally conceived of as "social" (such as welfare) and into the realm of culture. One of the social and cultural arenas where the breakdown of separate spheres was most apparent was in the movement's contribution to changes in French physical culture.

France's defeat in the Franco-Prussian war in 1871 and a growing pan-European interest in physical culture were two factors that drove the creation of gymnastic and sporting societies in the early Third Republic.[1] Indeed, the new Republic faced many challenges after the shock of defeat and the violence of the Paris Commune, which civic leaders met by creating a series of associations that emphasized physical challenge and sacrifice as they prepared young men to become citizen-soldiers.[2] The broadening of conscription laws in the 1880s helped bring about the integration of physical education into the curriculum of schools and the growth of physical education groups outside of schools.[3] While the first privately sponsored French sporting clubs were aimed at the bourgeoisie, Catholic parishes created clubs for the needy in an attempt to broaden their influence and contest the Republic's anticlerical measures; the Socialist Party developed its own sporting association in 1908 for members and opened it to all French men in 1911.[4]

By the interwar period, as many as four million women and men from all classes had joined sporting associations, and virtually all political groups had their own physical education programs or supported affiliated societies. The acceleration of interest in physical culture during the interwar period was rooted in several factors. The aftermath of the extraordinary destruction caused by the Great War left many Europeans mourning the dead and healing the millions of bodies damaged by physical and psychological trauma.[5] Moreover, an unprecedented influx of immigrants from Europe and the colonies added a new dimension to debates over how best to regenerate bodies comprising what many referred to as the "French race."[6] For these reasons, many believed that virile bodies, racial regeneration, and national rejuvenation were interconnected.[7] A Communist-affiliated sporting society explained it this way: "We don't want the race to degenerate. We want a strong and healthy youth."[8] The Popular Front expressed similar sentiments, asserting that the practice of sport should "be considered as one of the elements of the safeguarding of the race."[9] Women were central to debates over racial rejuvenation, although cultural attitudes toward bodily improvement were framed in stereotypical terms. State-run and Catholic physical education programs, for example, designed initiatives for women but tended to essentialize women's bodies by viewing them as weak and best suited for childbirth.[10]

Like most French, Croix de Feu/PSF supporters were concerned about the state of French physical culture, or conceptions of how the bodies of women and men should look, the best way to transform those bodies, and the implications of bodily health for national strength.[11] Despite such interest, the movement's intervention into physical culture remains understudied. The existing scholarship explores men's (not women's) physical education and locates its origins with male leaders rather than the Women's Section.[12] This chapter explores why the movement's supporters of both sexes believed that transforming French physical culture was a critical component of national rejuvenation and put emphasis on finding the ways in which the process of embodiment developed along gendered and racial lines.[13] While Joan Tumblety has shown that groups across the political spectrum developed similar programs based upon shared ideas, this was not the case with the Croix de Feu/PSF's approach to women's physical education.[14] The movement embraced conventional ideas about the military purpose of men's physical education, conflating masculinity with action, self-control, competition, and struggle, yet its approach to women's physical education was distinct. Influenced by contemporary scholarship suggesting that gender was culturally specific and based upon social norms, the movement's theorists created a physical education program that went beyond considering women's bodies as weak and conflating womanhood with child-rearing. The program emphasized general health initiatives such as vigorous training to increase women's circulation and heart rate, bodily movement that would build women's muscles throughout the body, and the competitive team sports of basketball and soccer. In these ways, the Croix de Feu/PSF created programs based upon the idea that women were fit, strong, and competitive.

While transgressive with regard to women's physical education, the Croix de Feu/PSF's approach to physical culture emphasized perfection and the ideal human form, which reflected the influences of eugenics and social Darwinian conceptions of hierarchy. Racial rejuvenation was a central component of the Croix de Feu/PSF's social model, which was based upon its supporters' ultra-nationalistic vision of a nation that was not a collection of individuals, but an organic whole. In this vein, ultranationalists believed that while European bodies were superior, those that were weak, flabby, or ugly threatened the nation's fate at the precise moment when national strength was critical to fight national and international threats. The Croix de Feu/PSF's approach to physical culture thus solidified existing racial hierarchies by obsessing over the state of French civilization, essentializing black bodies as "primitive" and French bodies as "civilized" yet in need of rejuvenation.

CIVILIZATION, PHYSIOLOGY, AND ANTHROPOLOGY: THE CROIX DE FEU/ PSF'S APPROACH TO TRANSFORMING FRENCH PHYSICAL CULTURE

"We are odiously ugly!" Doctor Jean Edward Ruffier proclaimed in 1914, arguing that it was this supposed ugliness that embodied a weakened nation and the social body's descent into decadence.[15] Paris, he bemoaned, while at one time renowned for its elegance and beauty, had become filled with "ridiculous stomachs, flushed jowls, rounded backs, pale faces, sloping shoulders, and hunched chests."[16] Ruffier was a leading physical culture advocate who would come to influence Croix de Feu/PSF technicians in developing the movement's physical education program, including the man who formulated its conceptual basis, Gaëtan Maire. Like Ruffier, Maire believed that French society was plagued by ugliness, which revealed one's true character. "Bodily ugliness is often due to negligence... Our body doesn't have to be ugly if we have the will to correct the imperfections. Not to devote oneself to these efforts is the mark of a great weakness of character," he opined.[17] This sentiment underpinned the Croix de Feu/PSF's entire approach to remaking France; *will* was an essential component of character. For France to regenerate itself, it needed women and men of strong morals. Ugliness symbolized laziness and was evidence of a significant threat facing French civilization, that of racial degeneration. Maire explained it this way: "Physical degeneration is the defect of civilized people who neglect the culture of the body."[18]

Conflating the state of civilization with race-thinking was pervasive in the Croix de Feu/PSF. Like most French, the movement's supporters believed that they were part of the "French race." The most common view of race held by supporters was articulated by La Rocque in *Service Public,* where he rejected biological and linguistic views of race. "The French race is a magnificent synthesis, disciplined, cultivated, and well-balanced. It forms a whole; no linguistic, no analysis of heredity can prevail against this fact," he wrote, adding, "France is more of an assimilating nation than any other. No other nation was or is better qualified to pacify, govern, and unify a vast intercontinental domain."[19] For La Rocque, fifteen hundred years of French history had demonstrated that a once linguistically diverse grouping of regions now spoke and thought of themselves as French. As the movement's leaders pointed out, the empire was still relatively young, and the French simply needed more time to let the civilizing project play itself out in France's new colonies, which stretched from Africa to Indochina. In this way, La Rocque linked race to culture, which provided the guidelines for assimilation and led the Croix de Feu to become the premier disseminator of cultural racism in the interwar period. Mere participation in the Croix de Feu/PSF exacerbated supporters' tendencies to think in racial terms. As Maire put it, "The physical perfecting of a race is indispensable to maintain [its place] in the first rank of great modern nations."[20]

The metropolitan Croix de Feu/PSF's emphasis on assimilation and its drive toward racial perfection centered around positive eugenics, which dominated French medical training and science and distinguished France from Nazi Germany and the United States.[21] Since an individual could be improved according to her or his environment and personal desire for change, one's life was neither genetically fixed nor predetermined. For Maire, if one man was bigger than another, it may have been "because he received more favorable genes, but also, perhaps because he benefited from better food when he was a child."[22] Indeed, Maire worked within the neo-Lamarckian tradition of eugenics that emphasized milieu, as he stated bluntly: "Positive eugenics presents the best means of human perfection."[23] A key component of positive eugenics was the rejection of biological theories positing that class was based upon genetic makeup in favor of the idea that education enabled an individual to seek self-improvement. On this point, metropolitan Croix de Feu/PSF supporters strongly agreed that the human body could be transformed regardless of ethnic, religious, or class background. In seeking to achieve perfection, the SPES leader in the Rhone, M. Thevenet, explained it this way: "We must make men of healthy body and spirit without the consideration of blood, money, religion, or [political] party."[24]

The movement's emphasis on positive eugenics was squarely in a social Darwinian tradition of using evolution to rank the civilizational state of a people. While all bodies could be improved, this did not mean that all bodies were equal. Maire framed his conception of evolutionary progress in this way: "Thanks to gesture, then language, then writing, then printing, successful initiatives, discoveries, and inventions spread from the elders to the young and from one group to another, so much so that knowledge and power accumulated through tradition and social heritage, which is without comparison in the animal kingdom."[25] For Maire, power, knowledge, and heritage were intermixed and formed the basis for the superiority of French civilization. Moreover, Maire not only argued that civilizational progress depended upon maintaining the superior intellectual and moral state of the people, but that robust ideas and programs were needed to halt decline.

Such interest in civilizational progress was one reason that interwar physical culture theorists such as Maire were drawn to the ideas and techniques of France's leading expert on physical education, Georges Hébert. During his time as an admiral stationed in French West Africa in the 1890s, Hébert was struck by the lack of development and industrialization that he saw, which he believed led to a less civilized state where nature still ruled. The inhabitants, those he called *"les primitifs,"* who by definition were inferior, nevertheless possessed natural traits that more "civilized" Europeans had forgotten. Discourses on primitivism were particularly charged during the 1930s and cast "primitive" peoples low on the evolutionary scale in terms of intelligence and ability to regulate their emotions and actions.[26] Absent such mental dexterity, *"les primitifs"* supposedly possessed more physical prowess. A brochure outlining Hébert's approach explained, "The reason the active *'primitif'* easily obtains his complete growth and maximum strength is that he produces a sufficient amount of bodily work. He does not reach the same result if he limits his effort."[27] For Hébert, while Europeans, or *"les civilisés"* as he called them, could learn from their African counterparts, a binary existed between them that was racial and hierarchical. Tumblety demonstrates that Hébert and other primitivists' conceptions of "the primitive" involved an implicit notion of hierarchy among "races" in which Europeans' place at the summit was naturalized.[28] Moreover, Hébert's ideas centered back to the concept of will, linking work with bodily strength. Because Europeans had already demonstrated their superior civilizational capabilities, they needed to remind themselves that they too could be physically strong. In this way, Hébert was one of many who believed that a negative effect of modern European civilization was the emergence of a sedentary and weak population incapable of defending itself. Only physical work could remind a man of his basic nature.

It is important to note that Hébert did not contribute to the most virulent scientific racism of the era, particularly the efforts of anthropologists who, as Alice Conklin explains, were driven to publicize "the findings of their science for racist political ends."[29] For Conklin, scientific racism developed in the West in the nineteenth century as anthropologists ranked human races, correlated intelligence to skin color, and then constructed hierarchies of civilization accordingly.[30] Rather than asserting the inferiority of Africans or comparing them to animals, Hébert admired the physical fitness of Africans but nevertheless reduced them to their bodies while recognizing the bodies *and* minds of the French. Hébert's primitivism stressed that the French needed to emulate the physical fitness of the black male body although he assigned it to permanent inferior status in comparison to *"les civilisés."*[31] Based upon his observations of *"les primitifs,"* Hébert suggested that certain movements came "naturally" to humans: walking, running, jumping, climbing, lifting, throwing, and self-defense. In creating what became known as the Natural Method, Hébert, and the many Hébertist societies established during interwar period, emphasized these movements as the basis for rejuvenating male French body. Combined with the intellectual capabilities of the French, Hébert believed that the movements would enable *"les civilisés"* to reach their full potential. A Hébertiste newspaper explained the racial binary in hierarchical terms, linking French racial heritage, temperament, and the body's physical condition: "We have a heritage to protect: that of our race, in which our mental spirit lacks nothing and includes in its beautiful history of heroic events resulting from its strength and virility."[32]

Hébert's emphasis on nature, racial rejuvenation, and the French "mental spirit" played a key role in why Croix de Feu/PSF leaders used his ideas to inform their own programs. In doing so, the Croix de Feu/PSF exacerbated the racism that was implicit in Hébert's primitivism by applying his methods to their own laudatory conceptions of French temperaments. One of the PSF's top-ranking medical professionals, Jeanne Latil, maintained, "Lieutenant Hébert created a method that perfectly adapted human physiology to the French temperament, which will be able to rejuvenate the race."[33] In identifying a distinct French temperament, the movement's leaders perpetuated the widespread sense of French exceptionalism. "It is on the essential principle of the return to Nature that Lieutenant Hébert has built his method," Maire stated, adding, "His doctrine centers around toughness, complete fitness, and utilitarianism... Hébert wants his subjects to resist fatigue and bad weather. He also wants them to be frugal and sober."[34] In listing physical traits and combining them with the mental traits of frugality and sobriety—two hallmarks of self-control—Maire articulated key markers of difference between "primitive" Africans and "civilized" French. Thevenet further perpetuated the notion of civilizational difference by lamenting that Hébert's eight movements "have been more or less abandoned by our civilization." The key to racial rejuvenation, he argued, was to combine the European self-control with the physical instincts of all humans: "Hébert's gestures are applied methodically, are reasoned and controlled because they cannot be executed by *'le civilisé'* in the same manner as *'le primitif.' 'Le primitif'* acts not methodically, but by instinct and need.... his living conditions require him to become strong. To develop the *'le civilisé,'* it is necessary to replace his instinct and need with that of steady, regular work, based... upon his strength and general state."[35] In this way, the Croix de Feu/PSF used Hébert's methods to allow French reason and self-mastery to flourish.

Beauty and Human Nature: the Influences of
Jean Edward Ruffier and Margaret Mead

While Hébert conflated embodiment with civilizational decline and rejuvenation, his ideas and methods privileged the male body. Due to the Croix de Feu/PSF's efforts to mobilize both sexes as agents of social action, the movement's leaders believed it was critical to prioritize strengthening women's bodies as well. In some ways the Croix de Feu/PSF perpetuated narrow gender stereotypes, yet more importantly, its theorists were influenced by cutting-edge scholarship that enabled them to break new ground with regard to women's physical education.

Diverging from the powerful pronatalist discourses, Croix de Feu/PSF theorists used the ideas of several prominent scholars, including Dr. Ruffier.[36] An adherent of cell theory, Ruffier examined organisms at the cellular level and determined that healthy muscle depended upon movement. In his study of the amoeba, for example, Ruffier documented its reaction to an exterior stimulus such as movement, heat, or contact with another body by contracting itself, making secretions, or dividing; these reactions were nonexistent in amoebas that did not move, or what Ruffier called "inert" amoebas.[37] Ruffier argued that since the human body was an "agglomeration" of microscopic cells, human cells needed to move lest they fall into an "inert" state.[38] Informed by Ruffier's findings, Maire stated that if one were to render "the most beautiful muscle possible" immobile for two or three months, it would become soft and deprived of energy, and would eventually "disintegrate."[39] Ruffier's contention that cells instinctively wanted to return to their nascent state spurred Croix de Feu/PSF leaders to create a program that emphasized movement as the key to bodily health. This physiological understanding of muscle formed a crucial component of the movement's program that was gender-neutral in the sense that all muscle was made from the same tissue and thus operated in a consistent manner regardless of sex. As we shall see, because Maire viewed movement as the basic way to transform muscle, he and his colleagues implemented many gender-neutral exercises that emphasized strength, coordination, and flexibility, which they believed would form a harmonious, healthy, and attractive body.

A second important influence on Croix de Feu/PSF physical culture theorists was the anthropologist Margaret Mead. They were fascinated by Mead's studies demonstrating that the behavior of men and women differed according to cultural and social norms. Based upon her observation of peoples living in the Sepik region of Papua New Guinea, the Arapesh, the Mundugumor (Biwat), and Tchambuli (Chambri), Mead concluded that temperament was not fixed but that women's and men's "nature" differed according to place and time. While Mead claimed that both sexes of the Arapesh were gentle and cooperative, traits she noted were consistent with Western conceptions of femininity, she characterized the temperaments of both sexes of the Mundugumor as aggressive and violent, which, she stated, the West viewed as masculine traits; and in the Tchambuli, Mead reported that women were dominant and emotionally distant whereas men were submissive and emotional.[40] Turning gender stereotypes on their head, these ideas underpinned key portions of the Croix de Feu/PSF's program. "According to the American Mead," Maire explained, "you [can] find women who have masculine behavior and men with feminine behavior."[41]

This evidence that sexual difference was not innate was critical to the Croix de

Feu/PSF's distinct approach to physical culture. Throughout the Third Republic, numerous social commentators had defined female bodies as weak and female minds as inferior to those of men.[42] However, Mead's ideas provided Maire with a language to contest such misogyny. "Weakness is not necessarily an attribute of women [and] biological differences between the sexes do not equate to an inequality in intelligence," Maire insisted, leading him to ask: "What [characteristics are] innate and what are acquired? What is hereditary and what is circumstantial? When one compares the man with the woman, we must remember that it is not a question of one of two natural and biological types, but two artificial and social types of which the divergence . . . lies in educational factors. From birth, society molds individual conformity to a certain conventional ideal."[43] As a feminist, Mead would have been concerned that far Right activists used her ideas for their own ends, but for theorists like Maire, Mead's view of human nature reinforced the notion that it was possible to mold women's bodies in new ways.

While Ruffier's attention to movement and muscle and Mead's findings that gender norms were culturally specific provided the basis for Croix de Feu/PSF theorists to create a distinct women's physical education program, they applied Mead's ideas selectively, insisting that certain traits were natural to women. Most significantly, Maire perpetuated a long-standing focus on physical attractiveness and beauty. He explained,

> Woman is naturally graceful; she has the instinct of elegance but the blossoming of her beauty cannot be complete if she remains a stranger to all physical exercise. Slenderness and weakness are not necessarily attributes of the woman. . . . Without physical education, the woman has only an ephemeral beauty; she oscillates between excessive scrawniness and portliness but never possesses the pure and well defined form that only a solid skeletal structure and a harmonious muscular development can provide in setting the contours of the body.[44]

Grace, elegance, and harmony were hallmarks of interwar discourses on ideal femininity. The idea that women could change and strengthen their bodies, however, reflected the intersection between physical education, will, and character that was pervasive in the movement. Maire warned, "All women must have the spirit of the cult of beauty. . . . One can momentarily give the appearance of beauty to a feeble body by deceptive means, but the woman who doesn't do physical education deprives herself of the only elements capable of maintaining her vigor and beauty."[45] Maire was not alone in his view, as a woman's body and her level of attractiveness was subject to judgment, debate, and scorn by groups across the political spectrum. The Communist women's youth group, for instance, instructed young women in how to apply makeup and achieve the perfect tan to become "pretty."[46] Maire was interested in beauty but wanted women's beauty to be rooted in their strength and health. Underlining the vital necessity of will power, Maire insisted, "By methodical exercise, each woman can become a healthy being of strength and beauty because congenital ugliness is not irreparable."[47] While perpetuating the insidious belief that ugliness and weakness marked a deficiency in one's character, Maire nevertheless emphasized health, which formed the basis for the women's portion of the movement's physical education programs.

Men too had a responsibility to work toward perfection as Croix de Feu/PSF physical education theorists sought to enhance their supposedly active nature and channel it through the use of reason and self-control. Perpetuating commonly held stereotypes that conflated masculinity with activity and femininity with passivity, Maire declared, "Man is generally more of a creator, more of a builder, and more adept at scientific studies, whereas the woman is more intuitive and more artistic. . . . Man is more aggressive, more proud, more nomadic, whereas woman is softer, more sensitive, more shy, more fine, more flirty."[48] In this sense, the movement perpetuated conventional ideas by seeking to prepare young men for action. Consequently, the movement's programs channeled youthful masculine energy into sport. Maire framed the intersections between the body, sport, and racial regeneration in this way: "The body, toned and fortified at the end of puberty, longs for performance. . . . It's the period of Sport, of individual sport, of team sport, the sport of combat. . . . Sport is essential for the formation of an energetic and robust race."[49] The competitive and team-oriented aspects of sport would prepare young men for a variety of challenges. According to Maire, boys and young men needed to be ready to "struggle against a definite element: a distance, a duration, an obstacle, a material difficulty, a danger, an enemy."[50] A negative consequence of competition and struggle was uncontrolled aggression, which Maire believed could be ameliorated by developing a sense of camaraderie, teamwork, altruism, and discipline among male youth. For Maire, these traits of self-control enabled young men to channel their instincts, which epitomized the best of French civilization and were crucial in reinforcing the social bonds that Croix de Feu/PSF ideologues sought to foster.[51]

THE CROIX DE FEU/PSF PHYSICAL CULTURE PROGRAM

For these ambitious ideas to be influential, Croix de Feu/PSF supporters needed to implement an effective physical education program. Physical education thus became central to the movement's social action. While women formulated and implemented the portions of its social program that concerned welfare, the two sexes worked together in physical education, which drew men into social action leadership and grassroots mobilization. As the 1930s progressed, the mix of ideology and structural organization were key factors in the Croix de Feu/PSF's mobilization of thousands to transform French physical culture. While France's largest women's physical education federation claimed 25,000 members in 565 affiliates and Communists mobilized roughly 30,000 youth, Croix de Feu/PSF supporters created 2,800 physical education societies serving 64,000 youth across Greater France, which included 1,100 basketball and 750 soccer teams by 1939.[52] In this way, the Croix de Feu/PSF's physical culture program became one of the largest and most dynamic of the interwar period.

The Women's Section and the Center for Physical Education, 1935–1936

The movement's first step in developing a physical education program was when Women's Section officials opened a Center for Physical Education in 1935. Préval appointed Maire as one of the Center's directors, and he worked with the Women's Section to create physical education centers for youth and adults throughout metropolitan France. In less than two years, the Croix de Feu had recruited twelve hundred children to its Parisian centers (Table 4), had opened ten provincial centers, and was in the process of creating centers in twenty more.[53] Croix de Feu/PSF activists viewed the physical education centers as the lynchpin in transforming the nation's physical culture. As the leadership repeatedly stated, physical education focused on not only physical but moral and intellectual development. Each center was around one hundred fifty square meters, the staff was approved by Women's Section headquarters, and the students, separated by sex, took daily lessons.[54] The physical layout of the centers reflected Women's Section priorities with regard to physical education, as they included space to perform exercises and a *foyer-bib-liothèque* for intellectual development. The Women's Section organized regular activities; talks on the French colonies, literature, and sports; a monthly film series; and annual fêtes celebrating gymnastics, water sports, and the French empire.[55]

TABLE 4. Croix de Feu Physical Education Centers in Paris, June 1936

Center	Male Supervisors	Female Supervisors	Boys Aged 7–13	Girls Aged 7–13	Boys Aged 14–16	Total Children
Rosalie	6	3	100	105	110	310
Reuilly	5	3	175	160	110	445
Madrid (Perronet)	5	3	125	75	75	275
Colombes	3	0	60	60	50	170

Source: CHSP LR 6, report, Gaëtan Maire, "Leçons données par semaine dans chaque groupe dans les centres de Paris," June 6, 1936.

This eclectic range of activities demonstrated that the Women's Section sought to make the centers fun so as to socialize youth into the movement's conception of what constituted the best aspects of French civilization.

As with all of the Croix de Feu's social services, the Popular Front's dissolution of the league had a limited impact on its growing physical education program. SPES replaced the Center for Physical Education and collaborated with the other social action groups that had evolved out of the Women's Section, namely Travail et loisirs, Social Action, and AMSJA. Additionally, Garrigoux's Social Studies Bureau created an offshoot—the SPES Study Bureau, which designed the SPES program. It was this body that Maire headed as he formulated the movement's physical culture program, although the entire SPES program required the approval of Garrigoux, Préval, and La Rocque.

While Tumblety has pointed out that SPES is "under-researched and highly significant," the new society could not operate on its own but only within the wider field of PSF social action.[56] Indeed, the PSF's efforts to regenerate French physical culture required the collective action of SPES, Travail et loisirs, Social Action, and AMSJA, which brought women and men together in organizing services. Préval wrote to a friend that she "had the honor of coordinating the efforts of all the past social works."[57] As the only leader who sat on the administrative council of all four organizations, Préval worked with Maire to formulate the SPES curriculum, appoint staff, and organize centers.[58] The coordination of services between the groups was to be "constant and tight," according to one circular, which warned, "If we neglect this essential coordination, we run the risks of a competition in recruitment, an overloading in the employment of children's time, a dispersion in effort, and useless expenses."[59] To this end, the leaders and staff of all four groups shared membership forms and medical files, which included notes on each child's medical history, temperament, educational level, disciplinary problems, and family members for recruiting purposes.[60] All of the groups also shared inspectors—both men and women—who traveled throughout metropolitan France and reported on the state of the movement's social services to the Social Studies Bureau.

In organizing their social programs, Croix de Feu/PSF supporters worked with SPES to determine the level of fitness of youth in their programs and the steps necessary for them to reach certain standards of health. For instance, the director of the Travail et loisirs social center at Saint Ouen, Madame Regnault, worked with the Center's head nurse, Madame Horaist, to implement the SPES curriculum. One of Horaist's primary responsibilities was to create a "strength index" file on each child by using thorough medical exams to calculate each individual's fitness level; based upon the findings, she placed each child into a group labeled as "strong, medium, or weak."[61] Staff supervisors catalogued in three-month intervals the changes in each child's height and weight and charted the increases in strength of their neck, shoulders, arms, abdomen, and thighs.[62] At Saint Ouen, Regnault's children, Jacqueline and Claude, were two of roughly twenty supervisors who supervised the groups and coached the boys' and girls' basketball and soccer teams, which were open to all youth deemed healthy enough to compete in team sports.[63] The supervisors were of vital importance due to their interactions with children, and for this reason, Maire, Préval, and other leaders spent a great deal of time looking for qualified young women and men who embodied Croix de Feu/PSF values. To be approved by the Social Studies Bureau, the supervisors had to be French citizens, were required to pass physical exams, and ideally were under thirty years of age.[64] Once approved, Préval and others at the Bureau assigned the supervisors wherever they were needed.

Not only did the supervisors function as intermediaries in socializing youth into Croix de Feu/PSF values, but the movement's leaders expected that they represent youthful symbols of ideal Frenchness. The SPES training manual dictated, "It is vital that the supervisors always be in good muscular shape and be trained perfectly in the practice of the exercises that they require of their students."[65] In addition to being fit and having perfect knowledge of SPES exercises, the supervisors were to exude a certain attitude as well. The training manual explained, "The supervisors must be examples and present themselves in front of their students in a manner that is always impeccable; they must demonstrate proof of absolute mastery and calm authority, and never allow themselves to become angry or use hurtful language."[66]

While the exercise curriculum that the SPES study bureau created was based primarily on Hébertist exercises, SPES leaders adapted the Natural Method to suit their own ideology and clientele. Since space was at a premium, SPES, like other interwar physical education societies, altered the exercises to the limited space available in their centers and summer camps and ensured that both sexes engaged in the exercises. As an SPES instructional booklet noted, "The same type of lesson applies to everyone: men, women, or children."[67] About one hundred exercises comprised the curriculum, all of which required students to combine strength, flexibility, balance, and coordination to strengthen muscles, coordinate breathing, and reduce flab. The diverse range of exercises were based on muscle movement and contraction that ranged from simple ones, like push-ups and sit-ups, to the complex, like the "walk like a duck" exercise, which required students to squat, place their hands on their knees or haunches, and move by alternating one foot in front of the other by straightening and bending their legs while gently moving their torso in a rotating motion.[68]

One of the most important goals of these exercises was to increase participants' circulation and heart rate. For women, this focus on general health differed notably from other physical education programs. Women's magazines and medical studies, for instance, emphasized the necessity of developing the muscles in the pelvic region to prepare girls for childbirth. In contrast, SPES sought to strengthen their entire body to promote stronger organ function and better health.[69] Girls from the ages of seven to thirteen focused on gymnastics and games, strengthening the muscles along the entire back and thoracic cavity, with secondary emphasis on the arms, legs, and neck. Girls from thirteen to sixteen continued to develop these muscles and added their abdominal ones to coordinate strength with flexibility through walking, running, jumping, and other exercises. Young women over sixteen continued to develop these muscles. Moreover, they could participate in team sports that emphasized physical contact such as basketball and soccer, which was unusual because many women's physical education programs assumed that women were docile and thus restricted young women from competition that was characterized by physical contact.[70] For example, Communists promoted gymnastics and swimming, and women's health guides encouraged them to play tennis and racquetball.[71] SPES leaders created the same expectations for girls and boys with regards to sprinting, medium-range running, long-jumping, and high-jumping abilities, which contested the widely held assumption that women were weak and should avoid prolonged or intense physical activity (Table 5).[72] SPES was not completely egalitarian, however, as its program followed the Hébertist belief that the female upper body was weak, which led it to exclude girls from climbing and lifting exercises.[73]

TABLE 5. SPES Performance Expectations for Girls and Boys

Activity	Age Range	SPES EXPECTATIONS (RANGES VARY ACCORDING TO AGE)	
		Girls	Boys
Sprinting	8–18	11–17 seconds depending on age for a 50-meter race; 100-meter for those 16–18	Same as girls
Medium-Distance Running	8–18	1.30–1.50 minutes depending on age for a 300-meter race; 500-meter for those 16–18	Same as girls
Running Long Jump	8–18	2.25 meters–3.50 meters depending on age	Same as girls
Standing Jump (straight up in the air)	8–18	0.55 meters–0.90 meters depending on age	Same as girls
Rope Climbing (with legs)	Boys only beginning at 14	NA	4.50–5.50 meters
Rope Climbing (without legs)	Boys only beginning at 14	NA	4–5 meters
Shot put	Boys only beginning at 14	NA	4.50–5.50 meters

Source: CARAN 451AP 155 G.A. Maire, "Rapport sur l'Education Physique, addressé à: Jean de Mierry, M. Danner, Mlle. Garrigoux," October 21, 1937.

The Croix de Feu/PSF's curriculum for men mirrored the one for women, emphasizing games, calisthenics, and gymnastics at earlier ages, and then, with the onset of puberty, the development of balance and strengthening core muscles through the Hébertist movements. The third stage, however, differed from the women's program.[74] While women continued to focus on exercises and calisthenics with the option of engaging in team sports, young men from sixteen to twenty were expected to embrace the competitive aspect of sport.[75] In this sense, the end goal of physical education was different for girls and boys. Boys needed to be physically ready for any sort of competitive struggle, which included boxing, rugby, basketball, soccer, and, of course, combat. If a young man happened to dislike sports or competition, not only would his masculinity be in doubt, but he would be considered a burden to the national community.

The Croix de Feu/PSF helped drive the national preoccupation with the relationship between the state of French bodies and the strength of the nation. Yet the transgressive nature of its gender ideology was the *least* influential component of its efforts to transform French physical culture. Once in power, the Vichy regime criticized interwar physical education programs that were overly egalitarian in providing opportunities for youth of both sexes. The regime emphasized that physical exercise needed to become distinct by the age of eight to prepare girls for childbirth and boys for competition. Its Commissariat General for Sports was especially critical of organizations like SPES whose programs for children did not diverge with the onset of puberty.[76] Moreover, the Croix de Feu/PSF never made physical education compulsory, unlike Vichy, which created the Chantiers de la Jeunesse for all young men twenty years of age to prepare them to become soldiers by building their moral character through hands-on work and physical education.[77] The Chantiers embodied Vichy's worldview, which championed the cult of masculine virility and emphasized that female bodies should not be "built" for national service but protected from excessive exertion in order to ready them for child rearing.[78]

CONCLUSION

While SPES flourished in metropolitan France, it struggled to such an extent in the Maghreb that it might well not have existed. Reasons for the dramatic differences included the absence of a sociocultural program in the North African Croix de Feu/PSF and distinctly different approaches to physical culture between the movement's metropolitan and settler supporters. Indeed, while both metropolitan and settler conceptions of race were hierarchical, the forms that the hierarchies took were different. The entire premise of the metropolitan movement's approach to physical culture—that French history was proof that different bodies could assimilate into Frenchness—was based upon a rejection of biological racism. Yet, SPES was social Darwinist in the sense that it cast black bodies as lower on the evolutionary scale than white ones. In contrast, as we shall see, Croix de Feu/PSF settlers based their political and social action on the idea that they were racially distinct from Jews, Berbers, and Arabs. In this way, the hypermasculinity and biological racism of the movement's North African sections were most apparent in the absence of SPES in the Maghreb; women could not contribute to physical culture, and even if they could have, the movement's racism would have precluded the possibility of creating a mass physical education program.

Figure 1. Croix de Feu Recruiting Poster (*Le Flambeau*, January 1934).
Courtesy Bibliothèque nationale de France.

Figure 2. The Croix de Feu's depiction of Joan of Arc (*Le Flambeau*, 1931). Courtesy Bibliothèque nationale de France.

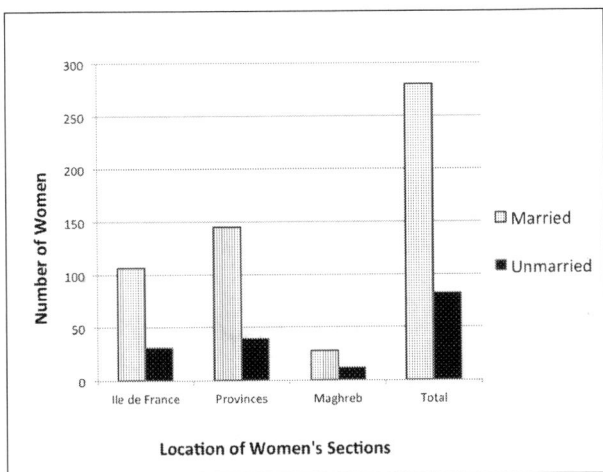

Figure 3. Marital status of Croix de Feu Women's Section Leaders
(October 1935). Source information given in Chapter 2, Note 43.

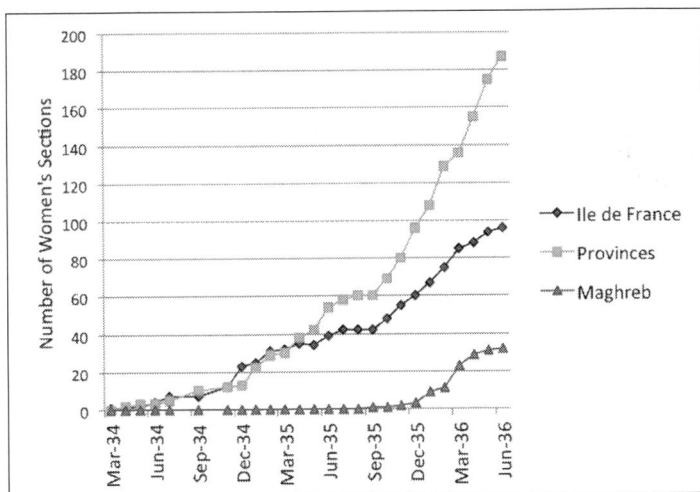

Figure 4. The growth of Croix de Feu Women's Sections from
April 1934 to June 1936. Source information given in Chapter 2, Note 46.

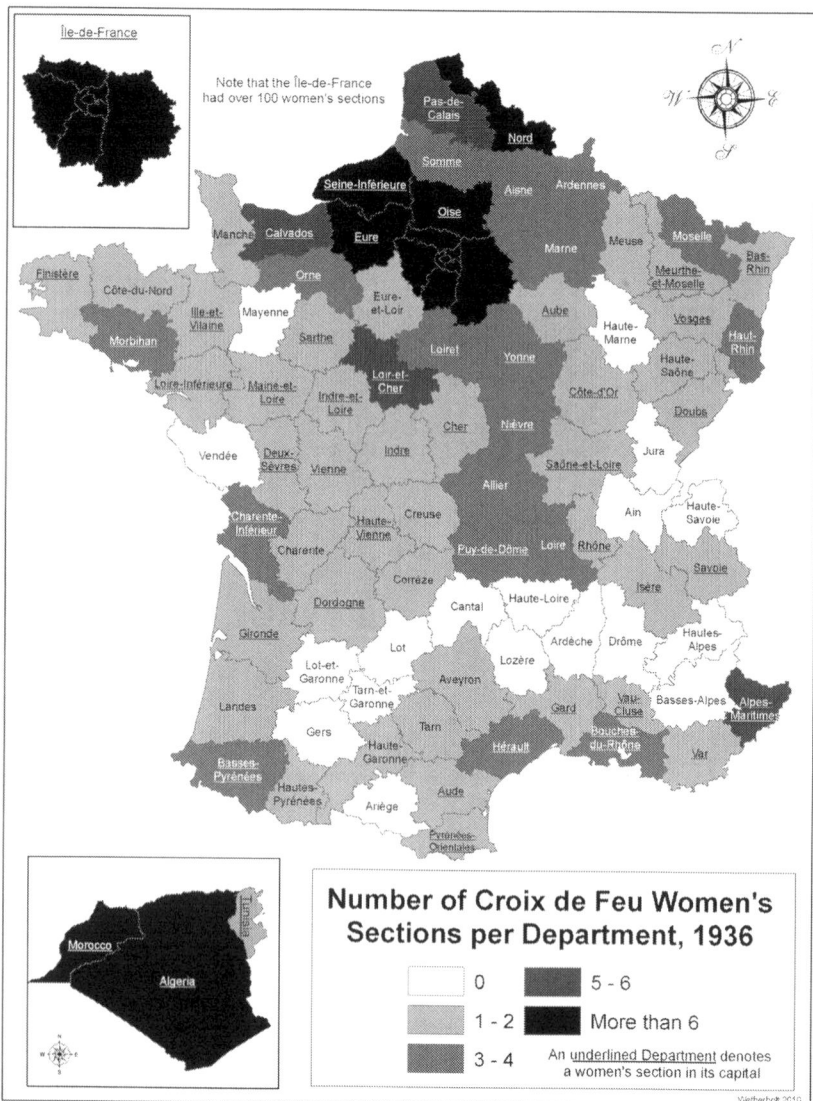

Île-de-France

Note that the Île-de-France had over 100 women's sections

Pas-de-Calais
Nord
Somme
Seine-Inférieure
Aisne
Ardennes
Oise
Manche
Calvados
Eure
Marne
Meuse
Moselle
Finistère
Orne
Meurthe-et-Moselle
Bas-Rhin
Côte-du-Nord
Ille-et-Vilaine
Mayenne
Eure-et-Loir
Aube
Haute-Marne
Vosges
Morbihan
Sarthe
Loiret
Yonne
Haut-Rhin
Haute-Saône
Loire-Inférieure
Maine-et-Loire
Loir-et-Cher
Côte-d'Or
Doubs
Indre-et-Loire
Cher
Nièvre
Jura
Vendée
Deux-Sèvres
Vienne
Indre
Saône-et-Loire
Charente-Inférieur
Haute-Vienne
Creuse
Allier
Ain
Haute-Savoie
Charente
Puy-de-Dôme
Loire
Rhône
Corrèze
Savoie
Dordogne
Cantal
Isère
Gironde
Lot
Haute-Loire
Ardèche
Drôme
Hautes-Alpes
Lot-et-Garonne
Tarn-et-Garonne
Aveyron
Lozère
Landes
Gard
Vau-cluse
Basses-Alpes
Alpes-Maritimes
Gers
Tarn
Hérault
Bouches-du-Rhône
Var
Basses-Pyrénées
Haute-Garonne
Hautes-Pyrénées
Aude
Ariège
Pyrénées-Orientales

Number of Croix de Feu Women's Sections per Department, 1936

	0		5 - 6
	1 - 2		More than 6
	3 - 4		An underlined Department denotes a women's section in its capital

Tunisia
Morocco
Algeria

Wetherholt 2010

Figure 5. Number of Women's Sections per French department (June 1936).
Source information given in Chapter 2, Note 43.

Action sociale

Mlle Fouché prononce sa conférence à Tunis

Figure 6. Despite the poor quality of the original photograph, it is a rare image of Suzanne Fouché as a key Croix de Feu/PSF activist; note that she is sitting. (*La Flamme*, February 19, 1938). Courtesy Les Archives nationales d'outre-mer, Aix-en-Provence, France.

La participation algérienne à la vente de charité
" Croix de Feu " de Paris

Figure 7. This picture of the Algerian pavilion reveals the opulence of the 1935 bazaar (*Bulletin de liaison du Movement Croix de feu du en Algérie*, Mai 1935). Courtesy of Les Archives nationales d'outre-mer, Aix-en-Provence, France.

Chaleureuse bienvenue aux « Soufflotines »
qui nous apporte le sourire de Paris

Nous sommes heureux, au nom de tous nos camarades P.S.F. d'Algérie, de présenter nos vœux fervents d'agréable séjour au groupe de « Soufflotines » qui est arrivé mercredi matin par « Ville d'Oran », sous la conduite de Mlle de Bellet, prési-

déplacements, dont le programme a été arrêté ainsi qu'il suit:

Du mercredi 13 au vendredi 15, visite d'Alger.

Du samedi 16 au mardi 19, circuit de la Mitidja.

Du mercredi 20 au vendredi 22,

dente du Foyer Universitaire des Étudiantes de Paris.

Nos charmantes camarades ont été invitées par la Fédération d'Alger, à passer leurs vacances de Pâques parmi nous. Elles seront cantonnées successivement chez plusieurs camarades bénévoles au cours de leurs

excursions à Tipasa et Cherchell.

Samedi 23, départ par le « G.-G.-Jonnart ».

Le prochain numéro de « La Flamme » relatera les randonnées des « Soufflotines » et leurs impressions sur notre belle Algérie.

Figure 8. The PSF's depiction of the Soufflotines as smiling tourists (*Le Flamme*, April 15, 1938). Courtesy of Les Archives nationales d'outre-mer, Aix-en-Provence, France.

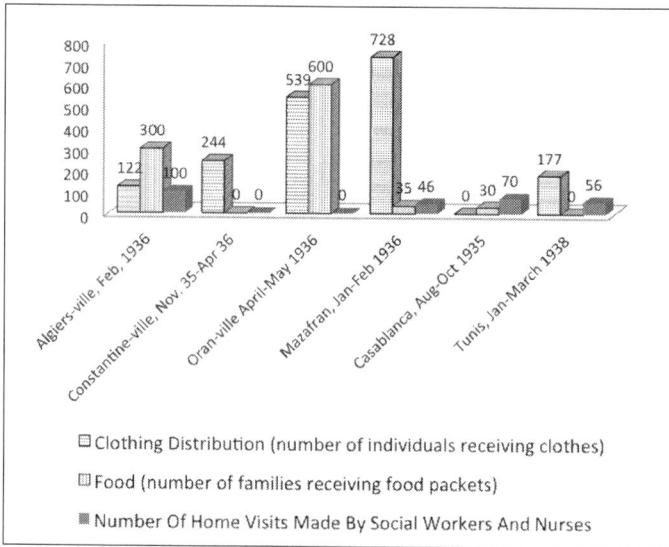

Figure 9. Croix de Feu/PSF social services in the French Maghreb.
Source information given in Chapter 6, Note 28.

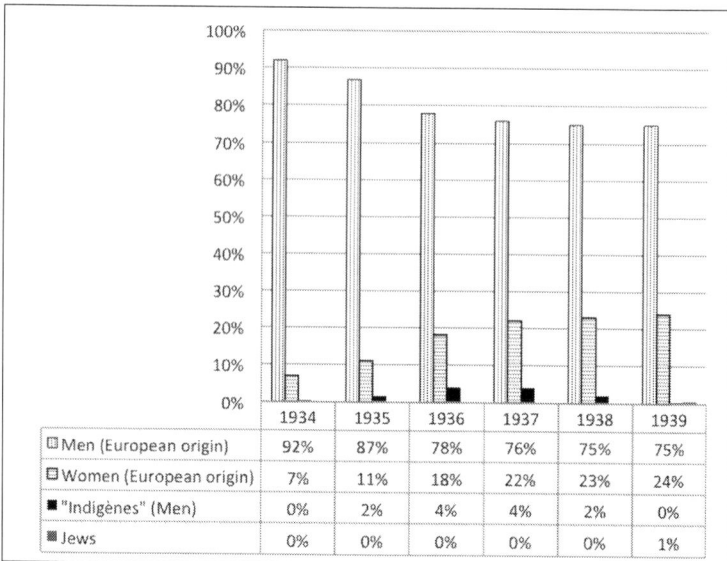

	1934	1935	1936	1937	1938	1939
Men (European origin)	92%	87%	78%	76%	75%	75%
Women (European origin)	7%	11%	18%	22%	23%	24%
"Indigènes" (Men)	0%	2%	4%	4%	2%	0%
Jews	0%	0%	0%	0%	0%	1%

Figure 10. Police reports of attendees at Croix de Feu/PSF meetings
in Algeria (1934–1939). Source information given in Chapter 6, Note 57.

5

WOMEN, RACE, AND CULTURE IN
THE CROIX DE FEU/PSF

ENTERTAINMENT, ENLIGHTENMENT VALUES, AND

THE CIVILIZING MISSION, 1934–1939

Croix de Feu/PSF supporters understood that culture was an important battle-ground between the Left and the Right to promote different ideas about race and argue that government policy needed to be based upon such conceptions. While historians have acknowledged the far Right's influence on culture by focusing on the Action Française, scholarly attention to the content and impact of the metro-politan Croix de Feu/PSF's cultural programs has been neglected.[1] Building upon the previous chapter, which sought to show that the metropolitan movement's Social First! strategy translated smoothly to physical culture, this chapter suggests that social action enabled the movement to intervene in entertainment because its supporters—primarily women—used social programs to organize charity bazaars, galas, concerts, expositions, and travel. Moreover, while racism in Croix de Feu/PSF physical education was relatively subtle, it was in the movement's entertainment that racism took its most explicit form.

Empire played a key role in the movement's social and cultural activities. Indeed, unquestioned support for colonialism was at the heart of the PSF's 1936 pro-gram: "France's colonial empire is an essential element of its economic strength, its military power, and its radiance in the world. Colonial questions should thus not be treated with secondary interest. They must pass to the forefront of national concerns."[2] In making the "radiance" of the empire central to national debates, the metropolitan Croix de Feu/PSF's entertainment emphasized a chauvinistic sense of French cultural superiority that was defined by Enlightenment conceptions of liberty, egalitarianism, rationality, reason, and work. Through sociocultural action, Croix de Feu/PSF supporters used colonial subjects to construct dichotomous models that illustrated the "advanced" state of French civilization against "inferior" peoples and cultures; they contrasted liberty with slavery, egalitarianism with war, rationality with superstition, reason with instinct, and work with laziness.

The Croix de Feu/PSF claimed to be the purist defender of these Enlightenment values, and used them to play a leading role in building and perpetuating hierarchies of difference that shaped the political culture of the late Third Republic.[3] The primary argument of this chapter is that the metropolitan Croix de Feu/PSF played a critical role in the increasing racism of the 1930s. Alice Conklin argues that not since the Dreyfus Affair had France experienced such "charged" racism at it did in the 1930s, which was due in large part to scientific racism.[4] While the Croix de Feu/PSF's physical education program was not characterized by scientific racism, the same cannot be said for its cultural programs. Comparing the Croix de Feu/PSF's treatment of the provinces with its portrayal of colonial subjects reveals the influence of scientific racism on the movement's supporters. Key leaders *intentionally* depicted colonial subjects in dehumanizing ways for political purposes: championing the civilizing mission to legitimate forced labor and the most dehumanizing aspects of colonialism.[5] Specifically, the Croix de Feu/PSF used culture to draw public attention away from growing anticolonial critiques of forced labor and demands to abrogate the *indigénat,* by insisting that colonial subjects were happy members of Greater France.[6]

Conklin demonstrates that the spike in racism in the 1930s spurred early formulations of antiracist sentiment by ethnologists such as Paul Rivet and Marcel Mauss, which lead to the first rejection of scientific racism in 1950 when UNESCO asserted that "race was less a biological fact than a social myth."[7] Not coincidentally, Mauss and Rivet were active Socialists. Rivet in particular railed against the Croix de Feu in his capacity as a founder of the CVIA. He maintained the Croix de Feu was alarming due to La Rocque's "pseudo-scientific" view of race and the ways in which the movement conflated race and temperament.[8] Rivet's assessments were accurate. The Croix de Feu/PSF defined itself in opposition to the Popular Front and not only became the period's premier defender of empire, but asserted that French temperament was shaped by the civilizing ideas of the Enlightenment. While historians have criticized the Popular Front's support of empire (even the Communist Party declared that colonial subjects were not ready for independence and Mauss and Rivet supported the empire) the leftist government nevertheless promoted reforms and generally displayed more respect for colonial subjects relative to the attitudes of the far Right.[9]

Such distinctions between the Left and the Right are especially clear in the Croix de Feu/PSF's cultural activities. The movement's entertainment provided an entrée for its supporters to use the colonial doctrines of assimilation and association to celebrate the civilizing mission and obscure the differences between them. Gary Wilder contends that during the interwar period, "French doctrines of colonial assimilation and association... remained interconnected. Neither was prior to the other, more real than the other, or a justification for the other... World War I did not mark the shift from a universalist republican colonialism committed to assimilation to a racist conservative colonialism committed to association."[10] As we shall see in this chapter and the next, Croix de Feu/PSF sociocultural action revealed that assimilation and association operated alongside one another and that the doctrinal boundaries between the two were malleable. The metropolitan Croix de Feu/PSF used culture to disengage from policy debates over the integration of colonial subjects and convince the public that the matter was self-evident: the French were a force for good throughout Greater France.

SHAPING HIERARCHIES IN FRENCH CULTURE: CHARITY BAZAARS AND THE 1937 WORLD'S FAIR

Beginning in 1935 the Croix de Feu Women's Section organized galas and soirées that featured live classical music, performers from the Comédie-Française, and singers from the Paris Opera such as the famous soprano Madeleine Grey. After the Croix de Feu's dissolution, many of these cultural activities fell under the purview of Travail et loisirs and Social Action. Travail et loisirs activities included planning salons on the topics of canonical French poets, playwrights, and writers, and organizing concerts by composers like Bizet, Berlioz, and Debussy. This emphasis on culture was important because, as a promotional brochure for Travail et loisirs stated, "music and literature [make up] the soul of a country."[11] The annual Christmas party was particularly significant, because the movement's supporters believed that the celebration of Christmas was an opportunity to remind families of France's Christian roots. These celebrations drew large numbers. For instance, the Women's Section restricted parents from attending the 1935 Christmas party in Paris at the 3,600-seat Cirque d'Hiver because the location was not big enough to hold entire families.[12]

Croix de Feu/PSF activists were open about the monetary significance of the movement's cultural events. One supporter explained that entertainment was a way "to provide a demonstration of our organization, our youth, our mass, and make money."[13] To this end, one of the most important funding sources was the movement's annual charity bazaar that was held each May. Croix de Feu women organized the first bazaar in 1932 to fund the league's only summer camp and the event grew in scope and sophistication thereafter. The one in 1935 at the Hotel Continental attracted 135,000 supporters from metropolitan France and the colonies and raised around 500,000 francs.[14] The opulence of the bazaar was reflected in the many pavilions that featured displays of high quality locally produced goods for sale from Paris; regions throughout the provinces, including Provence, the Basque region, Brittany, and Lorraine; and North Africa (fig. 7).[15]

Women used the bazaars for fund-raising and to promote an essentialized vision of French cultural identity that centered around the nation's integralist history. In preparation for the 1936 bazaar, Women's Section leaders emphasized that merchandise from both Paris and the provinces was to be treated equally, and they repeatedly cautioned that stalls featuring Parisian goods were not to dominate.[16] While Kevin Passmore has demonstrated that anti-southern prejudice was strong in elements of the French Right, such views were absent from the bazaars, due in large part to the movement's efforts to frame French identity in essentialized integrationist terms.[17] Indeed, the Right was far from unified on how to view the provinces. Passmore points out that some in the right-wing press mixed anti-southern prejudice with a dislike of the provinces in general, while others considered the Basque region positively for its Catholicism or followed the Action Française's tendency to downplay Paris as the capital of civilization in favor of emphasizing France's Greco-Roman roots.[18] The Croix de Feu's emphasis on reconciliation, dependence on grassroots support from across Greater France, and the provincial background of key leaders—including Préval's birth in Languedoc and La Rocque's ancestral home in Auvergne—all played a role in the lack of negative depictions of the provinces at cultural events such as the charity bazaars.

Held at the Berlitz palace, the 1936 bazaar was the most widely publicized and elaborately planned to date. It spread across three floors and featured thirty-one pavilions selling goods such as wine, flowers, fruits, and other perishables from provinces and Algeria, Morocco, and Tunisia, in addition to stalls that sold the movement's massive array of propaganda (stamps, pins, posters, postcards, brochures, guidebooks).[19] While the bazaar promoted provincial harmony through a shared sense of Frenchness, such unity did not extend to politics. The event was marked by the high political tensions that shook France in the lead-up to the spring general election. The bazaar was of such importance in the weeks preceding the election that *Le Flambeau*'s publicity for it *superseded* the newspaper's reporting of the election itself; it was the bazaar—not the election—that was featured more often and more prominently on its front page.[20] La Rocque and Préval wrote numerous circulars and letters asking delegates to publicize the sale as much as possible, while section presidents mentioned it months in advance and solicited volunteers to prepare goods to sell.

The charity bazaars thus became a proxy in the wider battle between the Popular Front and Croix de Feu to dominate France's political culture. Unlike many Popular Front events that were open to the public, entrance to the 1936 bazaar was by invitation only. Croix de Feu organizers stationed the *dispos* at the Berlitz entrances and instructed the shock troops to patrol the crowd inside to look for Popular Front supporters who crashed the event. On the bazaar's first day, La Rocque entered the hall to cries of *"Vive La Rocque,"* while an orchestra played the "Marseillaise" as he prepared to give a speech. On the second day, cars with the Popular Front logo harassed the people in line waiting to enter the palace while SFIO protestors shouted *"Vive le Front Populaire."*[21] The *dispos* reportedly removed twelve people from inside the halls that day.[22] Despite these tensions, organizers considered the bazaar a success because it brought in 1.4 million francs.[23]

The Women's Section's emphasis on celebrating the Frenchness of people from diverse regions, and bazaar organizers' use of the *dispos* to fight the Popular Front, reflected wider debates over the integralist character of French national identity. Indeed, the general population showed a growing interest in ethnography and folklore, which tended to promote the superiority of French cultural traditions and perpetuate the public's negative view of non-French people.[24] Squarely in this vein, the women organizing Croix de Feu/PSF bazaars and other funding events sometimes elicited feedback from experts on how to create "authentic" representations of the provinces and colonies. They sought to show that the Croix de Feu/PSF—not the Popular Front—best understood the essence of French culture. For its part, the Popular Front refused to cede ground in the battle to shape French national identity. To this end, the leftist coalition organized the 1937 World's Fair in Paris around the theme of folklore. In conjunction with the fair, the Popular Front created a folklore museum, the Musée des Arts et Traditions Populaires

(ATP). Led by Georges Henri Rivière, the ATP helped raised the prominence of folklore in French culture and legitimated it as a systematic method of understanding history and culture through its exhibits and outreach.

Travail et loisirs took advantage of the ATP's outreach to access spaces in civil society from which the early Croix de Feu—and its emphasis on politics—had been restricted. A typical example was the group's participation in a 1938 bazaar held in Paris that celebrated local crafts production called the Exposition artisanale. Jeanne Garrigoux urged La Rocque to increase the movement's involvement in such events, writing, "The PSF has specific reasons to take an interest in the current renaissance of regional decorative arts and hand-made crafts," which she maintained included respect for tradition that revealed "the richness of each province and the harmony that unites France."[25] To this end, Préval assigned Travail et loisirs member Madame Dutilh to organize a pavilion for the exposition. Dutilh was particularly interested in creating a pavilion filled with "real" provincial displays and sought the help of Rivière. He complied and connected her with craft producers from Savoie, Mervan, and the Ile-de-France, and most excitingly for Dutilh, ribbon manufacturers in Saint Etienne.[26] The area had a long tradition of handmade high-quality cloth ribbons of vibrant colors and creative patterns that included intricate designs of hand-stitched animals and plants.[27] The ribbon industry thus had been an economic pillar for Saint Etienne since the 1890s and exemplified perfectly the manner in which Dutilh sought to feature regional artwork for nationalistic purposes by selling the ribbons at the Travail et loisirs pavilion at the Paris exposition.

While PSF leaders wanted the Travail et loisirs pavilion to be authentic, they were equally interested in using the event to forge new connections with individuals and gauge their malleability when it came to political issues. In preparing for the Exposition artisanale, one report stated: "Madame Dutilh will correspond with everyone—PSF supporters and adversaries—using the Travail et loisirs letterhead, which after the exposition will allow us to distinguish knowledgeably one person's cause from another, and to push the PSF's emphasis on the production of artisanal crafts. It's the PSF, not Travail and loisirs who will do this [advocacy]."[28] Dutilh was happy to comply, especially when working with men of high clout like Rivière. As she put it, "Mr. Rivière is very influential and very Catholic."[29] In assessing Rivière's attitude toward Travail et loisirs, Dutilh was positive, explaining to her superiors that "Rivière warmly approved of everything I told him about Travail et loisirs."[30] While Dutilh considered Rivière a possible ally, especially because of his reputation as someone without political principles, she overestimated his willingness to support the PSF.[31] Indeed, much of Rivière's work centered around a refusal to reduce French identity to an essence. He used the ATP to promote a version of national identity that was cosmopolitan and syncretic, which was fundamentally at odds with the Croix de Feu/PSF's essentialized and unitary conception of France as a Christian civilization.[32] Despite Dutilh's efforts, he never supported the PSF.

In other cases Croix de Feu/PSF women used similar methods (the decorative arts) for similar ends (to promote the movement's integral nationalism). Yet the subject under consideration made all the difference in how they conceptualized cultural integration into the national community. Women like Préval and Dutilh no doubt considered people from the provinces "French" and believed that the goods they produced contributed positively to the nation. The fact that Travail et loisirs worked with ATP to promote France's ability to integrate provincial cultures attests to this drive for authenticity. However, conservative women's treatment of colonial cultures and people was quite different relative to that of people from the provinces. On one hand, pointing out that the Popular Front, ATP, and Croix de Fe/PSF worked together reflects similarities between the Left and the Right. More important, however, are the ways in which the production and content of key activities not only reveals fundamental differences between the Popular Front and Croix de Feu/PSF, but that Rivet and Mauss were at a disadvantage in trying to convince the public that Croix de Feu/PSF views of race were dangerous.

The French Save Tarzan: The 1937 World's Fair and the Fête Coloniale

By the late nineteenth and early twentieth centuries, World's Fairs had become popular among the European public and a primary way for nation-states to display their cultural, economic, and technological vitality. The 1937 exposition in Paris was no different. Popular Front organizers sought to showcase French cultural superiority and present French democracy as a force for peace amidst the deteriorating diplomatic conditions across the continent. Because of the international political conditions, PSF supporters believed that they had a stake in ensuring that French strength be demonstrated through the fair. The PSF's contributions to the exposition took two forms: thousands visited the party's welcome center, and Travail et loisirs produced several children's shows that won the gold medal for a children's production. Because the children in the PSF's social centers had spent months making the costumes, building the set, and preparing their performance, many of its organizers believed that the gold medal represented the superiority of Travail et loisirs and the PSF. Préval regularly mentioned the award in her writings, speeches, and applications to participate in other fairs and expositions.[33]

The 1937 World's Fair sold over thirty-one million tickets and dominated the social life of many Europeans during the spring, summer, and fall. The fairgrounds stretched 260 acres around the Eiffel tower and along the Seine River. The most famous symbol of the fair's fraught political tensions was the gigantic dueling pavilions, standing directly across from one another on the fairgrounds, that represented Nazi Germany and the Soviet Union. The Soviet pavilion featured a dramatic twenty-four-meter-tall sculpture of a socialist peasant and worker, striding—atop a thirty-three-meter-tall tower—confidently toward the future. Nazi architect Albert Speer had seen the plans for the Soviet pavilion before it was built and designed a structure that would dwarf it: an imposing building (fifty-four meters tall and twenty-two meters wide) that featured heavy pilasters and a nine-meter-tall Reich eagle on top that held a swastika in its talons.[34] The sheer size and prominent location of the two pavilions served as a stark reminder to Europeans that communism and fascism were forging deep divisions across Europe.

Amidst these tensions, the Popular Front sought to demonstrate the advanced state of French democracy by showcasing the superiority of the nation's culture and politics. It did so by emphasizing France's preeminent status as a colonial power.[35] Most infamously, the fair's colonial pavilion featured derogatory and demeaning portrayals of French colonial subjects by housing them in human displays that were akin to animals in a zoo. As we shall see, the PSF's participation in the exposition aligned with efforts by fair organizers to make fairgoers believe that they could travel to France's colonies without leaving Paris and become firsthand witnesses to the alleged "progress" that French rule brought to different parts of the world.[36]

As a part of the PSF's strategy to influence the fair and shape France's international image, Préval organized the children's entertainment shows on "Youth and Family" and the "Fête Coloniale." The former featured glorified depictions of the PSF's summer camps while the latter explored the origins and effects of French colonialism. The Fête Coloniale featured the artistic, dance, and singing talents of the youth in the movement's social centers.[37] Both Préval and Simone Marochetti communicated with each other and the centers' directors to ensure that preparations for the Fête proceeded according to plan.[38] The children in the centers' decorative arts studios made the costumes and sets, while those in the dance and chorus clubs performed in the show.[39] Jean d'Orsay, who was a key collaborator with Préval in organizing the PSF's many cultural initiatives, served as the narrator. Between the bright colors of the costumes and sets, sophisticated lighting displays, and the movement of the dances, the event was quite a spectacle.

The Fête Coloniale itself revealed the PSF's preoccupation with the indigenous societies that comprised the French empire by featuring a plot that focused on how the French brought "civilization" to "barbaric" peoples. To frame the story as one of progress, Travail et loisirs organizers decided that Tarzan and his monkeys would tour the world to show children what the French colonies looked like before and after the arrival of the French. In the first half of the show, Tarzan visited "Africa," "Asia," "Oceania," "Guyana," and "Morocco,"[40] as they appeared in the precolonial "uncivilized" state.[41] The turning point in the performance took place with a scene called "The Arrival of the French," while the last half of the show depicted each locale in its so-called civilized state. This format not only enabled PSF women to remind fairgoers and children that the scope of their empire extended across five continents, but depicted the temporal breadth of the empire as well, including a scene set in French Guyana, a colony dating back to the seventeenth century, and Morocco, which had recently been "pacified."

The organizers of the Fête Coloniale had specific reasons in choosing Tarzan as their protagonist. *Tarzan* was one of the best-selling comic books in France in the late 1930s and at the height of its popularity right before the war.[42] The organizers undoubtedly hoped that Tarzan would appeal to children; the children would have known that they were reading an American comic about an English lord. Tarzan's American and English background was especially critical, because Travail et loisirs organizers undermined Tarzan's masculinity throughout the performance, which would have been significant to those knowledgeable of Tarzan's Anglo-American roots. Tarzan himself was not French, but the French civilizers who arrived in the second half of the show exhibited a mastery over colonial subjects and their environment that the impotent Tarzan lacked.

The Fête's first scene, set in Africa, was representative of the racist stereotypes and complete disregard for geography that threaded their way throughout the entire performance and ran counter to Travail et loisirs's careful depictions of French provinces. The show opened with Tarzan and his monkey traveling companions in Africa, where they encountered, as the program put it, "war and slavery."[43] Tarzan was in the African savanna playing with a lion, crocodile, and giraffe, when he was interrupted by the entrance of "Pygmies" holding axes and clubs. The scene emphasized Tarzan's horror as he watched the Pygmies kill the animals that he had been playing with and eat them, highlighted by the Pygmies skinning and eating a giraffe. While the Pygmies feasted, members of the Bambara tribe, whom Travail et loisirs leaders called "the bravest of the Senegalese tribes," entered the scene armed with spears and shields and led by sorcerers.[44] The Bambara rushed at the Pygmies and the two engaged in battle, with the Bambara winning, leaving the scene by forcing the Pygmies into slavery. Tarzan and his monkeys reentered the scene to cry over the remains of the animals when Tarzan noticed the bodies of two Pygmies, which he took in his arms to lament their deaths. In the end, Travail et loisirs organizers used, as they put it, "murder and slavery" to reveal "human wickedness to Tarzan."[45]

The violence of this scene is striking for a children's production, especially considering that it was children who were engaged in the performance of battle and death, killing the animals, and skinning the giraffe. The adult organizers went to great extremes to convince children that Africa was a dangerous, brutal, and superstitious place, where the natural state of society was warfare, irrationality, and slavery. They perpetuated stereotypes of African ethnic groups prevalent in interwar French society, including a common one that promoted the Bambara as natural warriors.[46] Moreover, the geographical inaccuracies were stunning: as an ethno-linguistic group primarily living in West Africa, in particular in modern-day Mali, the Bambara would have had limited interaction with whatever ethnic group Travail et loisirs organizers had in mind when they referred to "pygmies," many of whom lived in the rain forest of central Africa. Neither group would have lived on the African savanna (most likely, Travail et loisirs envisioned the Serengeti), which was where the animals depicted in the Fête were concentrated. Instead, this portion of the plot reflected widespread caricatures of "Africa" in such popular publications as *Tin Tin in the Congo* (1931). Indeed, many plot points in the Fête mirrored those of *Tin Tin in the Congo,* including monkeys saving a protagonist, the slaughter of animals, and racist portrayals of distinct ethnic groups.

The rest of Tarzan's tour of precolonial locales proceeded along these schematic lines, following the adventures of Tarzan and his monkeys as they rode a magic carpet to four other places. He was nearly killed in Oceania and Guyana, only to be saved by his monkeys in both cases. In Oceania, the program stated that "lazy natives" lying on a beach tried to poison Tarzan with pineapples.[47] In Guyana, warlike natives engaged in sorcery tied Tarzan to a post, performed a "scalping dance," and called up a vampire and spider to kill Tarzan.[48] Diverging from the Popular Front–sponsored colonial pavilion not far away, which featured more peaceful activity—albeit in a zoo—Travail et loisirs women wanted children to fear "primitive" peoples by depicting them as naturally duplicitous and murderous. It would take real men—not the hapless Tarzan—to pacify them. In both of these scenes, while Tarzan exhibited emotional depth that colonial subjects did not, he was not the muscular brute so many children knew from their comics. Instead, he was dependent upon his monkeys to save him from a cruel death. This Tarzan was inept and continually emasculated by his circumstances. Travail et loisirs wanted children to know that such were the brutal and dangerous environments of each region and its people when left to their own devices, without the guidance of the French to enlighten them by demonstrating a proper work ethic and morals.

In addition to depicting the world before French colonization as filled with treacherous barbarians, Travail et loisirs women also used the Fête to warn the children about the danger of addictive substances by highlighting indigenous peoples' supposed lack of self-control juxtaposed with French mastery of their own bodies and minds. In Asia, revelers celebrating the Tet holiday indulged in opium, while in Guyana, the natives drank copious amounts of alcohol.[49] Here, Travail et loisirs women showed that indigenous peoples were too weak to resist addictive substances and morally inclined to indulge in them. These depictions were not original, as organizers used common stereotypes specific to each people: sub-Saharan Africans and Guyanese were warlike, Oceanians and Vietnamese were lazy, and Moroccans were exotic and mysterious.[50]

The plot's turning point came at the end of Tarzan's tour of each precolonial region. It was at this point, as he "took his head in his hands and give up hope for humanity," that he was suddenly startled out of his despair by the arrival of the French.[51] A man wearing the French flag entered, touched Tarzan's shoulders, and whispered, "Don't cry anymore, Tarzan. I am France. I bring peace, work, and liberty to the whole world. The people are going to become brothers. Slaves will be set free and work will give joy to all."[52] Inspired, Tarzan stopped weeping and stood to plant the French flag into the soil. This scene featured all of the colonial subjects from the previous scenes joining together as a narrator presented to them the emissaries of the French empire who would teach them how to become civilized: a doctor, soldier, missionary, teacher, and engineer.

The plot's turning point was thus defined by a vigorous French masculinity. The French civilizers in the Fête were nothing like the passive and weak Tarzan, but stood atop a hierarchy of masculinity through their "enlightened" colonial methods. France's male colonizers were the effective civilizers, from the doctor who brought "hygiene and health" to the "pioneering" soldier who exhibited bravery in the face of warlike and treacherous peoples. This mastery showed French domination of places in the world where Tarzan, representing his American and British progenitors, proved impotent.

The second half of the Fête featured wholly positive portrayals of colonialism by showing Tarzan's "wonder and delight" as he followed his French companions to each region and watched the effects of their civilizing capacities. In Africa ten nondescript "Africans" moved forward in line gesturing like lumberjacks, while ten others followed by packing down roads. Pygmies stood back-to-back in two columns using pickaxes to mine for gold and precious stones, which they deposited at the foot of the tricolor flag that Tarzan had planted in the last scene. Each scene from the second half of the show featured such synchronized and methodical movement of the newly "civilized" indigenous peoples. Oceanians were in canoes fishing for pearls, Asians worked in rice fields, and rural Moroccans plowed, sowed, and reaped wheat fields while unskilled urban workers labored in unison with stoneworkers and carpenters to build cities. In Guyana, gold was placed at the base of the French flag, which now stood next to an oil pipeline. Travail et loisirs organizers had reduced each society from one reified construct to another. Thanks to the French, work and economic exploitation had turned lazy and barbaric natives into colonial subjects adept at making use of their abundant natural resources.

These images clearly depicted the coercive and inhumane labor policies inherent in the interwar policy of *mise en valeur.* The last scenes foregrounded natural resources and left colonial subjects in the background. The resources that they extracted were not for their own benefit but for French economic gain. In this sense, the principles behind the Fête reflected colonial officials' belief that forced labor was good for colonial subjects because it helped them develop the work ethic of a civilized people.[53] Through work, order displaced disorder and violence while colonial subjects moved from adhering to their own customs to singing the "Marseillaise."

The PSF thus did not simply give tacit approval of forced labor as a temporary means to an end (helping colonized subjects to develop a good work ethic), but constructed a vigorous defense of the practice in the face of increasing calls from colonial reformers demanding humane treatment of colonial subjects. For the PSF, forced labor was not a temporary solution to the problem of a paucity of workers but a standard and acceptable method to maintain colonial control. Moreover, while primitivist entertainment was common during the interwar period and featured prominently at colonial exhibitions in Marseille in 1922, Paris in 1931, and the 1937 World's Fair, the Fête's use of ridiculous and demeaning stereotypes diverged from empirically and ethnographically based depictions of colonial subjects that attempted to re-create their authentic societies.[54]

The fact that Travail et loisirs organizers based the Fête upon their own conceptions of the civilizing mission, yet only several months later consulted with the ATP on how to accurately portray the French provinces, reveals their intentionality in portraying colonial subjects in a derogatory manner. Indeed, the PSF rejected in absolute terms the concerns of anticolonial activists and colonial reformers. Populations that PSF women deemed "French," such as those living in the provinces, merited careful and respectful treatment. People who were ethnically different from French citizens could never truly be French and remained at the bottom of racial hierarchy that the PSF worked diligently to preserve.

TRAVEL AND ETHNORELIGIOUS HIERARCHIES: PSF UNIVERSITY STUDENTS IN ALGERIA AND GERMANY

The schematic representations of colonial subjects in productions such as the Fête Coloniale influenced the practices of many Croix de Feu/PSF women and youth who organized the movement's programs. As youth on the cusp of adulthood, Croix de Feu/PSF leaders believed that university students were critically important because of their leadership potential. As she always did, Préval ensured that the young women who joined the Croix de Feu/PSF received the same opportunities as young men, or more. To this end, in 1935 the Women's Section established a university center for women students in Paris, called Le foyer universitaire (The Foyer), a month before they established a similar center for young men.[55] Women who participated in the Foyer published their own journal, which started a year before the men's journal, and enjoyed traveling opportunities not available to young men. Indeed, the sociability of the Foyer, the intellectual aspects of publishing a journal, and the independence inherent in travel reveal the high level of sophistication with which the Croix de Feu/PSF treated women university students in preparing them for leadership in French politics and society.

The Soufflotines and the Foyer Universitaire

Upon its creation, the Women's Section sought immediately to mobilize university students and socialize them into the movement's values. The women who attended the Foyer called themselves the "Soufflotines" because the Foyer was located on rue Soufflot, which was at the base of the Panthéon in the heart of the Latin Quarter.[56] Upon opening, the Foyer claimed 180 members and the number grew to nearly 500 by May 1937.[57] The university centers played a key role in the Croix de Feu/PSF's strategy of national reconciliation; by 1939 the movement had centers for both women and men in most major French and French colonial cities, including Algiers, Angers, Bordeaux, Casablanca, Dijon, Grenoble, Lille, Lyon, Aix-Marseille, Montpellier, Nancy, Nantes, Paris, Rennes, Rouen, and Strasbourg.[58] The provincial centers were based upon the same principles as the Parisian Foyer, which sought to develop a nationalistic cohort of university students while balancing respect for regional traditions. In provincial university centers, for instance, students learned the *"vieilles chansons"* along with local dance and artistic traditions.[59]

Since Croix de Feu/PSF leaders sought to create future leaders whose actions were informed by the movement's ultranationalistic principles, they made the Parisian Foyer a model of what the leadership expected of its university students. The Foyer's slogan, "work, joy, and mutual aid," revealed the traits that enabled the Soufflotines to develop a "fraternal" spirit that supposedly ignored class and religious backgrounds.[60] It provided space and training for the Soufflotines to develop intellectually through study, and socially by interacting with their peers in a multitude of intellectual and leisure activities.[61] If a young woman wanted to study at the Foyer, microscopes, dictionaries, blackboards, and a library were available to her. The Foyer was also a place of leisure; women could play ping-pong or the piano, drink tea, and relax and read newspapers and magazines. Finally, the Foyer was a cultural center; it organized concerts (usually of classical music), conferences, dinners, fêtes, and picnics.[62]

One of the most important aspects of being a Soufflotine was to publish the Foyer's journal, *Pourquoi S'en Faire* (Why Worry?), which sought to create a sense of groupness among university students. One author described the appearance and mannerisms of her peers in this way: "The Soufflotine is obviously of variable height. She has a clear eye, a pure conscience, a conquering allure, and a strong and sometimes fair voice. From her arrival in the Foyer, she acquires a great aptitude for never-ending discussions of all sorts."[63] This emphasis on speaking confidently from one's conscience and engaging in debate was a hallmark of the Soufflotines' self-depictions. Significantly, they maintained that such allure and reasoned debate revealed a key aspect of enlightenment rationality that only French republicanism enabled to flourish. Moreover, the archetypes reflected by these ideals included Joan of Arc and Nadine de La Rocque, who died supposedly murmuring, *"Je suis Jeanne d'Arc."* Not only did articles appear regularly in *Pourquoi S'en Faire* celebrating Joan of Arc's memory, but the Soufflotines wrote poetry admiring Joan's bravery in sacrificing herself for the *patrie*. Such nationalism and controlled expression of emotion were funneled into one of the most important aspects of the Soufflotine identity—work. According to *Pourquoi S'en Faire*, "[The Soufflotine] will always continue to cultivate a profound modesty which is . . . her most distinguished characteristic. The Soufflotine speaks a very pure, subtly colorful French. . . . Finally, a major point and incredible news: the Soufflotine works!!!!!"[64] Verging on sarcasm, the journal referred to a mindset rather than actual paid employment. It reflected the Croix de Feu/PSF's emphasis on the work ethic as a trait of the French temperament and a tactic to critique those whom the movement's supporters considered lazy, from colonial subjects to the Popular Front, which had shortened the work week and instituted paid vacations in 1936.

Préval assigned Mademoiselle Hélène de Bellet to run the Foyer. Like so many women engaged in the PSF's social action, Bellet worked with women and men as a liaison between the students of both sexes and PSF leaders, directing many of the Foyer's activities and acting as the editor-in-chief of *Pourquoi S'en Faire*. Préval believed that Bellet was the perfect model to lead young women because of her activist mindset, which emphasized women's empowerment. At the first PSF student congress in 1938, Bellet told her students, "The intellectual world has opened its ranks to women. . . . Since you, my friends, have chosen to profess your intelligence, it is with all your intelligence that you must be a member of the PSF and to radiate PSF values. . . . Your training is making you an elite. The duty of this elite is to be concerned about those who are less fortunate."[65]

While many of the Croix de Feu/PSF's male-centered activities had an anti-intellectual bias, women like Bellet emphasized intellectualism as the key to women's leadership in the national community.[66] In this sense, the PSF was a place where young women expanded their intellectual abilities, which would allow them to move into the elite ranks of society. Recognizing that the PSF promoted social mobility for young women, one Soufflotine proclaimed excitedly, "Soufflotines have all the rights!"[67]

The Soufflotines as PSF Emissaries in Algeria

The Soufflotines used the Foyer and *Pourquoi S'en Faire* for overtly political purposes, which included emphasizing spiritual renewal among the French public, staunch support for the French empire, and critiques of Nazism. In doing so, the Soufflotines' activism, intelligence, education, and vibrant advocacy for the PSF were clear to many leaders. These were key reasons why they deployed the Soufflotines as emissaries in 1938. While more trips were planned, the Munich Agreement of September 1938 curtailed the party's willingness to send youth beyond the borders of metropolitan France as the nation's attention shifted to preparing for war.

The Soufflotines' trip to Algeria was part of a wider trend in French society whereby rates of tourism increased in the first decades of the twentieth century. For example, travel to Algeria and Tunisia increased from 35,000 in 1910 to over 300,000 by 1923.[68] By the interwar period, tourism played a key role in imbuing French national identity with a sense of "imperial self-recognition" as tourists saw sites from ancient civilizations and new landscapes that previously they could only imagine.[69] While the PSF promoted activities in this vein, the party's leaders had additional reasons for sending the Soufflotines to Algeria. Most immediately, the Soufflotines sought to help the Algiers PSF establish its own Foyer for university students, which came to fruition later that year.[70] Doing so required a high level of interaction between the Soufflotines and the PSF leadership in Algiers. By deploying the Soufflotines as friendly and unassuming representatives of the party, metropolitan leaders sought to assuage severe tensions between the metropolitan and colonial branches of the movement that had arisen over the latter's use of physical violence, virulent anti-Semitism, and threats to overthrow the Republic. As we shall see in the next chapter, settler women were severely marginalized in the Algerian PSF, which led metropolitan leaders to hope that the youthful, joyful, ultranationalistic Soufflotines would show Algerian PSF leaders that women could be crucial agents in sociopolitical change (and was the same reason that Fouché had gone to Algeria and Tunisia several months earlier).

The Soufflotines' travels were led by Bellet and Marivic Duval, an advanced student on the verge of finishing her studies and the managing editor of *Pourquoi S'en Faire*. Travel between metropolitan France and Algeria had become relatively easy by the interwar period, and women were increasingly traveling independently of men. Indeed, Bellet and the Soufflotines had nearly complete autonomy throughout the trip. This independence and the remarkable sites that the Soufflotines toured made the trip a life-changing experience for many of them. Indeed, the excitement that they felt was replete in nearly all of their descriptions of the trip, including the first time they saw the North African coast. Sailing from Marseille to Algiers, Duval wrote, "The land comes into view. Forms take shape. Algiers appears. Slowly we approach. We greet Algiers with the Croix de Feu hymn, which the wind takes to those who are waiting on the quay. We disembark. We walk arm in arm. Some of us cry, others laugh. We are emotional. So many people [PSF members] have come to wait for us and they seem so happy."[71] In this way, the Soufflotines emphasized the emotional depth of their experiences, which were channeled in a positive and nationalistic manner through the "Song of the Croix de Feu."

Upon the Soufflotines' arrival in Algiers they stayed at the homes of PSF supporters and relied on them to become oriented within the city and its surroundings. Duval's enchantment with meeting PSF settlers was reflected in her description of a lunch at a supporter's home in M'sila: "[we] find our friends, the French, who welcome us with smiles... in a room decorated in the Arab style, and in the course of our meal, we felt the PSF miracle alive and strong."[72] Duval's emphasis on the humanity of the French compared to the inanimate nature of Arab culture, which was always in the background, was a dominant characteristic of the entire trip. Indeed, while Duval was delighted with Arab rugs and decorations, she expressed less excitement with actual people. On the few occasions when the Soufflotines mentioned Muslims themselves, it was nearly always in pejorative and paternalistic terms. A propaganda brochure celebrating the Soufflotines' trip, for example, showed a Soufflotine interacting with a young man; the caption read, "A student teaches an Arab shepherd to shout 'Long live France'!"[73] In suggesting that Arabs had the potential to be nationalistic, the PSF nominally demonstrated its support for assimilation, and thus, a key rationale of the civilizing mission. In contrast to this momentary instance of likeness between the Soufflotines and Arabs, it was more common for the students to avoid interacting with Muslims, as they emphasized cultural difference in demeaning ways. Upon visiting an Arab cemetery in Algiers, Duval referred with disdain to Arab women mourners, whom she called "veiled and prattling." At a souk, she described the crowds as "dirty and colorful," and found the streets to be "terribly narrow, dirty, swarming with children, with hennaed hair, dressed in rags."[74] In this way, Duval emphasized the strict division between the "conquering allure" of the Soufflotines and the separate spaces of the "dirty" Arab Other. These experiences reinforced the cultural racism that framed the Fête Coloniale: colonial subjects were fundamentally different from the French.

While the Soufflotines believed that indigenous Algerians who lived in French Algeria were insignificant in comparison to their "PSF friends," they admired the region's (altered) landscape and (Christian) history. Indeed, the Soufflotines perpetuated one of the "founding myths" of France's North African empire: that the French were modern-day heirs of the Roman's Latin empire.[75] Duval explained that seeing Algeria for themselves inspired awe in the Soufflotines. Such experience allowed them, as Duval put it, to "understand the colonizing efforts of so many generations of French who came here to make a Greater France."[76] For Duval, the magnificence of Greater France was reflected in the Soufflotines' tour of the Roman ruins, an oasis at Bou Saâda, a spa at Abziza, and Moorish baths at Blida. In Tipasa, home to a fifth-century Christian mausoleum and impressive Roman ruins, Duval was inspired "by the beauty of this corner of the African coast, by the variety of the landscape, the intensity of the colors . . . and the ruins of a Roman city."[77]

French treatment of the Algerian environment was a key component of the nation's efforts to recover the glory of the Roman Empire.[78] The centerpiece of this supposed environmental mastery was France's ecological exploitation of the Mitidja plain, which was located just south of Algiers and stretched nearly fifty kilometers to Blida, on the plain's southern edge. The Mitidja maintained a prominent place in colonial lore because the French identified themselves with their Roman progenitors by draining the Mitidja's marshlands for agricultural use and returning it to the "salubrious" condition reminiscent of Roman times.[79] For the Soufflotines, the Mitidja represented more than just a connection between the French and Roman empires. It imbued them with a deep respect for the vastness of the natural world, which contrasted with the urban Parisian environment in which they lived. Duval explained that they understood the contrast between Paris and the Mitidja this way: "When we have had enough of seeing only gray and dirty cobblestones at our feet [in Paris], we will close our eyes for an instant and see once again all the dazzling flowers of the Algerian countryside. When we tire of seeing every horizon as nothing but tall somber houses, we will think of the great plain of the Mitidja, so green, and so fresh."[80]

Algeria's Christian and Roman roots connected the colony with France's Latin heritage and enabled the Soufflotines to feel ownership in the places they visited, which for them, cultivated a deeper commitment to Greater France. It also reinforced their strong belief that Catholicism epitomized a rational type of religious faith because their religiosity was rooted in historical evolution and progress. In addition to the Christian mausoleum, Duval expressed wonder at the grandeur of the Grand Basilica, Notre Dame d'Afrique, in Algiers. The Basilica was rebuilt as a part of the French Church's efforts to link North Africa with its Augustinian legacy and symbolized the Catholic identity of the French empire.[81] For the Soufflotines, the Basilica was a place to practice their Catholic faith in a country dominated by Muslims. Duval noted that the Soufflotines prioritized praying at the Basilica, where they "asked the Virgin to bless all those who received us with such heart and devotion, and who sacrificed their time to us."[82]

In contrast to the areas near the coast where the concentration of French settlers was more dense, the Soufflotines were less enthusiastic about their experiences as they headed south into rural areas, which they cast as unenlightened and not yet civilized. Duval described Aumale, approximately seventy-five miles inland and closer to the desert, as being "in the middle of nowhere, far from Algiers, *far from France* ... a dump."[83] So long as the Soufflotines were surrounded by Algeria's Roman Catholic heritage, Algeria was "French"; however, upon their leaving the urban areas of French influence, Algeria was no longer "French." Further south, in El Hamel, Duval noted that there was "no trace of European life in this city with a Muslim seminary."[84] Notions of difference were paramount here and reflected the Soufflotines' perpetuation of racial hierarchies. Their experiences in Algeria only strengthened the binary distinctions between the French and Arabs, which reinforced widespread beliefs about the cultural incompatibility of the two groups.

Other facets of the trip were overtly political, specifically, their work to show the Algerian sections that university centers energized the PSF. It was this political action that garnered police attention. Indeed, the police had the Soufflotines under surveillance and monitored their movements throughout Algeria.[85] While Duval cast the trip in a lighthearted manner, the police understood that the Soufflotines were PSF political operatives. For example, Duval portrayed the lunch in

M'sila with PSF section leaders as casual and apolitical: "the lunch left us with a very profound impression ... one where all our hearts beat so well together in unison."[86] The police however considered the lunch quite dangerous. According to an informant, attendees "discussed leftist parties in an offensive manner" and expressed worry about PSF plans to act against Communists and Socialists.[87]

As the M'sila lunch reveals, Duval and other members sought to cover the Soufflotines' political activity by casting the group as cheery, optimistic, and girlish supporters of Greater France (Figure 8). Empire, like the Soufflotines, was benign. For example, Alfred Debay, the leader of the PSF in Algeria, who was notorious for his violent hatred of communism and anticolonialism, portrayed the Soufflotines as harmless apolitical nationalists. In thanking the Soufflotines for their visit, he wrote, "You have brought to the Algiers PSF something very young, very pure, very grand. We see you among us laughing, singing, acting, praying, and giving public witness, with such gallantry and love for your fatherland."[88] In this way, Debay cast the Soufflotines as joyful Catholics who represented a feminized and friendly version of the PSF. The Soufflotines were complicit in this messaging. In thanking the Algerian PSF for its hospitality, they referred to Debay as "Uncle Alfred" and cast supporters in gently parental terms: "With such smiling indulgence, you supported our childish whims, our fantasies, our foolishness, and our sometimes noisy cheerfulness!"[89] This exchange of thanks and politesse lasted for several months after the Soufflotines left Algeria. As *La Flamme* explained a few days after the Soufflotines returned to Paris, "We are happy that they fully enjoyed these past few days on African soil, that they will have precious memories of their vacation, and that they will diffuse 'the sense of empire' without resting."[90]

In transmitting the "sense of empire" the Soufflotines used the idea much like the organizers of Fête Coloniale: they emphasized French cultural superiority and used the rhetoric of the civilizing mission to justify French action while demonstrating that the civilizing mission remained incomplete. The Soufflotines suggested that the French had made great gains in spaces like the European quarters of Algiers and the Mitidja, yet work remained in Muslim rural spaces such as El Hamel and Aumale and the urban spaces of the souks and cemeteries of Algiers. The intermixing of assimilation and association was on display; while one propaganda brochure emphasized that the Soufflotines contributed to assimilation by purportedly teaching young Arab men French nationalism, most press coverage emphasized the separate spaces in which the French and Arabs lived (and evolved at separate rates), which was a hallmark of association. The Croix de Feu/PSF supporters who organized and publicized the trip cared less about doctrinal consistency than about using the civilizing mission to legitimate the empire and resist growing demands for reform.

The Soufflotines in Germany: Rational Catholicism versus Irrational Paganism

PSF leaders believed that the Algerian "vacation" was an effective way for the movement to recruit new members and propagandize its principles. They sent the Soufflotines on another trip only a few months later, this one to Nazi Germany, with a specific objective: to evaluate Nazi social policies and compare them with those of the PSF.[91] PSF leaders admired what they called Nazism's "resolute opposition to class struggle" and its ability to "unite the German people by intermixing the classes."[92] Indeed, PSF leaders were struck by, as they put it, the "preponderant" place of the Nazi Labor Service at public events throughout the 1930s.[93] For these reasons, they believed that the Nazis' "battle for work" and "schools of education" might have useful applications in the French context.

PSF leaders thus sent the Soufflotines to Germany in the summer of 1938 to evaluate the centerpiece of the Nazi "battle for work"—the work-service camps. To combat unemployment, the Weimar government had established the camps in 1932, which were expanded by the National Socialist regime under the auspices of the Labor Service (Reichsarbeitsdienst, RAD) to impart Nazi values of community building and racial education.[94] The Labor Service programs, including its work-service camps, were one of several factors that led to a decrease in unemployment from 34 percent in January 1933 to 7.4 percent by 1936.[95] Toward the end of 1936, Germany experienced a labor shortage, and the Labor Service turned to conscripting young people to work. The government sought to mobilize the labor that single women could provide and thus drafted women aged eighteen to twenty-six into the women's Labor Service to train them for domestic and agricultural work.[96] By the time the Soufflotines visited Berlin in the summer of 1938, the Women's Labor Service (Reichsarbeitsdienst-weibliche Jugend, RADwJ) ran about five hundred work-service camps for young women.

Upon arriving in Berlin, a Führer drove the Soufflotines to the camp where they stayed. It was there that they met the camp's Führerin, who served as their guide. The spokesperson for their travels was another Soufflotine, Madeleine, who was a regular contributor to *Pourquoi S'en Faire.*[97] According to Madeleine, leadership played an important role in each camp, which depended on the "personality of the Führerin."[98] Since the PSF trained supervisors for its own social centers and summer camps, PSF leaders asked the Soufflotines to evaluate the similarities and differences between Nazi and PSF training programs. Several of the Soufflotines served as supervisors and would have taken the PSF's training courses, although PSF courses (ten to twelve sessions) were not nearly as time-intensive as Nazi training (which took months) and, significantly, lacked the emphasis on racial education that was at the heart of Nazi programs.

The work-service camps across Germany required thousands of Führerinnen, and Madeleine stated that the young women she met had enthusiastic aspirations to join the leadership ranks of the women's Labor Service. Madeleine believed that many of the Germans seemed anxious to impress the Soufflotines, giving the impression that they enjoyed camp life and that they made valuable contributions to German society. The Führerin took the Soufflotines to the camp's impeccably kept barracks, where they were struck by the decorations, which included drawings, paintings, and a handmade wooden swastika. The Führerin then described a typical day at the camp, which included physical education, political classes, and primarily, doing farmwork, where the young women interacted with peasants. In the evening, when looking around the dinner table, Madeleine described seeing "a number of pleasant, intelligent, joyful faces."[99]

Overall, however, the Soufflotines were critical of the work-service camps and Nazism itself. They were most alarmed by Nazism's narrow view of womanhood and the inability of the Germans to debate issues freely. Underlining Hitler's conviction that women found ultimate fulfillment in their role as mothers, Madeleine derisively quoted him as saying, "When women of a nation aim towards other goals, then the soul of the nation dies."[100] Madeleine stated that the purpose of the camps was to teach young women how to aid overworked mothers (by acting as a maid, nanny, or cook), work in kindergartens, or help farmers in their fields. Indeed, the Soufflotines argued that the work-service camps showed that German society only valued women for two reasons: their ability to perform domestic work and to bear children. In this context, Soufflotine femininity was progressive in its emphasis on women's intellectual capabilities, social mobility, and refusal to reduce womanhood to motherhood.

Equally troubling to the Soufflotines was their belief that the Germans in the work-service camps lacked the ability to engage in independent thought and reasoned debate. Warning that the women who were training to become

Nazi teachers were in fact "seduced" by Nazism, Madeleine stated, "the teacher is transformed into a propaganda agent who works to excite the spirits and the youth only to know the political notions elaborated upon by the apostles of Hitlerism."[101] In contrast, the Soufflotines emphasized that they joined the Foyer of their own volition and that its intellectual nature demanded that participants exercise rationality in debating issues, which they believed was a hallmark of French republicanism.

Despite German attempts to portray their experiences positively, the Soufflotines met unhappy individuals who struggled with the difficult and labor-intensive work. Some of the Soufflotines saw that several women had trouble relating to the farmers, were "repulsed" by housekeeping duties, and did not receive enough food from the farmers for whom they worked. Perhaps most disturbing to the Soufflotines was the bullying that a practicing Catholic received, which bolstered the Soufflotines' most virulent critique of Nazism: that it was a pagan religion with no respect for tradition or Church authority. Such rational respect for authority demarcated the civilized French, who were willing to submit themselves to the Church, from the less civilized Germans, who the Soufflotines believed were swept away by the irrationalism of Nazism. In this way, Madeleine parroted a charge often levied against Nazism by its detractors, which discredited women who supported the Nazis as feminized fools who were willing to suspend rational judgment to follow a charismatic leader.

While the Soufflotines were not unique in their assessment of Nazism, they genuinely believed that a reasoned faith, versus a false religion, was a salient marker of difference. Madeleine made this critique most clearly in discussing the limits of Nazi social action: "Social achievements are good in themselves—one must fairly recognize this. What makes National Socialism attractive is the seductive quality of its social achievements, and, that it avoids awakening criticism in the people's soul because the crowd limits itself to the practical without considering the principles. The German people have the taste for the inexplicable and the irrational. For them, the symbol is stronger than argument and the will of the Führer takes precedence over the opinion of the majority."[102] These alleged German characteristics contrasted directly with the Soufflotines' portrayal of the French: a people informed by the Enlightenment principles of rationality, reason, and regard for the general will of the people. For the Soufflotines, these values were embodied by PSF social action, which was infused with the Catholic traditions that were at the heart of French identity.

CONCLUSION

While both the Nazis and PSF used their organizations for "community building" purposes and sought to subsume the individual into national community, PSF ethnoreligious nationalism did not aggressively seek to eradicate their "enemies" in the same manner as Nazism. Yet the Soufflotines did not criticize Nazism for its exclusionary practices but for its treatment of women and lack of respect for religion. The Soufflotines believed that republican civil society and the civic space in which PSF women operated provided them with multiple opportunities. The PSF's gender ideology thus contributed to the Soufflotines' belief that French culture was superior to that of the Germans. In terms of ethnoreligious hierarchies, unlike Travail et loisirs' portrayal of colonial subjects in the Fête and the Soufflotines' depictions of Arabs in Algeria, the Soufflotines recognized the humanity of their German peers by considering them as equals and empathizing with their goals and worries. Madeleine nevertheless expressed concern about the supposed German tendency to be drawn to the irrational. For Madeleine, French republicanism enabled young women to gain access to elite status, which was an opportunity that was missing in Nazism. In this way, the beliefs and actions of the Soufflotines revealed the ways in which the PSF used Enlightenment values to assert French superiority on the European continent and in Greater France.

6

SOCIAL AND POLITICAL ACTION IN NORTH AFRICA

THE FASCISM OF THE CROIX DE FEU/PSF IN THE

FRENCH MAGHREB, 1927-1940

One of the critical differences between metropolitan France and the colonies was the ways in which metropolitan women shaped republican civil society. It was this civic space that metropolitan Croix de Feu/PSF women captured and operated in so effectively. However, women's hard-won influence was challenged on a number of fronts. The grassroots nature of the movement's social program depended upon regional federations and local sections supporting the national leadership's approach to social renovation. If members refused to do so, women struggled to exert the influence that La Rocque and Préval envisioned when they initiated the movement's Social First! strategy.

Algeria, Tunisia, and Morocco's inclusion in Greater France was rooted in colonial warfare, and in the case of Algeria, what several historians have considered settler genocide.[1] The violence and racism of conquest carved out specific sets of ethnoreligious hierarchies in each place, which shaped the organization of settler communities and their relationship with the majority indigenous populations. These hierarchies enabled Croix de Feu/PSF ethnoreligious nationalism to thrive. While the violence of the early metropolitan Croix de Feu was justified through the veteran's mystique and a sense of purity and civic virtue, the North African Croix de Feu eschewed such ideas in favor of virulent attacks against Muslims and Jews. The political culture of the interwar French Maghreb was thus characterized by hypermasculinity, racialized thinking, and political violence, all of which were hallmarks of fascism. The political complexities of the 1930s—increasing rates of conflict due to political mobilization by indigenous activists, which spurred disdain from settlers and state repression—have led several historians to locate the early stages of decolonization not in World War II as was commonly believed, but during the interwar period.[2] The Croix de Feu/PSF played a key role in this process by helping to drive indigenous reformers toward anticolonialism.

The differences between the metropolitan and North African Croix de Feu reveal the "dual character" of republicanism in that metropolitan women operated in a civil society that was relatively more egalitarian, whereas settler women were inhibited by republican imperialism's authoritarian system of exclusions. While the metropolitan movement empowered women as agents of social action, the North African Croix de Feu/PSF marginalized women to such an extent that it lacked the social program that allowed the metropolitan movement to garner popular support. Sean Kennedy argues that the metropolitan Croix de Feu/PSF had an "impressive" capacity to attract working-class supporters despite significant challenges (workers comprised nearly 33 percent of the membership in the Nord by 1939).[3] As the previous chapters have sought to show, women's social action played a key role in the movement's ability to reach out to a variety of socio-economic groups. Yet, the extremism of the movement's North African branches limited its capacity to move beyond its bourgeois Catholic origins. For this reason, the metropolitan Croix de Feu/PSF leaders attempted to colonize the settlers as much as indigenous people; they sent Suzanne Fouché to Tunisia and Algeria to stress conciliatory forms of action and believed that the Soufflotines would demonstrate to the Algerian sections that women were critical sociopolitical actors. However, rather than using social services to attract support, the North African Croix de Feu/PSF used violence against forces they considered "anti-French" to defend the political, social, and economic privileges of settler communities. In North Africa, the movement's recruitment of indigenous men and women was abysmal in comparison to the metropolitan movement's recruitment of workers, only reaching 8 percent in one location (Constantine-*ville*) for a short time (several months).[4]

It is not simply that the Croix de Feu/PSF in North Africa was fascist, but that the political culture of colonial societies enabled settlers prone to the racialized, patriarchal, and violent forms of thinking to flourish in far Right groups. Gender was at the heart of these dynamics because it was central to the Croix de Feu/PSF's development in the French Maghreb. Most importantly, two of the associations that were central to the metropolitan Croix de Feu/PSF's Social First! strategy, Travail et loisirs and AMSJA, never existed in North Africa. SPES was exceedingly weak, and Social Action struggled immensely from the dearth of social workers and nurses in the Maghreb. Consequently, the programs that were at the heart of the metropolitan movement's sociocultural action—entertainment, physical education, social centers, health clinics, and summer camps—were severely lacking. Only the most rudimentary social services (clothing depots, food centers, and home visits) were left, which inhibited women's organizing and rendered them marginal in the North African Croix de Feu/PSF. While the metropolitan movement abandoned political violence and paramilitarism in favor of social action, the North African Croix de Feu's use of these hallmarks of fascism intensified.

REJECTING WOMEN AS CORNERSTONES: HYPERMASCULINITY AND THE ETHNORELIGIOUS HIERARCHY OF THE FRENCH MAGHREB, 1927–1936

While Croix de Feu/PSF men created sections in Tahiti, Madagascar, Saigon, Dakar, and even New York, Women's Sections were limited to North Africa. Just as in metropolitan France, colonial Women's Sections were constituted once fifty women expressed interest in the Croix de Feu/PSF. In many cases, the movement struggled to reach this threshold even in places where the presence of European settlers was particularly strong.[5] Croix de Feu women created the first metropolitan sections in March 1934 and proceeded to form forty-seven more before the first colonial section, located in Algiers, was created ten months later in January 1935. In Morocco, while the first Men's Section was created in May 1931, it was not until August 1935 that women created their own section in Casablanca, a city with a large settler population.[6] Women in Tunisia waited even longer, constituting their first section in early 1936.[7] As these dates suggest, women were more active in Morocco than in Tunisia; the Croix de Feu reported seven Moroccan sections in mid-1936 whereas women in Tunisia only created the same number by early 1938.[8] Since Algeria had the largest European settler population, the number of Women's Sections reflected those demographics. By June 1936 Croix de Feu women had created twenty-four sections in Algeria, which included twelve in the Department of Algiers, seven in the Department of Constantine, and five in the Department of Oran.[9] By the late 1930s, women constituted roughly one-third of the metropolitan movement's members, while in Morocco and Algeria, the numbers hovered between 20 and 25 percent.[10]

In comparison to metropolitan France, the delay in creating sections in North Africa led directly to the movement's inability to create an effective social program. Fewer women meant fewer social service providers, which inhibited the movement's ability to use social action effectively. While the metropolitan Women's Section organized charity bazaars to support their social programs beginning in 1934, one of the first activities that women in the Tunisian Women's Section organized was a fund-raiser in May 1936.[11] From there, the Tunisian Women's Section broadened their activities by opening a small food bank, clothing depot, and sewing room by 1938, the scope of which paled in comparison to those of many metropolitan sections and even those in Algeria.[12] In terms of health care, for instance, sixty-five individuals visited the Tunis health clinic and visiting nurses made fifty-six home visits in the first trimester of 1938.[13] Following the earlier creation of its Women's Sections, social services in the Moroccan Croix de Feu were established sooner than those in Tunisia. In Casablanca the league created its first clothing depot and sewing room in the fall of 1935, and in the two following months, they aided seventy needy families through the visiting social worker program and took thirty meals a day to the homes of the needy (soup kitchens were not widespread in Morocco).[14] Over the course of the next few months they expanded the services to include a clinic where doctors provided free medical exams, which sparked disdain by Croix de Feu enemies. The police remarked that the services were "heavily criticized" by the parties on the extreme Left.[15]

While many Croix de Feu women in the Maghreb sought to emulate their metropolitan counterparts by using social services to promote the movement's ultranationalist mission, the structures in which they operated limited their mobilization. Indeed, Préval repeatedly emphasized that the movement's organizational structure was the key to organizing effective social programs. The ways in which the movement's North African sections functioned demonstrated the wisdom of Préval's insight and leant credence to her worry that structural differences would lead to women's marginalization. In Morocco, women did not join their own section but the RNCF, which was defunct in metropolitan France due to its ineffectiveness. Within the RNCF they joined the Section Féminine d'Entr'aide, which fell under the purview of men's entr'aide.[16] Moreover, Moroccan entr'aide relied solely upon donations, leading to, as one circular put it, a "problem with resources."[17] Although the Tunisian Croix de Feu/PSF organized women slightly differently, it subordinated them in ways similar to those in Morocco. It wasn't until mid-1936—long after the metropolitan movement had rolled out its Social First! strategy—that its leader in Tunisia, Dr. Minguet, explained the structure of the Tunisian Croix de Feu and women's place in it. "The Croix de Feu and VN sections are essentially the active groups," he wrote. "Those who can't or don't want to take part in this activity can, upon their request, join the MSF."[18] In designating men as the movement's "active" members and women as inactive, Minguet diverged from the metropolitan movement, which was empowering women involved in social action. In Tunisia MSF section leaders did not organize or direct the league's social services as they did in metropolitan France. Instead, they performed administrative work that included registering new members, verifying membership applications, delivering membership cards and insignia, and collecting dues.[19]

In Algeria, the Croix de Feu structurally subordinated women in much the same way as in Tunisia, although unlike in Tunisia and Morocco, the league emphasized the medical component of social provisions by placing male doctors at the head of its social services and dividing them into medical and social branches. Within the social branch, the Women's Section only directed a sub-section of it that distributed clothing and was thus not expected to organize many social services, which included providing nurses, dentists, doctors, and midwives to assist members who were poor and ill.[20] Moreover, whereas in metropolitan France women often discussed the league's social services at Croix de Feu meetings, this was generally not the case in the league's North African sections. In Algeria, for example, the first leader of the league's social services, Doctor Lucien Colonieu, was the spokesman for the league's services, which reflected the masculinized social program that initially characterized the Algerian Croix de Feu.[21] He informed audiences that the league's social works were evidence of its growing power, which sought to "resuscitate the French France of the past."[22] Not surprisingly, Colonieu had trouble rounding up enough men to provide services that many considered to be women's work, much of which was administrative in nature: files needed to be organized to determine which members were eligible for aid and what type of aid, if any, was to be dispersed. Pleading for volunteers, Colonieu warned men that each section leader possessed his name, and that it was his duty to help: "EVERYONE MUST CONTRIBUTE TO THE SOCIAL SERVICE. EVERYONE NEEDS SOCIAL SERVICES AND THE SOCIAL SERVICES NEEDS EACH OF US."[23]

The masculinization of the bureaucracy organizing the Algerian social services meant that the league's welfare initiatives and youth development programs were initially either small or nonexistent. Each Men's Section created cards and dossiers for those in need, keeping this documentation on file at the local office. When a case required, the male section leader contacted the nearest doctor, who provided medicine and treatment to the patient, and if necessary, contacted a specialist. A female social worker—rare in Algeria as compared to metropolitan France—operated as a liaison between each section and individual homes to determine whether the family was eligible for aid. She submitted her findings to the league's social service office, which ultimately made decisions about aiding the sick individual and her or his family. It was at this point that the Women's Section provided clothing to the family in need, which revealed the degree to which the Women's Section was marginalized from social service provisions. Indeed, this marginalization was such that the Algerian Croix de Feu lacked one of the most vital aspects of the metropolitan Croix de Feu: a comprehensive youth development program. They did have a summer camp, although it received little publicity and few resources in comparison to the massive metropolitan propaganda drive that urged parents to send their children to the many Croix de Feu camps in France. The Algiers Men's Section—not the Women's Section—organized the first camp for the summer of 1935. Situated near a small village (Francis-Gornier), the camp was ideally located in a "salubrious" climate near both the Mediterranean Sea and the mountains.[24] Children were required to register with the FFCF, and supervisors of both sexes ran the camp. However, few children attended, which reflected the permanent struggles that the Algerian Croix de Feu would have in creating effective programs for youth.

To better organize its services, the Algerian Croix de Feu reorganized the Women's Section in early 1936—nearly two years after the same had been done in the metropolitan sections—and initiated a series of reforms that did not take place in Tunisia or Morocco. Most of these reforms would result in women earning slightly more influence in organizing social services. The Algerian Croix de Feu appointed its first woman leader to oversee its services by naming Madame Bernard the secretary general in early 1936. While Bernard had long been active in the Algiers section, this official designation granted her a degree of authority in becoming the lead organizer of Algerian social programs and working alongside Colonieu. Moreover, Bernard sought to strengthen connections across the Mediterranean by traveling occasionally to meet with metropolitan leaders and discuss how best to implement the social programs. To this end, Bernard—not male section heads—appointed upper-level adjutants, including Oran's secretary general, Mademoiselle Jeanne Martignier, who became a leading spokeswoman for the movement's social services. Her accomplishments were celebrated in the press and she was one of the few women who occasionally spoke at Croix de Feu meetings. Martignier articulated the movement's ideology with a sense of apolitical rhetoric similar to those of her comrades in the Hexagon, explaining to her Algerian colleagues, "the Women's Section occupies itself by relieving material and emotional miseries, outside of political and national discussions."[25]

Women's influence was growing in Algeria although they were at a structural disadvantage in comparison to metropolitan women. For example, the female heads of each metropolitan Women's Section appointed their own adjutants to each of the section's *seven* leadership positions, which reflected the categories of services they offered. In Algeria, however, female section heads had no such power; the male departmental delegate and male section chief assigned women to one of *three* leadership positions in each Women's Section.[26] The smaller number of lower-level leadership positions in the Algerian Women's Sections was a function of the smaller number of services offered by the Algerian Croix de Feu. One position, the adjutant to the female Women's Section leader, distributed membership cards and monthly bulletins. A second position, the director of social workers, registered social workers under her purview with each section's Social Service office. Finally, the clothing depot director gathered volunteers to organize and distribute clothing to individual families who carried a card with the signature from their social worker verifying that the family was in need of services. Each section also had a midwife on call and distributed food to those who were able to obtain cards from the Social Service office, which included instructions from the social worker on the amount of food for which the family was eligible.

While belated in comparison to metropolitan sections, the reorganization in Algeria did galvanize several highly motivated and energetic women to organize more effective social services at the local level. The Mazafran Women's Section in the Department of Algiers was one such section. Bernard and Colonieu inaugurated it in January 1936 and by March, the section's leader, Madame Nouvion, counted ninety members who organized the section's social services in the following manner.[27] Two principal centers in Mazafran's sector, Coléa and Castiglione, included an office, clothing and food depot, and small medical dispensary. The two centers employed a social worker, who visited homes and reported her findings to the female sector leader. Upon the approval of the social worker, the sector leader then distributed aid, which included medicine, food (obtained by donations from local shopkeepers), and clothing. Figure 9 shows that the Mazafran section—smaller in the number of women participants and overall population in comparison to the other cities—outstripped them in the distribution of key services.[28]

It should be noted that there are a number of difficulties in comparing the rates of social service provisions across sections. Surviving reports of North African Croix de Feu services are difficult to find, and the stray reports that remain in the historical record show that some sections reported bimonthly while others did so by trimester, which makes direct comparisons nearly impossible. Moreover, because the population and demographics varied wildly according to location, the clientele for services in a place like Oran—one of the few cities where settlers were the demographic majority—was greater than the majority of cities and towns where settlers constituted the minority; this distorts the Oran numbers and makes them proportionally less impressive than they appear at first glance. Despite these limitations, the data not only reveal the exceptional status of the Mazafran section but the struggles of sections elsewhere. For example, despite an extra two years in which to develop a social service network, the Tunis section still lagged behind where other sections were in the mid-1930s.

As the case of the Mazafran section demonstrates, it was possible for Croix de Feu supporters to commit to social action in North Africa—if local leaders had the will to do so. However, the movement's top leaders in the Maghreb were stuck between their rank-and-file members, who wanted dramatic and immediate action, and the metropolitan leadership's conciliatory and long-term approach to sociopolitical rejuvenation. Indeed, the vast majority of the movement's North African supporters not only expressed skepticism and hatred for democracy but were more overt than those in metropolitan France in stating their desires to destroy the Third Republic. As pressure from the league's central headquarters in Paris to put more emphasis on social programs mounted, many leaders in the Maghreb were more interested in pressing for immediate political change. Reflecting the beliefs of many, a Constantine section leader proclaimed at a meeting in 1935: "We must bring down the current regime, either by violence or legal means. For myself, I am ready to employ either method."[29]

French security services across North Africa understood that the Croix de Feu had the personnel and technological resources (airplanes, cars, weapons) necessary for a coup d'état if La Rocque called for one.[30] Police in Morocco, for example, were convinced that a coup was imminent in July 1935, when an informant told them that the Croix de Feu would use the July 14 national fête to demonstrate their patriotism by taking over the government. The informant added that the league's North African sections were awaiting the order from Paris and that once Croix de Feu shock troops took over points of strategic importance in the capital (post offices, telegraph and telephone centers, banks, buildings with government offices) they would do the same across Greater France. According to the informant, in Casablanca, two hundred members had cars that could carry up to six men, which in principle meant that as many as twelve hundred men—many with access to arms—could descend upon points of political, cultural, social, and economic importance in the city.[31] However, despite such preparations, La Rocque's order to overthrow the government never came.

The task of reconciling the divergent views of far Right settlers and the movement's leadership in Paris was left to Alfred Debay. Debay was at once the point man for leading the Social First! strategy and the voice of the movement's extremism. He sought to bridge these tensions by fusing the league's emphasis on social renovation with political revolution in much the same way as Nazism and Italian Fascism. He put it this way in February 1936 as tensions between the Popular Front and extreme Right were peaking:

> People often ask me this question: What will make La Rocque act like Hitler or like Mussolini? Invariably I respond: Our President would act like Mussolini in Italy, and like Hitler in Germany. But in France, in the French milieu, he will act like the French.... Some are impatient and find our progress too slow. Hitler wanted to act too quickly, and spent two years in prison. To act, we must have the adherence of the vast majority of the country.[32]

In this way, Debay cultivated more fertile ground for the movement's principles to take hold. However, his emphasis on patience was a position that the movement's more radical members found untenable. In metropolitan France, these factions were in the minority, which spurred many of them to leave for more radical movements such as Doriot's PPF and the Cagoule, which initiated a bombing campaign in 1937.[33] In Algeria, however, extremists were in the majority, which played a key role in the virulence of its politics.

La Rocque regularly attempted to convince Algerian sections to take social services seriously, although due to women's marginalization they lacked the expertise and grassroots activists necessary to implement them. The most urgent calls for social action came not from Algerian section heads but when local leaders *read* directives from La Rocque. At a meeting in Constantine in early 1936, for example, the head of the Constantine Croix de Feu, Colonel Gros, read a La Rocque circular that insisted on the centrality of women to the Croix de Feu: "The women's movement must be the *cornerstone* of our movement. It is the very base of our success."[34] However, only weeks later, Gros told another audience that social workers had the important duty of coming into their homes with portraits of La Rocque, which families were to put in a "place of honor."[35]

While La Rocque and other metropolitan male leaders regularly visited the North African sections, they could not apply constant pressure in the same manner as they did in the areas where they lived. Combined with the sense of *algérian-ité* among settlers, metropolitan calls for social action lacked resonance for settlers who sought direct confrontation with their enemies. After visiting with La Rocque in Paris in June 1935, Debay returned to Algiers to read a set of instructions. Debay stated that if the movement were to expand, it needed to "profoundly penetrate" the social layers of society, which was why La Rocque wanted to institute soup kitchens and other aid.[36] Debay continued emphasizing the relationship between social action and social penetration at virtually all of the meetings he led, including an important Oran general assembly meeting attended by over one thousand audience members in November 1935. At the meeting Debay urged supporters to aid people "like them" by emulating metropolitan services such as summer camps, which he claimed led parents to join the Croix de Feu instead of Communist organizations.[37] This comparison to Paris was telling because metropolitan summer camps were run by women. However, Debay's sincerity was tenuous at best; as late as 1938 no child from the Oran section had registered for a summer camp.[38]

Despite La Rocque's best efforts, only a minority of supporters in Algeria would agree with him that women should constitute the cornerstone of the Croix de Feu. As political conditions deteriorated in 1935 and 1936, La Rocque's directives to mobilize women became increasingly difficult to achieve. The election of the Popular Front in May 1936 confirmed the worst fears of many of the movement's supporters and exacerbated tensions within the movement over its direction and its ability to save Greater France. After the election, many of the league's top leaders in Algeria used apocalyptic language to express their fear that Greater France would cease to exist. Casting France's political problems as a matter of life and death, the movement's head in Algiers argued that "The country is beginning to understand where the Popular Front will lead: to ruin, insurrection, war, and death."[39] This fear over the fate of the very existence of Greater France was a key reason why none of the Algerian leaders was willing to cede strategic and tactical control to women. The section head in Marengo (Algiers), on behalf of many male settlers, said: "In the PSF, we reckon that women are made for mending socks and staying at home."[40] The Croix de Feu/PSF's "social turn" in the Maghreb was thus isolated to cases where especially energetic women such as Madame Nouvion, the Mazafran section's leader, were able to withstand the disdain of men and were given leeway by supportive section presidents.

A New "Cornerstone"? Croix de Feu Attempts to Recruit Muslims, 1927–1936

The energy that the North African Croix de Feu/PSF might have committed to galvanizing women and engaging in social action went instead to mobilizing men from indigenous communities and fighting the Popular Front and anticolonial nationalist groups. The movement made no effort to recruit indigenous women, whom North African leaders considered even less suitable political actors than women from settler communities. Many Croix de Feu/PSF supporters believed that recruiting indigenous men would not only undermine colonial reformers, but serve as proof that the civilizing mission remained a central justification for empire.[41] However, indigenous men faced restrictions in joining the movement that European settlers did not. While male and female French citizens were admitted to the Croix de Feu/PSF with the approval of section leaders, indigenous men could only join the Croix de Feu with special permission of the movement's administrative council in Paris.[42] The narrow parameters for membership were based upon prospective members' proving their Frenchness, which was most often demonstrated through military service and renunciation of one's personal status.

Croix de Feu/PSF attempts to recruit indigenous men took many forms that varied according to locale. The Tunisian Croix de Feu/PSF's recruitment of native Tunisians was ineffective, and the movement there was essentially bereft of indigenous members.[43] Such struggles were not surprising given Minguet's biologically based hostility toward indigenous Tunisians: "Tunisian workers belong to different races, and because of this, their habits, religions, and aptitudes are different; above all they have neither the same needs nor the same productivity.... Everyone knows that the Muslims, when they earn some money, voluntarily rest and go spend their days in contemplative inaction at Moorish cafes, which would not be suitable to the French temperament."[44]

In contrast, sections in Morocco and Algeria initiated sustained recruiting campaigns to draw indigenous veterans and elites to the movement. In Casablanca, for instance, in response to a November 1935 recruiting campaign aimed at veterans conducted by the pro-democracy Republican Veterans, Croix de Feu section presidents attempted to convince indigenous veterans that they were the true representatives of veterans' interests.[45] Section heads believed that the campaign paid off because around a dozen men joined.[46] Encouraged by this slight degree of interest, sections across Morocco continued to emphasize that the Croix de Feu fought for veterans' rights regardless of ethnoreligious background. Most Moroccan veterans, however, were skeptical about these claims given the movement's hostility to Islam, resistance to colonial reforms, and strident opposition to the Popular Front and anticolonial nationalist groups. The limited effectiveness of the Moroccan Croix de Feu/PSF recruiting efforts dwindled into the late 1930s. The Meknès section, for example, essentially failed in its attempt to attract indigenous notables: only one man joined in the first half of 1938.[47]

The Croix de Feu/PSF's recruiting of indigenous men was the most sustained in Algeria. For a brief moment in the mid-1930s it appeared as if the movement might actually attract *évolués* and anticommunist Muslims, or at the very least, form a working partnership with high-profile Muslims.[48] In the municipal elections of May 1935, it is likely that the Constantine Croix de Feu colluded with Dr. Mohamed-Salah Bendjelloul's Fédération des Élus Musulmans (FEM) in Batna, Sétif, and Khenchela (a commune that had a majority settler population) to elect anticommunist councilors.[49] The departmental prefect stated that in Sétif, five Croix de Feu members were elected directly due to the indigenous Algerian vote.[50] Bendjelloul was perhaps the most influential Muslim activist at the time, and the FEM drew high levels of support around Constantine for its moderate program that initially emphasized easing the political, economic, and legal restrictions on Muslims to pursue Franco-Algerian integration.[51] Before the municipal elections took place, a leader in the Constantine Croix de Feu, Professor Stanislaus Devaud, approached Bendjelloul about a potential alliance. However, it is unlikely that Bendjelloul wanted a long-term partnership because he had refused to see several lower-level Croix de Feu men whom FEM members had brought to him several months prior. The prefect nevertheless played up the notion of a "tentative *rapprochement*" between the FEM and Croix de Feu based in large part on both group's anti-Semitic sentiments. As Joshua Cole points out, colonial officials consistently overstated anti-Semitic sentiments in Muslim communities as a way to blame them for anti-Jewish violence and thus divert attention from the government's failure to maintain order.[52] By late 1936 Bendjelloul regularly denied colluding with the Croix de Feu. He put it this way to an audience of 2,200 Muslims: "Some people want you to think that I was a Croix de Feu and my number was 113. That's false . . . I'm not a socialist, radical socialist, communist or Croix de Feu. I'm the Algerian Bendjelloul, who defends his Algerian brothers."[53]

From the perspective of far Right settlers, the possibility of collaboration with indigenous Algerians was demonstrated when several of them rose to prominence in the Croix de Feu. The most influential was the president of the Tizi-Ouzou section, Augustin Iba-Zizen. For the Croix de Feu, Iba-Zizen was an exemplar of the ideal *évolué* because he was a veteran and had converted to Catholicism. Iba-Zizen's speeches at meetings across Algeria were publicized widely, and he often drew large numbers of indigenous supporters. For instance, indigenous attendance at Croix de Feu meetings in Constantine-*ville* reached 8 percent in 1936, a figure that was unmatched (and temporary) in Greater France.[54] However, as will be discussed later in this chapter, Iba-Zizen evinced disdain for Islam that became more pronounced with the election of the Popular Front and the emboldening of anticolonial sentiment among key Muslim groups, including the FEM, which drove indigenous veterans from the movement in the late 1930s.

However, before these significant changes took place, authorities believed that the Croix de Feu's inroads among Muslim populations constituted a threat to state security. As Governor General Georges le Beau warned in late 1935, "Associating our Muslim subjects with the political quarrels of French citizens" endangered "our very sovereignty."[55] Le Beau instructed the Oran prefect to "take all useful measures to attempt to slow if not jam the rate of adhesions and to keep me informed of the size of the *indigène* contribution to the different parties."[56] Despite Le Beau's worry, indigenous support for the Croix de Feu throughout Algeria was quite small, clustered around the *évolués,* and peaked at around 4 percent of meeting attendees in 1936 and 1937 before dropping to zero in 1939 (Figure 10).[57] As for the exceedingly small number of indigenous Algerians who joined, a number of them expressed hatred for communism and referred to their own life experiences as proof of the success of France's civilizing mission. Indeed, Iba-Zizen was not alone in seeking to drive a wedge between the indigenous elites and the masses. In Constantine, for instance, at a meeting attended by 2,500, which included 250 indigenous Algerians, an M. Bouchedja stated that communists were seeking to take advantage of the "masses of ignorant *indigènes.*" Worried about the outbreak of the Spanish Civil War, he warned Algerian Muslims that they needed to reject communist propaganda coming out of Radio Barcelona that, as he explained, "called upon the Muslims of North Africa—from Tunis to Tangier—to take up arms and throw off the yoke of France." Claiming the orders were coming from

Moscow, Bouchedja summed up the feelings of virtually all who joined the Croix de Feu/PSF: "Communism is War!"[58] In this way, Bouchedja was one of many who feared that the civil war in Spain would spill over to North Africa. Like virtually all Croix de Feu supporters, he believed that the Spanish fascists—as "good nationalists"—were the best line of defense against the spread of communism.

In addition to its discriminatory admissions process and efforts to divide further the *évolués* and the masses, the Croix de Feu/PSF's divisive approach to providing social services constituted a third aspect of its hierarchical conception of North African societies. In distributing aid to the needy, Croix de Feu/PSF policy was to privilege those they considered French. In a November 1935 policy statement to social service providers in Morocco, the head of the Casablanca section sounded very much like Préval in explaining who was entitled to social services: "Your aid must go first to the French, and among them, to Croix de Feu, Briscards, and VN in need."[59] While this policy was blatantly discriminatory, there were occasions when individual women offered aid to Algerian families. The Women's Section in l'Arba, for example, established a soup kitchen and clothing depot for the indigenous community in late 1935 to act as favorable propaganda for the league.[60] Likewise, the Women's Section in Tiaret provided aid to indigenous Algerians on an occasional basis.[61] Far more typical, however, were the actions of the Cité Ausas Women's Section, which explicitly declared that it would only provide aid to Algerians who were PSF members.[62]

THE POPULAR FRONT, INDIGENOUS ACTIVISM, AND THE RACISM OF THE PSF

The Croix de Feu/PSF's failed attempts to recruit Muslims must be contextualized within the wider changes that took place in the political cultures of North Africa in the 1930s. Jonathan Wyrtzen argues that the rise of anti-French protest movements in the Muslim world "demonstrated the potential for the internationalization of anti-colonial protest within the unique transnational ecosystem that flourished in the interwar period."[63] A confluence of events in Tunisia, Algeria, and Morocco in 1930 and 1931 sparked indigenous protests, which exacerbated long-standing tensions between colonial subjects, settlers, and the state. Elaborate celebrations of the centennial conquest of Algeria took place in metropolitan France and Algeria in 1930 and featured triumphalist parades and speeches. The spectacle culminated with the huge 1931 colonial exhibition in Paris. In Tunisia, protectorate officials celebrated the semicentennial of conquest in a similar manner in 1931, while the Catholic Church organized an international Eucharist congress that conflated Tunisian history with Catholicism and featured youths dressed as crusaders who distributed pamphlets written in Arabic that promoted conversion.[64] In Morocco, a turning point in anticolonial activism occurred in 1930 with what became known as the Berber Dahir (a decree issued by the sultan), which was written in French and mandated that Berbers be governed according to their own laws and customs and not Islamic law, which applied to Arabs. Both Arabs and Berbers saw the dahir as part of the long-standing French plan to divide indigenous communities and privilege Berbers in preparing them for citizenship.[65] La Rocque's beliefs about the rise of indigenous activism and the threat it posed to Greater France reflected the racist fears of many in the Croix de Feu/PSF, which centered around Islam and its alleged ability to confront "Christian" Europe. He put it this way in *Service Public:* "A superficial observation of the Mohammedan world reveals that Islam is fully awakened and that today its vibrations spread almost instantaneously over thousands of kilometers."[66]

The election of the Popular Front played a key role in exacerbating settler fears and accelerating indigenous activism. John Ruedy explains the significance of the elections this way: "Overnight the political climate changed."[67] As the only interwar government to emphasize colonial reform in its election platform, the Popular Front had promised to end the worst excesses of colonialism.[68] To the Croix de Feu/PSF's dismay, the new government was particularly concerned about forced labor, colonial subjects' inadequate access to welfare, and the imprisonment of indigenous political leaders. The Popular Front's openness to reform spurred two major events in Algeria that galvanized indigenous reformers and further radicalized many settlers. First, indigenous Algerians organized the Algerian Muslim Congress, the first of its kind, in June to formulate a set of demands that would broaden the political, social, civic, and economic rights of Muslims.[69] Second, Popular Front officials offered a more moderate proposal that became known as the Blum-Violette bill, which promised full citizenship rights for Algeria's Muslim elites (around 25,000, or 2 percent of the population) without forcing them to abandon their personal status. These two events prompted virulent reaction by settlers who believed that the reforms would destroy French control of Algeria.

The Algerian Muslim Congress was a turning point in indigenous activism as individuals and groups who had divergent agendas came together to demand fundamental reforms. While the unity of the coalition was tenuous, the outcome of the Congress demonstrated to many settlers that indigenous activists were mobilizing in new ways. One of the organizers was the Algerian-based Association des Ulama Musulmans Algériens (AUMA), which was founded in 1931 and led by Shaykh Adb al-Hamid Ben Badis. The Ulama were religiously oriented cultural nationalists who emphasized the Islamic revivalism of the pan-Maghrebi *salafiyya* movement. Initially, the Ulama were willing to work with the French to expand Islamic teachings, emphasize the dignity of Islam, and promote equitable systems of justice.[70] In doing so, the AUMA articulated what became a central tenet of Algerian and Arabophone nationalism. In a 1932 work, *The Book of Algeria,* one of the leaders of the AUMA, Ahmad Tawfik al-Madani, put it this way: "Islam is my religion, Arabic is my language, Algeria is my fatherland."[71] Amidst the oppression of colonialism, the Ulama led the indigenous struggle for social authority by propagating this singular view of national identity, which erased Berber and Jewish contributions from North African history. While this assertion of Arab-Muslim nationalism would lead to state suppression and the Ulama's concomitant rejection of French colonialism in 1938, the opening created by the Popular Front led Shaykh Ben Badis and the AUMA to believe that negotiation with the French was possible.[72]

The other group that organized the Congress was Dr. Bendjelloul's FEM, which championed elite interests at the expense of the poor. While the Ulama were a part of a transnational colonial reform movement, the FEM developed within the context of Algeria's integration with France and the concomitant development of the colonial classification of the *élus.* The bulk of the FEM's rural support came from wealthy Muslim landowners who backed its integralist politicians.[73] While the FEM emphasized assimilation by demanding that the government expand Muslim access to French citizenship, it converged with the Ulama by highlighting the value of Islamic institutions and learning.[74]

A third group, Messali Hadj's ENA, attended the Congress as individuals, but its leaders were excluded from participating in its organization. While the ENA shared the Ulama's transnationalism, Messali diverged from the clerics in his secularism. Created in Paris in 1926 and initially aligned with the PCF, the ENA was especially interested in the plight of the poor and urban workers. Moreover, the ENA was one of the best-organized groups at the inaugural congress of the League against Imperialism and Colonial Oppression held in Brussels in 1927. It was here that the ENA distinguished itself by becoming the first to call for an independent Algeria, which helped Messali earn the distinction of being a "founding father" of Algerian nationalism.[75] For Ben Badis and Bendjelloul, while Messali's supposedly extremist calls for independence endangered the potential for reform, the ENA's metropolitan organization and Messali's personal prestige lent legitimacy to the Congress.[76]

Led by Ben Badis, Bendjelloul, and Ferhat Abbas (a leading reformer who used the rhetoric of republicanism to claim universal rights for all Muslims within French Algeria), the Congress produced an official program, the Charter of Demands, which called for an end to the structures that had subordinated Muslims throughout the colonial period. Significantly, the Charter was reformist—not anticolonial—in nature.[77] It demanded the suppression of the *indigénat* and pressed for significant legal reform to the *senatus consulte* by demanding that Muslims gain access to citizenship without ceding their personal status. It also insisted upon a reorganization of the Muslim judiciary, free teaching of the Arabic language, freedom of the Arab press, and equitable suffrage rights for men.[78] For his part, Messali rejected the notion that Muslims would ever achieve equity with the French, as the ENA began a campaign to reject the "attachment" of Algeria to France. At a public meeting in August at a stadium in Algiers, Messali "irrupted" at the Congress's delegation, demanding an end to the racial division and hatred embodied by the *indigénat* and proclaiming that only independence would free Algerians.[79] Messali's speech was a critical turning point for populist anticolonialism. From this point on, the ENA moved from being an émigré organization to a significant force in Algerian politics, establishing over sixty sections in only two months.[80]

While the indigenous coalition that comprised the Congress gradually fell apart, the Charter mobilized European settlers. According to the PSF's incendiary mouthpiece, *La Flamme,* Muslims sought to create an "eighty-million-strong Arab caliphate."[81] The first issue of *La Flamme* appeared in October 1936 as the movement's bimonthly press organ in North Africa. Its purpose, as its masthead proclaimed, was to serve as "the North African organ of French reconciliation." The paper's anti-Semitism, attacks on Muslims, defense of violence, and misrepresentation of facts to provoke readers' fear made it the most extreme of the movement's over sixty regional newspapers. Intended for readers in Algeria, Tunisia, and Morocco, it played a key role in radicalizing settlers and in the movement's growth. *La Flamme* charged that North African Muslims were conspiring to create an Arab empire based in Cairo and that the delegates at the Congress were in fact "agents" of pan-Islamism.[82] The PSF used this rhetoric regularly as the party became one of the most outspoken critics of the Charter, calling it a "monument of pretentious recklessness" that would never be realized.[83] PSF press outlets and speakers vilified Ben Badis, Messali, Abbas, and their one-time potential ally, Bendjelloul. Despite the radical differences between the Ulama, FEM, and ENA that contributed to the disintegration of the Congress, most PSF supporters believed that each group supported the Charter, which made all Arabs one in the same: anticolonialists conspiring to put an end to Greater France.

The second event that drove settler radicalization in 1936 was the Blum-Violette bill. A top member of the Popular Front government was the prominent Socialist, Maurice Violette, whom Blum named as the new minister of state. Violette had been the governor-general of Algeria in the 1920s, where he came to believe that continued French control of Algeria depended upon easing the draconian restrictions that affected most indigenous Algerians. Moreover, Violette knew that the settlers would oppose any change that they perceived would threaten their privileged status. For these reasons, he took a conservative approach to reform that characterized the bill by only addressing the issue of citizenship and only opening access to elite Muslims. Despite Violette's caution, the proposal nevertheless provoked virulent outrage among settlers because it recognized the possibility that practicing Muslims could have the same rights and status as French citizens. Assimilationist reformers like Bendjelloul and Abbas supported the bill. Islamists such as Ben Badis, believing that the proposal was evidence of a "workable partnership" with the French, supported it as well.[84] Predictably, Messali rejected the bill's entire premise and seized the opportunity to criticize its division of elite Algerians from poor peasants and urban workers. For ENA activists, the initiative was further evidence that only independence would emancipate indigenous Algerians.

Faced on two fronts with the prospect of Muslims gaining citizenship rights and expanding their sociopolitical influence, the PSF led the charge against growing demands for reform. The manner in which PSF supporters conflated the diverse agendas of Arab and Muslim reformers and activists into one threat to Greater France exhibited a mix of familiarity with the complexities of Maghrebian political culture and a paranoid fear that Muslims were plotting against Christians. Claiming, for example, that the Ulama would create an Islamic caliphate, *La Flamme* characterized what it would look like: "Tyranny by Terror! Here's the regime that the Ulama seek to impose on Algeria: inquisition, denunciation, boycotts, corporal punishment, the ax or the dagger."[85] Ignoring the fact that in 1936 the

AUMA accepted the possibility of a French Algeria, many PSF supporters believed that the Ulama were the Algerian agents of a wider Islamic revivalist movement that engulfed the Mediterranean world. The lead player in this new type of nationalism was the head of the Syro-Palestinian Congress, Emir Shekib Arslan. Delegates from the Congress challenged the British and French mandates in the Levant, which led to Arslan's exile and settlement in Geneva.[86] The PSF charged that because of Arslan, Geneva had become the center of Arab nationalism.[87] The PSF fixated on Arslan precisely because of his emphasis on Islamic revivalism and Europe-based internationalism. From Geneva, Arslan wrote numerous books and articles and published a newspaper called *La Nation arabe*, which made him an international figure that attracted Muslim and Arab nationalists from across Europe and the Mediterranean.[88] While Arslan emphasized Islamic unity he nevertheless attracted secular nationalists such as Messali Hadj, who worked with Arslan in 1935 when Messali fled French territories to escape a one-year jail sentence for urging Muslim soldiers to desert the French army.[89] In 1935, Arslan organized the first European Muslim Congress, which attracted Muslims and Arabs from across Europe, many of whom were living in exile or as émigrés. One of the largest contingents was a Paris-based group who envisioned the Congress as an opportunity to promote intellectual, social, and educational unity among Muslims.[90] The ENA also attended, encouraged by Arslan's demands for Muslim independence from Western occupation.[91]

The PSF press repeatedly claimed that Arslan sought to unify Muslims and anticolonial Europeans against Western occupation of North Africa and the Levant. The party believed that Arslan was "an agent of trans-alpine fascism" due to his support of Fascist Italy and Nazi Germany.[92] Arslan knew Mussolini personally and was impressed by the dictator's demands at the League of Nations that the British and French mandates in the Levant be abolished and local populations granted independence.[93] While Italy's brutal invasion of Libya in 1931 diminished Arslan's enthusiasm, by the mid-1930s he still believed that Mussolini's desire to reconstitute an Italian Mediterranean empire on Italy's "Fourth Shore" was the best way to rid it of French and British forces.[94] For this reason, Arslan sought the support of Mussolini and accepted donations from the Fascists. The Germans, Arslan believed, would never allow the Italians to create an excessively powerful empire and would thus keep Mussolini's power in check.[95]

For PSF supporters, Arslan's internationalism, calls for Muslim independence, and support of Italian interests against the French made him and his associates a dire threat to Greater France. PSF supporters also believed that the pan-Islamism of the Ulama made Ben Badis and his colleagues Arslan's top agents in the Maghreb. *La Flamme* warned readers that the language that Ben Badis used in his French language newspaper echoed Arslan's message. Attempting to incite fear, *La Flamme* quoted Arslan's newspaper: "We work equally for our neighbors, Tunisia and Morocco, which form with Algeria a nation with a common language and traditions, and where the populations have the same belief, the same spiritual formation, the same history, and the same interests. After these provinces comes the ARAB NATION, THE MUSLIM NATION, AND FINALLY THE ENTIRETY OF HUMANITY."[96] In claiming falsely that Arslan sought to create a caliphate, PSF supporters believed that he was the puppeteer behind an alliance between the Ulama and ENA and was maneuvering nationalists in the Maghreb to align with the fascists in Germany and Italy. As *La Flamme* put it, "the anti-French work is directed from Geneva by Shekib Arslan, from which, as everyone knows, is for the profit of Germany and Italy."[97]

For the PSF, this anticolonial coalition was international, and its leaders had complete freedom of movement inside and outside of metropolitan France. Arslan's reach, for example, extended into Paris. *La Flamme* periodically referenced a Paris restaurant in Montparnasse, Tlemcen, that was frequented by Arslan, Messali Hadj, and Habib Bourguiba, leader of the Tunisian nationalist Néo-Destour, implying that the restaurant was a hub for anti-French forces.[98] This anti-French coalition was bolstered by the ENA, which the PSF press noted led a series of anti-French demonstrations on July 14, 1935, in Paris, Lyon, and Toulon.[99] La Rocque himself questioned the loyalty of practicing Muslims in Paris and charged that the Paris mosque was a locus for anticolonial plotting. "The most worldly men and the humanitarians of our society continue to speak positively about the Paris Mosque," La Rocque warned sarcastically in criticizing the Popular Front's support for the mosque; instead, La Rocque proclaimed that the mosque was a "shelter where the enemies of our civilization meet."[100]

In addition to pan-Arabism, pan-Islamism, and European fascism, the last set of links that the PSF made between forces it considered anti-French connected the Ligue Internationale Contre l'Antisémitisme (LICA) to the Ulama and the PCF. Alfred Debay claimed that because "the majority of indigenous Algerians love France," it was a minority of troublemakers that sewed discontent with French rule.[101] *La Flamme* explained, "The best ally of communism in North Africa is LICA," whose leader, Bernard Lecache, wanted to create a "Judeo-Muslim block."[102]

Established in France in 1926, LICA's mission was to promote inclusion among different ethnoreligious groups. In doing so, Lecache was an outspoken opponent of the extreme Right and the Croix de Feu/PSF in particular. Consequently, he drew venomous reactions from the PSF, which derisively called him "the apostle for the union of the races."[103] Just as the PSF press selectively quoted Muslim press outlets to scare its readers, it did the same for the Jewish press. The PSF was particularly appalled by Lecache's influence in Muslim communities. At a 1937 meeting with native Algerians in Constantine, *La Flamme* derisively quoted Lecache as saying: "My indigenous comrades, know where to find your true friends. There are those who deny you from recovering your rights within the French family. Muslims must have their place beside us."[104]

Evidence of this so-called Judeo-Muslim bloc was supposedly everywhere. The PSF monitored every event where the Ulama and LICA worked together. At a conference that featured Lecache and one of the Ulama leaders, El Okbi, the PSF claimed that the two had unified and were plotting against the French. "Lecache advocated tight solidarity with Algerian Muslims," *La Flamme* noted, while "El Okbi also recalled the historical bonds that always united Muslims and Jews."[105] This was the type of solidarity that the PSF sought to undermine. After a municipal election in the summer of 1937 sent twelve Communists to the Algiers municipal council, the PSF stepped up its critiques. The election returns, it claimed, were the "result of too long of a period of egoism with regard to our Muslim brothers as well as a weakness towards foreign propaganda that exercises itself with impunity here against the French ... the guilty are the Jewish LICA, the communists, the Muslim Congress, the Ulama, and the ENA."[106]

Most PSF supporters believed that the Jewish presence in this "anti-French" coalition was the most pernicious because, they falsely claimed, Jews exercised a disproportionate political influence. One of the top PSF leaders explained it this way: "The PSF is against racism. However, it demands that the Jew enjoy all of our French rights in equally accepting all of the duties and acquiring the French soul. Blum doesn't have a French soul ... the PSF is against Blum-Violette and the creation of a Free Federation of Republics of North Africa, the goal of the Ulama and the Jews."[107] This anti-Semitism was common in PSF sections across Algeria. The PSF leader in Oran, for example, stated: "The Jewish question is neither a question of religion nor race but one of mentality and spirit. The Jewish spirit manifests itself in three characters: idealism, arrogance, and worry, to which one adds, the taste for revenge and the desire for power." The speaker added that the Jew was a "revolutionary by birth" and sought to "transform society by a total and violent revolution." Noting that the "Jewish spirit" was the basis for the Popular Front, which was represented by Lecache and LICA, he stated: "The Jewish question consists of two civilizations that oppose each other: ours, which seeks to model men on the world and theirs, which seeks to model the world on men. France doesn't want to reject those who would ask for refuge, but those who would come into its foyer must give sermons that champion French heritage and the Christian civilization."[108] PSF supporters thus feared that Jews and Muslims represented civilizations that were fundamentally opposed to the Christian civilization of Greater France.

THE PSF'S SOCIOPOLITICAL STRATEGY IN NORTH AFRICA: INTEGRAL CITIZENSHIP AND "ADAPT AND ASSIMILATE"

In confronting these alleged threats, the North African PSF was devoted to the movement's social mission, although North African leaders recast it for their own ends. At the party's first meeting after its creation in August of 1936, Alfred Debay explained its purpose to a raucous audience of twenty-eight hundred in Algiers: "the PSF's program is summed up in two words: Social French. Social First, because it's the root that places itself at the right to life and happiness of each of our fellow citizens."[109] An influential metropolitan report less than a year later outlined the PSF's ideological basis along similar lines by stating that the party sought to bring about social betterment across Greater France: "Our most important ideal and our practical goal is the SOCIAL, that is to say, the establishment of a better society and a more just and fraternal lifestyle between the most diverse elements of the Nation and of the French Empire."[110] The racism and violence in which settlers engaged illustrated a major problem for the North African Croix de Feu/PSF's strategy to seek social betterment. It refused to consider women as sociopolitical agents and was thus unable to obtain the support of women and men outside of settler communities. Moreover, the election of the Popular Front, the Algerian Muslim Congress, and the Blum-Violette proposal made debates over ethnoreligious integration a top political issue after June 1936.

La Rocque created a Commission for Indigenous Affairs in the summer of 1936 to craft the party's policy toward integrating indigenous Algerians into the French national community. While it was initially created to address Algerian problems, La

Rocque believed that the Commission's recommendations could apply to Tunisia and Morocco as well. The Commission's head was Augustin Iba-Zizen. As a Berber who converted to Catholicism, Iba-Zizen not only fulfilled long-standing stereotypes of the assimilable Muslim but embodied the movement's stance that France exerted a liberating force among oppressed peoples.[111] His religious, ethnic, and veteran status not only aligned with ideals preached by the movement's supporters but illustrated its approach to integrating Muslim subjects into Greater France: the French enlightened Muslims by revealing to them Algeria's Christian heritage. Debay explained it this way, writing that Iba-Zizen was "a Frenchman of the race of Saint Augustin … a lawyer, brilliant speaker, a Berber of pure blood who came to the Christian religion of his ancestors, and a *Tirailleur* officer decorated during the war."[112]

In his staunch defense of the French empire, Iba-Zizen saw himself as proof of the glories of the civilizing mission and a bridge between the settler and indigenous communities. His presence at meetings often drew large numbers of indigenous Algerians (especially Berbers when meetings took place around Tizi-Ouzou, in the heart of Kabylia). For example, at a PSF meeting in Constantine that was attended by four thousand, which included five hundred women and one hundred fifty indigenous Algerians, he said this to the settlers in the audience: "You came to Algeria to teach us to love France and convince us to assimilate to your culture and your civilization. … Let me remind you of the words of the great African, Saint Augustine, to whom the faithful came seeking advice. 'I have only one thing to give you' replied the bishop of Hippo, 'go everywhere and relight the fire of your faith.'"[113]

Iba-Zizen's assertion that France's Catholic heritage extended to North Africa and his disdain for Muslim culture had significant ramifications for the Maghreb because of the key role that the Commission played in crafting the PSF's political strategy in North Africa. The Commission submitted its findings to La Rocque in May 1937, and the party published its reports in prominent press outlets such as *Le Petit Journal* and *La Flamme* beginning in June 1937. La Rocque introduced the Commission's findings by defining the PSF's political strategy in Algeria: "Some may say 'Economics First' or 'Politics First,' to which the PSF responds, 'Social First.' This axiom applies to the Algerian problem *par excellence*."[114] Defining "Social First" in Algeria as "Adapt and Assimilate," La Rocque explained: "Adapt means raising by degree the standards of education and instruction of native civilization. Assimilate leads to progressively but effectively opening the door towards the exercise of integral civic rights and duties." Purposely avoiding the loaded term *association,* La Rocque nevertheless argued that a basis for association—evolution alongside but separate from settler societies—was a key to the social progress of indigenous communities.

Using the words *integral citizenship* and basing them upon the policy of "Adapt and Assimilate," the PSF sought to bridge the assimilation/association divide. If the Muslim Congress used the concept of assimilation liberally, and the Popular Front more conservatively through the Blum-Violette proposal, then the PSF carved out the space that reflected the beliefs of most French in the metropole and colonies: a Muslim's Frenchness was dependent upon abandoning his cultural and religious particularism (the PSF mentioned Muslim women only as objects of Muslim men's polygynous behavior). Debay explained it this way: "We think that what many have called 'the indigenous problem' is above all a social problem."[115] For Debay, the problems were rooted in what several top leaders, including La Rocque and Iba Zizen, referred to as the "indigenous temperament." Two of the major social problems that Debay cited—common in rhetoric claiming that subjects were not ready for citizenship—were the practice of polygyny (which was not widespread) and higher divorce rates among Muslim families than among French families (which Debay asserted based upon skewed statistics). Because the PSF was one of many groups that cast the family as the basic cell of the French nation, the supposed problems with which Muslim families struggled were convenient justifications to limit Muslim access to citizenship. Such alleged differences between French and Muslim families were where the "adapt" portion of the PSF's program applied; the Commission maintained that before the government could consider reforms such as abrogating the *indigénat,* it was first the responsibility of Muslims to change their own behavior.

The meat of the Commission's findings rejected Blum-Violette and the Charter and instead proposed a PSF "counter-project" that sidestepped the issue of granting rights in favor of bringing about a new *union sacrée.*[116] Essentially a defense of the 1865 *senatus consulte,* the counter-project was based upon what Iba-Zizen called "social harmonization," which centered around mutual understanding between Christians and Muslims. Iba-Zizen pointed out that Muslims were free to become French. All they had to do, as he had, was to cede their personal status. Iba-Zizen heaped criticism on reformers like Ben Badis, calling him a Muslim agitator who irrationally defended Muslims' personal status, which Iba-Zizen claimed legislation and jurisprudence had "reduced to almost nothing" that "no longer has a moral value." He added that "sycophants" lacking sincere faith used the personal status as a smokescreen to organize resistance to French rule. For Iba-Zizen, this "secular apathy" characterized the culture of Algerian Muslims, which he derogatorily maintained was the "daughter of the climate and decadence of a dying civilization."[117]

Explaining the PSF's policy, Iba Zizen identified four barriers that needed to be destroyed for harmonization between Christians and Muslims to occur: the attitude of the French in general, policies of the French administration, indigenous temperaments, and the behavior of indigenous elites. Iba-Zizen admitted that the French had not always acted properly, but that the changes necessary on both sides were in *attitude*, not in law, institutions, education, or any of the other structural sources of subjugation. The problems plaguing indigenous communities such as poverty, low literacy rates, and unemployment were not a result of oppressive politics and law codes but a social problem. "The Algerian problem is a problem of harmonization," he explained, arguing that the civil societies of settler and indigenous communities needed to be integrated by "creating a spirit of agreement" that would bring about "social evolution."[118] While Iba-Zizen argued that the French needed to acknowledge that indigenous communities faced numerous petty injustices, he heaped scorn on Algerian Muslims. He wrote: "There is the weight of blind fanaticism and prejudice that agitators and individuals cultivate against enterprises of the French spirit."[119]

Hope for the future of Greater France and the Algerian Muslims living under French rule, Iba-Zizen argued, was based upon convincing indigenous elites to embrace the social impetus of the French imperial project and reject nationalist causes. Emphasizing the superiority of French education and methods of bureaucracy, he explained, "it's a sociological principle that a people is transformed by its elite ... it is essential for us, the French of indigenous origin, nourished by French vigor, to assimilate ourselves to the best of the French spirit." For Iba-Zizen, true assimilation occurred when elites embraced a social approach to assimilation and, as he put it, "understand that social values cannot be neglected and that France has the duty to incorporate."[120] The key role that elites played in integration, according to Iba-Zizen, was the reason the PSF wanted to reward certain narrowly defined groups of indigenous Algerians for their loyalty to France by granting them citizenship rights so long as they abandoned their personal status: veterans, *évolués,* and functionaries.[121]

The Commission's proposal was presented by Stanislaus Devaud to the Chamber of Deputies in February 1938, in part as an alternative to Blum-Violette, but more importantly to appease the wide-ranging views of the PSF's membership. Indeed, the movement's conception of integral citizenship had something for everyone in its creation of the policy of "Adapt and Assimilate" and its rhetoric of social harmonization. Settlers who aligned with the *algérianiste* movement hailed the associationist elements of the proposal that preserved the status quo and denied Muslims citizenship.[122] The movements' North African leaders pointed to its assimilationist components, which retained the promise of the civilizing mission, and thus, the rationale of French colonialism and justification to resist reform. Metropolitan supporters of the civilizing mission could point to the long-term possibility of assimilation to claim that France's universal republicanism remained intact. In sum, the PSF crafted a political strategy based upon the universalist promise and ethnoreligious distinctions of republican imperialism.

THE FASCISM OF PSF SETTLERS IN NORTH AFRICA

The Commission's proposals revealed the PSF's racism, which when combined with violence, misogyny, and hatred of communism and socialism, led the North African PSF to have much in common with other European fascist movements. Samuel Kalman has pointed out that in Algeria the movement's use of violence was so pervasive that it constituted a strategy.[123] Indeed, racist attitudes and violence were widespread in Tunisia and Morocco as well. Rather than depend upon women's social action, the movement systematically deployed violence in rhetoric and action against those it deemed enemies, which rendered it a dangerously sectarian force throughout North Africa.

Anti-Semitism was a key component of Croix de Feu/PSF's contribution to the political violence that structured the interwar Maghreb. For example, many of the movement's sections in Tunisia, Morocco, and Algeria organized economic boycotts of Jewish businesses, and in the most extreme cases, encouraged members to buy only from businesses run by Croix de Feu/PSF members. The boycotts against Jewish businesses included those in Tiaret in July 1935, in Casablanca in 1936, in Batna in 1937, in Tunis in 1937, in Marrakech in 1938, and against all non-Croix de Feu/PSF businesses in Oran in February 1936 and in Meknès in 1939.[124] The movement's leader in Oran explained the rationale behind the Oran boycott in this way: "The principles of solidarity and entr'aide must exist between the movement's members; only buy from the Croix de Feu and boycott everything that's not Croix de Feu."[125] In some cases Jewish boycotts were accompanied by swastikas being painted on city walls and appearing on posters.[126] Indeed, Croix de Feu/PSF meetings throughout Tunisia, Algeria, and Morocco often ended with chants of "Down with Jews!," the fascist salute, and the singing of the "Marseillaise." Police in Morocco reported that copies of the *Protocols of the Elders of Zion* were floating around far Right circles in Fès.[127] La Rocque went so far as to place sanctions against members of the Sidi-bel-Abbès section for their anti-Semitism, but the sanctions failed, just as had La Rocque's directives to make women the cornerstone of the Algerian Croix de Feu.[128]

The most dramatic cases of violence were those that were politically oriented and physical. The largest loss of life occurred in Constantine in 1934 when twenty-five Jews and three Muslims were killed in anti-Jewish rioting in which Croix de Feu members likely played an inciting role.[129] In contrast to this dramatic display of violence, smaller bursts of violence occurred and worsened after the Popular Front's election; street fights themselves were nearly too numerous to count. Shootouts between the far Right and Popular Front rocked Tiaret, Tlemcen, Oran, and Algiers in the mid- to late 1930s. Nineteen were wounded in Ain-Temouchant after the July 14, 1936, national fête, four were wounded in Perrégoux, and eight wounded and two killed in Sidi-Bel-Abbès in March 1937.[130] *La Flamme* placed the blame for the March 1937 violence on PSF enemies, claiming that nationalists were attacked by a "howling pack of reds."[131] After the PSF did not do well in cantonal elections that took place in October 1937, the director of the Oran PSF's political bureau, Marcel Sarrochi, claimed that the party's poor showing was due to skirmishes caused by "an armed band of maniacs" that kept nationalists from voting.[132] Sarrochi perpetuated the widely held belief that PSF members were always victims and combined it with issuing threats: "The people of Oran will no longer tolerate being persecuted. If the methods employed continue, the Nationalists will be forced to reestablish order themselves."[133]

This sustained violence led to frequent crackdowns by the state in its attempts to preserve public order. On a regular basis, mayors banned Croix de Feu/PSF public meetings in Tiaret, Tlemcen, Tunis, Casablanca, and Oran; after riots in Rabat, authorities there banned Croix de Feu public meetings and restricted the league's flags and insignia in public spaces.[134] Algerian governor general Le Beau asked the interior ministry for a police state in Oran in early June 1936 after the Popular Front's victory led to riots between the leftist coalition and extreme

Right militants, who proceeded to go on a spree of violence throughout the city, attacking their opponents, injuring twelve, and killing one.[135] However, the state's actions to quell the violence had little effect, in large part because the Croix de Feu had supporters in local governments and on the police force.

It was not a coincidence that the place where Croix de Feu/PSF women and indigenous men were the most marginalized—Tunisia—also experienced the highest degree of repression and violence in French North Africa during the interwar period.[136] The Tunisian resident general had the authority to approve the formation of any political group, ban political and religious meetings and unauthorized assemblies, and detain those suspected of sedition without trial.[137] The residency's suppression of indigenous activism combined with the economic struggles and barriers faced by the indigenous population contributed to the rise of anticolonialism during the interwar period.[138] One of the most influential groups was the Confédération Générale des Travailleurs Tunisiens (CGTT), which was created in 1924. Discontented workers created the group in the aftermath of a dock strike, and they established a platform that rejected gradual reforms and the notion of French sovereignty altogether.[139] Like Messali's ENA, the CGTT was one of the first groups in Tunisia to insist that reforming a colonial system based upon ethnoreligious subordination was impossible. The growing numbers of Tunisians who supported such principles led the metropolitan government to broaden the residency's authority to arrest political activists and ban newspapers that expressed hostility to the French, the protectorate, and the bey, in 1926.[140] The CGTT was joined in 1933 by the secular anticolonialist Néo-Destour (which broke off from Destour, an elite reformist movement), led by Habib Bourguiba, which called for an end to settler dominance by demanding increased access to the franchise for Muslim men, reforms to the tax structure, and equitable pay.[141] As *La Flamme* pointed out, Bourguiba traveled in transnational anticolonial networks that included Arslan, Messali, and leaders of the Moroccan National Action Bloc. However, contrary to what *La Flamme* claimed, Bourguiba's demands were specific to the Tunisian protectorate, centering around a rejection of French sovereignty and the preservation of Muslims' personal status.

Néo-Destour's strong influence and increasingly public disdain for French rule led the residency to govern more and more through decree powers. Colonial officials regularly imprisoned nationalist leaders like Bourguiba, sentenced them to internal exile, and banned Néo-Destour and the CGTT along with their press outlets. The Croix de Feu/PSF was a champion of the resident general behind the most repressive measures, Marcel Peyrouton, who had no qualms about jailing Bourguiba to suppress nationalist sentiment. As *La Flamme* put it, "Peyrouton understood the danger" of Arabs who demanded full political rights, and it insisted that Peyrouton was right to jail them for anti-French activity.[142]

The election of the Popular Front further radicalized the Tunisian Croix de Feu/PSF in much the same way as it did in Algeria and Morocco. The leftist coalition appointed a new resident general in Tunisia to replace Peyrouton, Armand Guillon, who applied the government's amnesty of political prisoners quicker than other North African colonial administrators.[143] The freeing of leaders like Bourguiba, combined with Guillon's lifting of press restrictions and broadening of the freedom of assembly, further infuriated most settlers.[144] *La Flamme* proclaimed: "While Peyrouton assured long months of social peace in Tunisia with the exile of Bourguiba and his lieutenants, Armand Guillon believed himself to be a shrewd policy-maker when he opened up the sheep's pen with reverence to his wolves and closed his eyes to their maneuvers."[145]

The Croix de Feu/PSF's support of Peyrouton and disdain for the Popular Front's reforms were rooted in the movement's campaign to deny the expansion of rights to anyone that its supporters considered "anti-French." For the Croix de Feu/PSF, the pervasive presence of anti-French forces in Tunisia underlined its hatred of democratic forms of government. Shortly after the May 1936 election, the Croix de Feu/PSF's leader in Tunisia, Dr. Minguet, proclaimed that elections featured "favoritism and rancor," which engendered "jealousy, plotting, and covetous" behavior.[146] The Popular Front and Guillon lacked legitimacy, Minguet believed, because they catered to the wishes of anti-French forces like Néo-Destour and the CGTT rather than French nationalists who sought to preserve French sovereignty, and more importantly, he claimed, peace.

The PSF's authoritarianism, incessant criticism of the Popular Front, and defense of settler interests made it one of the largest political groups in Tunisia by 1937. The PSF blamed Bourguiba and the Popular Front for riots near Bizerte that killed six in March of 1937, for a phosphate miners' strike near Metlaoui that killed sixteen later that month, and for four other incidents that resulted in dozens of injuries and several deaths.[147] The PSF itself instigated violence numerous times, including during the Bastille Day celebration in July 1937. Joined by the PPF, PSF supporters descended on the parade routes in major Tunisian cities seeking to demonstrate ultranationalist dominance of the Tunisian streets and assert the permanency of the French presence in Tunisia. The PSF and PPF lambasted anyone they considered enemies, making the fascist salute and shouting "Power to La Rocque!" and "Down with Guillon!"[148] Popular Front supporters responded by holding a counterdemonstration, and violent clashes ensued, injuring as many as sixty. Claiming that its supporters were simply preserving public order and their right to celebrate the national fête, the PSF blamed "Leftist extremists" for the violence.[149]

The PSF's strident opposition to the Popular Front and Néo-Destour led the party to become the largest group on the Right in Tunisia by 1938.[150] This growth only exacerbated the violence. Néo-Destour was frustrated with the Popular Front's failure to fulfill its promises concerning political and social reforms and the government's tepid response to reining in the PSF and PPF. Bourguiba thus called for a general strike that April. In what became a watershed moment, the strike degenerated into a riot as the PSF and PPF supporters provoked Néo-Destour activists with the fascist salute and chanting of fascist slogans. Attempting to secure order, the police fired at the rioters; while authorities stated that twenty-two were killed, demonstrators claimed the death toll was closer to two hundred.[151] Néo-Destour was banned and as many as three thousand of its activists were arrested, yet the PSF did not face any severe repercussions. Instead, it focused on the violence that had occurred since the Popular Front took power by claiming that forty-three people had been killed and over three hundred injured in eleven outbreaks of violence.[152] Placing the blame squarely on the Popular Front and chiding Resident General Guillon for his pie-in-the-sky optimism, *La Flamme* recounted what took place during the April riots in Tunis: "Rabid and howling hordes surrounded the Palace of Justice, swarming security services with sticks, daggers, and revolvers, throwing stones at cars, burning tramways.... These are the results of the so-called 'crowning dignity' of the optimistic politics of Armand Guillon and his lackeys."[153] It was not until a riot broke out in Tunis at the Bastille Day celebration of 1938 that the residency ended its leniency toward the PSF, banning all parades, the party's insignia, and *La Flamme*.[154]

The Croix de Feu/PSF was thus a key player in the extreme violence that crippled Tunisia after the Popular Front took power. As Martin Thomas points out, security forces were called out more often in Tunisia than in Morocco and Algeria, and the repressive measures in place in Tunisia in 1939 were the most severe anywhere in the empire since the Yen Bay mutiny in 1930–1931.[155] Despite the residency's leniency toward the PSF, it was only in Tunisia that *La Flamme* was banned, and the PSF catalogued more deaths and injuries due to political violence there than in Algeria and Morocco.

CONCLUSION

The North African Croix de Feu/PSF's use of violence and its insistence that the civilizing mission was the central rationale for empire enabled the movement to play a leading role in rejecting reforms proposed by indigenous activists and the Popular Front. In Algeria, the PSF helped to discredit the Charter and defeat the Blum-Violette bill, which drove the AUMA's shift from seeking negotiation with the French to anticolonial activism. Increasing numbers of reformers came to agree with the ENA's supposedly "extreme" stance: the only path toward emancipation was independence. In Morocco, whereas in 1934 the National Action Bloc issued a moderate list of constitutional reforms that broadened indigenous access to the franchise, loosened economic restrictions, and called for better access to education and health care, their willingness to seek a partnership had diminished by 1937.[156] Indeed, 1937 was a turning point in Moroccan nationalism; as in Tunisia, the residency cracked down on activists by jailing and exiling leaders and banning press outlets. Nationalists thus came to believe that pursuing reforms was a "dead end."[157] Ultimately, the growth of the Croix de Feu/PSF into the largest far Right movement in North Africa played a key role in driving many indigenous activists from reformism to anticolonialism. While women's influence led the metropolitan Croix de Feu/PSF to moderate tactically, their marginalization in North Africa directly influenced the latter's radicalism. It would be a mistake, however, to consider the metropolitan and North African Croix de Feu/PSF fundamentally different. While their practices may have taken different forms in the imperial nation-state, the movement's anticommunism, staunch Catholicism, and assertion of a unique French temperament defined the Social First! mission and was consistent across the borders of the Mediterranean. Such extremism had dire consequences in North Africa and metropolitan France alike.

7

"THE ARMY OF THE GOOD"

VICHY AND THE FEMINIZATION OF THE

CROIX DE FEU/PSF, 1939–1945

While Croix de Feu/PSF leaders railed against the ineffectiveness of the Third Republic throughout the 1930s, they rarely offered specific proposals as to what a Croix de Feu/PSF government might look like. The movement's Social First! strategy to achieve national reconciliation was ideally suited to garner support from the many bourgeois French who were disillusioned with the Third Republic's inability to grapple with economic problems, internal division, and foreign aggression, without offering a specific plan as to how its leaders would actually govern. The German invasion of France, the evacuations that followed, and the fall of the Third Republic, confirmed the beliefs of many Croix de Feu/PSF supporters that secular parliamentary republicanism had weakened the French nation. In contrast, the new Vichy leader, Marshal Henri Philippe Pétain, represented what the movement had called for throughout the previous decade: a military man of discipline who would save France based upon his belief in authoritarian hierarchy and Greater France's status as a Christian civilization. Despite the disaster and tragedy of 1940, Vichy's initial popularity led many Croix de Feu/PSF supporters to believe that the Social First! strategy was working (albeit applied differently in metropolitan France and North Africa) because increasing numbers of French women and men supported the movement's basic principles.

Emboldened by the public's acceptance of an authoritarian regime, the PSF's political director, Edmond Barrachin, offered one of the clearest statements ever provided by a top leader in terms of how the movement would govern France. In March 1942 he informed the U.S. State Department that three prominent political tendencies existed in Vichy France: the Pétainists (Vichyites), the Gaullists (resisters), and collaborationists (fascists).[1] As Pétainists, Barrachin explained that he and his fellow supporters were distinct from the latter two because the PSF was motivated by purely French considerations. They sought to defend French political and territorial sovereignty, which they believed was Pétain's goal as well. Yet this avowed support for the Marshal was misleading. Barrachin went on to tell the U.S. official that with the death of the elderly Pétain or some other crisis, the PSF would immediately step in and take control of the government. Barrachin stated exactly what would happen: the PSF would set up an "authoritarian form of government with a dummy parliament having an upper and lower house, the members of which would be appointed rather than elected."[2] This would be a legitimate action, he claimed, because the PSF represented the general will of the French people. While the U.S. official explained to Barrachin that he had not described a democratic government, Barrachin rejected him outright and insisted that the PSF embodied an authoritarian republic.

While the PSF fragmented under Vichy, women's influence continued to grow. Several leaders joined the government as collaborators, others joined the resistance, and some (including Barrachin) defected to the Allies.[3] In metropolitan France, however, the movement's social action remained intact and adapted to the changing conditions brought about by the German occupation, widespread material shortages, and Vichy's persecution of minorities and political dissidents. The metropolitan movement channeled nearly all of its energy into social action and became one of the premier aid organizations during the Vichy period, while the North African branch was unable to transform itself and declined as an organization. The influence of the metropolitan movement thus continued to increase due to women's social action, which was all the more important after around one hundred fifty of the movement's male leaders were arrested and deported in 1943, leaving it effectively feminized. Women's high status was recognized by the Allies as they prepared for the D-Day invasion. Not only did they categorize the movement as one of the most important organizations in France, but the Supreme Headquarters of the Allied Expeditionary Force called it "a social welfare organization ... run mainly by women."[4] This was a far cry from the Croix de Feu of 1927.

This chapter seeks to show that the feminization of the Croix de Feu/PSF was rooted in two interrelated factors that were central to the movement's actions since the early 1930s.[5] First, the movement's leaders had always believed that they alone represented and protected the interests of the national community. This belief defined the veteran's mystique of the early Croix de Feu and was a key reason why La Rocque did not join the right-wing coalitions that formed to fight the Popular Front, including the National Front in 1935 and the Liberty Front in 1937. Refusing to cede autonomy, he preferred to emphasize the movement's status as the leading defender of true France. So long as Croix de Feu/PSF supporters believed that Vichy protected French territorial and political sovereignty, they supported collaboration. However, once they—like many French—saw that Vichy capitulated to the Germans and had limited control over French foreign and domestic interests, their support dwindled, which led some of them to engage in resistance activities. Indeed, Simon Kitson has argued that the concept of sovereignty is as analytically important in understanding the Vichy period as collaboration, accommodation, and resistance.[6] The Croix de Feu/PSF fits clearly in this vein. The growth of its social action, and the folding of collaboration and resistance into social action, were rooted in the movement's efforts to protect French sovereignty.

Second, like many collaborators, the movement's supporters understood political and territorial sovereignty in the context of the culture of war. Their tendency to conceive of themselves as good soldiers fighting evil accelerated dramatically with the German invasion and was a pervasive component of their speeches and writings thereafter. Both women and men used terms such as army, soldier, post, fight, and battle to insist that their social action would save France. In doing so, Croix de Feu/PSF activists, like so many French, were faced with a series of morally wrought choices concerning how to survive, whom to support, and what would be the most effective way to maintain the movement's influence.

THE EVACUATIONS, EXODUS, AND CREATION OF THE ADP,
SPRING 1939–JUNE 1940

Nazi Germany's aggressive foreign policy, its *"Anschluss"* with Austria, and its seizure of the Sudetenland made many French fear that war was inevitable. Remembering the horrors brought about by the German occupation of northern France during the Great War and the establishment of the western front across some of France's most populated and economically significant areas, public and private officials began to organize defense strategies, which included the creation of a new association, Passive Defense. The group's officials worked with the government by distributing gas masks, providing instructions to individuals on how to bombproof their homes, organizing evacuation plans, and preparing the public for a German onslaught by teaching them how to respond to firebombing, shelling, and gas attacks.[7] These plans included driving evacuees and refugees to train stations, accompanying evacuation convoys on foot, and directing refugees to welcome centers. Planning focused on urban areas whereby evacuations would take place on a block-by-block basis, led by women and men who would guide children, the elderly, and the infirm out of major cities and villages toward refugee shelters set up at sites along evacuation networks.[8]

PSF leaders were torn over the best way to capitalize on public sentiment, which they believed was receptive to a new *union sacrée*. The PSF could either maintain the autonomy of its extensive social service network or coordinate its services with Passive Defense. To strike a balance, PSF leaders created a new group in May 1939, the Auxiliaries to Passive Defense (ADP), which worked with public and private officials to expand the PSF's influence and, La Rocque and Préval hoped, make them dependent upon ADP services and personnel. Initially, the ADP's mission centered around providing material assistance by establishing welcome centers, using the centers to help in planning for orderly evacuations, and creating aid stations in vulnerable cities and towns.

This was when the ADP created a crucial partnership with Secours National, an aid organization that had close ties with the government. During the Great War, Secours National had played the leading role in coordinating welfare services; it was revived for similar purposes in 1939. While the ADP's relationship with Secours National would change over the course of the following years, initially the two groups worked together to find, collect, transport, and warehouse vital materials such as scrap iron, tin, woolens, and paper. La Rocque believed that this action was critical because it would demonstrate that the government and civil society were dependent upon the ADP.[9]

Because PSF social action dotted the entirety of northern France, the movement was in a unique position to contribute to the government's passive defense strategies. Upon its creation, ADP supporters of both sexes transformed their social centers and summer camps into welcome centers that could house refugees and provide rudimentary medical care. ADP social action in Calvados, for instance, comprised four centers with the capacity to hold around one thousand beds, dispense material provisions (food and blankets), and offer triage services to as many as ten thousand refugees.[10] This combination of material aid and medical care distinguished the ADP from Secours National, which provided welfare services such as soup kitchens, clothing depots, kindergartens, and workshops for the unemployed, and the Red Cross, whose mission focused on public health and finding missing persons.[11] As a part of this massive planning, the ADP emphasized the mobility of its personnel. They could distribute Passive Defense instructional brochures, transport the infirm to train stations, and drive them out of towns and cities. ADP delegates and nurses who ran the centers could become part of a network to guide refugees out of danger and point them to the next center, taking them further south toward safety.

The evacuation plans were put into effect when the Germans attacked Poland in September 1939, dragging the reluctant French into the war. Panic and fear followed for some people living on the northern borders, particularly those in Alsace and Lorraine. The ADP worked with Passive Defense, Secours National, and the Red Cross to help the refugees flee to central France, particularly the Indre, Haute-Vienne, Vienne, Charentes, and Dordogne. ADP officials claimed to have provided fifty tons of goods, including blankets, clothing, layettes, undergarments, hats, and toys, through their welcome centers located in those departments. Large clothing depots in Paris and Lyon provided additional materials, which ADP members transported by train and car.[12]

Working with the government was more chaotic than ADP delegates had expected, which intensified their disgust with republican officials. PSF activists were just some of many who accused public officials of being grossly unprepared for war, citing "grave" and "urgent" problems.[13] Of particular concern were numerous cases where refugees had fled their homes in Alsace and returned several months later to find them looted and the remaining materials inside, such as linens, deteriorating because the inhabitants had left their windows open to depressurize their dwelling in case of bombings.[14] In some cases, life savings and family heirlooms were either stolen or destroyed. Refugees who did not return home, those in the Haute-Vienne for instance, found themselves moved repeatedly to different refugee centers. ADP officials charged that local prefects either refused or were too incompetent to collaborate with different aid groups, which resulted in an uneven distribution of basic services.[15]

The Phony War was thus characterized by a hardening of disdain toward the government on the part of many ADP supporters and PSF leaders' weakening resolve to work with it. While the ADP still collaborated with other public and private aid groups, its leaders sought to increase their autonomy by subsuming all PSF social action into the ADP. *Travail et loisirs* was temporarily suspended so that its personnel, offices, social centers, and summer camps could operate under the purview of the ADP; AMSJA's health services and personnel were redirected to run ADP dispensaries; Social Action organized ADP welcome centers to provide food and clothing to refugees and evacuees.[16]

La Rocque and Préval believed that the transformation of the ADP necessitated a slight restructuring so that supporters could clearly understand the organization's hierarchy and purpose. The Executive Council that organized PSF social action now headed the ADP, with La Rocque as its president. The Executive Committee included Préval, who continued to direct social services and was outranked only by La Rocque and Jeanne Garrigoux, who continued to organize staffing and coordinate social services. One of Préval's most important duties with the ADP was to balance the organization's autonomy and work with private and public aid organizations.[17] Of all the members of the Executive Committee, it was Préval who was the most indispensable. The colonel explained, "It's Mademoiselle de Préval who has completely animated all this work and who is charged at the same time with the coordination of all our social works.... Without her, the ADP would not be able to succeed."[18]

ADP leaders were determined to increase the organization's ability to aid evacuees and refugees in northern and central France. To this end they expanded their efforts to reach beyond local social centers and summer camps by increasing the number of aid stations. Run by personnel who had worked for Travail et loisirs, AMSJA, and Social Action, the ADP created eighteen hundred aid stations by early 1940. Most were located in train stations and staffed by certified nurses, stretcher bearers, telephone operators, agents who coordinated with other aid groups, and individuals with bicycles and cars to facilitate movement and transportation.[19] In describing ADP initiatives, Garrigoux urged staffers to make ADP centers feel like home. "These offices, or 'the house,'" she said, "is the center of our action, open and welcoming, where radiance meets action.... It's the information provided, the welcome, the smile, the outstretched hand, the fraternal sharing of sorrow and joy, the friendship that comforts and [helps] recovery."[20]

ADP supporters believed that these aid offices were at the frontlines for the defense of France and that the social delegates who staffed each station were like soldiers assigned to a post. Garrigoux explained that the first priority of a social delegate was to "remain loyal and present at her post," so that she could fight in the "struggle against the elements of disintegration and disorder."[21] For Garrigoux, faith was a key motivating factor, which she explained comprised learning about the Croix de Feu "mystique" and its legacy of defending France from all threats. Garrigoux explained that faith was "formed in the climate of honor and fidelity, providing the apostles for all the generous causes that they use today to defend the frontiers of France."[22] In likening ADP social delegates to apostles, Garrigoux emphasized the values of Christianity, soldierly duty, and nationalism that motivated many Croix de Feu/PSF supporters.

Garrigoux's unwavering belief that she and her fellow social delegates were soldiers for France was tested in the most dramatic way possible with the German attack in May 1940 and subsequent exodus of eight million civilians from northern France. As the scope of these evacuations dwarfed those from the previous fall, the PSF leaders believed that government ineptitude was on display once again. The unanticipated volume of refugees overwhelmed public and private officials. As French defenses crumbled, ADP leaders urged their supporters to maintain an "intensive organization" and "spirit of solidarity." However, it quickly became clear that the scope of the evacuations was more massive than anyone had anticipated, especially in rural areas and small villages.[23] Only those ahead of German troop advances believed they could stay and fight. As the heads of the ADP in Clermont-Ferrand informed Préval, "We are ready to fight using our Social Action bases in order to establish the indispensable union between all French that will maintain France."[24] Once they saw that the German military was overwhelming the French, however, ADP personnel fled. ADP activists in Lille, for instance, evacuated the city along with the rest of the population on May 21, giving their clothing depot keys to the Sisters of Saint Vincent de Paul.[25] When members returned two days after the armistice agreement, they found wounded soldiers in hospitals and schools in dire need of medical care, food, and clothing, although they lacked the materials necessary to alleviate widespread misery.

The violence and chaos of the exodus would be difficult for many to forget and became a formative experience for many in the Croix de Feu/PSF. Those living in the North did not return to their homes for a significant period of time; La Rocque and Préval fled with the government to Bordeaux before they settled in unoccupied Clermont-Ferrand. Communications broke down throughout northern France, and ADP personnel were forced to operate on an ad hoc basis. One of the most devastating moments for Préval came when she learned that Garrigoux had been killed as she accompanied an evacuee convoy to a refugee station. It was Préval who wrote Garrigoux's obituary, which appeared in the movement's regional press: "[Garrigoux] considered her professional life not a job but a calling. Her openly Christian existence was marked by a sign of faith. In service to God, she served the French family... modest and enthusiastic, this sister of work died accompanying people who were suffering and menaced. Soldier of God, she was killed on our homeland as an apostle of Christian civilization."[26] Both Préval and La Rocque had to endure further pain upon learning of the death of one of La Rocque's sons, Jean-François, who was killed when his plane was shot down during the Battle for France (another son, Gilles, was wounded). Their lives uprooted, many supporters learned of the death of loved ones, worried over the fate of those who were missing, and grappled with the shock of France's quick defeat to Nazi Germany after only six weeks of fighting. Their already low trust in public officials disintegrated completely, and their long-standing fears of an existential threat that France might cease to exist became a reality.

THE ADP AND VICHY: EXPANSION AND CAPITULATION

On one hand, the events of May and June 1940 embodied the worst fears of many PSF supporters. France had fallen, the nation was literally divided into various sectors, and the *patrie* was occupied by a foreign power that many regarded as pagan. On the other hand, the new regime at Vichy epitomized their ideal vision of the best type of government. Finally, a military man of integrity was the head of an authoritarian government that had no patience for Communists, Socialists, and foreigners whose loyalty to France was questionable. Perhaps most promising, many supporters believed that their efforts to promote France's Catholic heritage had helped pave the way for the Catholic precepts of Vichy's National Revolution. In this way there was hope that this was the beginning of national rejuvenation.

As per Vichy's dissolution of political parties, La Rocque simply dropped what was left of the movement's political arm in favor of social action and renamed it the Progrès Social Français (PSF). Convinced that social action and the National Revolution were inextricably intertwined, the PSF's administrative committee issued a revealing pronouncement: "Before the war and since its creation, all forms of social activity represent just under seventy-five percent of the PSF's effort; since September 2, 1939 ... social activity represents one hundred percent of the PSF's activity. ... National renovation depends exclusively on generalized civic and social activity inspired from the principles adopted by the Government of Marshal Pétain."[27] This was the first of many pro-Pétain statements emanating from the PSF's leadership.[28] Several PSF leaders joined Pétain's cabinet and La Rocque took on a role as a consultant. Despite this early collaboration, La Rocque never abandoned one of his most important concerns: maintaining the PSF's autonomy. As La Rocque put it in a letter to the movement's supporters, "the PSF is established across the entire country … it has the best organization among all the private groups and it's the one that can be most useful."[29]

Stripped of all political vestiges, La Rocque and Préval reorganized the renamed PSF and its most important affiliated group, the ADP (renamed the Artisans du Devoir Patriotique), to operate in the occupied and unoccupied zones. The movement had experienced dramatic upheaval as many of its members had been mobilized, several of its largest and most vibrant sections were under German occupation, and its leadership had been scattered across the country.[30] To adapt to these new circumstances, the organization maintained a headquarters in German-occupied Paris and added one in the free zone at Clermont-Ferrand. La Rocque headed the eight-member executive committee, which included Gérus and Préval; Renée Binet, a top Travail et loisirs official and long-time director of the Billancourt social center, was named the technical director of the ADP in the occupied zone. Departmental delegations organized the administrative and technical details of running ADP centers, which included the establishment of directors who ran each center and provided its services.

While ADP leaders were in mourning and struggled to replace Garrigoux, the ADP's leadership structure remained relatively intact. Several administrative changes, however, had direct implications for the ADP's role in collaboration. Pétain placed Secours National under his personal patronage and required all French aid organizations to work under its purview.[31] In September 1940 the French received permission from the German armistice commission for Secours National to operate in the occupied zone. The Germans placed Secours National under the auspices of the French Red Cross, which was controlled by the German Red Cross, and in theory, "put all civilian aid in France under German authority."[32] Such a structure was especially important because the ADP was now dependent on subsidies from Secours National to fund its social services. Consequently, every ADP departmental delegation appointed a delegate to work with what was now Vichy's civilian aid organization.[33] While the ADP's dependence on Secours began before Vichy—in early 1940, it wrote a 100,000 franc check to Préval to finance ADP welcome centers—it was now beholden to it because the ADP lost its autonomy in determining budgetary priorities.[34]

The ADP still managed to expand its social services despite a range of challenges. A key reason for its success was that the sole aspect of PSF activity—its social action—was by and large done by women who were able to remain at their posts. Moreover, by the 1940s, many of them had become experienced in finding resources, publicizing services, organizing staff, and distributing aid. In addition to the eighteen hundred aid stations they had created as a part of the Passive Defense strategy, from 1941 to 1944 ADP social centers increased from around fifty to two hundred fifty and its sewing rooms increased from around five hundred to four thousand.[35] Supporters also started several new initiatives, including ADP-affiliated restaurants that offered reduced-price meals and roughly three thousand "worker's gardens," or small plots of land that could be used to grow vegetables. The largest initiative was to send desperately needed care packages to prisoners in France and Germany. To accomplish the daunting mission of gathering up goods during times of scarcity, ADP leaders created a network of "Jean Mermoz" centers, most of which were located in the southern zone.[36] The contents of the packages that women created at the centers included corned beef, dried fish, dried fruits, jams, sugars, chocolate, tobacco, soaps, books, and blankets. However, local leaders often had trouble locating enough foodstuffs to constitute a package. The Jean Mermoz center in Marseille, for instance, blamed the head of the local Red Cross for refusing to help the ADP gather enough goods.[37] In this case, the ADP and Red Cross were more of competitors than collaborators. Nevertheless, the ADP established around twenty-four centers and 260 branches.[38]

The armistice agreement and establishment of the Vichy government brought a degree of stability back to French society—so long as one was not Jewish—which led the PSF to lift the suspension of its associations and place them under the purview of the ADP. SPES, for instance, was now headed in the occupied zone by Binet.[39] While Travail et loisirs reinstituted its summer camps, SPES reestablished its physical education programs, and AMSJA reconstituted its clinics, the effectiveness with which the services functioned was uneven. In many cases across France, centers were understaffed and had trouble attracting participants. One SPES section head complained to Gaëtan Maire that the Germans inhibited his group's ability to function effectively. The center would have to temporarily close, he noted, because his section was unable to attract enough participants.[40] The military requisitioned AMSJA's convalescent home in Pau in August 1939; in July 1940 the Paris prefecture ordered AMSJA's Parisian health clinic to dispense fresh milk, which it did, averaging around two hundred liters per day. It also continued to provide health care, but without several critical funding sources it struggled to maintain the full range of services for its clients, most of whom were on social assistance and could barely pay their rent. Despite a lack of money and personnel, during 1943 the clinic was still able to help 1,370 families and conduct 2,377 consultations.[41]

"THE ARMY OF THE GOOD" AND THE METAMORPHOSIS OF THE CROIX DE FEU/PSF

Aside from Vichy's authoritarianism, the regime's most attractive feature for PSF supporters was its strident, pervasive, and exclusionary Catholicism. Indeed, most members believed that Vichy had opportunistically taken advantage of a general will that had been shaped by Croix de Feu/PSF's ethnoreligious nationalism. For this reason, many of them continued to believe that the PSF remained at the vanguard of preserving France's status as a Christian civilization. One ADP member explained it this way: "The social activity of the ADP . . . and the inspiration that animates it proceeds with the same spirit: profoundly Christian, passionately French, and always Croix de Feu."[42]

Préval remained the driving force to frame the movement's social services in Christian terms and pointed to activists like Garrigoux as proof that ADP supporters were soldiers willing to die as martyrs. Indeed, Préval's tendency to see the world in terms of good and evil was magnified by the war. As she explained in a speech at the ADP congress in October 1942, "The ADP are *soldiers* in the *Army of the Good,* where one loves to suffer cheerfully, sometimes often, for the benefit of the general interest."[43] Préval admired Garrigoux's devotion to France and referred to the concepts of war and duty to influence supporters who struggled to cope with the pressures they faced as ADP members. For example, addressing a social delegate in the Haute-Savoie (Annecy), Madame Barrucand, who was considering leaving the ADP, Préval cast "the social" as the singular duty for all good French. While Barrucand's reasons for considering leaving were unclear, Préval was determined to keep personnel whom she considered indispensable, and she used the language of battle to do so: "The social assistant is made to suffer from repeated sadness and attempt to redress it invisibly; it's the palliative of life. In these tragic hours we must give the example of unity despite everything that's against us. A true woman like yourself must understand. As for leaving your post in these present moments (!!!!) it's unbelievable. I've known soldiers in the trenches who couldn't do it."[44] Préval insisted that the social assistant's duty was to lose herself in her mission, whereby she could transcend the daily grind of emotional distress by focusing on the greater cause of her work. This type of dedication and sense of conviction were key reasons why ADP services continued to grow as women drew significance from their patriotic sacrifice.

Perhaps most significantly for Préval, the advent of Vichy had issued in a new phase in the movement's ability to bring about social rejuvenation. At the ADP Congress in 1942, Préval thanked her social teams in the occupied and unoccupied zones and praised those who managed to obtain papers to move between both to facilitate better communication between ADP offices. She noted that the values of the Croix de Feu mystique were infused in the ADP and contended that the war had brought about what she called a "metamorphosis." It was not enough, she said, to simply nominate an army officer or male doctor as a social delegate or administrator because the nominations were too often made in haste and resulted in unqualified men obtaining positions of power. While these men possessed administrative skills they lacked the technical ones necessary for social action. Indeed, for Préval, the ADP's metamorphosis was rooted in men learning the techniques and values of social action. Explaining the evolution in men's attitudes, Préval stated: "The metamorphosis is seeing men who are ignorant of everything social, first training with social questions without hampering our action and not providing formal opinions based upon exceptional incompetence, adapting themselves, studying, and once gaining a *mastery* of the subject, coming into their own as administrators, then first class advisors."[45]

Préval hailed men who acquired the professionalism necessary to engage in effective social action. They needed to learn a body of knowledge and technical skills to become true collaborators with women. For Préval, men's recognition of the technical precision that effective social action required, played a critical role in the growth of the ADP's ability to provide aid. Moreover, while the metamorphosis began with men, it transformed women as well. Ultimately, Préval argued, it created a new relationship between them:

In the ADP you will see men who no longer believe that 'the social' is our Chief's useless and inefficient wearing of petticoats; you will see men effectively participating in the *true National Revolution*. You will see some female social assistants no longer taking on an air of superiority based upon the depth of technical knowledge that they enjoy … precise intellectual collaboration takes effect between them [men and women] for the good of everyone. Of this metamorphosis we will be proud.[46]

Operating under Vichy and the German occupation fulfilled Préval's hopes that the movement was on the frontlines to shape French society into an environment where a true spirit of teamwork took precedence, the equality of souls was reified, and a hierarchy of values came about. Moreover, for the first time, Préval publicly declared that national rejuvenation required a profound change in French women's and men's attitudes toward roles in French society. Throughout the 1930s, Préval had created structures to mobilize women for social action and had not only suffered a great deal of scorn from men who believed that social action was women's work, but argued that it was a wrongheaded path to power. With the changes brought about by the fall of France and Nazi occupation, Préval believed that finally, the majority of men embraced the potential of social action to bring about national rejuvenation.

Historian Laura Downs has demonstrated that the frontiers between the sexual division of labor epitomized by the movement's social and political action were constantly shifting and became increasingly blurred during the Vichy period.[47] Indeed, Downs argues that during the war, "the social" became an "identity" for increasing numbers of bourgeois men and women disillusioned with the divisions of parliamentary politics, seeking instead what they believed was political neutrality.[48] As we have seen, the growing support for social action was brought about by the structures that women built in the 1930s, which facilitated men's ability to participate in social action that was more widely construed than traditional welfare services and included a range of cultural activities. Whether through the University Centers, SPES, or the movement's many entertainment activities, men like Gaëtan Maire, Jean Mermoz, Pierre Suire, and Jean d'Orsay (none of whom had a counterpart in North Africa) played a key role in the movement's social action. When Préval stated in an October 1944 speech, "I represent the social direction of the PSF and its affiliated groups," she believed that the PSF was leading France into a new era whereby "the social"—an army of Christians protecting French sovereignty in an authoritarian Catholic framework—would permanently transcend the petty politics of the secular parliamentary republic.[49]

SOCIAL ACTION AND RESISTANCE

While Préval was encouraged that the ADP changed women's and men's understanding of their role in French society, her reference to the "true National Revolution" revealed a growing disenchantment with Vichy. Sean Kennedy argues that the PSF was one group of many that identified with what François Bédarida called the "Vichy of Illusions."[50] These groups were not collaborationists but supported the precepts of the National Revolution. Moreover, the PSF also differed from conservatives who initially supported Vichy but came to disagree with the policy of collaboration because of their disdain for aiding Nazi Germany. Rather, La Rocque's disillusion stemmed from his belief that Vichy was incapable of fulfilling the promises of the National Revolution. Préval fell into this category as well and came to believe that Vichy was incapable of protecting French political and territorial sovereignty.

Préval and other ADP members' support for Vichy diminished as the regime's policy of collaboration led to unpopular measures like the brutal roundups of Jews at Vel d'Hiv in July 1942 and the February 1943 Service du travail obligatoire (STO), which drafted French workers for German factories. These capitulations to German demands spurred many ADP supporters to believe that the regime lacked the independence that it had promised. Equally important was the Allied invasion of North Africa, which led the Germans to occupy all of France in November 1942. In these ways, some of the movement's supporters believed that Vichy's claims to protect French political and territorial sovereignty had collapsed and its campaign to rechristianize France had failed. As La Rocque lamented in 1943, "an essential cause of our misfortune is the dechristianization of our country."[51]

The Vel d'Hiv roundups, the German occupation of all of France, and the STO pushed some French toward resistance activities; ADP members were no different. Key leaders realized that it was possible to use the movement's social action as a cover to participate in resistance activities. Conflicting reports make it difficult to determine precisely when resistance activities began. Several members, including La Rocque, claimed that top leaders laid the groundwork for resistance by identifying personnel who might be willing to engage in intelligence gathering in 1940.[52] Several historians, however, have argued that the network was not established until early 1942.[53] Despite the disparity of these dates, the historians and militants agree that the movement's supporters provided intelligence that would undermine the German occupiers and Vichy collaborators *before* the three events that turned public opinion against the regime. This sequence of events suggests that the movement's tendency to value its own autonomy, and hence its ability to represent the national community, remained paramount.

While existing records may not exist to determine the precise date, it is clear that La Rocque and Préval had organized what would later be called the "Klan" resistance network by spring 1942. Under the cover of ADP social action, the PSF's resistance activities centered around providing intelligence to the Allies to help prepare for an invasion. The Klan network's structure was based upon La Rocque's time as the head of French intelligence services in Morocco during the 1925 Rif war in Morocco. In undermining Berber independence fighters, La Rocque believed that the most effective intelligence networks were well organized, had "cloistered" areas of knowledge, and were decentralized.[54] Préval's long-standing and detailed knowledge of all aspects of the movement's social action, combined with her position as the director of the ADP, enabled her to have intricate knowledge of how to structure the network in terms of which personnel could be trusted agents, what types of ADP social action lent themselves to resistance work, and how paperwork could be crafted for use in a clandestine manner. Indeed, few individuals in France at this time possessed Préval's unique combination of leadership power, ability to manage a large bureaucracy, and deep knowledge of grassroots action.

La Rocque and Préval subsequently organized the Klan network in "cloisters" to protect the network and its agents from discovery and capture by Vichy intelligence officials, the Gestapo, and the SS. The cloisters were based upon four levels of knowledge about the resistance activities. At the first level were those who knew of the existence of the Klan network and all of its activities. The second level consisted of social action activists who received directives to gather intelligence against the German occupiers but were ignorant about the network's formal existence. The third level comprised those who were aware of the details of the network's functioning but did not engage in intelligence gathering. At the fourth level were those who knew of the Klan's liaison methods with the Allied agents, which required knowledge of the formal network itself. Only eight people knew of all four levels; they comprised the network's central leadership—the "central organ"—which included La Rocque, Préval, Ottavi, Jean d'Orsay, Pierre le Tanneur, Pierre Robert, and Ottavi's secretary Marie Jouanneau, and Préval's secretary Antoinette Pinet. Knowledge at level two—the existence of general resistance activity—was more widespread, as over one hundred regional and departmental administrators and coordinators knew that they were gathering intelligence against the Germans.[55]

Because of its structure, the Klan's intelligence gathering depended upon *both* women and men, although women's participation and Préval's central role have not been explored by historians. The ADP provided cover for the Klan through its aid restaurants; medical, social and physical education centers; schools for social assistants and rhythmic dance; and teams that helped clear debris from aerial bombardments. The male and female agents themselves were divided into two groups: *cadres nomades,* who were traveling ADP inspectors and administrators, and *cadres fixes,* who provided ADP social services on site.[56] Each intelligence-gathering project began when a Klan official met with an Allied contact who requested information about the activities and movements of German troops in French villages and towns, the existence and scope of arms depots, and the attitude of the local populations toward the Germans. The Allied agent was usually Georges Charaudeau, founder of the British-linked Alibi resistance network. He typically met with La Rocque, although Charaudeau noted that he also met with Préval, Ottavi, le Tanneur, and Robert.[57] The Klan was thus essentially a sub-network of the Alibi network, which employed relatively common practices in terms of espionage and counterespionage tactics: formulating and transmitting questionnaires produced in London that requested information about troop and police activities and public opinion.[58]

Préval used these questionnaires to generate what La Rocque called "research plans." Jean d'Orsay coordinated the research plans with ADP inspectors and administrators *(cadres nomades),* who then required local ADP social services providers *(cadres fixes)* to fill out a series of forms related to the research plans. These members may not have known that they were gathering intelligence, especially if Préval requested information about trends in public opinion to detect support for resistance. In this regard, the SPES section head who informed Maire that he was forced to close his physical education center due to German harassment, which spurred a high level of resentment toward the Germans among supporters in the area, provided the type of information that the Allies requested. The section head was in the position to pass key information along per Préval's request and remain unaware that he was participating in the intelligence gathering process. The reports were then passed back up to Préval and La Rocque, who synthesized them for submission to the Allies.[59]

Because the Klan's intelligence gathering was based on ADP social action, much of its intelligence gathering, some of which was quite dangerous, was done by women. Simon Kitson has noted that Vichy's counterespionage officials regarded the British Intelligence Service as amateurish.[60] If the British were in the practice of contacting French resistance networks that employed women as agents, Vichy may have been seeking to diminish the legitimacy of the British service and undermine the intelligence that it gathered. Préval's research plans typically depended upon the women directors and staff of social centers, summer camps, health clinics, and aid stations who comprised the *cadres locaux* to report upon whatever information was requested. While the records pertaining to Préval's research plans have not survived, it is possible to reconstruct the way in which they worked based upon the network's structure and personnel. Préval would generate a research plan that would be passed along to an ADP departmental inspector of Travail et loisirs social centers, whereby the inspector would then submit the plan to a director of a social center such as the Saint Ouen center, which was led by Madame Horaist. Horaist, who was the head nurse for several years at Saint Ouen before becoming its director in 1939 and was a long-time Préval collaborator and trusted adjutant. She was also one of the hundreds of *cadres fixes* who participated in intelligence gathering but was unaware of the network itself. Horaist would then monitor German activities around the Saint Ouen center, gather the information according to the parameters established by Préval, and submit her findings to the inspector who passed the report along to Préval and La Rocque.[61]

One of the key features of ADP resistance activities was the sub-networks created by regional and departmental administrators across France. These sub-networks operated independently of the Klan's central organ, which illustrates another facet of the network's system of cloistered knowledge and decentralized operations.[62] The Jean Mermoz centers played a key role in sub-network resistance. One member of the resistance attested that centers in Clermont and Saint Etienne provided him with false papers and clothing that he used to disguise himself as either a military official or an ordinary person. Dying the clothing was a key factor in making what he called "the costume" look believable to the police, milice (the Vichy secret police), and Gestapo. He stated that the dyes were formed into balls and coated in chocolate; the clothing was a typical part of the care packages, and false papers and money were hidden in toys.[63] In this way, not only would Vichy and German officials have had a difficult time distinguishing between care packages and resistance aid, but it was also possible for ADP supporters of both sexes to gather materials for the resistance without knowing officials were doing so.

Préval's research plans were often divided into parcels by the *cadres nomades* to hide the totality of the intelligence requests, which led to varying levels of knowledge among ADP supporters about their participation in resistance activities.

Some played a double game while others believed that they were only providing social services. Simone Marochetti, for example, was reportedly kept in complete ignorance of all resistance activities, but still filled out aspects of the parceled research plans that were helpful to the Klan, such as who was receiving ADP aid, and reported on local attitudes toward the Germans. Other women, such as the former heads of Travail et loisirs's rhythmic dance programs, Gisèle Biehler and Lisette Roux, both lived in Clermont-Ferrand and were registered with the central organ as intelligence agents. Biehler and Roux transmitted some of the most sensitive components of the research plans to the *cadres locaux*. Passing along these secret and illegal documents made their work especially dangerous, not only because of the materials they carried, but because their constant movement from center to center was suspicious, making them vulnerable to detection. Mademoiselle Strohl, another longtime Croix de Feu social action militant, was charged with monitoring the organization and movement of German troops in the coastal zones of occupied Landes and the Basses-Pyrénées, which required interactions with German troops that were more extensive than those required of other agents.[64]

In addition to supporting the Allies, ADP members may have provided aid to Jews, although sufficient documentation does not exist to evaluate its scope.[65] It is highly likely that resistance aid to Jews was not structured at an organizational level but left to individual initiative. While it appears that top PSF leaders themselves played key roles in personally providing shelter to Jews, some of the very same people backed Vichy's anti-Semitism. Kennedy has shown that La Rocque endorsed Vichy's first *Statut des juifs* in October 1940, arguing that Jewish refugees constituted an "undesirable multitude."[66] This legislation and some fifty laws that followed, including the second *Statut des juifs* of June 1941, created a system of identification, segregation, and exclusion, by defining Jewishness as someone's having at least two Jewish grandparents, establishing quotas for certain professions, revoking citizenship of Jews naturalized under the 1927 law, and restricting their access to public spaces such as parks, cinemas, and libraries.[67] These measures opened the door for Vichy to arrest, intern, and deport tens of thousands of Jews living in France. In a speech to PSF supporters on June 29, 1941, not long after the announcement of the second Jewish statute, La Rocque argued that the "evident lack of assimilation" was justification to deprive families of citizenship. He insisted that Vichy needed to be more aggressive in stripping naturalizations, arguing, "in [terms of] practical execution my suggestions surpass what the most severe ones have ever called for."[68]

Just as Préval was supportive of her Jewish friends, whom she called "non-sectarian," whose devotion to France was demonstrated by driving children for their first communion, La Rocque advocated for "longer-established" Jews who accepted France's Christian heritage.[69] In this way, the movement was entirely consistent in its denial of individual particularism in favor of a religiously based universalism: anybody could be French so long as they accepted that France was a Christian civilization. It was not until the July 1942 Vel d'Hiv roundups that La Rocque—like most French—appeared to change his mind about Vichy's treatment of Jews. The head of the ADP in Rennes, Madame Bourrut-Lacouture, reported that at a private meeting in her home, La Rocque expressed outrage at the "inhumane" treatment of Jewish families.[70]

The visceral reaction of many French to the brutality of the Vel d'Hiv roundups was what spurred some of them, including a few PSF members, to help Jewish individuals. Testimony from two Jewish sisters indicated that Préval provided them shelter at her home in Clermont-Ferrand until the liberation.[71] Stray reports suggest that La Rocque used his connections to find places for Jews to hide at *Le Petit Journal* and at the Faculté de Médecine de Lyon, which was led by a friend of La Rocque's.[72] Moreover, since hundreds of ADP centers were active across France and some of its personnel had experience operating clandestinely through the Klan, it is clear that the ADP had the organizational structure and personnel to operate as a multi-pronged resistance network. It is possible that individual ADP members helped Jews by procuring false papers, providing places for Jewish refugees to hide, and guiding them along rescue networks to escape France.[73] Indeed, the ADP was positioned perfectly to help Jews move clandestinely into Spain via their social centers in Biarritz and Perpignan and into Switzerland via their centers in Annemasse and Annecy.[74] The case of the latter is particularly plausible because not only was the director of those two centers, Madame Barrucand, a registered agent with the Klan, but the ADP in Lyon, Haute-Savoie, and Savoie provided clothes and foodstuffs to the *foyer social français* in Lausanne and Geneva.[75] Established as early as May 1940 to aid refugees fleeing France, these two Swiss *foyers* could have served as the endpoints of cross-border refugee routes between France and Switzerland, which would have constituted a viable underground network for Jews to escape persecution in France. Despite these possibilities, it is clear that the ADP did not devote its activities to aid Jews as did famous rescue groups like the Jewish Oeuvre de Secours aux Enfants, the Catholic Amitié Chrétienne, the Protestant CIMADE, and resistance journals like *Témoignage Chrétien*.

The Klan's resistance activity, combined with La Rocque's increasingly skeptical editorials in *Le Petit Journal* toward the policy of collaboration, led to a crackdown on the PSF by the German authorities and the arrest of its leadership. Kennedy notes that German actions against the PSF occurred at the same time as those against other groups expressing political dissent against the occupiers even if they supported Vichy.[76] In March 1943 the Gestapo arrested 152 members of the PSF's national and regional leadership, including La Rocque, the head of the ADP in the North, Mademoiselle Binet (a registered Klan agent), and Ottavi's secretary, Marie Jouanneau, who ended up surviving the Ravensbrück concentration camp. The daughter of an army officer, Binet was a close friend of Préval's.[77] Upon learning of Binet's arrest, Préval wrote to the German ambassador to France, Otto Abetz, demanding her release: "I alone am responsible for Mademoiselle Binet's social activities.... If it is necessary [to hold her] hostage, I ask—as the *chef* responsible for Mademoiselle Binet—to replace her in Fresnes and hold me at the disposal of the occupying authorities."[78] In the context of the massive arrests, this letter was brave but futile. Binet would spend the next twelve and a half months in the French prison at Fresnes. Although Préval had escaped the arrests that netted most of the Klan's central organ and much of the PSF's male leadership, she herself was under tight surveillance and expected to be arrested.

While the arrests decimated the entire PSF male leadership and were yet another devastating moment for Préval, who worried about the fate of her closest comrades, the ADP's female leadership remained relatively intact, and those like Binet who were arrested were replaced. Such continuity enabled the organization's social action to continue. Despite the arrests, six months later the police called the ADP a "breeding ground" for recruiting and worried that the organization was subversively taking on a political character.[79] ADP supporters' ability to sustain their activities in the face of worsening persecution was a key reason why the head of the Gestapo, General Oberg, banned Travail et loisirs that December. While Travail et loisirs leaders simply renamed several of their centers, this decree forced Préval to go into hiding at the Saint Ouen social center along with the center's director, Madame Horaist.[80] Consequently, Préval made arrangements to ensure that the ADP's social programs could still run in her absence by drawing up contingency plans in case all of the ADP's female leaders were arrested, putting Simone Marochetti in charge of technical direction of the ADP.[81]

Maintaining ADP social action was especially important to Préval because it provided significant material aid to a population that was experiencing severe deprivation. The fact that the Gestapo's arrest of the PSF's male leadership did not diminish the ADP's capacity to provide services is evidence of its solid organizational structure and the autonomy and authority with which ADP women worked. The balance sheet on the amount of ADP aid between 1939 and 1944 was impressive and included fourteen million meals provided in their Restaurants d'Entr'aide, sixteen thousand tons of care packages sent to prisoners, offices that welcomed an estimated 3.4 million women and the elderly, and 44,000 small plots of land for gardening that they rented out.[82] As Shannon Fogg has shown, material deprivation was one of the greatest challenges facing the French populace.[83] In comparison with other aid groups, the scope and amount of ADP aid stands out. It made a real difference in helping to alleviate the miseries of thousands. Concerned about the relationship between aid and popular support, the police put it this way: "it is undeniable that the number and diversity of the ADP's works have increased knowledge in all social milieus, where they have found new supporters who will go naturally to the PSF if it is reconstituted."[84]

When the D-Day landings in June 1944 commenced the brutal process of liberating France from German occupation and the purge of suspected collaborators, liberation authorities were faced with the question of what to do with organizations that flourished under Vichy. Because it was the latest incarnation of the Croix de Feu and its president was La Rocque, the ADP faced hostility from the Communists and Socialists who dominated the provisional government. Laura Downs has shown that the new Socialist interior minister, Adrien Tixier, was determined to reconstitute a republican France and was thus exceedingly hostile toward the PSF/ADP.[85] While in 1936 Popular Front leaders assumed they could eradicate the ideas of the Croix de Feu by banning the league and ignoring its social action, Tixier was not going to make the same mistake. The government banned *Le Petit Journal,* dissolved the PSF, and sought to kill the ADP by ending its subsidies. The ADP was in severe debt at the time, and dependent upon the 400,000 franc subvention from Secours National to support some of its operations. Préval worried that losing the subsidy would irreparably harm the ADP, especially because the provisional government classified it as a collaborationist group.[86]

While a top Secours National official urged the authorities to allow the ADP's "humanitarian work" to continue, Secours itself was stained by its collaboration with Pétain and Nazi aid services.[87] In an attempt to rescue the reputation of Secours National, Father Pierre Chaillet was appointed to help run the organization, which was renamed Entr'aide Français. During a time when the majority of French accommodated the Vichy regime and displayed "benign neglect" toward the plight of Jewish men, women, and children, Chaillet stands out as a genuine resister.[88] He was one of only a handful of Catholics to immediately denounce the first Statut des Juifs in October 1940 and thereafter repeatedly and publicly railed against Vichy's anti-Semitism. He founded the resistance journal *Temoignage Chrétien* to call attention to Vichy's moral depravity when it came to the regime's treatment of Jews, and on these grounds, he urged the French to resist Vichy by aiding Jews. Notably, the journal was in the possession of some ADP activists.[89] He also founded and helped run the Jewish rescue group L'Amitié Chrétienne. For this work, the Yad Vashem named Chaillet one of the Righteous Among Nations in 1981.[90]

These resistance credentials played a major role in Chaillet's high-ranking position in Entr'aide Français. Indeed, he played a key role in deciding whether to continue to subsidize the ADP and summoned its highest-ranking leader, Préval, for a discussion of its fate. Préval knew that the ADP would not survive without the subsidies and thus touted the organization's many achievements throughout the war. Chaillet was more sympathetic to Préval and the ADP than Tixier, telling her that the ADP's work was "admirable in principle as well as in action."[91] However, he was highly critical of the fact that La Rocque remained the president of its administrative council and informed Préval that Entr'aide Français would pull the ADP's subsidies unless La Rocque was removed. As Chaillet explained to Préval, "Colonel de La Rocque represents a particularly virulent form of political action in the country. In France, he is the symbol of fascism."[92] Chaillet went on to question why the ADP was so effective under Vichy: "The fact that the ADP's work was able to blossom under this regime [Vichy] proves that the politics of the PSF were not contrary to it."[93] Préval was thus faced with a choice between abandoning her long-standing loyalty to La Rocque, and obtaining Chaillet's endorsement and all the benefits therein. Attempting to walk a middle ground, Préval fell back upon the old argument that neither her political enemies nor her competitors believed but that she herself felt wholeheartedly: the ADP was only involved in social action, and therefore was not a political organization and could not be fascist. Chaillet, incredulous at this type of thinking, proclaimed "The [social] question is uniquely political," and repeated his stance that La Rocque represented the worst of French politics. Indeed, he insisted that any group affiliated with La Rocque was "fascism in disguise."[94]

Reflecting the stance of the provisional government and Entr'aide Français, Chaillet's ultimatum presented a gut-wrenching dilemma for Préval. Arrested and deported to prisons in Bohemia and Italy, La Rocque had only returned to France the previous month and was in very poor health. Malnourished, he was confined by the provisional government to a police barracks in Versailles, where his health deteriorated to such an extent that he died from surgery to repair an esophageal ulcer in April 1946.[95] For Préval, the prospect of watching the ADP disintegrate after so many of her friends had made profound sacrifices to maintain its work was unbearable. Moreover, she believed that the ADP still had much to do. Millions still needed aid, the ADP was poised to lead a spiritual renaissance, and Préval knew from experience that the ADP could be effective without La Rocque. Consequently, before he died, La Rocque resigned as the ADP's president, remarking bitterly that his actions were forced upon him by exterior forces.[96] ADP leaders expressed outrage that Entr'aide Français would put such conditions on their group, but were powerless to do anything except register their protest.[97] That September, Tixier officially removed the ADP from the government's list of official social service providers, ending the ADP's subsidies. This action effectively ended the Croix de Feu/PSF/ADP movement, and more broadly speaking, a massive endeavor to empower women as agents of social action who sought to transcend politics by reminding the French people that their very identity was embedded in France's heritage of Christian civilization.

BALANCE SHEET: A MORAL QUAGMIRE

From a moral point of view, Chaillet's attitude toward La Rocque, Préval, and the ADP is revealing in terms of examining the complexities of the concepts of fascism, collaboration, and resistance. Chaillet's resistance credentials were something that many French in the following decades wished they had. His harsh judgment of La Rocque was indicative of his disgust with the actions of some of his fellow Frenchmen and women. As for the ADP, he admired its aid work, questioned its politics, and rejected Préval's contention that it was not political. Chaillet admonished La Rocque for his role in cultivating the ideological conditions whereby Vichy's ethnoreligious nationalism flourished. Yet Chaillet's harsh view of the movement fell on deaf ears for most of its supporters. Ultimately, La Rocque, Préval, and virtually all Croix de Feu/PSF supporters refused to acknowledge that their conception of France as a Christian civilization played any role in Vichy's persecution of people whom the regime considered foreign to the national community, including Jews, Communists, and anticolonial nationalists. They believed that the Croix de Feu/PSF's championing of authoritarianism and militarism remained legitimate because Vichy betrayed the movement's principles by ceding sovereignty to the Germans. The ADP willingly collaborated with Secours National, which Vichy gave a "monopoly on charitable fund-raising," and differentiated them from the likes of Chaillet, who refused what he believed was dirty money.[98]

On the other hand, collaboration with Secours National enabled the ADP to aid hundreds of thousands and provided cover for their resistance work. When it came to action under Vichy, Croix de Feu/PSF supporters often engaged in what can only be called brave and dangerous work. Indeed, it is striking that the Klan network provided intelligence to the Allies. As Simon Kitson has found, many individuals who held political beliefs similar to those of ADP supporters—a hatred of communism, staunch anti-Germanism, and support for the National Revolution—worked *with* Vichy to hunt down Nazi spies and Allied agents because they believed that Vichy protected French sovereignty.[99] Moreover, a number of Croix de Feu activists were shot, arrested, or deported to French prisons, foreign prisons, and concentration camps precisely because of their resistance activities.[100] Others, however, were shot for collaboration. Added to the war-related deaths of Garrigoux and Jean-François de La Rocque, the war's toll on the Croix de Feu was immense. When the likes of Préval, La Rocque, and Garrigoux compared themselves to soldiers ready to die for France, they meant it.

There is another way to view the actions of Croix de Feu/PSF supporters aside from the concepts of collaboration, accommodation, and resistance. The Klan's intelligence gathering for the Allies was to rid France of the occupation and policy of collaboration, not to pursue democratic principles. As Kennedy has pointed out, throughout the war, La Rocque praised Nazism's ability to bring about social unity and admired the dictatorships in Spain and Portugal because they were based upon a "patriotic and spiritual formula."[101] Préval, so focused on social reform, never wrote such overtly political statements, but nevertheless worked relentlessly to bring about a spiritual renaissance based upon authoritarian principles. Ultimately, support for the Croix de Feu/PSF reflected the beliefs held by many French women and men that authority and Christianity defined what it meant to be French. They consistently challenged the legitimacy of governments that they claimed betrayed the "collective soul" of the people, which was epitomized by their movement's conception of Catholic authoritarian principles. In this way, one of the top concerns of the women and men who supported the Croix de Feu/ PSF was to protect French political and territorial sovereignty from forces they conceived of as anti-French *and* from entities that failed to protect France from foreign forces: the pacifists of the early 1930s, the Popular Front coalition of the mid-1930s, and the Vichy government of 1942–1944.

While the provisional government dealt a deathblow to the movement that began as the Croix de Feu, 1945 was only the beginning of its supporters' efforts to rehabilitate La Rocque's memory by positioning the movement as a conservative forerunner to Gaullism instead of the fascist precursor to Vichy. Préval played the leading role in this endeavor to shift attention away from the movement's ethnoreligious nationalism and toward the positive accomplishments of its social action. Rather than spending the remaining thirty years of her life devoted to social Catholic organizing or the politics of the Christian democratic MRP or Gaullist RPF, she retreated to La Rocque's ancestral home in Auvergne (Cantal) and created a complex of buildings that came to be known as the Préval hamlet: the Aérium des Croix, Notre Dame des Croix, and the Maison du Souvenir.[102] Préval remained true to her actions of the 1930s and 1940s: her loyalty was to the Croix de Feu, and she believed that social action transcended politics. The hamlet became a site of memory formation as former members gathered to commemorate their efforts to "save France" during the 1930s by providing social services, laud their resistance activities, and make annual pilgrimages to La Rocque's grave. An association to this end, called Les amis de La Rocque, was created in 1954. In 1969 Préval and two other former members started a biannual bulletin of the same name to announce events and promote sociability among the membership. Préval died in 1977 and was buried not at her birthplace in the Languedoc but in Auvergne near the hamlet that she built.[103] The bulletin was last published in 2002. It is still possible to visit the graves and museum in the Cantal, and the contested memory over the fascism or Gaullism of the Croix de Feu—and what such debates reveal about French "identity"—remain.

CONCLUSION

GENDER, RACE, AND EMPIRE IN THE SOCIOCULTURAL

ACTION OF THE CROIX DE FEU/PSF

One of the most consequential mistakes that the Popular Front made when it was elected to power in May 1936 was to identify the Croix de Feu/PSF as male and assume that banning the league would end its activities and the ideas behind them. While the ban dramatically undermined the other leagues, the Popular Front never fully recognized that Croix de Feu/PSF women had become the cornerstone of the metropolitan movement and that its social and cultural action would continue regardless of whether the state cracked down on paramilitarism or extra-parliamentary political organizing was illegal. In misunderstanding women's central role, Popular Front leaders underestimated the seriousness with which metropolitan Croix de Feu/PSF leaders used sociocultural action to promote the organization's authoritarian, hard-line Catholic principles. The provisional government did not make the same mistake during the social turmoil and political chaos of 1945. Socialists and Communists understood that the Croix de Feu/PSF's sociocultural action garnered good will among large segments of the population and that its leaders were attempting to reconstitute the movement under yet another new name. For this reason, the provisional government believed that women's activities were a significant threat to the reemerging Republican state, and Tixier ended the ADP's subsidies.

Ethnoreligious nationalism was central to the Croix de Feu/PSF's sociocultural action, which played a key role in the dramatic spike in racism of the 1930s and its horrific manifestations during the Vichy period and early stages of decolonization. While in many situations the religious aspects of Croix de Feu/PSF nationalism were more prevalent in other circumstances, nationalistic expression tilted toward an exclusivist focus on ethnicity and race. Regardless of the extent to which Frenchness was understood in religious or ethnic terms, many Croix de Feu/PSF supporters believed that the French race was real and that it determined one's character and temperament. Popular Front leader Paul Rivet recognized that this view of race was dangerous and spoke out vehemently against it in 1935 as the leader of the CVIA. Indeed, Croix de Feu/PSF conceptions of race were a key reason why most Popular Front supporters and progressive Catholics like Father Chaillet believed the movement was fascist.

While race theory was not embedded in Croix de Feu/PSF ideology as it was in Nazism, ethnoreligious hierarchies determined a great deal of the Croix de Feu/PSF's sociocultural action. In metropolitan France, Croix de Feu/PSF racism ranged from exceedingly rigid assimilation to scientific racism. The best example of the relationship between assimilation and religion was the Croix de Feu/PSF's efforts to align with Catholic Action to support rechristianization, which played a key role in the movement's broader agenda to uphold France as a Christian civilization. Préval welcomed Jews in the movement so long as they did not reference their religious difference; Jews and Protestants could speak at major events so long as they ignored the particular aspects of their own religious identity; the small number of Jewish members were expected to accept that they lived in the Occidental civilization and that it was Christian. Such hierarchies structured the belief held by many women that it was ethical to provide social services to the French first, and only after that to anyone deemed "non-French." Moving toward modes of thinking that were reflected in scientific racism, the Croix de Feu/PSF celebrated the most egregious aspects of colonialism by maintaining that forced labor was good because it compelled colonial subjects to learn the value of work and advance upward on the evolutionary ladder. Most Croix de Feu/PSF supporters thus believed that France's civilizing mission was an unquestioned force for good and needed to be defended at all costs. Unflinching support for the civilizing mission was at the heart of the PSF's political program and its "adapt and assimilate" policy proposal, which provided the language for PSF supporters to undermine proposals for reform and become the leading defenders of the glory and prestige of the French empire.

In flocking to the Croix de Feu/PSF, metropolitan women rose to the top of its leadership ranks, helped to formulate its innovative Social First! mission, and worked alongside men in sociocultural action. The idea of Social First! was so powerful that, despite women's marginalization in the movement's North African branches, it became the organizing principle for the movement's "adapt and assimilate" policy: Muslims needed to evolve socially before they could assimilate. In this way, Croix de Feu/PSF racism was more explicit and extreme in the Maghreb, where it was characterized by strong ethnolinguistic sentiments that were rooted in the demographic minority status of settlers. The movement's North African newspaper derided cases when Jews and Muslims worked together, claiming that such solidarity represented a dangerous "union of the races." The head of the Croix de Feu/PSF in Tunisia claimed that indigenous Tunisians belonged to a different race, which supposedly explained their lazy habits, limited aptitudes, and superstitious religion. Croix de Feu/PSF leaders in Algeria spoke on behalf of many supporters by not only claiming that the "Jewish spirit" was shaped by a desire for power and taste for revenge, but that Islam was a "dying and decadent" civilization. Croix de Feu/PSF section meetings in Morocco regularly ended with the fascist salute, and the movement's leader there greatly admired Mussolini. As indigenous rights activists argued, Croix de Feu/PSF action made even the smallest proposals for reform exceedingly difficult to achieve, which played a key role in driving the AUMA, Néo-Destour, and the National Action Bloc toward anticolonial calls for independence. Moreover, while each of these cases reveal the ways in which race-thinking was pervasive in the Croix de Feu/PSF's North African branches, the examples reflect the movement's hierarchical conception of human societies. Participants with such broad backgrounds as the Soufflotines, Suzanne Fouché, and La Rocque had few qualms about working with the very same individuals who believed that race determined human potential despite key Popular Front supporters' questioning of race-thinking.

The ideas that structured Croix de Feu/PSF Social First! mission and the ethno-religious nationalism that was at the heart of it thus circulated throughout the French imperial nation-state and were applied in different ways according to local conditions. Indeed, each of the examples mentioned above came back to an idea that was popular among supporters: will was an important marker of character and revealed where one fit on a social Darwinist scale of "civilization." Germans, for example, were supposedly drawn to Nazi paganism, which revealed the ways in which German "character" lacked the Enlightenment value of rationality. For Croix de Feu/PSF supporters, such rationality was manifested by the intellectual rigor required to engage in reasoned debate. In other cases, colonial subjects were supposedly too morally weak to resist addictive substances and needed to be taught a stronger work ethic by the French to become more "civilized." Depending upon the situation, Croix de Feu/PSF sociocultural action used ethnographic methods to depict why one group of people had the will to assimilate into Frenchness, and in another case, deployed wildly racist stereotypes to explain why integration was difficult for another group. In this context, Suzanne Fouché's experience with disability is illuminating because she was not denigrated but celebrated for her difference. Fouché insisted that suffering was good in that it strengthened her resolve, which allowed her to transcend her body and become closer with God. While Fouché intended her message to promote Catholic conceptions of suffering, she had no control over how her audiences would use it for their own ends. The Tunisian Croix de Feu, for instance, used Fouché's ideas to denigrate the idea of individual freedom in favor of solidarity, mass harmony, and an allegedly joyful binding together of individuals into a collective. Combined with the Tunisian Croix de Feu/PSF's belief that humanity was hierarchically organized according to race, this emphasis on the collective provided a powerful rationale to undermine indigenous activists who cited the sufferings of colonial subjects to press for reforms. Ultimately, Nadine de La Rocque could not have been more prescient when she stated that the tenets of republicanism were broad enough that they could morph into fascism depending upon the general will of the people and the actions of movements they supported.

NOTES

INTRODUCTION

1. On the Croix de Feu/PSF's status as the largest political movement in French history, see Jean-Paul Thomas, "Les effectifs du Parti social français," *Vingtième siècle* 62 (avril–juin 1999): 61. For sociologists' perspective on the concept of a movement versus other forms of organizing, see Kathleen Blee, *Women of the Klan: Racism and Gender in the 1920s* (Berkeley: University of California Press, 1991); Jeff Goodwin, James M. Jaspar, and Francesca Polletta, eds., *Passionate Politics: Emotions and Social Movements* (Chicago: University of Chicago Press, 2001). This scholarship, combined with the fact that Croix de Feu members referred to the organization as a movement, is why I refer to the Croix de Feu (1927–1936) as a league or organization, but use the term *movement* in reference to Croix de Feu/PSF, which existed in various forms from 1927 to 1947, beginning as a league (1927–1936), shifting to a political party (1936–1940), a social service organization (1940–1945), and back to a political organization (1945–1947).

2. Marivic Duval, "Une lettre des 'Soufflotines,'" *La Flamme,* May 20, 1938.

3. Centre d'histoire de Sciences Po, Paris (hereafter CHSP), Fonds La Rocque (hereafter LR) 52, letter from Nadine de La Rocque to her cousin Hubert, May 10, 1934.

4. Alice Conklin, Sarah Fishman, and Robert Zaretsky, *France and its Empire since 1870* (Oxford: Oxford University Press, 2010), 8–9.

5. Osama Abi-Mershed, *Apostles of Modernity: Saint-Simonians and the Civilizing Mission in Algeria* (Stanford, Calif.: Stanford University Press, 2010), 2, 6.

6. Jennifer E. Sessions, *By Sword and Plow: France and the Conquest of Algeria* (Ithaca, N.Y.: Cornell University Press, 2011), 304.

7. Ibid., 311–12.

8. Sarah A. Curtis, *Civilizing Habits: Women Missionaries and the Revival of French Empire* (Oxford: Oxford University Press, 2010), 5–7.

9. Ibid., 101, 123–24.

10. Ibid., 128; Patricia Lorcin, *Imperial Identities: Stereotyping, Prejudice, and Race in Colonial Algeria* (London: I.B. Tauris, 1995), 178–79.

11. Julia Clancy-Smith, *Mediterraneans: North Africa and Europe in an Age of Migration, c. 1800–1900* (Berkeley: University of California Press, 2010), Chapter 7.

12. J.P. Daughton, *An Empire Divided: Religion, Republicanism, and the Making of French Colonialism, 1880–1914* (Oxford: Oxford University Press, 2006), 121–24.

13. Todd Shepard, *The Invention of Decolonization: The Algerian War and the Remaking of France* (Ithaca, N.Y.: Cornell University Press, 2006), 26.

14. John Ruedy, *Modern Algeria: The Origins and Development of a Nation,* 2nd ed. (Bloomington: Indiana University Press, 2005), 89; Martin Thomas, *The French Empire Between the Wars: Imperialism, Politics, and Society* (Manchester: Manchester University Press, 2005), 6; Emmanuel Saada, "The Empire of Law: Dignity, Prestige, and Domination in the 'Colonial Situation,'" *French Politics, Culture and Society* 20, no. 2 (2002): 98–120.

15. Gregory Mann, "What was the *indigénat?* The 'Empire of Law' in French West Africa," *Journal of African History* 50, no. 3 (November 2009): 333.

16. Ruedy, *Modern Algeria,* 89.

17. Mann, "What was the *indigénat?*," 343.

18. On migration, see Tyler Stovall, "National Identity and Shifting Imperial Frontiers: Whiteness and the Exclusion of Colonial Labor After World War I," *Representations* 84, no. 1 (November 2003): 52–72; Clifford Rosenberg, *Policing Paris: The Origins of Modern Immigration Control Between the Wars* (Ithaca, N.Y.: Cornell University Press, 2006); Jennifer Anne Boittin, *Colonial Metropolis: The Urban Grounds of Anti-Imperialism and Feminism in Interwar Paris* (Lincoln: University of Nebraska Press, 2010). On popular culture and support for empire, see Edward Berenson, *Heroes of Empire: Five Charismatic Men and the Conquest of Africa* (Berkeley: University of California Press, 2011), 13–24; Naomi Davidson, *Only Muslim: Embodying Islam in Twentieth-Century France* (Ithaca, N.Y.: Cornell University Press, 2012); Ellen Furlough, "Une leçon des choses: Tourism, Empire, and the Nation in Interwar France," *French Historical Studies* 25, no. 3 (Summer 2002): 441–73; Dana Hale, *Races on Display: French Representations of Colonized Peoples, 1886–1940* (Bloomington: Indiana University Press, 2008); Patricia Morton, *Hybrid Modernities: Architecture and Representation at the 1931 Colonial Exhibition, Paris* (Cambridge: Massachusetts Institute of Technology, 2000); Brett A. Berliner, *Ambivalent Desire: The Exotic Black Other in Jazz-Age France* (Amherst and Boston: University of Massachusetts Press, 2002).

19. Robert Aldrich, "Colonial Man," in *French Masculinities: History, Culture and Politics,* ed. Christopher Forth and Bertrand Taithe (New York: Palgrave Macmillan, 2007), 125; Sessions, *By Sword and Plow,* 305; Margaret Cook Andersen, "Creating French Settlements Overseas: Pronatalism and Colonial Medicine in Madagascar," *French Historical Studies* 33, no. 3 (Summer 2010): 417–44.

20. Patricia M.E. Lorcin, *Historicizing Colonial Nostalgia: European Women's Narratives of Algeria and Kenya, 1900–Present* (New York: Palgrave Macmillan, 2012), 22–23, 77, 107; Marie-Paule Ha, "'La femme française aux colonies': Promoting Colonial Female Emigration at the Turn of the Century," *French Colonial History* 6 (2005): 206.

21. Oissila Saaïdia, "Le cas de l'Eglise catholique en l'Algérie avant la première guerre mondiale," in *Religions et colonisation, Afrique-Asie-Océanie-Amériques XVIe–XXe siècles,* eds. D. Borne and B. Falaize (Paris: Les éditions de l'atelier, 2009), 166–76; Darcie Fontaine, "Treason or Charity? Christian Missions on Trial and the Decolonization of Algeria," *International Journal of Middle East Studies* 44, no. 4 (November 2012): 739.

22. Clifford Rosenberg, "The International Politics of Vaccine Testing in Interwar Algiers," *American Historical Review* 117, no. 3 (June 2012): 690; Jennifer Boittin, "Feminist Meditations of the Exotic: French Algeria, Morocco, and Tunisia, 1921–1939," *Gender and History* 22, no. 1 (April 2010): 139.

23. Julia Clancy-Smith and Frances Gouda, eds., *Domesticating the Empire: Race, Gender and Family Life in French and Dutch Colonialism* (Charlottesville: University of Virginia Press, 1998); Ellen Amster, "'The Harem Revealed,' and the Islamic-French Family: Aline de Lens and a French Woman's Orient in Lyautey's Morocco," *French Historical Studies* 32, no. 2 (Spring 2009): 279–312.

24. Ann Laura Stoler, *Carnal Knowledge and Imperial Power: Race and the Intimate in Colonial Rule* (Berkeley: University of California Press, 2002); Judith Surkis, *Sexing the Citizen: Morality and Masculinity in France, 1870–1920* (Ithaca, N.Y.: Cornell University Press, 2006).

25. Ha, "La femme française aux colonies," 2005.

26. Alice Conklin, *In the Museum of Man: Race, Anthropology, and Empire in France, 1850–1950* (Ithaca, N.Y.: Cornell University Press, 2013), 1; Jennifer Dueck, "The Middle East and North Africa in the Imperial and Post-Colonial Historiography of France," *Historical Journal* 50, no. 4 (December 2007): 943, 944; Lorcin, *Historicizing Colonial Nostalgia,* 96.

27. Jonathan K. Gosnell, *The Politics of Frenchness in Colonial Algeria 1930–1954* (Rochester, N.Y.: University of Rochester Press, 2002), 9; Samuel Kalman, *French Colonial Fascism: The Extreme Right in Algeria, 1919–1939* (New York: Palgrave Macmillan, 2013); Lorcin, *Imperial Identities;* Lorcin, "Mediating Gender, Mediating Race: Women Writers in Colonial Algeria," *Culture, Theory, and Critique* 45 (2004): 45; Lorcin, *Historicizing Colonial Nostalgia,* 4, 79, 112; Ruedy, *Modern Algeria,* 69.

28. Kalman, *French Colonial Fascism,* 2.

29. Kenneth Perkins, *A History of Modern Tunisia* (Cambridge, England: Cambridge University Press, 2004), 40; C.R. Pennell, *Morocco Since 1830: A History* (New York: New York University Press, 2000).

30. Perkins, *A History of Modern Tunisia,* 82.

31. Albert Ayache, "Les grèves de juin 1936 au Maroc," *Annales. Histoire, Sciences Sociales,* 12e Année, No. 3 (July–September 1957): 418.

32. Boittin, "Feminist Meditations," 133.

33. Mary D. Lewis, *Divided Rule: Sovereignty and Empire in French Tunisia, 1881–1938* (Berkeley: University of California Press, 2013), 4.

34. Jonathan Wyrtzen, "Constructing Morocco: The Colonial Struggle to Define a Nation, 1912–1956," (PhD diss., Georgetown University, Washington, D.C., 2009).

35. James McDougall, *History and the Culture of Nationalism in Algeria* (Cambridge, England: Cambridge University Press, 2006); Mahfoud Kaddache, *Histoire du nationalisme algérien,* Vol. 1 (Paris: Editions Paris-Méditerranée, 2003).

36. Boittin, "Feminist Meditations," 141; Carolyn J. Eichner, "*La citoyenne* in the World: Hubertine Auclert and Feminist Imperialism," *French Historical Studies* 32, no. 1 (Winter 2009): 64, 76.

37. Boittin, "Feminist Meditations," 132, 145; for more on the suffrage, see Lorcin, *Historicizing Colonial Nostalgia,* 127–30; Margaret Cook Andersen, "French Settlers, Familial Suffrage, and Citizenship in 1920s Tunisia," *Journal of Family History* 37, no. 2 (April 2012): 213–31.

38. Boittin, "Feminist Meditations," 136; Carolyn J. Eichner, "*La citoyenne* in the World," 64, 76; Sara L. Kimble, "Emancipation through Secularization: French Feminist Views of Muslim Women's

Condition in Interwar Algeria," *French Colonial History* 7 (2006): 109–28; Natalya Vince, "Transgressing Boundaries: Gender, Race, Religion, and 'Françaises Musulmanes' during the Algerian War of Independence," *French Historical Studies* 33, no. 3 (Summer 2010): 446.

39. Richard C. Keller, *Colonial Madness: Psychiatry in North Africa* (Chicago: University of Chicago Press, 2007), 96–97.

40. Ibid., 103.

41. On employment in the sevice sector, see Lorcin, *Historicizing Colonial Nostalgia,* 107.

42. Keller, *Colonial Madness,* 97.

43. Ruedy, *Modern Algeria,* 139; McDougall, *History and the Culture of Nationalism in Algeria,* 97, 98.

44. Testis, "L'Etendard du Congrès Musulman Algérien tourne du rouge au vert," *La Flamme,* August 1, 1937.

45. Gary Wilder, *The French Imperial Nation-State: Negritude and Colonial Humanism between the Two World Wars* (Chicago: University of Chicago Press, 2005).

46. Frederick Cooper, *Colonialism in Question: Theory, Knowledge, History* (Berkeley: University of California Press, 2005).

47. Wilder, *The French Imperial Nation-State,* 25.

48. On the antinomious nature of republican universalism and exclusion, see Spencer D. Segalla, *The Moroccan Soul: French Education, Colonial Ethnology, and Muslim Resistance, 1912–1956* (Lincoln: University of Nebraska Press, 2009), 10; Elisa Camiscioli, *Reproducing the French Race: Immigration, Intimacy, and Embodiment in the Early Twentieth Century* (Durham, N.C.: Duke University Press, 2009); Surkis, *Sexing the Citizen,* 2006.

49. Kalman contends that settlers "rejected" republicanism, Abi-Mershed states that republicanism was "deferred" in Algeria, and Trumbell argues that the colonial project and republicanism were "fundamentally opposed" (Kalman, *Colonial Fascism,* 2; Abi-Mershed, *Apostles of Modernity,* 3; George Trumbell, *An Empire of Facts: Colonial Power, Cultural Knowledge, and Islam in Algeria, 1870–1914* [Cambridge, England: Cambridge University Press, 2009], 7–8).

50. On the elite/mass distinction, see especially Kevin Passmore, *The Right in France from the Third Republic to Vichy* (Oxford: Oxford University Press, 2013); and Jessica Wardhaugh, *In Pursuit of the People: Political Culture in France, 1934–1939* (New York: Palgrave Macmillan, 2009).

51. On the antidemocratic nature of the Croix de Feu/PSF, see Sean Kennedy, *Reconciling France Against Democracy: The Croix de Feu and Parti Social Français, 1927–1945* (Montreal: McGill-Queen's University Press, 2007).

52. Alice L. Conklin and Julia Clancy-Smith, "Introduction: Writing Colonial Histories," *French Historical Studies* 27, no. 3 (Summer 2004): 499–500.

53. Sean Kennedy, "The End of Immunity? Recent Work on the Far Right in Interwar France," *Historical Reflections* 34, no. 2 (Summer 2008): 25–45. For discussion on the future of the field, see Brian Jenkins, "Conclusion: Beyond the Fascism Debate," in *France in the Era of* Fascism, 200–215; Roger Griffin, "Studying Fascism in a Postfascist Age. From New Consensus to New Wave?" *Fascism: The Journal of Comparative Fascist Studies,* no. 1 (2012): 1–17. For the view that fascism was weak in France, see René Rémond, *Les Droites en France, de 1815 à nos jours,* 4th ed. (Paris: Aubier-Montaigne, 1982); Serge Berstein, "La France des années trente allergique au fascisme: à propos d'un livre de Zeev Sternhell," *Vingtième siècle* 2, no. 2 (1984): 83–94. For challenges to this view, see Michel Dobry, "Février

1934 et la découverte de l'allergie de la société française à la 'Révolution fasciste,'" *Revue française de sociologie* 30, no. 3/4 (July–December 1989): 511–33; Zeev Sternhell, *Ni droite ni gauche: l'idéologie fasciste en France* (Paris: Seuil, 1983); Robert Soucy, *French Fascism: The Second Wave, 1933–1939* (New Haven, Ct.: Yale University Press, 1995); William Irvine, "Fascism in France and the Strange Case of the Croix de Feu," *Journal of Modern History* 63, no. 2 (June 1991): 271–95. For debates on how to define fascism, see Kevin Passmore's emphasis on the anti-Marxism and antifeminism of fascism (*Women, Gender and Fascism in Europe, 1919–1945* [Manchester: Manchester University Press, 2003], 8–10; *Fascism: A Very Short Introduction* [Oxford: Oxford University Press, 2002], 118, 132); Roger Griffin's insistence that fascism was revolutionary and characterized by a palingenetic ultranationalism (*The Nature of Fascism* [London: Pinter, 1991], 38–39); and Robert Paxton's emphasis on examining fascism in stages, which includes its birth after World War I, the establishment of a movement, and the creation of a government (*The Anatomy of Fascism* [New York: Random House, 2004]).

54. For the former view, see especially Raymond Betts, *Assimilation and Association in French Colonial Theory, 1890–1914* (Lincoln: University of Nebraska Press, 2005); and Alice Conklin, *A Mission to Civilize: The Republican Idea of Empire in France and West Africa, 1895–1930* (Stanford, Calif.: Stanford University Press, 1997). For the latter view, see especially Wilder, *The French Imperial Nation-State;* Trumbell, *An Empire of Facts;* and Abi-Mershed, *Apostles of Modernity.*

55. On the French Revolution and rights, see Lynn Hunt, *Inventing Human Rights: A History* (New York: W.W. Norton, 2007).

56. Carla Hesse, *The Other Enlightenment: How French Women Became Modern* (Princeton, N.J.: Princeton University Press, 2001).

57. Suzanne Desan, *Reclaiming the Sacred: Lay Religion and Popular Politics in Revolutionary France* (Ithaca, N.Y.: Cornell University Press, 1990).

58. Steven C. Hause, with Anne R. Kenney, *Women's Suffrage and Social Politics in the French Third Republic* (Princeton, N.J.: Princeton University Press, 1984), 260.

59. There is extensive debate over the French Revolution and its effect on women. For the view that it closed off spaces that had been opening to women and created paradoxes of republican citizenship that denied women's political activism, see Carol Pateman, *The Sexual Contract* (Stanford: Stanford University Press, 1988); Joan Landes, *Women in the Public Sphere in the Age of the French Revolution* (Ithaca: Cornell University Press, 1988); Joan Scott, *Only Paradoxes to Offer: French Feminists and the Rights of Man* (Cambridge, Mass.: Harvard University Press). For the view that the Revolution opened doors for women by enabling them to make significant gains in terms of rights outside of politics and in broadening their ability to challenge male authority, see Karen Offen, *European Feminisms, 1700–1950: A Political History* (Stanford, Calif.: Stanford University Press, 2000); Hesse, *The Other Enlightenment;* Hunt, *Inventing Human Rights;* Jennifer Popiel, *Rousseau's Daughters: Domesticity, Education, and Autonomy in Modern France* (Lebanon: University of New Hamphire Press, 2008).

60. Caroline Ford, *Divided Houses: Religion and Gender in Modern France* (Ithaca, N.Y.: Cornell University Press, 2005), 10.

61. Bonnie Smith, *Ladies of the Leisure Class: The Bourgeoises of Northern France in the Nineteenth Century* (Princeton, N.J.: Princeton University Press, 1981).

62. Sylvie Fayet-Scribe, *Associations féminines et catholicisme: De la charité à l'action sociale, XIXe–XXe siècle* (Paris: Editions de l'Atelier, 1990). On Protestant and Jewish organizations, see Emily

Machen, "Traveling with Faith: The Creation of Women's Immigrant Aid Associations in Nineteenth and Twentieth-Century France," *Journal of Women's History* 23, no. 3 (Fall 2011): 89–112.

63. Passmore, *The Right in France,* 73; Magali Della Sudda, "Socio-histoire des formes de politisation des femmes conservatrices avant le droit de suffrage en France et en Italie. La Ligue patriotique des Françaises (1902–1933) et l'Unione fra le donne cattoliche d'Italia (1909–1919)" (PhD diss., Ecole des Hautes Etudes en Sciences Sociales, Paris, 2007), 79.

64. Evelyne Diébolt, "Les femmes catholiques: entre Eglise et société," in *Catholicism, Politics, and Society in Twentieth-Century France,* ed. Kay Chadwick (Liverpool: Liverpool University Press, 2000), 219.

65. Odile Sarti, *The Ligue Patriotique des Françaises (1902–1933): A Feminine Response to the Secularization of French Society* (New York: Garland, 1992); Della Sudda, "Socio-histoire des formes de politisation des femmes conservatrices," 83–85.

66. Bruno Dumons, *Les Dames de la Ligue des femmes françaises, 1901–1914* (Paris: Editions du Cerf, 2006), 26.

67. Ibid.

68. Ibid.

69. Timothy B. Smith, *Creating the Welfare State in France, 1880–1940* (Montreal and London: McGill-Queen's University Press, 2003), 13.

70. Harry W. Paul, *The Second Ralliement: The Rapprochement between Church and State in France in the Twentieth Century* (Washington, D.C.: Catholic University of America Press, 1967); René Rémond, *Religion et société en Europe: La sécularisation au xix et xx siècle, 1780–2000* (Paris: Seuil, 1998).

71. Anne Cova, *"Au service de l'église, de la patrie et de la famille": Femmes catholiques et maternité sous la IIIe République* (Paris: l'Harmattan, 2000), 160.

72. The UNVF reached a membership of 100,000 in 1939; the UFCS reached a membership of 10,000 in the 1930s.

73. Ford, *Divided Houses,* 15–16; on women's political action during this time, see Offen, *European Feminisms;* Claire Goldberg Moses, *French Feminism in the Nineteenth Century* (Albany: State University of New York Press, 1985); Naomi Andrews, *Socialism's Muse: Gender in the Intellectual Landscape of French Romantic Socialism* (Lanham, Md.: Lexington, 2006); Alain Corbin, Jacqueline Lalouette, and Michèle Riot-Sarcey, *Femmes dans la cité, 1815–1871* (Grâne: Editions Créaphis, 1997); Whitney Walton, *Eve's Proud Descendants: Four Women Writers and Republican Politics in Nineteenth-Century France* (Stanford, Calif.: Stanford University Press, 2000); Linda Clark, *The Rise of Professional Women in France: Gender and Public Administration since 1830* (Cambridge, England: Cambridge University Press, 2000).

74. Hause, *Women's Suffrage,* 8.

75. Boittin, "Feminist Meditations of the Exotic," 133.

76. Sonya Michel and Seth Koven, "Womanly Duties: Maternalist Politics and the Origins of Welfare States in France, Germany, Great Britain, and the United States, 1880–1920," *American Historical Review* 95, no. 4 (October 1990): 1076–1108.

77. Laura Levine Frader, *Breadwinners and Citizens: Gender in the Making of the French Social Model* (Durham, N.C.: Duke University Press, 2008), 1–3; Della Sudda, "Socio-histoire des formes de politisation des femmes conservatrices," 212–426.

78. Elinor A. Accampo, Rachel Fuchs, and Mary Lynn Stewart, eds., *Gender and Politics of Social Reform in France, 1870–1914* (Baltimore: Johns Hopkins University Press, 1995), 8–9.

79. Paul Smith, *Feminism in the Third Republic: Women's Political and Civil Rights in France, 1918–1945* (Oxford: Clarendon, 1996), 13.

80. Ibid.

81. See Karen Offen's influential definition of the differences between individual and relational feminism (*European Feminisms,* 21–22).

82. Della Sudda, "Socio-histoire des formes de politisation des femmes conservatrices," 12, 18–20.

83. Smith, *Feminism in the Third Republic,* 193–200.

84. See especially ibid., 133.

85. Herman Lebovics, *True France: The Wars over Cultural Identity, 1900–1945* (Ithaca, N.Y.: Cornell University Press, 1992), 13.

86. Rachel G. Fuchs, *Contested Paternity: Constructing Families in Modern France* (Baltimore: Johns Hopkins University Press, 2008), 125, 194.

87. Karen Offen, "Depopulation, Nationalism and Feminism in Fin-de-Siècle France," *American Historical Review* 89, no. 3 (1984): 648–76.

88. Mary Louise Roberts, *Civilization Without Sexes: Reconstructing Gender in Postwar France, 1917–1927* (Chicago: University of Chicago Press, 1994).

89. Christine Bard, *Les femmes dans la société française au 20e siècle* (Paris: A. Colin, 2001), 68.

90. Susan Pedersen, *Family, Dependence, and the Origins of the Welfare State: Britain and France, 1914–1945* (Cambridge, England: Cambridge University Press, 1993), 396–97.

91. Christine Bard, dir., *Un siècle d'antiféminisme* (Paris: Fayard, 1999), 180.

92. Kristen Stromberg Childers, *Fathers, Families, and the State in France, 1914–1945* (Ithaca, N.Y.: Cornell University Press, 2003).

93. Wardhaugh, *In Pursuit of the People,* 10.

94. Sarah Maza, *Violette Nozière: A Story of Murder in 1930s Paris* (Berkeley: University of California Press, 2011), 55–56.

95. Wardhaugh, *In Pursuit of the People,* 8.

96. Ibid., 10.

97. Paul Dutton, *Origins of the French Welfare State: The Struggle for Social Reform in France, 1914–1947* (Cambridge, England: Cambridge University Press, 2002); Bard, *Les femmes dans la société française,* 54.

98. Daniella Sarnoff, "Domesticating Fascism: Family and Gender in French Fascist Leagues," in *Women of the Right: Comparisons and Interplay across Borders,* ed. Kathleen M. Blee and Sandra McGee Deutsch (University Park: Pennsylvania State University Press, 2012), 164–66; Magali Della Sudda, "Gender, Fascism, and the Right-Wing in France between the Wars: The Catholic Matrix," *Politics, Religion, and Ideology* 13, no. 2 (June 2012): 194; Passmore, *The Right in France,* 221–23.

99. Smith, *Feminism and the Third Republic,* 216.

100. The Jeunesses Patriotes grew to 65,000 members in 1926 before its membership declined when the *cartel des gauches* left power; its numbers grew to around 100,000 following the election of the second *cartel des gauches* in 1932.

101. Passmore, *The Right in France,* 244.

102. While the PDP mobilized women during its creation, the Fédération Républicaine and Radicals waited until 1935 to create their own Women's Sections.

103. The Faisceau claimed up to 60,000 members, Solidarité Française claimed around 180,000 in 1933; and the PPF may have had around 75,000 in 1936/37 (Passmore, *The Right in France,* 235; Soucy, *French Fascism: The Second Wave,* 61; Passmore, "Class, Gender, and Populism: The Parti Populaire Française in Lyon," in *The Right in France: From Revolution to Le Pen,* ed. Nicolas Atkin and Frank Tallett [London: I.B. Tauris, 2003], 183).

104. Della Sudda, "Gender, Fascism, and the Right-Wing in France between the Wars," 190.

105. Daniella Sarnoff, "Interwar Fascism and the Franchise: Women's Suffrage and the *Ligues,*" *Historical Reflections* 34, no. 2 (Summer 2008): 114.

106. Samuel Kalman, *The Extreme Right in Interwar France: The Faisceau and the Croix de Feu* (Aldershot, England, and Burlington, Vt.: Ashgate, 2008).

107. Sarnoff, "Domesticating Fascism," 165.

108. Ibid., 169.

109. Passmore, "Class, Gender, and Populism," 201.

110. The definitions of feminism that have been the most influential in the study of the French Third Republic are those proposed by Steven C. Hause, Paul Smith, Christine Bard, and Karen Offen (Hause, *Women's Suffrage and Social Politics in the French Third Republic,* 6; Bard, *Les filles de Marianne: histoire des féminismes 1914–1945* [Paris: Fayard, 1995]; Smith, *Feminism in the Third Republic,* 5; Offen, *European Feminisms,* 21–22).

111. For an international perspective on the relationship between the far Right and feminism, see the forum in the 2004 issue of the *Journal of Women's History* ("Right-Wing Women in Women's History: A Global Perspective," *Journal of Women's History* 16, no. 3 [Fall 2004]).

112. Passmore, *The Right in France,* 103, 145.

113. Ibid., 244.

114. Della Sudda, "Socio-histoire des formes de politisation des femmes conservatrices," 24.

115. Cova, *Au service de l'église, de la patrie et de la famille,* 16.

116. On the numbers of women's participation in the Croix de Feu, see Jean-Paul Thomas, "Les droites, les femmes et le mouvement associatif, 1902–1946," in Claire Andrieu, Gilles Le Béguec, and Danielle Tartakowsky, eds., *Associations et champs politique: La loi de 1901 à l'épreuve du siècle* (Paris: Publications de la Sorbonne, 2001), 524.

117. On the unprecedented numbers of the Croix de Feu/PSF's women membership, see Caroline Campbell, "Women and Men in French Authoritarianism: Gender in the Croix de Feu and Parti Social Français, 1927–1945" (PhD diss., University of Iowa, 2009), 18–23.

118. On methodology and gender essentialism, see Paola Bachetta and Margaret Power, eds., *Right-Wing Women: From Conservatives to Extremists Around the World* (New York: Routledge, 2002).

119. Mary Jean Green, "Gender, Fascism and the Croix de Feu: The 'Women's Pages' of *Le Flambeau,*" *French Cultural Studies* vii (1997): 229–39, and "The Bouboule Novels: Constructing a French Fascist Woman," in *Gender and Fascism in Modern France,* ed. Melanie Hawthorne and Richard J. Golsan (Hanover, N.H.: University Press of New England, 1997).

120. Samuel Kalman, *The Extreme Right in Interwar France,* 122.

121. Kennedy, *Reconciling France,* 99–101, 175–77, 208.

122. Kevin Passmore, "'Planting the Tricolor in the Citadels of Communism': Women's Social Action in the Croix de feu and Parti social français," *Journal of Modern History* 71, no. 4 (December

1999): 815–51; Laura Lee Downs, "Each and every one of you must become a chef: Toward a Social Politics of Working-Class Childhood on the Extreme Right in 1930s France," *Journal of Modern History* 81, no. 1 (March 2009): 1–44, and "'Nous plantions les trois couleurs,' Action sociale féminine et la recomposition des politiques de la droite française: Le mouvement Croix-de-Feu et le Parti social français, 1934–1947," *Revue d'histoire moderne et contemporaine* 58, no. 3 (2011): 118–63.

123. For more on conservative beliefs in a fundamental opposition between the elite and the mass, see Passmore, *The Right in France*, 13–17, 14.

124. An emphasis on continuity is central to the landmarks on Vichy history: Robert Paxton, *Vichy France: Old Guard New Order*, rev. ed. (New York: Columbia University Press, 2001); Julian Jackson, *France, the Dark Years, 1940–44* (Oxford: Oxford University Press, 2001). For a recent analysis, see Debbie Lackerstein, *National Regeneration in Vichy France: Ideas and Policies, 1930–1944* (Aldershot, England, and Burlington, Vt.: Ashgate, 2012).

125. Thomas, "Les effectifs du Parti social français," 1999.

126. Wardhaugh, *In Pursuit of the People*, 21.

127. Passmore, *The Right in France*, 345.

128. Patrick Weil, *How to be French: Nationality in the Making since 1789*, trans. Catherine Porter (Durham, N.C.: Duke University Press, 2008), 128.

129. Miranda Pollard, *Reign of Virtue: Mobilizing Gender in Vichy France* (Chicago: University of Chicago Press, 1998).

130. Francine Muel-Dreyfus, *Vichy and the Eternal Feminine: A Contribution to a Political Sociology of Gender*, trans. Kathleen A. Johnson (Durham, N.C.: Duke University Press, 2001), 9.

CHAPTER ONE

1. Le Centre d'accueil et de recherche des Archives nationales, Paris (hereafter CARAN), Fonds La Rocque (hereafter 451AP) carton 83, dossier 32, *La Relève*.

2. See, for example, Antoine Prost, *Les anciens combattants et la société française, 1914–1939*, 3 vols. (Paris: Presses de la Fondation nationale des sciences politiques, 1977); Leonard V. Smith, *The Embattled Self: French Soldiers' Testimony of the Great War* (Ithaca, N.Y.: Cornell University Press, 2007).

3. Chris Millington, *From Victory to Vichy: Veterans in Interwar France* (Manchester: Manchester University Press, 2012), 113–20; Soucy, *French Fascism*, 220–21.

4. Several historians have pointed out that it would be more accurate to refer to the plurality of "cultures of war" rather than one monolithic "culture" of war. See, for example, Antoine Prost and Jay Winter, *The Great War in History: Debates and Controversies, 1914 to the Present Day* (Cambridge, England: Cambridge University Press, 2005), 162–66; David Hopkin, Yann Lagadec, and Stéphane Perréon, "The Experience and Culture of War in the Eighteenth Century: The British Raids on the Breton Coast, 1758," *French Historical Studies* 31, no. 2 (Spring 2008): 225–27; John Horne, "Demobilizing the Mind: France and the Legacy of the Great War, 1919–1939," *French History and Civilization: Papers from the George Rudé Seminar* 2 (2009): 102–103.

5. Jean-Jacques Becker, *1914: Comment les Français sont entrés dans la guerre* (Paris: Presses de la Fondation nationale des sciences politiques, 1977).

6. Stéphane Audoin-Rouzeau, *Men at War, 1914–1918: National Sentiment and Trench Journalism in France during the First World War,* trans. Helen McPhail (Oxford and Providence: Berg, 1992); Leonard V. Smith, *Between Mutiny and Obedience: The Case of the French Fifth Infantry Division during World War I* (Princeton, N.J.: Princeton University Press, 1994).

7. Leonard V. Smith, Stéphane Audoin-Rouzeau, and Annette Becker, *France and the Great War 1914–1918* (Cambridge, England: Cambridge University Press, 2003).

8. Stéphane Audoin-Rouzeau and Annette Becker, *14–18: Understanding the Great War* (New York: Hill and Wang, 2002), 134–52; Annette Becker, *La Guerre et la foi* (Paris, 1994); Alan Kramer, *Dynamic of Destruction: Culture and Mass Killing in the First World War* (Oxford: Oxford University Press, 2007), 175–80; Smith, *The Embattled Self.*

9. Rachel Chrastil, *Organizing for War: France 1870–1914* (Baton Rouge: Louisiana State University Press, 2010), 153, 156–58; Millington, *From Victory to Vichy,* 13–15, 182–85; Kéchichian, *Les Croix de feu à l'âge des fascismes,* 43, 160–61; Horne, "Demobilizing the Mind," 108; David Bell, *The First Total War: Napoleon's Europe and the Birth of Warfare as We Know It* (Boston: Houghton Mifflin, 2007).

10. Chrastil, *Organizing for War,* 157.

11. Geoff Read, "'He Is Depending on You': Militarism, Martyrdom, and the Appeal to Manliness in the Case of France's 'Croix de feu,' 1931–1940," *Journal of the Canadian Historical Association/Revue de la Société historique du Canada* 16, no. 1 (2005): 261–91.

12. On masculinity, see George Mosse, *The Image of Man: The Creation of Modern Masculinity* (Oxford: Oxford University Press, 1996); Robert Nye, *Masculinity and Male Codes of Honor in Modern France* (New York: Oxford University Press, 1993); Klaus Theweleit, *Male Fantasies,* Vol. 1. *Women, Floods, Bodies, History* (Minneapolis: University of Minnesota Press, 1987); Christopher Forth, *The Dreyfus Affair and the Crisis of French Manhood* (Baltimore: Johns Hopkins University Press, 2004); Stromberg Childers, *Fathers, Families, and the State in France*; David Slavin, *Colonial Cinema and Imperial France, 1919–1939: White Blind Spots, Male Fantasies, Settler Myths* (Baltimore: Johns Hopkins University Press, 2001).

13. Prost, *Les anciens combattants et la société française.*

14. For more on the veteran's mystique, see Prost, *ibid.;* Millington, *From Victory to Vichy,* 3–9; Soucy, *French Fascism: The Second Wave,* 102–103; Kennedy, *Reconciling France Against Democracy,* 20–22.

15. Millington, *From Victory to Vichy,* 40.

16. Prost, *Les Anciens Combattants et la société française*; Kéchichian, *Les Croix de feu à l'âge des fascismes.*

17. Andrieu, Le Béguec, and Tartakowsky, eds., *Associations et champs politique.*

18. Kevin Passmore, "Boy Scouting for Grown-Ups? Paramilitarism in the Croix de Feu and the Parti Social Français," *French Historical Studies* 19, no. 2 (Autumn 1995): 531–32, 538–542.

19. Matt Perry, *Memory of War in France, 1914–1945: Cesar Fauxbras, the Voice of the Lowly* (New York: Palgrave Macmillan, 2011), 100–122.

20. CARAN 451AP 81, circular, G. Henry, July 14, 1930.

21. Jacques Nobécourt, *Le colonel de La Rocque 1885–1946: Ou les pièges du nationalisme Chrétien* (Paris: Fayard, 1996), 243.

22. Pozzo di Borgo, "L'appel, Filles des Croix de Feu," *Le Flambeau,* July 1933.

23. La Rocque, "L'appel, Filles des Croix de Feu," *Le Flambeau,* September 1933.

24. Kennedy, *Reconciling France,* 37.

25. The figure for women comes from Green, "Gender, Fascism and the Croix de Feu," 232.

26. For the view that the female holders of the *carte* achieved equal status to veteran men, see Kéchichian, *Les Croix de feu à l'âge des fascismes,* 34.

27. Susan Whitney, *Mobilizing Youth: Communists and Catholics in Interwar France* (Durham, N.C.: Duke University Press, 2009); Millington, *From Victory to Vichy,* chapter 5; Kalman, *The Extreme Right in Interwar France,* 145–84.

28. François de La Rocque, *Service Public* (Paris: Editions Bernard Grasset, 1934), 49, 68.

29. CHSP LR 6, Croix de Feu Statutes, "Le Regroupement National autour des Croix de Feu," n.d. (but probably 1933).

30. Forth, *The Dreyfus Affair and the Crisis of French Manhood;* Elizabeth Everton, "Scenes of Perception and Revelation: Gender and Truth in Antidreyfusard Caricature," *French Historical Studies* 35, no. 2 (Spring 2012): 386.

31. Everton, "Antidreyfusard Caricature," 411; Ruth Harris, *Dreyfus: Politics, Emotion, and the Scandal of the Century* (New York: Metropolitan, Henry Holt, 2010).

32. CHSP, LR 6, Croix de Feu Statutes, "Le Regroupement National autour des Croix de Feu," n.d. (but probably 1933), emphasis mine.

33. CARAN 451AP 81, circular, November 14, 1934; CARAN 451AP 81, meeting of May 11, 1935.

34. CARAN 451AP 82, letter, La Rocque to Hermann-Paul, November 25, 1933.

35. Peter H. Merkl, "Approaches to the Study of Political Violence," in *Political Violence and Terror: Motifs and Motivations,* ed. Peter Merkl (Berkeley: University of California Press, 1988), 20.

36. Prost, *Les anciens combattants et la société française.*

37. Chris Millington, "Political Violence in Interwar France," *History Compass* (2012): 1–14.

38. For debates over the danger that Croix de Feu paramilitarism posed, see Rémond, *Les droites en France;* Michel Winock, "Retour sur le fascisme français: La Rocque et les Croix de Feu," *Vingtième siècle* 90 (2006): 6–8; Passmore, "Boy Scouting for Grown-Ups?," 527–57; Sean Kennedy, "Pitfalls of Paramilitarism: The Croix de Feu, Parti Social Français, and the French State, 1934–1939," *Journal of Conflict Studies* (Winter 2007), 64–79; Soucy, *French Fascism: The Second Wave,* 167–75; Irvine, "Fascism in France and the Strange Case of the Croix de Feu," 271, 274; Kéchichian, *Les Croix de Feu à l'âge des fascismes,* 78–83, 333–42.

39. Paul Chopine, *Le Colonel de la Rocque veut-il la guerre civile?* (Paris: Gallimard, 1936), 43.

40. CARAN F7 13306, police report, reprinted circular, May 1, 1930.

41. Chopine, *Le Colonel de la Rocque veut-il la guerre civile?,* 69–70.

42. Ibid., 4.

43. Richard Bessel, "Violence as Propaganda: The Role of the Storm Troopers in the Rise of National Socialism," in *The Formation of the Nazi Constituency,* ed. Thomas Childers (London: Croom Helm, 1986), 131–46.

44. On Lyautey's infuence on La Rocque, see Downs, "'Nous plantions les trois couleurs,'" 126–31; Kéchichian, *Les Croix de Feu à l'âge des fascismes,* 36, 90–93, 105–107; Kennedy, *Reconciling France Against Democracy,* 31–32.

45. Passmore, "Boy Scouting for Grown-Ups?," 543.

46. Archives de la préfecture de police, Paris (hereafter APP) B/a 1973, police surveillance of a meeting organized by the "Fils de Croix de Feu" and the "Volontaires Nationaux," February 28, 1934 (emphasis mine).

47. Millington, "Political Violence in Interwar France," 7; Kennedy, "Pitfalls of Paramilitarism," 78.

48. CARAN 451AP 93/34, poster, "insignes qu'il faut connaitre," n.d.

49. APP B/a 1901, police report, prefecture of police, October 31, 1935.

50. CARAN F7 12962, police reports, 1930–1933.

51. Passmore, "Boy Scouting for Grown-ups?," 529–30.

52. Avner Ben-Amos, *Funerals, Politics, and Memory in Modern France, 1789–1996* (Oxford: Oxford University Press, 2000); Antoine Prost, "Monuments to the Dead," in *Realms of Memory: The Construction of the French Past.* Vol. 2: *Traditions,* dir. Pierre Nora, trans. Arthur Goldhammer, ed. Lawrence D. Kritzman (New York: Columbia University Press, 1997), 308; Michel Winock, "Joan of Arc," in *Realms of Memory,* Vol. 3, 433.

53. On how the sacrifices of the *poilu* overtook those made by women, see Margaret H. Darrow, *French Women and the First World War: War Stories of the Home Front* (Oxford: Berg, 2000), 15.

54. Kéchichian locates the Croix de Feu's emphasis on purity in its medieval codes of Christian chivalry, nostalgic view of trench fraternity, and its denial of heroism (*Les Croix de feu à l'âge des fascismes,* 42, 49).

55. The traits of the Croix de Feu veteran mirrored those valued by antidreyfusards (Everton, "Antidreyfusard Caricature," 383–88).

56. CARAN 451AP 81, "Note aux présidents de section CF & VN, aux secrétaires générales, et déléguées des groupes féminines, chant des CF et VN," July 5, 1935.

57. Michel Vovelle, "La Marseillaise: War or Peace," in *Realms of Memory,* Vol. 3, 29–76.

58. CARAN 451AP 82, sheet music, *Chant des Croix de Feu et des Volontaires Nationaux,* lyrics by Gabriel Boissy, music by Claude Delvincourt, Verse 3, n.d.

59. For the invitations, see the entire carton in CARAN 451AP 86.

60. APP B/a 1973, police report, October 1935, p. 12.

61. André Vauchez, "The Cathedral," in *Realms of Memory,* Vol. 2, 37–70.

62. CARAN 451AP 86, speech, R.P. Vauplane, May 7, 1933.

63. Ibid.

64. Prost, "Monuments to the Dead," in *Realms of Memory,* Vol. 2, 307–32.

65. Chrastil, *Organizing for War,* 93.

66. For debates over the extent to which memorials were consensus-building, see Daniel J. Sherman, *The Construction of Memory in Interwar France* (Chicago: University of Chicago Press, 1999); Jay Winter, *Sites of Memory, Sites of Mourning: The Great War in Cultural History* (New York: Cambridge University Press, 1995).

67. CARAN 451AP 81, circular, Croix de Feu Propaganda Bureau, n.d.

68. Winock, "Joan of Arc," in *Realms of Memory,* Vol. 3: *Symbols,* 433–82.

69. See, for example, Martha Hanna, "Iconology and Ideology: Images of Joan of Arc in the Idiom of the Action Française, 1908–1931," *French Historical Studies* 14, no. 2 (Autumn 1985): 215–39; Eric Jennings, "'Reinventing Jeanne': The Iconology of Joan of Arc in Vichy Schoolbooks, 1940–44," *Journal of Contemporary History* 29, no. 4 (October 1994): 711–34.

70. CARAN F7 13306, report, May 1925.

71. CARAN F7 13306, *L'Humanité,* May 13, 1929.

72. CARAN F7 13306, chart, prefecture of police, 1934; APP B/a 1973, police report, October 1935, p. 12.

73. CARAN 451AP 81, "Cérémonie de Jeanne d'Arc: Instructions pour les sections Croix de Feu et Volontaire Nationaux," May 1934.

74. "La Fête de Jeanne d'arc," *Le Flambeau,* June 1930.

75. Carlier's letter, reprinted in *Le Flambeau,* "Au sujet de Jeanne d'arc," June 1930.

76. La Rocque, "Au sujet de Jeanne d'arc," *Le Flambeau,* June 1930.

77. Green, "Gender, Fascism and the Croix de Feu," 238.

78. "Ce qu'une femme doit savoir," *Le Flambeau,* September 1931.

79. "Ce qu'une femme doit savoir," *Le Flambeau,* January 1933.

80. On conservatism and women's marginalization, see Cheryl Koos, "Engendering Reaction: The Politics of Pronatalism and the Family in France" (PhD diss., University of Southern California, Los Angeles, 1996); on women's agency in restrictive discourses, see Roberts, *Civilization without Sexes,* 1994.

81. Yver, "La Section Féminine du R.N.C.F.," *Le Flambeau,* December 1933.

82. Chopine, *Six ans chez les Croix de feu* (Paris: Gallimard, 1935), 132.

83. While Kéchichian suggests that individual Croix de Feu sections offering small-scale services was evidence that the league was committed to social action, I would suggest that the ad hoc nature of the activities revealed a *lack* of commitment in light of the sophisticated program that women began to develop in 1934 (Kéchichian, *Les Croix de feu à l'âge des fascismes,* 31, 35, 108–109).

84. APP B/a 1901, letter, Madame Hidieu to the Police Préfect, March 1932.

85. Ibid.

86. Bard, *Un siècle d'antiféminisme,* 22.

87. Richard J. Evans, "German Women and the Triumph of Hitler," *Journal of Modern History* 48, no. 1, On Demand Supplement (March 1976), 126–27.

88. Theweleit, *Male Fantasies.*

89. Robert Brasillach, quoted in Jackson, *France, the Dark Years,* 202.

CHAPTER TWO

1. Photographs of Préval are in *Servir,* April 27, 1939; "Une conférence de Mlle de Préval sur l'Action Sociale du PSF," *Le Flambeau de Flandre, Artois, Picardie,* May 15, 1938. For more on Préval's biography, see Downs, "Nous plantions les trois couleurs," 118–26.

2. John Rymell, "Militants and Militancy in the Croix de Feu and Parti Social Français: Patterns of Political Experience on the French Far Right (1933–1939)" (PhD diss., University of East Anglia, 1990).

3. The social turn terminology comes from Albert Kéchichian, who has shown that Croix de Feu social programs were central to its political endeavors. In tracing this shift, Kéchichian focuses on the actions of male supporters, arguing that the social turn's roots were in La Rocque's efforts to bring about national reconciliation by emphasizing the social bonds that held a society together (*Les Croix*

de Feu à l'âge des fascismes, 38–41, 105, 333–39). For Downs's view that La Rocque was the impetus behind the social turn, see "Each and every one of you must become a *chef,"* 6–7, 17, 19, 20, 21, and 23. Passmore too has emphasized La Rocque's role but highlights that of women as well ("Planting the Tricolor in the Citadels of Communism," 819, 824–26, 847).

4. Florence Rochefort, dir., *Le pouvoir du genre: Laïcités et religions, 1905–2005* (Toulouse: Presses universitaires du Mirail, 2007), 16.

5. On the riots, see Kennedy, *Reconciling France against Democracy,* 44–49; Chris Millington, "February 6, 1934: The Veterans' Riot," *French Historical Studies* 33, no. 4 (2010): 545–72; Serge Berstein, *Le six février 1934* (Paris: Gallimard, 1975).

6. Brian Jenkins, "Plots and Rumors: Conspiracy Theories and the *Six Février 1934," French Historical Studies* 34, no. 4 (Fall 2011): 650n4.

7. John Hellman, "Vichy Background: Political Alternatives for French Catholics in the Nineteen-Thirties," *Journal of Modern History* 49, no. 1, On Demand Supplement (March 1977): D1125, ft. 22.

8. Popiel, *Rousseau's Daughters*; Hunt, *Inventing Human Rights*; Hesse, *The Other Enlightenment,* 2001.

9. CHSP 52, letter from Nadine de La Rocque to her cousin Hubert, May 10, 1934 (underlined in original).

10. Ibid.

11. La Rocque, *Service Public,* 76 (emphasis mine).

12. Ibid.

13. Stanley Payne, *A History of Fascism, 1924–1945* (Madison: University of Wisconsin Press, 1995), 38–39.

14. Chopine, *Six ans chez les Croix de feu,* 146. The other advisor to whom Chopine referred was Noël Ottavi.

15. CARAN 451AP 87, speech by Préval at the meeting of First Delegates and General Secretaries, October 26 and 28, 1936.

16. CARAN 451AP 87, speech by Madame Gouin at the meeting of First Delegates and General Secretaries, October 26, 1936; 451AP 87, speech by Préval at the meeting of First Delegates and General Secretaries, October 26 and 28, 1936.

17. CARAN 451AP 87, speech by Préval at the meeting of First Delegates and General Secretaries, October 26 and 28, 1936.

18. See especially Kalman, *The Extreme Right in Interwar France,* 125; Green, "Constructing a French Fascist Woman," 62.

19. "Section Féminine du Regroupement National autour des CF," *Le Flambeau,* April 1934.

20. CARAN 451AP 81, tract, "Buts Généraux des CF," n.d.

21. Steven Hause, "Anti-Protestant Rhetoric in the Early Third Republic," *French Historical Studies* 16, no. 1 (Spring 1989): 183–84.

22. On whiteness, see Frader, *Breadwinners and Citizens,* 124–25, and "From Muscles to Nerves: Gender, 'Race' and the Body at Work in France, 1919–1939," *International Review of Social History* 44, supplement 7 (1999): 130; Camiscioli, *Reproducing the French Race,* 12–13; Tyler Stovall, "National Identity and Shifting Imperial Frontiers: Whiteness and the Exclusion of Colonial Labor after World War I," *Representations* 84 (Autumn 2003): 52–53, 65.

23. La Rocque, "Section Féminine du Regroupement National," *Le Flambeau,* April 1934.

24. Marie-Claire de Gérus, "Allocution de Madame de Gérus," *Le Flambeau,* April 1934.

25. Ibid.

26. Ibid.

27. Pastor Durleman, speech, "La femme au foyer," *Le Flambeau,* April 1934.

28. Ibid. (emphasis mine).

29. Rabbi Kaplan, speech, "La femme dans la cité," *Le Flambeau,* April 1934.

30. Ibid.

31. Ibid.

32. R.P. Dieux de l'Oratoire, speech, "la femme dans la nation," *Le Flambeau,* April 1934.

33. Ibid. (emphasis mine).

34. Germaine Féraud, speech, "Allocution de Mademoiselle Féraud," *Le Flambeau,* April 1934.

35. Ibid.

36. Speech by Féraud, "Le congrès social de la section féminine," *Le Flambeau,* November 2, 1935; also in CARAN 451AP 87/62, report, "Action Social de Croix de Feu: Résumé des Oeuvres Sociales de la Section Féminine du Mouvement Social des Croix de Feu," n.d.

37. CARAN 451AP 87, report, "Oeuvres sociales Croix de Feu," Fall 1935. Requirements to register for the Women's Section are in "Règlement de la section féminine," *Le Flambeau,* November 1934.

38. CARAN 451AP 82, tract, "Femmes Françaises," 1934.

39. APP B/a 1901, police report, "Section Féminine du Mouvement Social Français des Croix de Feu," June 2, 1936; CARAN F7 12964, police report, March 11, 1936.

40. APP B/a 1901, police report, "Section Féminine du Mouvement Social Français des Croix de Feu," June 2, 1936.

41. CARAN 451AP 87, "Instruction provisoire pour le fonctionnement de la Section Féminine du RNCF," April 1934. Also printed under the same title in the April 1934 issue of *Le Flambeau.*

42. CARAN 451AP 87, report, "Oeuvres sociales Croix de Feu," Fall 1935.

43. Women's Sections across France sent in short reports that listed the announcement of a section's creation, its activities, and nominations for leadership positions. Gérus and Féraud collected these reports and submitted them for publication in *Le Flambeau.* Active sections reported more often while those that were less active only reported a few times. It is important to note that these figures are based on *Le Flambeau's* reporting of new sections; it is possible that not all newly created sections were announced in the newspaper. Data for Figure 3 were compiled from these reports that were printed monthly from March 1934 to February 1935, then weekly from February 1935 to June 1936. The data for women in North Africa stretch from October 1935 to June 1936 and come from *Le Flambeau,* and the Archives nationales d'outre-mer, Aix-en-Provence (hereafter ANOM) 30 134 *Bulletin des Associations Croix de Feu du Département d'Alger* (May 1935–October 1935), and *Bulletin de Liaison du Croix de Feu en Algérie* (October 1935–June 1936).

44. "Règlement de la section féminine," *Le Flambeau,* November 1934.

45. Passmore, "'Planting the Tricolor in the Citadels of Communism,'" 832, 834.

46. Caroline Campbell, "Women and Gender in the Croix de Feu and Parti Social Français: Creating a Nationalist Youth Culture, 1927–1939," *Proceedings of the Western Society for French History* 36 (2008): 253.

47. "Règlement de la section féminine," *Le Flambeau,* November 1934.

48. APP B/a 1901, police report, "Section Féminine du Mouvement Social Français des Croix de Feu," June 2, 1936.

49. CARAN F7 13320, police report on Croix de Feu meeting, January 1935.

50. "Dans nos Fédérations," *Le Flambeau du Sud-Ouest,* December 25, 1937.

51. My survey of the Croix de Feu/PSF's regional press has shown that there were not Women's Sections in the Basses-Alpes, Cantal, Hautes-Alpes, Haute-Loire, Lot, Lozère, and Tarn-et-Garonne (*L'Heure Française; La Flamme du Midi; L'Auvergne nouvelle; Le Volontaire 36*).

52. I am defining "most active" as five sections or more. On the number of sections in each department and how the figures correlated to Popular Front and feminist activism, see Campbell, "Women and Men in French Authoritarianism," 104–106. The figure of 45 percent comes from Croix de Feu electoral planners' analysis of the 1932 general election that brought the *cartel des gauches* to power; see the CHSP LR 56, "le Front Populaire," *Le Document,* 1935.

53. Ibid. For the Women's Section, I am defining "less active" as having two sections or less.

54. Ibid.

55. Hause, *Women's Suffrage and the Social Politics in the French Third Republic,* 271.

56. Madame Merle, "Le Rôle civique de la femme," *La Flamme du Midi,* May 14, 1937.

57. The 1935 figures come from APP B/a 1901, police report from the General Secretary of the Parisian Police Prefect, n.d. (but probably August 1935).

58. APP B/a 1901, police report, "Effectif des Groupements Nationaux," August 1935.

59. Julian Jackson, *The Popular Front in France: Defending Democracy, 1934–1938* (Cambridge, England: Cambridge University Press, 1988), 219–20.

60. Smith, *Feminism in the Third Republic,* 78–79.

61. Ibid., 84; Whitney, *Mobilizing Youth,* 207–208.

62. Cova, *Femmes catholiques et maternité sous la IIIe République,* 160.

63. Services from 1927 to 1934 were reported in *Le Flambeau;* services from April 1934 to October 1935 are based on Women's Section reports in: CARAN 451AP 87/10, report, "Oeuvres Sociales CF, Section Féminine du Mouvement Social des CF," n.d. (probably October 1935); CARAN 451AP 87/13, Report, "Oeuvres Sociales réalisées dans nos association," n.d; CARAN 451AP 87/16, Report, "Compte Rendu du Vestiaire Central," n.d. (probably 1936); CARAN 451AP 87/25, Report, "Centre Médical," 1936; CARAN 451AP 87/39, Report to the Croix de Feu General Assembly, February 17, 1935; CARAN 451AP 87/62, Report, "Action Social de Croix de Feu: Résumé des Oeuvres Sociales de la Section Féminine du Mouvement Social des CF," n.d. (probably late 1935); CARAN 451AP 87/20, "exposé de Madame de Gérus," November 7, 1935; CHSP LR 6, report on Croix de Feu social activities, 1935; CARAN 451AP 93, statutes, "Centre Social Universitaire, 11 rue Soufflot, Paris, 6th," October 1935; CHSP LR 6, report, Gaëton Maire, "Leçons données par semaine dans chaque groupe dans les centres de Paris," June 6, 1936.

64. Madame Buisset, "Compte Rendu de l'Assemblée Générale Annuelle des Sections de Charleville," *Le Flambeau ardennais,* February 1936.

65. CARAN 451AP 81, La Rocque, *Le Flambeau,* November 16, 1935 (emphasis mine).

66. APP B/a 1973, police report synthesizing major Croix de Feu activities, October 1935, p. 21.

67. CARAN 451AP 87, Circular on the MSF to Regional and Departmental Delegates, Croix de Feu and VN Section Presidents, and Commissioners and Representatives of the Croix de Feu and MSF, January 22, 1936.

68. CARAN 451AP 93, circular, Charles Varin, "Défilé de Jeanne d'Arc," May 10, 1936.

69. *Le Flambeau*, "Section Féminine," December 1934, January 1935, April 1935.

70. APP B/a 1902, police report on Croix de Feu activity, February 28, 1936.

71. Ibid.

72. APP B/a 1902, police report on Croix de Feu activities, March 30, 1936.

73. Ibid.

74. Kennedy, *Reconciling France*, 69.

75. CARAN 451AP 102, Charles Vallin, brochure *Aux Femme du PSF*, 1937.

76. CARAN 451AP 133, La Rocque, monthly bulletin *Service Social*, February 1, 1938.

77. Bruno Dumons, "L'Action française au féminine; Réseaux et figures de militantes au début du XXe siècle," in *L'Action française: culture, société, politique*, ed. Michel Leymarie and Jacques Prévotat (Lille: Presses Universitaires du Septentrion, 2008), 235–36.

78. CARAN 451AP 87, Préval speech at the meeting of First Delegates and General Secretaries, October 26 and 28, 1936.

79. APP B/a 1902, report from the prefecture of police, December 27, 1935.

80. Whitney, *Mobilizing Youth*, 116, 240.

81. CHSP LR 56, letter, La Rocque to Cardinal Verdier of Paris, March 7, 1936 (emphasis mine).

82. Ibid.

83. Ibid.

84. CARAN 451 AP 130, Bulletin d'information No. 52, October 14, 1937.

85. See also François Veuillot, *La Rocque et son parti: comme je les ai vus* (Paris: Librairie Plon, 1938).

86. CHSP LR 52, J. Daujat, *Orientations*, "Chronique: les Catholiques et la Politique," 3éme Année, 5–6, March–April 1936, p. 6.

87. CHSP LR 31, Jean Daujat, "Service de presse régionale du PSF, Quelques Principes, Civilisation Chrétienne de Mission de la France," August 1, 1939.

88. Ibid.

89. Ibid.

90. David Curtis, "True and False Modernity: Catholicism and Communist Marxism in 1930s France," in *Catholicism, Politics and Society in Twentieth-Century France*, ed. Chadwick, 76–77.

91. CARAN 451AP 121, Michel-P. Hamelet, "Les Catholiques dans la cité: Le Colonel de La Rocque nous dit," *Sept*, February 26, 1937.

92. Michael Kelly, "Catholicism and the Left in Twentieth-Century France," *Catholicism, Politics and Society in Twentieth-Century France*, ed. Chadwick, 151.

93. CARAN 451AP 87, speech by Préval at the meeting of First Delegates and General Secretaries, October 26 and 28, 1936. Quoted also in Downs, "Nous plantion les trois couleurs," 120–21.

94. CARAN 451AP 87, circular, Simone Marochetti, "Le groupe 'C' et les Cours du Social Service," October 10, 1935.

95. CHSP LR 56, letter, La Rocque to Cardinal Verdier of Paris, March 7, 1936.

96. Mauriac, quoted by Louis Desobeau, "Action Sociale et Entr'aide: Conférence de Mlle Fouché," *Le Flambeau du Sud-Ouest,* June 5, 1937.

97. Edward Welch, *François Mauriac: The Making of an Intellectual* (Amsterdam, N.Y.: Editions Rodopi BV, 2006), 13; Pascal Ory and Jean-François Sirinelli, *Les Intellectuels en France: de l'affaire Dreyfus à nos jours* (Paris: Parrin, 2004).

98. Frantz Fanon, *The Wretched of the Earth* (New York: Grove Press, 2005), 8.

99. CHSP LR 31, Suzanne Fouché, *J'espérais d'un grand espoir* (Editions du Cerf, 1981), 141–42.

100. Kéchichian, *Les Croix de feu à l'âge des fascismes,* 345.

101. CHSP LR 29, circular from La Rocque to presidents of local committees and sections, March 18, 1937, p. 7.

102. My description of Fouché's social sense conferences is synthesized from articles that appeared in the PSF's regional press. The most useful are: Madame S. d'Arras, "Le sens social: La première conférence de Mlle Fouché," *La Flamme,* January 29, 1938; Madame S. d'Arras, "Les 2e et 3e conférences d'action social ont été consacrées à la psychologie de l'enfant et à celle du malade," *La Flamme,* February 5, 1939; Dr. G. Minguet, "Action Sociale: Mlle Fouché à Tunis," *La Flamme,* January 15, 1939; Suzanne Lacomme, "Action Sociale: La semaine sociale des cours sociaux de Mlle Fouché," *Le Flambeau du Sud-Ouest,* June 19, 1937; "Cours de formation sociale de Suzanne Fouché," *Le Flambeau des Vosges,* January 1939; "Le Service Social et La Charité"; *La Flamme tourangelle: Organe hebdomadaire du Parti social français pour le département d'Indre-et-Loire,* January 7, 1939: "Le rôle de l'auxiliaire sociale," *Servir* (Bourogne, Nivernais), June 8, 1939.

103. CARAN 451AP 133, "Résumé de la Réunion de Travail du Bureau d'Etudes Sociales," April 23, 1937; CARAN 451AP 87, circular, Suzanne Fouché, "Cours Elémentaires de Formation Sociale," September 1, 1936.

104. Fouché, quoted by Madame S. d'Arras, "Le sens social: La première conférence de Mlle Fouché," *La Flamme,* January 29, 1938.

105. Dr. G. Minguet, "Mlle Fouché à Tunis," *La Flamme,* January 15, 1938.

106. Fouché, quoted by Madame S. d'Arras, "Le sens social: La première conférence de Mlle Fouché," *La Flamme,* January 29, 1938. For more on collectivism and feminism, see Hause, *Women's Suffrage and the Social Politics in the French Third Republic;* Cova, *"Au service de l'église, de la patrie et de la famille."*

107. CARAN 451AP 134, Fouché speech at the Premier Congrès Social du PSF, "le Rôle de l'Auxiliaire Sociale," May 1939.

108. Madame S. d'Arras, "Le sens social: La première conférence de Mlle Fouché," *La Flamme,* January 29, 1938.

109. Ibid.; Dr. G. Minguet, "Mlle Fouché à Tunis," *La Flamme,* January 15, 1938.

110. Dr. G. Minguet, "Mlle Fouché à Tunis," *La Flamme,* January 15, 1938.

111. Madame S. d'Arras, "Le sens social: La première conférence de Mlle Fouché," *La Flamme,* January 29, 1938.

112. Suzanne Lacomme, "Action Sociale: La semaine sociale des cours sociaux de Mlle Fouché," *Le Flambeau du Sud-Ouest,* June 19, 1937.

113. Janet R. Horne, "In pursuit of Greater France: Visions of Empire Among Musée Social Reformers, 1894–1931," in *Domesticating the Empire,* ed. Clancy-Smith and Gouda, 33, 38–39.

114. On Catholicism and suffering, see Brenna Moore, *Sacred Dread: Raissa Maritain, the Allure of Suffering, and the French Catholic Revival, 1905–1944* (South Bend: University of Notre Dame Press, 2013).

115. Fouché, quoted by Louis Desobeau, "Action Sociale et Entr'aide: Conférence de Mlle Fouché," *Le Flambeau du Sud-Ouest,* June 5, 1937.

116. Madame S. d'Arras, "Les 2e et 3e conférences d'action social ont été consacrées à la psychologie de l'enfant et à celle du malade," *La Flamme,* February 5, 1939.

117. Ibid.

118. Catherine J. Kudlick, "Disability History: Why We Need Another 'Other,'" *American Historical Review* 108, no. 3 (June 2003): 766.

119. My use of the phrase "rhetoric of pity" comes from Rebecca Scales, "Radio Broadcasting, Disabled Veterans, and the Politics of National Recovery in Interwar France," *French Historical Studies* 31, no. 4 (Fall 2008): 651, 662.

120. Henri-Jacques Stiker, *A History of Disability,* trans. William Sayers (Ann Arbor: University of Michigan Press, 1999), 185.

121. Fouché, *J'espérais d'un grand espoir.* (Les Editions du Cerf: Paris, 1981), 141.

122. Kudlick, "Why We Need Another 'Other,'" 765.

123. Smith, *Creating the Welfare State in France,* 23–25.

124. Ibid., 13.

125. Dutton, *Origins of the French Welfare State,* 7–8 and 121–22.

126. Frader, *Breadwinners and Citizens.*

127. Brochure, "Les Croix de Feu, leur chef, leur programme," Le Comité de vigilance des intellectuels antifascistes.

128. Le Centre des Archives contemporaines, Fontainebleau (hereafter CAC), 19940500 art 207 dossier 3458, "Circulaire aux préfets des départements et au Préfet de police au sujet du rapport de l'arrêté relatif à la dissolution de l'organisation fasciste 'Croix de Feu,'" July 22, 1936.

129. CARAN 451AP 163, report, "Réunion Constitutive de l'Association—statuts initiaux," December 23, 1936.

130. CARAN 451AP 130, report, "Action Sociale et Politique dans le Nord," 1938.

131. CARAN 451AP 171, "Conseil d'Administration," 1936; CARAN 451AP 163, List of Personnel, n.d. (probably 1937–1938); CARAN 451AP 163, report, "Réunion Constitutive de l'Association—statuts initiaux," December 23, 1936; CARAN 451AP 153, anon. "Qu'est-ce que SPES?," n.d.; CARAN 451AP 187, Report by M. Danner for M. Le Tanneur, "Compte-Rendu de Notre Entretien avec le Bureau d'Etudes Sociales, SPES, et l'Office du Tourisme," October 14, 1937.

132. CARAN 451AP 171, series of Travail et loisirs reports, n.d; CARAN 451AP 189, Travail et loisirs report, "Nos Centres Sociaux sont en constant progrès—inscriptions—accroissement des présences," June 1939.

133. CHSP LR 29, circular from La Rocque to presidents of local committees and sections, March 18, 1937.

134. Ibid.

135. CARAN 451AP 133, "Note sur la Visite faites par Mlle Garrigoux à Compiègne le 28 Octobre 1937."

136. CARAN 451AP 133, letter to Garrigoux from Préval.

137. CHSP LR 31, Suzanne Fouché speech at the PSF's First Social Congress, "Le Rôle de L'Auxiliaire Sociale," May 1939.

138. On integral nationalism, see Lebovics, *True France;* David Carroll, *French Literary Fascism: Nationalism, Anti-Semitism, and the Ideology of Culture* (Princeton, N.J.: Princeton University Press, 1995), 10, 88–92; Martha Hanna, *The Mobilization of Intellect: French Scholars and Writers During the First World War* (Cambridge, England: Cambridge University Press, 1996); Payne, *A History of Fascism.*

139. Pedersen, *Family, Dependence, and the Origins of the Welfare State,* 137; Timothy Smith, *Creating the Welfare State in France,* 5.

140. APP B/a 1901, police report, "Section Féminine du Mouvement Social Français des Croix de Feu," June 2, 1936.

141. Reprint of a La Rocque circular from April 24, 1937 in "Aux Président de Sections," *Le Flambeau de Franche-Comté et Territoire de Belfort,* June 15, 1938.

142. Ibid.

143. Ibid. (emphasis mine).

144. CARAN 451AP 172, letter and questionnaire from J. Bruyas to Préval, February 4, 1939.

145. Ibid.

146. Ibid.

147. CARAN 451AP 184, letter from Préval to Madame Roland-Gosselin, February 8, 1939.

148. CARAN 451AP 162, letter from Préval to Ducrocq, February 1, 1937.

149. CARAN 451AP 171, "Statuts de Travail et loisirs," 1936.

150. "Une conférence de Mlle de Préval sur l'Action Sociale du PSF," *Le Flambeau de Flandre, Artois, Picardie,* May 15, 1938.

151. Ibid.

152. CARAN 451AP 174, letter from Antoinette de Préval to Madame Hirsch, July 6, 1937.

153. CARAN 451AP 172, letter and questionnaire from J. Bruyas to Préval, February 4, 1939; quoted also in Downs, "'Each and every one of you must become a *chef,*'" 29.

154. CARAN 451AP 172, Préval letter to Mademoiselle Frandaz, October 19, 1937; quoted also in Downs, "'Each and every one of you must become a *chef,*'" 23.

155. On the relationship between the red zones and Lyautey's social theories about the pacification of "savage" peoples, see Downs, "Nous plantions les trois couleurs," 126–33.

156. CHSP LR 59, Stamp Booklet, "Timbre de la Victoire," attached to a circular by Verdier, May 25, 1937.

157. CARAN 451AP 187 (Saint Ouen Dossier), "Relations de 'Travail et Loisirs' avec le 'P.S.F.' (1937–1938)," letter, Saint Ouen section president Henry Goubier to Paul Iltis, president of the St. Denis local committee, 27 October 1937; quoted also in Passmore, "'Planting the Tricolor in the Citadels of Communism,'" 848.

158. CARAN 451AP 184, "correspondance de centre Aubervilliers," newspaper clipping, *L'Echo du Monfort: Bulletin Mensuel des Communistes du Quartier,* n.d. Quoted also in Downs, "Each and every one of you must become a *chef,*" 28.

159. CARAN 451AP 188, Préval speech at the 1938 Travail et loisirs General Assembly.

160. CARAN 451AP 182, letter from M. Metman, to le Procureur de la République, Paris, January 18, 1938, and letter from M. Metman, to Monsieur la Commissaire de Police, Saint-Ouen, January 19, 1938.

161. CARAN 451AP 188, Préval speech at the 1938 Travail et loisirs General Assembly.

162. Simon Kitson, "The Police and the Clichy Massacre, March 1937," in Richard Bessel and Clive Emsley, eds., *Patterns of Provocation: Police and Public Disorder* (New York: Berghahn, 2000), 31.

163. Ibid., 32.

164. CAC 19940496 Article 12 Dossier 310, Police Report, 1937.

165. Kennedy, "Pitfalls of Paramilitarism," 72.

166. Ibid.

167. CARAN 451AP 115, circular, anon. "The Aspirations of the Student and the PSF Spirit," n.d.

168. Kennedy, *Reconciling France Against Democracy,* 210.

169. CARAN 451AP 114, anon. report, "la Gestion de *l'Etudiant Social,"* June 12, 1939.

170. Kennedy, "The Croix de Feu, the Parti Social Français, and the Politics of Aviation, 1931–1939," *French Historical Studies* 23, no. 2 (Spring 2000): 383.

171. CARAN 451AP 115, Jean Bernard, "His Example," *L'Etudiant Social,* December 1938.

172. Ibid.

173. CARAN 451AP 114, Pierre Suire, "The Social Student," *L'Etudiant Social,* April 1938.

174. CARAN 451AP 115, Pierre Suire, Speech, "The Student and Social Action," First National Congress of PSF Students, January 27–28, 1938.

175. CARAN 451AP 114, Andre Blanchet, "November 23 Meeting of Cadres," *L'Etudiant Social,* December 1938.

CHAPTER THREE

1. R. Loustau, brochure, *Notre doctrine devant le problème sociale,* n.d.

2. On the similarities between the PSF and PPF, see Laurent Kestel, *La conversion politique: Doriot, le PPF, et la question du fascisme français* (Paris: Editions Raisons d'Agir, 2012).

3. Goy, quoted in Christopher Millington, "The French veterans and the Republic: The Union nationale des combattants, 1933–1939" (PhD diss., University of Cardiff, 2009), 107.

4. Anon., "Le PSF et le Vote des Femmes," *Le Flambeau de Flandre, Artois, Picardie,* November 13, 1937.

5. Ibid.

6. Downs, "Nous plantions les trois couleurs," 127, 136.

7. CARAN 451AP 87, letter from Dr. Maurice Chiray to Préval, November 22, 1934.

8. CARAN 451AP 87, Medical Center Report: January 1935–March 1936.

9. CARAN 451AP 163, report, "Réunion Constitutive de l'Association—statuts initiaux," December 23, 1936.

10. CARAN 451AP 163, List of Personnel, n.d. (probably 1937–1938); CARAN 451AP 161, Tract, "Association Médico-Sociale Jeanne d'Arc," n.d.

11. CARAN 451AP 162, letter from Préval to Madame Perrineau, April 26, 1937.

12. Ibid.

13. CARAN 451AP 163, Pau Guidebook, n.d; Ruth Harris, *Lourdes: Body and Spirit in the Secular Age* (New York: Penguin Compass, 1999).

14. CARAN 451AP 163, statutes, "Conditions d'Admission à la Maison de Repos 'Les Allées,'" n.d.

15. Ibid.

16. CARAN 451AP 164, Tract, "Les Allées," n.d.

17. CARAN 451AP 164, Report, M. Hecht at the AMSJA General Assembly, January 31, 1938.

18. CARAN 451AP 164, Report, Mademoiselle de Gimard at the AMSJA General Assembly, January 31, 1938.

19. Ibid.

20. CARAN 451AP 163, letter from de Gimard to Préval, January 6, 1938.

21. CARAN 451AP 162, unsigned inspection report, February 3, 1937.

22. CARAN 451AP 162, confidential letter from Préval to Perrineau, March 26, 1937.

23. CARAN 451AP 162, report, Mademoiselle Vieira, July 21, 1937.

24. CARAN 451AP 162, letter from Préval to Madame Perrineau, April 26, 1937.

25. Ibid.

26. Ibid.

27. Ibid.

28. CARAN 451AP 163, report from M. Lerecouvreur to Préval, September 9, 1937.

29. Ibid.

30. CARAN 451AP 161, unsigned inspection report, June 20, 1939.

31. Ibid.

32. CARAN 451AP 161, unsigned inspection report, September 28, 1939.

33. CARAN 451AP 163, letter from Ducrocq to Mademoiselle Guithard, January 26, 1938.

34. CARAN 451AP 162, letter from Préval to Ducrocq, August 25, 1937.

35. CARAN 451AP 162, confidential report, Ducrocq, October 7, 1938.

36. Ibid.

37. Ibid.

38. CARAN 451AP 162, letter from Préval to Perrineau, January 29, 1937.

39. CHSP LR 15, regulation booklet, "Groupes d'Action Sociale," n.d (probably fall 1936).

40. CARAN 451AP 175, letter from Marochetti to Madame Dutihl, September 26, 1938.

41. CARAN 451AP 162, letter from Préval to M. Danner, August 26, 1937.

42. CARAN 451AP 162, letter from Préval to Ducrocq, August 25, 1937.

43. CARAN 451AP 182, confidential letter from Préval to Madame Leonardi, April 27, 1938.

44. CARAN 451AP 131, series of reports by Social Action Delegate P.F. Bouaine, "PSF Fédération de Tunisie; Rapport du groupe féminin d'Action Sociale," April–September 1938.

45. CARAN 451AP 179, anon. report, "Réunion du Conseil d'Administration," 1937.

46. CARAN 451AP 133, Garrigoux circular, "Colonies de vacances," June 17, 1937.

47. CARAN 451AP 133, *Service Social,* January 1939, p. 1; CARAN 451AP 175, Travail et Loisirs report, "Observations et Suggestions devant servir à l'étude de l'organisation des loisirs," January 1938.

48. CARAN 451AP 172, letter from A. Gendre (Isère PSF Federation president), December 14, 1938.

49. CARAN 451AP 172, letter from Madame Carpano to Préval, December 2, 1938.

50. CARAN 451AP 172, letter from Aimé Lefevre (Isère PSF section chief) to Préval, December 2, 1938.

51. CARAN 451AP 172, letter from M. Carpano to La Rocque, December 3, 1938.

52. CARAN 451AP 172, letter from anon. to A. Gendre, n.d.

53. CARAN 451AP 172, letter from A. Gendre to La Rocque, December 14, 1938.

54. Ibid.

55. CARAN 451AP 172, "Plan d'Action Civique Féminine," n.d (probably early 1937).

56. Ibid.

57. CHSP LR 29, circular from La Rocque to Social Action Delegates, March 18, 1937.

58. Ibid.

59. CHSP LR 29, circular from La Rocque to presidents of local committees and sections, March 18, 1937.

60. Ibid.

61. CHSP LR 15, circular from La Rocque to presidents of Regional Councils, Departmental Federations, Local Committees, and Sections, January 15, 1937.

62. CHSP LR 29, circular from La Rocque to presidents of local committees and sections, March 18, 1937.

63. CHSP LR 29, circular from La Rocque to Social Action delegates, March 18, 1937.

64. CHSP LR 15, circular from La Rocque to presidents of Regional Councils, Departmental Federations, Local Committees, and Sections, January 15, 1937.

65. CHSP LR 29, circular from La Rocque to presidents of local committees and sections, March 18, 1937.

66. CARAN 451AP 102, Published Brochure, Garrigoux, *Le PSF et l'action social: Rapport presenté au 1ière congrès national,* 1937.

67. CARAN 451AP 134, Garrigoux speech at the Social Action Congress, May 17, 1939.

68. CARAN 451AP 172, "Plan d'Action Civique Féminine," n.d (probably early 1937).

69. CARAN 451AP 131, anon., "Compte-Rendu du Région de Bourgogne, Fédération de la Nièvre," April–June 1938.

70. CARAN 451AP 172, "Plan d'Action Civique Féminine," n.d (probably early 1937).

71. CHSP LR 15, regulation booklet, "Groupes d'Action Sociale," n.d (probably fall 1936).

72. CARAN 451AP 133, anon., "Rôle de la Déléguées Civiques," n.d.

73. Casanova's struggles are also discussed in Kennedy, *Reconciling France Against Democracy,* 206–207.

74. CARAN 451AP 133, report, Casanova to Préval, July 31, 1939.

75. Ibid.

76. CARAN 451AP 172, Garrigoux inspection report on Péronne section, March 28, 1940.

77. S. Desmons, "La Femme et la Politique," *Le Flambeau de Lorraine: pour la réconciliation française,* April 1, 1939.

78. Odette Bernard, "Votre devoir civique Mesdames?" *La Flamme des Deux-Sèvres,* April 1939.

79. Anon., "Action Civique," *L'Heure Française: organe hebdomadaire de la réconciliation française pour la région provençale,* March 5, 1938.

80. L.N., "Au Foyer: Les Femmes et le PSF," *Liberté du Maine: organe du P.S.F. de la Sarthe et de la Mayenne,* June 1938.

81. Jean-Marie Gautier, "Vous Mesdames," *La Flamme des Deux-Sèvres,* May 1939.

CHAPTER FOUR

1. Chrastil, *Organizing for War,* 112–13, 125–26; Eugen Weber, "Pierre de Coubertin and the Introduction of Organised Sport in France," *Journal of Contemporary History* 5, no. 2 (1970): 7.

2. Chrastil, *Organizing for War,* 125.

3. Ibid., 113, 119.

4. Eugen Weber, "Gymnastics and Sports in Fin-de-Siècle France: Opium of the Classes?," *American Historical Review* 76, no. 1 (February 1971): 92–93.

5. See, for example, Joshua Cole, *The Power of Large Numbers: Population, Politics, and Gender in Nineteenth-Century France* (Ithaca, N.Y.: Cornell University Press, 2000); Eugen Weber, *The Hollow Years: France in the 1930s* (New York: W.W. Norton, 1994).

6. Rosenberg, *Policing Paris,* 2006; Boittin, *Colonial Metropolis,* 2010.

7. See for example, Whitney, *Mobilizing Youth,* 177–79; Joan Tumblety, "The Soccer World Cup of 1938: Politics, Spectacles, and *la Culture Physique* in Interwar France," *French Historical Studies* 31, no. 1 (Winter 2008): 81–82; Christopher Forth, *Masculinity in the Modern West: Gender, Civilization and the Body* (New York: Palgrave Macmillan, 2008); Mosse, *The Image of Man.*

8. Quoted in Whitney, *Mobilizing Youth,* 178.

9. Quoted in Tumblety, "The Soccer World Cup of 1938," 93.

10. Mary Lynn Stewart, *For Health and Beauty: Physical Culture for Frenchwomen, 1880s–1930s* (Baltimore: Johns Hopkins University Press, 2001) 1, 147–50, 158–60.

11. Tumblety defines interwar physical culture as a set of ideas and fields of practices that ranged from gymnastics and bodybuilding to team sports (*Remaking the Male Body: Masculinity and the uses of Physical Culture in Interwar and Vichy France* [Oxford: Oxford University Press, 2012], 4).

12. Ibid., 179–91; Kalman, *The Extreme Right in Interwar France,* 175–79.

13. For more on the concept of embodiment, see Kathleen Canning, *Gender History in Practice: Historical Perspectives on Bodies, Class, and Citizenship* (Ithaca, N.Y.: Cornell University Press, 2006); and Camiscioli, *Reproducing the French Race.*

14. Tumblety, *Remaking the Male Body,* 14.

15. Jean Edward Ruffier, *Soyons fort! Manuel de culture physique elémentaire* (Paris: Librairie de "Portez-vous bien," 1914), 3. For more on conceptions of ugliness during the Third Republic, see Rae Beth Gordon, *Dances with Darwin, 1875–1910: Vernacular Modernity in France* (Aldershot, England, and Burlington, Vt.: Ashgate, 2009), 103–44.

16. Ruffier, *Soyons fort!,* 3.

17. CARAN 451AP 153, Med. A. Bleu and Maire, "SPES Education Physique Féminine Technique et Programme," n.d.

18. CARAN 451AP 155, Maire speech, "Les SPES et Leur Programme," October 1938.

19. La Rocque, *Service Public,* 157, 46–47.

20. CARAN 451AP 134, Maire speech at the First PSF Social Congress, "Rapport sur les SPES," May 1939.

21. Henry Friedlander, *The Origins of Nazi Genocide: From Euthanasia to the Final Solution* (Chapel Hill: University of North Carolina Press, 1995), 1–22.

22. CARAN 451AP 155, Maire presentation, "Biologie Elémentaire: L'Hérédité, L'Influence du Milieu," n.d.

23. Ibid.

24. CARAN 451AP 156, Thevenet, SPES program, "SPES du Rhône: Cours de Pédagogie à l'usage des Moniteurs d'Education Physique," n.d.

25. CARAN 451AP 155, Maire, "L'Homme et La Civilisation," n.d.

26. Conklin, *In the Museum of Man*, 1, 5.

27. CARAN 451AP 155, Hébertist brochure, n.d.

28. Tumblety, *Remaking the Male Body*, 37.

29. Conklin, *In the Museum of Man*, 6.

30. Ibid., 3–6.

31. Tumblety, *Remaking the Male Body*, 35–37.

32. CARAN 451AP 155, Henri Sirolle, "Une France Fort, Une jeunesse heureuse," *La Vie Hébertiste*, November 1937.

33. CARAN 451AP, Report by Mlle le Docteur Jeanne Latil to Garrigoux, "Surveillance Médico-Sociale de l'Enfant et de l'Adolescent, Rapports avec la SPES," May 2, 1939.

34. CARAN 451AP 155, SPES Instructional Booklet, "Education Physique," n.d.

35. Ibid.

36. Tumblety and Kalman have explored the influences of Hébert on SPES but not the influences of other scholars on the CF/PSF (Tumblety, *Remaking the Male Body*, 182–86; Kalman, *The Extreme Right in Interwar France*, 176–77).

37. CARAN 451 AP 155, Maire report, "Principes Elémentaires de Physiologie, selon le Docteur Ruffier," n.d.

38. Ibid.

39. Ibid.

40. Margaret Mead, *Sex and Temperament in Three Primitive Societies* (New York: W. Morrow, 1935).

41. CARAN 451AP 155, Maire presentation, "Biologie Elémentaire: Différenciation des Sexes," n.d.

42. See, for example, Stewart, *For Health and Beauty*, 147, 156; Frader, *Breadwinners and Citizens*, 79, 126.

43. CARAN 451AP 155, Maire presentation, "Biologie Elémentaire: Différenciation des Sexes," n.d.

44. CARAN 451AP 153, Med. A. Bleu and Maire, "SPES Education Physique Féminine Technique et Programme," n.d.

45. Ibid.

46. Whitney, *Mobilizing Youth*, 201.

47. CARAN 451AP 153, Med. A. Bleu and Maire, "SPES Education Physique Féminine Technique et Programme," n.d.

48. CARAN 451AP 155, Maire presentation, "Biologie Elémentaire: Différenciation des Sexes," n.d.

49. CARAN 451AP 156, pamphlet, Maire, "SPES Un Programme d'Education Physique," n.d.

50. Ibid.

51. Ibid. For more on the Croix de Feu/PSF's emphasis on team at the expense of the individual, see Kalman, *The Extreme Right in Interwar France,* 176–78.

52. Stewart, *For Health and Beauty,* 171; Whitney, *Mobilizing Youth,* 181; CARAN 451AP 189/5, Travail et Loisirs report, "Centres d'Education Physique," June 1939.

53. CHSP LR 6, report, Gaëtan Maire, "Leçons données par semaine dans chaque groupe dans les centres de Paris," June 6, 1936.

54. CHSP LR 39, Brochure, "Le Centre Social Paris-Sud"; CARAN 451AP 93, Women's Section Circular, "Centres D'éducation Physique Avec Foyer-Bibliothèque," October 1935.

55. CARAN 451AP 93, Women's Section Circular, "Centres D'éducation Physique Avec Foyer-Bibliothèque," October 1935.

56. Tumblety, *Remaking the Male Body,* 15.

57. CARAN 451AP 162, letter from Préval to Madame Perrineau, January 29, 1937.

58. CARAN 451AP 174, letter from Maire to Préval, June 1938.

59. CARAN 451AP 153, SPES statutes, "Qu'est-ce que SPES," n.d (probably late 1936).

60. CARAN 451AP 187, Report by M. Danner for M. Le Tanneur, "Compte-Rendu de Notre Entretien avec le Bureau d'Etudes Sociales, SPES, et l'Office du Tourisme," October 14, 1937.

61. CARAN 451AP 172, form, "Service des Examens Médico-Physiologiques de Travail et Loisirs." For Downs's analysis of how children's level of fitness was used to exclude them from the movement's summer camps, see "'Each and every one of you must become a *chef,*'" 29–32.

62. CARAN 451AP 172, form, "Service des Examens Médico-Physiologiques de Travail et Loisirs."

63. CARAN 451AP 155, dossier "Cartes de Moniteurs d'Education Physique."

64. CARAN 451AP 153, SPES statutes, "Qu'est-ce que SPES," n.d (probably late 1936); CARAN 451AP 154 *bis,* Maire, "Conditions d'Admission, SPES de France, EP: Ecole de Moniteurs," n.d.

65. CARAN 451AP 153, SPES training manual, "Conseils aux Moniteurs et Monitrices," n.d.

66. Ibid.

67. CARAN 451AP 155, SPES Instructional Booklet, "Education Physique," n.d.

68. Ibid.

69. On developing girls' bodies for childbirth, see Stewart, *For Health and Beauty,* 156–62.

70. CARAN 451AP 153, Med. A. Bleu and Maire, "SPES Education Physique Féminine Technique et Programme," n.d.

71. Whitney, *Mobilizing Youth,* 200; Stewart, *For Health and Beauty,* 167.

72. CARAN 451AP 155, Report, Maire, at the "Réunion des Responsables Féminines PSF," March 8, 1939; Stewart, *For Health and Beauty,* 168.

73. Stewart, *For Health and Beauty,* 168.

74. CARAN 451AP 156, pamphlet, Maire, "SPES Un Programme d'Education Physique," n.d.

75. Ibid.

76. Muel-Dreyfus, *Vichy and the Eternal Feminine,* 294–95.

77. Lackerstein, *National Regeneration in Vichy France,* 194.

78. Stromberg Childers, *Fathers, Families, and the State in France,* 113–18; Muel-Dreyfus, *Vichy and the Eternal Feminine,* 251–54; Pollard, *Reign of Virtue,* 86–97.

CHAPTER FIVE

1. On the far Right and culture, see especially Lebovics, *True France;* Conklin, *In the Museum of Man;* Wardhaugh, *In Pursuit of the People;* Jane F. Fulcher, *The Composer as Intellectual: Music and Ideology in France, 1914–1940* (Oxford: Oxford University Press, 2005).

2. CARAN 451AP 102, brochure, *PSF, Une mystique, un programme,* 1936.

3. On using culture to study process, empire, and the construction of hierarchies, see Sessions, *By Sword and Plow,* 12–15.

4. Conklin, *In the Museum of Man,* 6.

5. For more on the legitimizing power of the civilizing mission see Morton, *Hybrid Modernities,* 7.

6. For a discussion of different types of anticolonialism, see J.P. Daughton, "Behind the Imperial Curtain: International Humanitarian Efforts and the Critique of French Colonialism in the Interwar Years," *French Historical Studies* 34, no. 3 (Summer 2011): 504–505.

7. Conklin, *In the Museum of Man,* 1–5.

8. Brochure, "Les Croix de Feu, leur chef, leur programme," Le Comité de vigilance des intellectuels antifascistes, 1935.

9. This is not to say the Left was "humanist" but that their views must be contextualized against those of the Croix de Feu/PSF (Thomas, *The French Empire between the Wars,* 8–11).

10. Wilder, *The French Imperial Nation-State,* 81, 116; Lebovics, *True France,* 69n26; Lorcin, *Imperial Identities,* 7–8.

11. CARAN 451AP 188, Brochure, "L'Association TL a deux buts," n.d.

12. APP, B/a 1902, report, General Secretary of the Police Prefecture, December 21, 1935.

13. CARAN 451AP 187, Travail et loisirs report, "Etude d'Un projet de Fêtes Françaises," December 20, 1938.

14. CARAN 451AP 87, report, "Action Social de Croix de Feu: Résumé des Oeuvres Sociales de la Section Féminine du Mouvement Social des Croix de Feu," n.d. (but probably late 1935).

15. See the map of the Hotel Contintental in CARAN 451AP 87.

16. CARAN 451AP 87, various correspondence on the "vente de 1935."

17. Kevin Passmore, "Crowd Psychology, Anti-Southern Prejudice, and Constitutional Reform in 1930s France: The Stavisky Affair and the Riots of 6 February 1934," in *The French Right between the Wars: Political and Intellectual Movements from Conservatism to Fascism,* ed. Samuel Kalman and Sean Kennedy (New York: Berghahn, 2014), 31–38.

18. Ibid., 37–38

19. *Le Flambeau,* map of the setup at the Berlitz Palace, May 16, 1936.

20. See weekly issues of *Le Flambeau* from April and May 1936.

21. CARAN 13983, police report, Sûreté nationales-Documentation Politique "Bleus de la Préfecture de police" et de la Sûreté nationale, May 23, 1936.

22. Ibid.

23. CARAN 13983, police reports, Sûreté nationales-Documentation Politique "Bleus de la Préfecture de police" et de la Sûreté nationale, May 22–25, 1936; *Le Flambeau,* "Notre Kermesse," May 30, 1936.

24. Lebovics, *True France,* 135–40; Daniel Sherman, "'Peoples Ethnographic': Objects, Museums, and the Colonial Inheritance of French Ethnography," *French Historical Studies* 27, no. 3 (Summer 2004): 669–70.

25. CARAN 451AP 188, Bureau d'Etudes Sociales to the Cabinet du Président, "Note sur l'Exposition Artisanale," January 7, 1938.

26. CARAN 451AP 188, Dutilh report, February 16, 1938.

27. Brigitte Reynaud, *L'industrie rubanière dans la région stéphanois, 1895–1975* (St-Etienne: Centre d'Etudes Foréziennes, Université Jean Monnet, 1991).

28. CARAN 451AP 188, unsigned note, January 27, 1938.

29. CARAN 451AP 188, Dutilh report, February 16, 1938.

30. CARAN 451AP 188, "Rapport de Mdm Dutilh sur les préparatifs de la Vente Comptoir Artisanal," n.d.

31. On Rivière's politics, see Conklin, *In the Museum of Man,* 105; on Rivière, folklore, ethnology, and ethnography, see Chapter 3.

32. Lebovics, *True France,* 140.

33. For the title of the show, see CARAN 451AP 186, poster, "Exposition Internationale, 1937," n.d; for the award letter, see CARAN 451AP 189, letter from Jury President of Class 8A, International Exposition to Travail et loisirs, April 18, 1938; for one of Préval's references to the medal, see CHSP LR 29, Préval letter, June 20, 1965.

34. Shanny Peer, *France on Display: Peasants, Provincials, and Folklore in the 1937 Paris World's Fair* (Albany: State University of New York Press, 1998), 44–47; Karen Fiss, *Grand Illusion: The Third Reich, the Paris Exposition, and the Cultural Seduction of France* (Chicago: University of Chicago Press, 2009), 58, 60.

35. Thomas G. August, "Paris 1937: The Apotheosis of the Popular Front," *Contemporary French Civilization* 5, no. 1 (1980): 51.

36. Elizabeth Ezra, *The Colonial Unconscious: Race and Culture in Interwar France* (Ithaca, N.Y.: Cornell University Press, 2000), 30–32.

37. CARAN 451AP 182, anon., "Notes de service pour le Centre Guynemer," October 12, 1937.

38. CARAN 451AP 189, letters in dossier called "Travail et loisirs à l'Exposition Internationale Paris 1937."

39. CARAN 451AP 182, anon., "Réunion des Directrices," October 2, 1937.

40. In each of the five scenes (particularly Africa, Oceania, and Asia) I will use the original terminology in the instructions for the Fête Coloniale, which reflect Travail et loisirs's schematic conception of each region.

41. CARAN 451AP 189, Travail et loisirs instructions, "Divertissement Colonial en 11 tableaux: I, Afrique," 1937.

42. Richard I. Jobs, "Tarzan under Attack: Youth, Comics, and Cultural Reconstruction in Postwar France," *French Historical Studies* 26, no. 4 (Fall 2003): 692, 693.

43. CARAN 451AP 189, Travail et loisirs instructions, "Divertissement Colonial en 11 tableaux: I, Afrique," 1937.

44. Ibid.

45. Ibid.

46. Myron Echenberg, *Colonial Conscripts: The Tirailleurs Sénégalais in French West Africa, 1857–1960* (Portsmouth, N.H.: Heinemann, 1991), 14.

47. CARAN 451AP 189, Travail et loisirs instructions, "Divertissement Colonial en 11 tableaux: II, Océanie," 1937.

48. CARAN 451AP 189, Travail et loisirs instructions, "Divertissement Colonial en 11 tableaux: IV, La Guyane," 1937.

49. CARAN 451AP 189, Travail et loisirs instructions, "Divertissement Colonial en 11 tableaux: III, Asie," 1937.

50. Hale, *Races on Display*.

51. CARAN 451AP 189, Travail et loisirs instructions, "Divertissement Colonial en 11 tableaux: IV, Afrique du Nord," 1937.

52. CARAN 451AP 189, anon. instructions, "Divertissement Colonial en 11 tableaux: L'appel de la France," 1937.

53. Conklin, *A Mission to Civilize*, 212–14.

54. Wilder, *The French Imperial Nation-State*; Lebovics, *True France*; Ezra, *The Colonial Unconscious*; Furlough, "Une leçon des choses"; Morton, *Hybrid Modernities*.

55. CARAN 451AP 87, anon. circular, "Action Social de Croix de Feu: Résumé des Oeuvres Sociales de la Section Féminine du Mouvement Social des Croix de Feu," 1935.

56. Ibid.

57. The figure of 180 is from CHSP Paris, LR 6, anon. report of Croix de Feu social activities, 1935. The figure of 490 is from CARAN 451AP 114, announcement, *Pourquoi S'en Faire,* May 1937.

58. CARAN 451AP 114, anon., "Le Mois Passe, Vie en Foyer," *Pourquoi S'en Faire,* June 1938.

59. CARAN 451AP 114, Hélène de Bellet, special issue of *Pourquoi S'en Faire,* Winter 1938.

60. CARAN 451AP 93, statutes, "Centre Social Universitaire, 11 rue Soufflot, Paris, 6th," October 1935.

61. Ibid.

62. List of activities at the Foyer listed in 451AP 114, tract, "Etudiantes, Le Foyer Universitaire Des Etudiantes PSF," n.d.

63. CARAN 451AP 114, anon., "Une Soufflotine," *Pourquoi S'en Faire,* June 1938.

64. Ibid.

65. CARAN 451AP 115, Hélène de Bellet, speech "L'Etudiante," First National Congress of PSF Students, 27–28 January 1938.

66. On the movement's anti-intellectualism, see Kennedy, *Reconciling France Against Democracy,* 211.

67. CARAN 451AP 114, *Pourquoi S'en Faire,* August/September 1938.

68. Furlough, "Une leçon des choses," 451.

69. Ibid., 443.

70. "Les étudiantes PSF ont inauguré leur foyer," *La Flamme,* December 4, 1938.

71. CARAN 451AP 114, Marivic Duval, "Notre Voyage en Algérie," *Pourquoi S'en Faire,* May 1938.

72. Ibid.

73. CARAN 451AP 114, anon., "Reportage photographique sur la vie et les activités des étudiantes PSF," *L'étudiante de France,* February 1939.

74. CARAN 451AP 114, Marivic Duval, "Notre Voyage en Algérie," *Pourquoi S'en Faire,* May 1938.

75. Patricia Lorcin, "Rome and France in Africa: Recovering Colonial Algeria's Latin Past," *French Historical Studies* 25, No. 2 (Spring 2002): 297, 317.

76. Marivic Duval, "Une lettre des 'Soufflotines,'" *La Flamme,* May 20, 1938.

77. CARAN 451AP 114, Marivic Duval, "Notre Voyage en Algérie," *Pourquoi S'en Faire,* May 1938.

78. Diana Davis, *Resurrecting the Granary of Rome: Environmental History and French Colonial Expansion in North Africa* (Athens: Ohio University Press, 2007).

79. Lorcin, "Recovering Colonial Algeria's Latin Past," 308; Caroline Ford, "Reforestation and Anxieties of Empire in French Colonial Algeria," *American Historical Review* 113, no. 2 (April 2008): 352.

80. Marivic Duval, "Une lettre des 'Soufflotines,'" *La Flamme,* May 20, 1938.

81. Lorcin, "Rome and France in Africa," 313–15.

82. CARAN 451AP 114, Marivic Duval, "Notre Voyage en Algérie," *Pourquoi S'en Faire,* May 1938.

83. Ibid. (emphasis mine).

84. Ibid.

85. ANOM 93 B3 635, special report, commissaire de police to the Prefect and Directeur de la Sécurité Générale, April 23, 1938.

86. Marivic Duval, "Une lettre des 'Soufflotines,'" *La Flamme,* May 20, 1938.

87. ANOM 93 B3 635, special report, commissaire de police to the Prefect and Directeur de la Sécurité Générale, April 23, 1938.

88. CARAN 451AP 114, Alfred Debay, "Aux Soufflotines de la Caravane d'Alger," *Pourquoi S'en Faire,* May 1938.

89. Marivic Duval, "Une lettre des 'Soufflotines,'" *La Flamme,* May 20, 1938.

90. "Les Soufflotines parmi nous," *La Flamme,* April 22, 1938.

91. CARAN 451AP 114, Madeleine, "Jeunesse de Notre Temps: Camps de Travail," *Pourquoi S'en Faire,* August/September 1938.

92. Author cited as "une Soufflotine," "Camps de service du travail en Allemagne," *La Flamme,* September 15, 1938.

93. Editor's note, "Camps de service du travail en Allemagne," *La Flamme,* September 15, 1938.

94. Elizabeth Harvey, *Women and the Nazi East: Agents and Witnesses of Germanization* (New Haven, Ct.: Yale University Press, 2003), 45–46.

95. Statistics from Dan P. Silverman, "Fantasy and Reality in Nazi Work-Creation Programs, 1933–1936," *Journal of Modern History* 65, no. 1 (March 1993): 113, 115.

96. Elizabeth Heineman, *What Difference Does a Husband Make? Women and Marital Status in Nazi and Postwar Germany* (Berkeley: University of California Press, 1999), 40, 42.

97. I have been unable to find biographical information on Madeleine, including her last name.

98. CARAN 451AP 114, Madeleine, "Jeunesse de Notre Temps: Camps de Travail," *Pourquoi S'en Faire,* August/September 1938.

99. Ibid.

100. Ibid.

101. Ibid.

102. CARAN 451AP 114, Madeleine, "Jeunesse de Notre Temps: Camps de Travail," *Pourquoi S'en Faire,* August/September 1938.

CHAPTER SIX

1. Ben Kiernan, *Blood and Soil: A World History of Genocide and Extermination from Sparta to Darfur* (New Haven, Ct.: Yale University Press, 2007).

2. See especially Thomas, *The French Empire Between the Wars*, 10; Cole, "Anti-Semitism and the Colonial Situation in Interwar Algeria," 100–101; Kalman, "Fascism and Algérianité."

3. On the complexities of determining Croix de Feu/PSF membership and the degree of work-ing-class support for the movement, see Kennedy, *Reconciling France against Democracy*, 191, 195–97.

4. Kennedy, *Reconciling France*. On the figure of 8 percent, see the discussion of the recruitment numbers for indigenous Algerians later in this chapter.

5. ANOM Oran 466, police report on a Croix de Feu meeting, May 17, 1935.

6. Centre des Archives diplomatiques de Nantes (hereafter CADN), Maroc, région de Casablanca 29, police report on a Croix de Feu meeting, June 23, 1931; "Programme d'Action" for the RNCF attached to a police report, November 29, 1935.

7. Minguet, "Le mouvement social français: ses origines, sa constitution, sa direction, son rôle," *Bulletin de Liaison du Croix de Feu en Algérie*, June 15, 1936.

8. CHSP LR 6, anon. report, "Maroc," n.d; CARAN 451AP 131, series of reports by Social Action Delegate P.F. Bouaine, "PSF Fédération de Tunisie; Rapport du groupe féminin d'Action Sociale," April–September 1938.

9. Data on the dates and location of the Women's Sections come from issues of *Le Flambeau* (1934–1936) and the *Bulletin des Associations Croix de Feu du Département d'Alger* (May 1935–October 1935), which became the *Bulletin de Liaison du Croix de Feu en Algérie*, October 1935–June 1936.

10. For the metropolitan figure of one-third, ses Thomas, "Les Droites, Les Femmes et le Mouve-ment Associatif, 1902–1946," 524; Nobécourt, *Le colonel de La Rocque*, 640. For the colonial figures, ANOM 91/F/405–406, 93/B3/707, 522, 635, 323, 327, 700, Oran 70, Oran 466, 92/F/2413, police reports listing attendees at meetings, 1934–1939; CHSP LR 6, anon. report, "Maroc," n.d.

11. "La première Kermesse du Mouvement social français à Tunis," *Bulletin de Liaison du Croix de Feu en Algérie*, May 15, 1936.

12. CARAN 451AP 131, series of reports by Social Action Delegate P.F. Bouaine, "PSF Fédération de Tunisie; Rapport du groupe féminin d'Action Sociale," April–September 1938.

13. Ibid.

14. CADN, Maroc, région de Casablanca 29, report by the Chef de Section, Le Délégué au Service d'Entr'aide, November 29, 1935.

15. Ibid.

16. CADN, Maroc, région de Casablanca 29, "Programme d'Action" for the RNCF attached to a police report, November 29, 1935.

17. Ibid.

18. Minguet, "Le mouvement social français: ses origines, sa constitution, sa direction, son rôle," *Bulletin de Liaison du Croix de Feu en Algérie*, June 15, 1936.

19. Ibid.

20. Lucien Colonieu, "Le Service Social des C. de F. et V.N.," *Bulletin des Associations Croix de Feu du Département d'Alger*, May 1935.

21. ANOM 91/F/405–406, police report from Le Chef de la Sûreté Départementale, March 5, 1935; 91/F/405–406, report from Le Commissaire de Police, to le Secrétaire Général administration Préfecture, November 25, 1935.

22. ANOM 93/B3/707, report on a Croix de Feu meeting from the Bône Commissaire Central to the Directeur de la Sécurité Générale de Algérie; Le Préfet de Constantine; le Sous-Préfet de Bône; Le Maire de la Ville de Bône, December 30, 1935. The "French France" quote is from 93/B3/707, confidential police report on a Croix de Feu meeting from Le Chef de la Sûreté Départementale, December 31, 1935.

23. Lucien Colonieu, "Service Sociale," *Bulletin des Associations Croix de Feu du Département d'Alger,* September 15, 1935.

24. "Notre camp de vacances," *Bulletin des Associations Croix de Feu du Département d'Alger,* June 15, 1935.

25. "La Section Féminine a entendu une intérassante conférence de Mlle Martignier," *Bulletin de Liaison du Croix de Feu en Algérie,* June 15, 1936.

26. "Comment fonction le mouvement social à Alger," *Bulletin de Liason du Croix de Feu en Algérie,* March 15, 1936.

27. "La brillante activité de la jeune section féminine du Mazafran," *Bulletin de Liaison du Croix de Feu en Algérie,* March 15, 1936.

28. The data for figure 9 are based upon documents in ANOM 30 134 *Bulletin de Liaison du Croix de Feu en Algérie:* "L'activité de la Section féminine d'Alger en Février," March 15, 1936; Nouvion, "La brillante activité de la jeune section féminine du Mazafran," March 15, 1936; Mlle Tréfumus, "Chez les Constantinois," April 15, 1936; "La Section Féminine a entendu une intérassante conférence de Mlle Martignier," June 15, 1936; ANOM 93 B3 323, confidential report from le Chef de la Sûreté Départementale, December 27, 1935; CADN, Maroc, région de Casablanca 29, "Programme d'Action" for the Regroupement National autour du Mouvement Croix de Feu, attached to a report by the Chef de Section, Le Délégué au Service d'Entr'aide, addressed to Monsieur le Contrôleur, Chef de la Région civile, Casablanca, November 29, 1935; CARAN 451AP 131, series of reports by Social Action Delegate P.F. Bouaine, "PSF Fédération de Tunisie; Rapport du groupe féminine d'Action Sociale," April–September 1938.

29. ANOM 93/B3/707, report by the prefect of the Constantine Department, August 3, 1935, p. 40.

30. ANOM 91/F/405–406, report on Croix de Feu weekly meeting by le Chef de la Sûreté Départementale to Préfect (Cabinet) and Directeur Sécurité Générale, January 22, 1935, and June 19, 1935.

31. CADN, Maroc, région de Casablanca 29, confidential report from the chef de la police mobile to the Délégué à la Résidence Générale, July 12, 1935.

32. ANOM 93/B3/707, report on a private meeting of the Constantine Croix de Feu by le chef de la Sûreté Départementale, February 4, 1936 (emphasis mine).

33. Gayle K. Brunelle and Annette Finley-Croswhite, *Murder in the Metro: Laetitia Toureaux and the Cagoule in 1930s France* (Baton Rouge: Louisiana State University Press, 2012).

34. ANOM 93/B3/707, police report on a Constantine Croix de Feu meeting from le chef de la Sûreté Départementale, January 23, 1936 (emphasis mine).

35. ANOM 93/B3/707, police report on the Croix de Feu in Constantine from le chef de la Sûreté Départementale, February 3, 1936.

36. ANOM 93/B3/707, Constantine police report from le Chef de la Sûreté Départementale to le Gouverneur Général et le Préfet (Cabinet) and le Préfet de la Police Générale, June 19, 1935.

37. ANOM Oran 466, police report on Croix de Feu general assembly meeting, November 4, 1935 (emphasis mine).

38. CARAN 451AP 131, "Rapport sur l'Action l'activité de l'Action Sociale en 1938–1939."

39. ANOM 91/F/405–406, police report on a speech by Roumégous (head of the PSF's Algiers Federation) at PSF meeting, August 2, 1936.

40. ANOM 91/F/405–406, police report on a PSF meeting, February 8, 1937.

41. For more on Croix de Feu/PSF efforts to recruit in indigenous communities, see Kalman, "Fascism and Algérianité," 115–19.

42. Minguet, "Le mouvement social français: ses origines, sa constitution, sa direction, son rôle," *Bulletin de Liaison du Croix de Feu en Algérie,* June 15, 1936.

43. CADN, Tunisie, RG 1723, note from the Special Commissar to the head of the General Security Service, April 15, 1937; Amira Sghaier, *La droite française en Tunisie entre 1934 et 1946* (Tunis: Institut supérieur d'histoire du mouvement national, 2004), 74.

44. Minguet, quoted in Sghaier, *La droite française en Tunisie,* 143.

45. CADN, Maroc, région de Casablanca 29, report by Le Commissaire Divisionnaire to Le Commissaire Résident Général de la République Française au Maroc, November 18, 1935.

46. CADN, Maroc, région de Casablanca 29, report by Le Commissaire Divisionnaire to Le Commissaire Résident Général de la République Française au Maroc, November 16, 1935.

47. CADN Maroc, Direction de l'Intériur 315, report by le Contrôleur Civil, Chef des Services Municipaux, June 3, 1938.

48. Kalman argues that the Croix de Feu/PSF's shift away from recruiting évolués and Algerian veterans was rooted in how the Depression made communism and colonial nationalism more appealing to indigenous Algerians ("Fascism and Algérianité," 125).

49. ANOM 93 B3 707, report by the prefect of the Constantine Department, August 3, 1935.

50. Ibid.

51. Thomas, *Empires of Intelligence,* 265; Cole, "Anti-Semitism and the Colonial Situation," 88.

52. ANOM 93 B3 707, report by the prefect of the Constantine Department, August 3, 1935; Cole, "Anti-Semitism and the Colonial Situation," 97–98.

53. ANOM 93 B3 700, report from Section des Affaires indigènes et de la Police Géneralé, October 26, 1936.

54. This figure is based upon police reports on Croix de Feu/PSF meetings in the Departments of Algiers, Oran, and Constantine: ANOM Oran 70, Oran 466, Oran 92/F/2413, Alger 91/F/405–406, Constantine 93/B3/323, 93/B3/327, 93/B3/522, 93/B3/635/, 93/B3/700, 93/B3/707.

55. ANOM Oran 466, confidential note from Governor General Georges Le Beau to the Oran prefect, November 23, 1935.

56. Ibid.

57. The data for figure 10 are based upon police reports on Croix de Feu/PSF meetings in the Departments of Algiers, Oran, and Constantine: ANOM Oran 70, Oran 466, Oran 92/F/2413, Alger 91/F/405–406, Constantine 93/B3/323, 93/B3/327, 93/B3/522, 93/B3/635/, 93/B3/700, 93/B3/707.

58. ANOM 93/B3/327, police report on PSF meeting, September 27, 1936.

59. CADN, Maroc, région de Casablanca 29, "Programme d'Action" for the RNCF, attached to a police report, November 29, 1935.

60. ANOM 91 F 405–406, report on Croix de Feu meeting from Le Commissaire de Police de l'Arba to le Préfet Police Générale à Alger, December 1, 1935.

61. ANOM Oran 466, police report on the Croix de Feu, August 2, 1935.

62. ANOM 93/B3/635, police report on the Croix de Feu, May 15, 1937.

63. Wyrtzen, "Constructing Morocco: The Colonial Struggle to Define a Nation, 1912–1956," 159–60.

64. Perkins, *A History of Modern Tunisia,* 89–90.

65. Susan Gilson Miller, *A History of Modern Morocco* (Cambridge, England: Cambridge University Press, 2013) 126–27.

66. La Rocque, *Service Public,* 44–45.

67. Ruedy, *Modern Algeria,* 140.

68. Thomas, *The French Empire Between the Wars,* 278.

69. Kaddache, *Histoire du nationalisme algérien,* Vol 1, 2003.

70. McDougall, *History and the Culture of Nationalism in Algeria,* 65.

71. Ruedy, *Modern Algeria,* 134–35.

72. Thomas, *The French Empire Between the Wars,* 251, 258, 264; McDougall, *History and the Culture of Nationalism in Algeria,* 64–66.

73. Ruedy, *Modern Algeria,* 133–47; Thomas, *The French Empire Between the Wars,* 253.

74. Ibid., 258–59.

75. McDougall, *History and the Culture of Nationalism,* 64; Thomas, *The French Empire Between the Wars,* 258.

76. Benjamin Stora, *Nationalistes algériens et révolutionnaires français au temps du Front populaire* (Paris: Editions l'Harmattan, 1987).

77. McDougall, *History and the Culture of Nationalism in Algeria,* 76.

78. For a full list, see Ruedy, *Modern Algeria,* 141.

79. Ibid., 142.

80. McDougall, *History and the Culture of Nationalism in Algeria,* 98.

81. "L'imbroglio de la politique musulmane en Algérie," *La Flamme,* February 15, 1937.

82. Ibid.

83. Testis, "L'Etendard du Congrès Musulman Algérien tourne du rouge au vert," *La Flamme,* August 1, 1937.

84. McDougall, *History and the Culture of Nationalism in Algeria,* 64.

85. Testis, "La tyrannie par la terreur," *La Flamme,* March 3, 1938.

86. William Cleveland, *Islam Against the West: Shakib Arslan and the Campaign for Islamic Nationalism* (Austin: University of Texas Press, 1985).

87. "Comment l'Algérie qui n'a jamais formé une nation devient la proie de nationalismes importés de l'étranger," *La Flamme,* March 22, 1937.

88. Cleveland, *Islam Against the West,* 1985.

89. Kaddache, *Histoire du nationalisme algérien,* 176.

90. William Kramer, *Islam Assembled: The Advent of the Muslim Congresses* (New York: Columbia University Press, 1986), 143.

91. Ibid., 151.

92. "La conjuration antifrançaise se précise en Afrique du Nord," *La Flamme,* March 22, 1937.

93. Kramer, *Islam Assembled,* 147–48.

94. Ibid.

95. Cleveland, *Islam Against the West,* 1985.

96. "Comment l'Algérie qui n'a jamais formé une nation devient la proie de nationalismes importés de l'étranger," *La Flamme,* March 22, 1937.

97. Ibid.

98. "La conjuration antifrançaise se précise en Afrique du Nord," *La Flamme,* March 22, 1937.

99. "L'imbroglio de la politique musulmane en Algérie," *La Flamme,* February 15, 1937.

100. La Rocque, *Service Public,* 46.

101. Alfred Debay, "La désillusion des indigènes nord-africains," *La Flamme,* October 3, 1937.

102. "Comment l'Algérie qui n'a jamais formé une nation devient la proie de nationalismes importés de l'étranger," *La Flamme,* March 22, 1937.

103. Ibid.

104. Ibid.

105. "La conjuration antifrançaise se précise en Afrique du Nord," *La Flamme,* March 22, 1937.

106. Testis, "Les élections municipales indigènes d'Alger ne doivent pas être exploitées contre l'accession de nos frères musulmans aux droits civiques," *La Flamme,* July 16, 1937.

107. ANOM Const 635, police report, speech by Ribère, chef de la propagande du PSF du Département d'Alger, April 12, 1938.

108. ANOM Oran 70, police report, speech by Sarrochi, April 23, 1938.

109. ANOM 91/F/405–406, police report on PSF meeting, August 2, 1936.

110. CHSP LR 29, PSF report, "Le PSF devant les Problèmes Algériens," Spring 1937, p. 2.

111. For the development of the myth that Berbers were more assimilable than Arabs, see Lorcin, *Imperial Identities,* 1999.

112. CHSP LR 52, Alfred Debay, unpublished manucript, "Sous l'Insigne Croix de Feu: Alger, 1930–1945," December 1951.

113. ANOM 93/B3/635, police report on a PSF meeting, August 14, 1936.

114. La Rocque, "Le Problème Algérien," *La Flamme,* June 1, 1937.

115. Debay, "Blum-Violette-Sarraut," *La Flamme,* February 12, 1938.

116. Iba Zizen, "La citoyenneté intégral doit être conférée d'office à certaines catégories d'indigènes," *La Flamme,* February 12, 1938. While not locating Iba-Zizen's rhetoric within the Croix de Feu/PSF's wider social program, Kalman finds that it shows a disconnect between the movement's assimilationist rhetoric and associationist practice ("Fascism and Algérianité," 130).

117. Ibid.

118. Iba-Zizen, "Chrétiens et musulmans d'Algérie comprenez-vous," *La Flamme,* November 11, 1938.

119. Ibid.

120. Ibid.

121. Iba Zizen, "La citoyenneté intégral doit être conférée d'office à certaines catégories d'indigènes," *La Flamme,* February 12, 1938. The PSF placed complex conditions for citizenship on each of these groups.

122. Philippe Machefer, "Autour du problème algérien en 1936–1938: La doctrine algérienne du P.S.F.: Le P.S.F et le projet Blum-Violette," *Revue d'histoire moderne et contemporaine* 10 (1963): 156; Kalman, "Fascism and Algérianité," 130.

123. Kalman, "Le Combat par Tous les Moyens," 127.

124. CADN Maroc, Direction de l'Intériur 315, confidential note from Le Commissaire Chef de la Sûreté Régionale, February 13, 1939; ANOM Oran 466, police report on the Croix de Feu, February 21, 1936; 93/B3/635, police report on PSF activities, April 27, 1937; CADN Maroc, Direction de l'Intérior 315, Marrakech, police report on a Croix de Feu meeting, July 2, 1939; Sghaier, *La droite française en Tunisie,* 114–50; Kalman, "Le Combat par Tous les Moyens," 135.

125. ANOM Oran 466, police report on a speech by Richard at a Croix de Feu meeting, February 21, 1936.

126. Kalman, "Le Combat par Tous les Moyens," 135–37.

127. CADN, région de Meknès, 251, police report on anti-Semitic activities, 1937–1947.

128. For more on the context of the sanctions, see Richard Millman, "Les Croix-de-feu et L'antisémitisme," *Vientième Siècle* 38 (1993): 55.

129. Cole, "Anti-Semitism and the Colonial Situation in Interwar Algeria," 55.

130. Kalman, "Le Combat par Tous les Moyens," 146, 150; ANOM Oran 70, police report on the Croix de Feu, March 1, 1937.

131. "Est-ce un plan concerté?" *La Flamme,* March 1, 1937.

132. ANOM Oran 70, police report on the PSF, Oct 27, 1937.

133. Ibid.

134. Kalman, "Le Combat par Tous les Moyens," 134; ANOM Oran 466, le sous préfet de Tlemcen to le préfet d'Oran, October 9, 1935; CADN, région de Marrakech, 936, police report on Croix de Feu activities, June 1934.

135. Kalman, "Le Combat par Tous les Moyens," 146.

136. Thomas, *Empires of Intelligence,* 273; Thomas, *The French Empire Between the Wars,* 271.

137. Thomas, *The French Empire Between the Wars,* 57.

138. Perkins, *A History of Modern Tunisia,* 10.

139. Thomas, *The French Empire Between the Wars,* 265.

140. Ibid., 57.

141. Thomas, *Empires of Intelligence,* 269.

142. Minguet, "Peyrouton avait raison," *La Flamme,* December 7, 1937.

143. Thomas, *Empires of Intelligence,* 268.

144. Ibid., 269.

145. Pierre-Louise Ganne, "Pour l'onzième fois en un an le sang coule en Tunisie," *La Flamme,* April 15, 1938.

146. Minguet, "Le mouvement social français: ses origines, sa constitution, sa direction, son rôle," *Bulletin de Liaison du Croix de Feu en Algérie,* June 15, 1936.

147. "Le calme règne en Tunisie … et cependant," *La Flamme,* September 3, 1937. See also Thomas, *The French Empire Between the Wars,* 269–70.

148. Sghaier, *La droite française en Tunisie,* 150.

149. "Le calme règne en Tunisie … et cependant," *La Flamme,* September 3, 1937.

150. Sghaier, *La droite française en Tunisie,* 70.

151. Thomas, *The French Empire Between the Wars,* 270.

152. Pierre-Louise Ganne, "Pour la onzième fois en un an le sang coule en Tunisie," *La Flamme,* April 15, 1938.

153. Ibid.

154. CADN, Tunisie, RG 1723, decree from the Resident-General, August 27, 1938; RG 1723, note from the Resident-General, July 6, 1938.

155. Thomas, *Empires of Intelligence,* 273; Thomas, *The French Empire Between the Wars,* 271.

156. Pennell, *Morocco Since 1830,* 233; Thomas, *Empires of Intelligence,* 223, 270.

157. Wyrtzen, "Constructing Morocco," 136n1.

CHAPTER SEVEN

1. CHSP, LR 35, Confidential Report from J. Rives Childs, chargé d'affaires ad interim, to the U.S. Secretary of State, March 18, 1942.

2. Ibid.

3. Kennedy, *Reconciling France,* 250.

4. CHSP, LR 35, Supreme Headquarters Allied Expeditionary Force, Counter Intelligence Glossary, April 1944.

5. For some of the key works that emphasize continuity between the 1930s and Vichy, see: Paxton, *Vichy France;* Jackson, *France, the Dark Years, 1940–44;* Lackerstein, *National Regeneration in Vichy France.*

6. Simon Kitson, *The Hunt for Nazi Spies: Fighting Espionage in Vichy France,* trans. Catherine Tihanyi (Chicago: University of Chicago Press, 2008).

7. CHSP LR 30, Association déclarée Les Volontaires de la Défense passive, "Extraits des Statuts," n.d (probably 1939).

8. Ibid.

9. CHSP LR 15, La Rocque circular, February 13, 1940.

10. CHSP LR 31, Instructional, "Défense passive du PSF," n.d. (probably 1939).

11. Julia Torrie, *For Their Own Good: Civilian Evacuations in Germany and France, 1939–1944* (New York: Berghahn, 2010), 45–46.

12. CHSP LR 32, speech by Madame Witasse at ADP Conference, "Les ADP," April 6, 1940.

13. CHSP LR 29, Confidential Report from the office of the PSF President, December 7, 1939; Hanna Diamond, *Fleeing Hitler: France 1940* (Oxford: Oxford University Press, 2007).

14. CHSP LR 29, Confidential Report from the office of the PSF President, December 7, 1939.

15. Ibid.

16. CHSP LR 32, speech by Madame Witasse at ADP Conference, "Les ADP," April 6, 1940; CHSP LR 32, Madame Verrier, "Deuxième Cours de Documentation," February 20, 1940.

17. CHSP LR 31, Instructional, "Défense passive du PSF," n.d. (but probably 1939).

18. CHSP LR 32, speech by La Rocque at an ADP Congress, "Intervention du Colonel après Madame Wistasse," April 6, 1940.

19. CHSP LR 32, speech by Madame Witasse at an ADP Congress, "Les ADP," April 6, 1940.

20. CHSP LR 32, speech by Mademoiselle Garrigoux at an ADP Congress, "Une Méthode de travail social à l'intérieur des fédérations et des sections P.S.F.," April 6, 1940.

21. Ibid.

22. Ibid.

23. CHSP LR 32, circular from Pierre Latrobe, Member of the PSF Executive Committee to Regional Delegates, Federation Presidents, and Section Presidents, May 24, 1940.

24. CHSP LR 32, letter from Joseph Levet, Pierre Latrobe, and de Lespapis to Préval, June 17, 1940.

25. CARAN 451AP 129, Report, "Progrès Social Francais, Section de Lille Nord Est," n.d. (probably late 1940–early 1941).

26. Antoinette de Préval, "Jeanne Garrigoux Morte pour la France," *Le Volontaire 36,* August 1940.

27. CHSP LR 33, circular, "Résolution prise par la Commission administrative permanente du PSF," August 8, 1940.

28. For more on La Rocque's ongoing support of Pétain, see Kennedy, *Reconciling France,* 234–36, 248.

29. CHSP LR 15, letter from La Rocque to PSF Federation and Section presidents, February 13, 1940.

30. Kennedy, *Reconciling France,* 230, 234.

31. Torrie, *For Their Own Good,* 45.

32. Ibid., 46–47.

33. CHSP LR 34, Georges Riché and André Portier, "Instructions Générales Pour Une Délégation Départemental en Zone Occupée," 1941.

34. CHSP LR 32, La Rocque speech at an ADP Congress, "Le Colonel après l'exposé de Madame Witasse sur les ADP," April 6, 1940; CHSP LR 34, Georges Riché and André Portier, "Instructions Générales Pour Une Delegation Départemental en Zone Occupée," 1941.

35. The figures for 1940 come from CHSP LR 32, speech by Madame Witasse at ADP Conference, "Les ADP," April 6, 1940; the figures for 1944 come from CARAN F7 15284 police report on the ADP, July 18, 1944.

36. CHSP LR 33, La Rocque, "Observations Générales, ADP, Département 'Colis du Prisonnier,' Centre Jean Mermoz," June 5, 1941.

37. CHSP LR 34, unsigned, "Rapport sur le fonctionnement du Centre Jean Mermoz de Marseille (Colis du Prisonnier), 1941.

38. CARAN F7 15284 police report on the ADP, July 18, 1944.

39. CARAN 451AP 153, SPES meeting minutes from September 27, 1941.

40. CARAN 451AP 155, unsigned letter to Maire, January 22, 1941.

41. CARAN 451AP 161, undated, unsigned report.

42. CHSP LR 34 unsigned report, "Rapport sur l'Activité Sociale des Départements de l'Ain, de l'Ardèche, de l'Allier, de la Drôme, de l'Isère, de Jura, de la Loire, des Savoie, du Puy-de-Dôme, et du Rhône," June 28, 1941.

43. CHSP LR 34, Préval speech at ADP congress, "Rapport sur l'Esprit d'Equipe ADP," October 1942.

44. CHSP LR 34, Préval letter to Barrucand, December 18, 1942.

45. CHSP LR 34, Préval speech at ADP congress, "Rapport sur l'Esprit d'Equipe ADP," October 1942 (emphasis mine).

46. Ibid. Quoted also in Downs, "Nous plantions les trois couleurs," 148.

47. Downs, "Nous plantions les trois couleurs," 142–50.

48. Ibid., 150.

49. CHSP LR 39, Préval speech, October 1944.

50. Kennedy, *Reconciling France,* 226.

51. CARAN 451AP 102, La Rocque, *France d'aujourd'hui, France de demain,* 1943.

52. CHSP 37, La Rocque, "Note au Sujet du Réseau 'Klan,'" late June–early July 1945.

53. For a summary, see Kennedy, *Reconciling France,* 246.

54. CHSP LR 32, undated, unsigned note/report.

55. CHSP LR 37, unknown author, "Supplément à la Note au Sujet du Réseau 'Klan.'"

56. CHSP LR 37, Confidential Questionnaire by the Renseignement Généraux for François de La Rocque, March 1946.

57. CHSP LR 37, letter from Charaudeau to Captain Thomas, June 25, 1945.

58. Nobécourt, *Le Colonel de La Rocque,* 822. For more on intelligence gathering and public opinion, see Kitson, *The Hunt for Nazi Spies,* 158.

59. CHSP 37, La Rocque, "Note au Sujet du Réseau 'Klan,'" late June–early July 1945.

60. Kitson, *The Hunt for Nazi Spies,* 161.

61. CHSP LR 37, La Rocque, "Note au Sujet du Réseau 'Klan,'" late June–early July 1945.

62. CHSP LR 37, Report for the Paris Police Commissioner, Jean Joba, Médaille de la Résistance and member of the Samson resistance network, April 15, 1950.

63. CHSP LR 34, Attestation by François Kemlin, Médaillé de la Résistance, July 5, 1948.

64. CHSP LR 37, La Rocque, "Note au Sujet du Réseau 'Klan,'" late June–early July 1945.

65. CARAN 451AP 102, letter from Henri Hermann, "Préval pendant la guerre," October 5, 1946.

66. Quoted in Kennedy, *Reconciling France,* 238.

67. Conklin, Fishman, and Zaretsky, *France and its Empire since 1870.*

68. Quoted in Kennedy, *Reconciling France,* 241.

69. Ibid., 239.

70. CHSP LR 32, "Extrait des cahiers de Mme Bourrut-Lacouture," September 12, 1942; also reported in CHSP LR 34, "Procès-Verbal," M. Villebrun to Paris Police Commissar, December 3, 1945.

71. This evidence comes from a series of very short accounts (around five) compiled by Gilles de La Rocque in CHSP 32, "L'aide apportée par La Rocque et son œuvre aux Juifs persécutées," n.d. These accounts reference a June 29, 1948, letter by a Mademoiselle Bernheim attesting that she and her sister obtained refuge with Préval through the liberation.

72. CHSP LR 32, "Temoignage du Doyen Hermann de la Faculté de Médecine de Lyon," n.d.; LR 32, "Temoignage de Mme Devise," n.d.

73. CHSP LR 34, letter, Robert Garric to Gilles de La Rocque, May 28, 1948.

74. CHSP LR 32, unsigned, untitled typed document, dated April 28, 1956.

75. CHSP LR 34, "Rapport sur l'activité du foyer social Français de Genève et Lausanne," May 1940–May 1941.

76. Kennedy, *Reconciling France,* 248. Jacques Nobécourt, on the other hand, suggests that the Milice denounced the PSF (Nobécourt, *Le Colonel de La Rocque,* 881–84). Given Nobécourt's hagiographical account of La Rocque and dismissal of the significance of women's social action, it is likely that Kennedy's dates are based upon stronger evidence.

77. CARAN 451AP 132, Speech, Préval, October 1944.

78. CHSP LR 36, letter from Préval to Ambassador Abetz, April 5, 1943.

79. CARAN F7 15284, police report on the ADP, September 4, 1943.

80. CARAN 451AP 132, speech by Préval, October 1944; CHSP LR 34, letter from Horaist to M. Querenet, Avocat à la Cour, June 25, 1948.

81. CHSP LR 38, Préval, note, (month illegible) 1943.

82. CHSP LR 39, Robert Garric, Commissaire Générale du Secours National, "Attestation," November 15, 1965.

83. Shannon Fogg, *The Politics of Everyday Life in Vichy France: Foreigners, Undesirables, and Strangers* (Cambridge, England: Cambridge University Press, 2008).

84. CARAN F7 15284, police report on the ADP, July 18, 1944.

85. Downs, "Nous plantions les trois couleurs," 157–60.

86. Ibid., 158.

87. CHSP 39, Roger Traub, General Secretary of Secours National, "Attestation," July 1, 1944.

88. For more on accomodation, see Philippe Burrin, *France under the Germans: Collaboration and Compromise* (New York: New Press, 1995); for more on the concept of "benign neglect," see Susan Zuccotti, *The Holocaust, the French, and the Jews* (New York: Basic Books, 1993).

89. CARAN 451AP 128, "La Mission de Jeanne d'Arc," *Témoignage Chrétien* 11 July 14, 1944.

90. For more on Chaillet, see Wilfred D. Halls, *Politics, Society, and Christianity in Vichy France* (Oxford: Berg, 1995).

91. CHSP LR 34, Simone Marochetti Report, "Entrevue de Mademoiselle de Préval avec le Père Chaillet," June 27, 1945.

92. Ibid.

93. Ibid.

94. Ibid.

95. For more on La Rocque's fate, see Kennedy, *Reconciling France,* 255–60.

96. CHSP LR 39, "Procès-Verbal d'Assemblée Générale Ordinaire des ADP," July 20, 1945.

97. Ibid.

98. Torrie, *For Their Own Good,* 46.

99. Kitson, *The Hunt for Nazi Spies,* 2008.

100. Nobécourt provides a list of around twenty of the arrested militants, which includes their background and how they died (*Le Colonel de La Rocque,* 817).

101. Kennedy, *Reconciling France,* 249–50.

102. "La Vie d'Association," *Les Amis de La Rocque,* December 1978.

103. Ibid.

BIBLIOGRAPHY

PRIMARY SOURCES

Archives
Archives de la préfecture de police (APP), Paris, France
Archives nationales d'outre-mer (ANOM), Aix-en-Provence, France
Le Centre d'accueil et de recherche des Archives nationales (CARAN), Paris, France
    451 Archives Privées (AP), Fonds François de La Rocque
    F2 Ministère de l'intérieur adminstration départemental
    F7 Police Générale
Le Centre des Archives contemporaines (CAC), Fontainebleau, France
Centre des Archives diplomatiques de Nantes (CADN)
Centre d'histoire de Sciences Po (CHSP), Paris, France
    Les Fonds Colonel François de La Rocque (Archives Privées, LR)

Newspapers, Journals, and Bulletins
Agir: organe mensuel du Parti social français pour le département de l'Indre
Les Amis de la Rocque
L'Auvergne nouvelle
Bulletin des Associations Croix de Feu du Département d'Alger
Bulletin de la Fédération des Deux-Sèvres
Bulletin d'information du Parti social français, Fédérations de la Sarthe et de la Mayenne
Bulletin de liaison du Croix de Feu en Algérie
Bulletin de liaison de la Fédération PSF de Vaucluse
Bulletin de la Section de Lunéville
Croix de Feu du Gard, Bulletin de liaison des sections
Les Croix de feu de Rouen et de Normandie
L'Espoir de l'Est
L'Espoir lorrain
L'Etudiant Social

Le Flambeau

Le Flambeau ardennais

Le Flambeau des Bouches-du-Rhône

Le Flambeau de Bourgogne

Le Flambeau de Cannes

Le Flambeau de l'Est

Le Flambeau de Franche-Comté et Territoire de Belfort

Le Flambeau de Flandre, Artois, Picardie

Le Flambeau du Gard

Le Flambeau d'Indochine

Le Flambeau d'Isère

Le Flambeau de Lorraine

Le Flambeau du Midi

Le Flambeau du Sud-Est

Le Flambeau du Sud-Ouest

Le Flambeau des Vosges

La Flamme

La Flamme Catalane

La Flamme des Deux-Sèvres

La Flamme du Midi

La Flamme tourangelle

La Flamme vendéenne

L'Heure française

L'Humanité

La Liaison PSF: bulletin de la Fédération de la Charente-Inférieure

La Liberté du Maine: Organe du P.S.F. de la Sarthe et de la Mayenne

Le Petit Journal

Pour sauver la France: bulletin périodique de la Moselle

Pourquoi S'en Faire

PSF: Bulletins d'informations

PSF: Section du canton de Maromme

Réalité

La Réconciliation

La Relève

La Rénovation républicaine

Samedi de France

Samedi de l'Ouest

Service Social

Servir: servir ... et non se servir

Le Trait d'union du Val de Loire
Le Volontaire 36
Le Volontaire du Centre-Est
La Volonté bretonne
La Volonté du Centre

Published Primary Sources

Aucouturier, Marcel. *Programme du Parti Social Français: Pour la reconstruction de l'Etat Social Français.* Ardennes: Imprimerie P. Anciaux, 1938.

Barrachin, Edmond. *La politique du PSF: Rapport présenté au Deuxième Congrès National.* Lyon, 1937.

Chopine, Paul. *Le Colonel de la Rocque veut-il la guerre civile?* Paris: Gallimard, 1936.

——. *Six ans chez les Croix de feu.* Paris: Gallimard, 1935.

Comité de vigilance des intellectuels antifascistes (Paul Rivet). *Les Croix de feu, leur chef, leur programme.* Paris, 1935.

Creyssel, Paul. *La Rocque contre Tardieu.* Paris: Fernand Sorlot, 1938.

L'Espoir Français: Le Congrès National du PSF. Paris, 1937.

"France sera sauvée par le PSF." *Le Petit Journal, Numéro Spécial Illustre:* Octobre 1937.

Forest, Pierre. *Le PSF et le syndicalisme: Rapport présenté au Deuxième Congrès National.* Lyon, 1937.

Fouché, Suzanne. *J'espérais d'un grand espoir.* Les Editions du Cerf: Paris, 1981.

Garrigoux, Jeanne. *Le PSF et l'action social: Rapport présenté au Deuxième Congrès National.* Lyon, 1937.

de Hauteclocque, François. *Grandeur et décadence des Croix de Feu.* Paris: Editions la Bourdonnais, 1937.

Lacretelle, Jacques de. *Qui est La Rocque.* Paris: Flammarion, 1937.

La Rocque, Colonel François de. "Le complot communo-socialiste: l'insurrection armée dans l'Unité d'action." Paris: Grasset, 1935.

——. *Disciplines d'action.* Clermont-Ferrand: Editions du Petit journal, 1941.

——. "'Le secret' de l'action Croix de feu au 6 février 1934 vu par un ancien Croix de Feu." Paris: Poirier, 1945.

——. *Service Public.* Paris: Grasset, 1934.

La Rocque, Edith de, et Gilles de La Rocque. *La Rocque: Tel qu'il était.* Paris: Fayard, 1962.

Léotard, Pierre de. "Mes souvenirs politiques." Extrait de la revue *Recherches contemporaines,* n 5, 1998–1999.

Malherbe, Henri. *La Rocque un chef, des actes, des idées.* Paris: Plon, 1934.

Manifeste Croix de Feu: Pour le peuple, par le peuple. Supplément du *Flambeau:* 1936.

Mead, Margaret. *Sex and Temperament in Three Primitive Societies.* New York: W. Morrow, 1935.

Le mouvement Croix de feu et l'ordre social. Publication du *Flambeau:* Aout 1935.

L'Oeuvre Sociale dans le mouvement Croix de feu. Supplément illustre du *Flambeau:* May 1936.

Olivier-Martin. *Le PSF et les Fonctionnaires: Rapport présenté au Deuxième Congrès National.* Lyon, 1937.

Le Paysan sauvera la France avec le PSF. Paris: S.E.D.A., 1937.

Petit, Jacques. *De La Rocque est-il un chef?* Paris: Société française de Librairie et d'Editions, 1938.

Pourquoi J'ai adhère au PSF. Paris: S.E.D.A., 1937.

Pourquoi nous suivons La Rocque. Paris, March 1945.

Pozzo di Borgo, Joseph Jean (Joseph duc). *La Rocque: Fantôme à vendre.* Paris: Fernand Sorlot, 1938.

Préval, Antoinette de. *Deux prières de La Rocque déporté.* Imprimerie des Tournelles, 1947. *In Memoriam: Conférence du 6 octobre 1946.*

Le PSF devant les problèmes de l'heure, Rapports présentés au Premier Congrès National du PSF. S.E.D.A., December 1936.

Le PSF et la semaine de Quarante Heures. Paris: S.E.D.A., 1936.

Le PSF: Une Mystique, Un Programme. Paris: S.E.D.A., 1936.

Pujo, Maurice. *Comment la Rocque a trabi.* Paris: Fernand Sorlot, 1937.

Ruffier, Jean Edward. *Soyons fort! Manuel de culture physique elémentaire.* Paris: Librairie de "Portez-vous bien," 1914.

Suarez, Georges. *Que veulent, que peuvent, les Croix de feu?* Paris: Editions Denoël et Steele, 1935.

Vallin, Charles. *L'activité du PSF: Rapport présenté au Deuxième Congrès National.* Lyon, 1937.

———. "Aux femmes du Parti Social Français." Conférence faite aux déléguées des Groupes d'Action Sociale du PSF, Paris, 1937.

Veuillot, François. *La Roque et son parti: Comme je les ai vus.* Paris: Librairie Plon, 1938.

Ybarnegaray, Jean. *Le PSF et la politique extérieure: Rapport présenté au Deuxième Congrès National.* Lyon, 1937.

SECONDARY SOURCES

Abi-Mershed, Osama. *Apostles of Modernity: Saint-Simonians and the Civilizing Mission in Algeria.* Stanford, Calif.: Stanford University Press, 2010.

Accampo, Elinor A., Rachel Fuchs, and Mary Lynn Stewart, eds. *Gender and Politics of Social Reform in France, 1870–1914.* Baltimore: Johns Hopkins University Press, 1995.

Adler, Jacques. *The Jews of Paris and the Final Solution: Communal Responses and Internal Conflicts, 1940–1944.* Oxford: Oxford University Press, 1987.

Adler, Karen H. *Jews and Gender in Liberation France.* Cambridge and New York: Cambridge University Press, 2003.

Aldrich, Robert. "Colonial Man." In *French Masculinities: History, Culture and Politics,* edited by Christopher Forth and Bertrand Taithe. New York: Palgrave Macmillan, 2007.

Allen, Ann Taylor. *Feminism and Motherhood in Germany, 1800–1914.* New Brunswick, N.J.: Rutgers University Press, 1991.

Allwood, Gill, and Khursheed Wadia. *Women and Politics in France, 1958–2000.* London: Routledge, 2000.

Amster, Ellen. "'The Harem Revealed,' and the Islamic-French Family: Aline de Lens and a French Woman's Orient in Lyautey's Morocco." *French Historical Studies* 32, no. 2 (Spring 2009): 279–312.

Andersen, Margaret Cook. "A Colonial Fountain of Youth: Imperialism and France's Crisis of Depopulation, 1870–1940." PhD diss., University of Iowa, 2008.

———. "Creating French Settlements Overseas: Pronatalism and Colonial Medicine in Madagascar." *French Historical Studies* 33, no. 3 (Summer 2010): 417–44.

———. "French Settlers, Familial Suffrage, and Citizenship in 1920s Tunisia." *Journal of Family History* 37, no. 2 (April 2012): 213–31.

Andrews, Naomi. *Socialism's Muse: Gender in the Intellectual Landscape of French Romantic Socialism.* Lanham, Md.: Lexington, 2006.

Armus, Seth. *French Anti-Americanism 1930–1948: Critical Moments in a Complex History.* Lanham, Md.: Lexington, 2007.

Arnal, Oscar. "Catholic Roots of Collaboration and Resistance in France in the 1930s." *Canadian Journal of History* 1982 (17): 87–110.

———. "Emmanuel Mounier as a Paradigm of the Catholic Avant-Garde (1930–1950)." *Historical Reflections* 10, no. 3 (1983): 377–86.

Attwood, Lynne. *Creating the New Soviet Woman: Women's Magazines as Engineers of Female Identity, 1922–53.* New York: St. Martin's, 1999.

Audoin-Rouzeau, Stéphane. *Men at War, 1914–1918: National Sentiment and Trench Journalism in France during the First World War.* Translated by Helen McPhail. Oxford and Providence, R.I.: Berg, 1992.

Audoin-Rouzeau, Stéphane, and Annette Becker. *14–18: Understanding the Great War.* New York: Hill & Wang, 2002.

August, Thomas G. "Paris 1937: The Apotheosis of the Popular Front." *Contemporary French Civilization* 5, no. 1 (1980): 43–60.

Ayache, Albert. "Les grèves de juin 1936 au Maroc." *Annales. Histoire, Sciences Sociales, 12e Année,* no. 3 (July–September, 1957): 418–29.

Bachetta, Paola, and Margaret Power, eds. *Right-Wing Women: From Conservatives to Extremists Around the World.* New York: Routledge, 2002.

Bard, Christine. *Les femmes dans la société française au 20e siècle.* Paris: A. Colin, 2001.

———. *Les filles de Marianne: Histoire des féminismes 1914–1945.* Paris: Fayard, 1995.

———. (dir.) *Un siècle d'antiféminisme.* Paris: Fayard, 1999.

Baumel, Judith. *Double Jeopardy: Gender and the Holocaust.* London and Portland, Ore.: Vallentine Mitchell, 1998.

Becker, Annette. *La Guerre et la foi.* Paris: Armand Colin, 1994.

Becker, Jean-Jacques. *1914: Comment les Français sont entrés dans la guerre.* Paris: Presses de la Fondation nationale des sciences politiques, 1977.

Bédarida, Renée. *Les Catholiques dans la guerre, 1939–1945: Entre Vichy et la Résistance.* Paris: Hachette, 1998.

Bell, David. *The Cult of the Nation in France: Inventing Nationalism, 1680–1800.* Cambridge, Mass.: Harvard University Press, 2001.

———. *The First Total War: Napoleon's Europe and the Birth of Warfare as We Know It.* Boston: Houghton Mifflin, 2007.

Ben-Amos, Avner. *Funerals, Politics, and Memory in Modern France, 1789–1996.* Oxford: Oxford University Press, 2000.

Berenson, Edward. *Heroes of Empire: Five Charismatic Men and the Conquest of Africa.* Berkeley: University of California Press, 2011.

Bergen, Doris. *Twisted Cross: The German Christian Movement in the Third Reich.* Chapel Hill: University of North Carolina Press, 1996.

Berliner, Brett A. *Ambivalent Desire: The Exotic Black Other in Jazz-Age France.* Amherst and Boston: University of Massachusetts Press, 2002.

Berstein, Serge. "La France des années trente allergique au fascisme: A propos d'un livre de Zeev Sternhell." *Vingtième siècle* 2, no. 2 (1984): 83–94.

———. *Le 6 février 1934.* Paris: Gallimard, 1975.

Bessel, Richard. "Violence as Propaganda: The Role of the Storm Troopers in the Rise of National Socialism." In *The Formation of the Nazi Constituency,* edited by Thomas Childers. London: Croom Helm, 1986.

Betts, Raymond. *Assimilation and Association in French Colonial Theory, 1890–1914.* With a new preface by the author. Lincoln: University of Nebraska Press, 2005.

Blee, Kathleen. *Women of the Klan: Racism and Gender in the 1920s.* Berkeley: University of California Press, 1991.

Blee, Kathleen, and Sandra McGee Deutsch, eds. *Women of the Right: Comparisons and Interplay Across Borders.* University Park: Pennsylvania State University Press, 2012.

Blinkhorn, Martin. *Fascists and Conservatives: The Radical Right and the Establishment in Twentieth-Century Europe.* Cambridge, England: Cambridge University Press, 1990.

Blom, Ida. "Gender and Nation in International Comparison." In *Gendered Nations: Nationalisms and Gender Order in the Long Nineteenth Century,* edited by Ida Blom, Karen Hagemann, and Catherine Hall. Oxford and New York: Berg Publishers, 2000.

Bock, Gisela. "Equality and difference in National Socialist racism." In *Beyond Equality and Difference: Citizenship, Feminist Politics and Female Subjectivity,* edited by Gisela Bock and Susan James. London: Routledge, 1992.

Boittin, Jennifer Anne. *Colonial Metropolis: The Urban Grounds of Anti-Imperialism and Feminism in Interwar Paris.* Lincoln: University of Nebraska Press, 2010.

——. "Feminist Meditations of the Exotic: French Algeria, Morocco, and Tunisia, 1921–1939." *Gender and History* 22, no. 1 (April 2010) 131–50.

Bourdieu, Pierre. *Réponses: Pour une anthropologie réflexive.* Paris: Editions du Seuil, 1992.

Brubaker, Rogers, and Frederick Cooper. "Beyond Identity." *Theory and Society* 29, no. 1 (February 2000): 1–47.

Brunelle, Gayle K., and Annette Finley-Croswhite. *Murder in the Metro: Laetitia Toureaux and the Cagoule in 1930s France.* Baton Rouge: Louisiana State University Press, 2012.

Burrin, Philippe. *France under the Germans: Collaboration and Compromise.* New York: New Press, 1995.

Burton, Antionette. *Burdens of History: British Feminists, Indian Women, and Imperial Culture, 1865–1915.* Chapel Hill: University of North Carolina Press, 1994.

Camiscioli, Elisa. *Reproducing the French Race: Immigration, Intimacy, and Embodiment in the Early Twentieth Century.* Durham, N.C.: Duke University Press, 2009.

Campbell, Caroline. "Building a Movement, Dismantling the Republic: Women and Political Extremism in the Croix de Feu/Parti Social Français, 1927–1940." *French Historical Studies* 35, no. 4 (Fall 2012): 691–726.

——. "Women and Gender in the Croix de Feu and Parti Social Français: Creating a Nationalist Youth Culture, 1927–1939." *Proceedings of the Western Society for French History* 36 (2008): 249–64.

——. "Women and Men in French Authoritarianism: Gender in the Croix de Feu and Parti Social Français, 1927–1945." PhD diss., University of Iowa, 2009.

Canning, Kathleen. *Gender History in Practice: Historical Perspectives on Bodies, Class, and Citizenship.* Ithaca, N.Y.: Cornell University Press, 2006.

Caron, Vicki. *Uneasy Asylum: France and the Jewish Refugee Crisis, 1933–1942.* Stanford, Calif.: Stanford University Press, 1999.

Carroll, David. *French Literary Fascism: Nationalism, Anti-Semitism, and the Ideology of Culture.* Princeton, N.J.: Princeton University Press, 1995.

Chadwick, Kay, ed. *Catholicism, Politics, and Society in Twentieth Century France.* Liverpool: Liverpool University Press, 2000.

Chrastil, Rachel. *Organizing for War: France 1870–1914.* Baton Rouge: Louisiana State University Press, 2010.

Chritchlow, Donald. *Phyllis Schlafly and Grassroots Conservatism: A Woman's Crusade.* Princeton, N.J.: Princeton University Press, 2005.

Clancy-Smith, Julia. *Mediterraneans: North Africa and Europe in an Age of Migration, c. 1800–1900.* Berkeley: University of California Press, 2010.

Clancy-Smith, Julia, and Frances Gouda, eds. *Domesticating the Empire: Race, Gender and Family Life in French and Dutch Colonialism.* Charlottesville: University of Virginia Press, 1998.

Clark, Anna. *The Struggle for the Breeches: Gender and the Making of the British Working Class.* Berkeley: University of California Press, 1995.

Clark, Linda L. *The Rise of Professional Women in France: Gender and Public Administration since 1830.* Cambridge, England: Cambridge University Press, 2000.

Clarke, Jackie. *France in the Age of Organization: Factory, Home, and Nation from the 1920s to Vichy.* New York: Berghahn, 2011.

Clément, Jean-Louis. "L'Episcopat, les democrates-chrétiens et les croix de feu: 1930–1936." *Revue historique* 298, no. 1 (1997): 103–13.

Clements, Barbara Evans. *Bolshevik Women.* Cambridge, England: Cambridge University Press, 1997.

Cleveland, William. *Islam Against the West: Shakib Arslan and the Campaign for Islamic Nationalism.* Austin: University of Texas Press, 1985.

Coffin, Judith. *The Politics of Women's Work: The Paris Garment Trades, 1750–1915.* Princeton, N.J.: Princeton University Press, 1996.

Cole, Joshua. "Anti-Semitism and the Colonial Situation in Interwar Algeria: The Anti-Jewish Riots in Constantine, August 1934." In *The French Colonial Mind: Violence, Military Encounters, and Colonialism,* edited by Martin Thomas. Lincoln: University of Nebraska Press, 2011.

———. *The Power of Large Numbers: Population, Politics, and Gender in Nineteenth-Century France.* Ithaca, N.Y.: Cornell University Press, 2000.

Conklin, Alice. *In the Museum of Man: Race, Anthropology, and Empire in France, 1850–1950.* Ithaca, N.Y.: Cornell University Press, 2013.

———. *A Mission to Civilize: The Republican Idea of Empire in France and West Africa, 1895–1930.* Stanford, Calif.: Stanford University Press, 1997.

Conklin, Alice L., and Julia Clancy-Smith. "Introduction: Writing Colonial Histories." *French Historical Studies* 27, no. 3 (Summer 2004): 497–505.

Conklin, Alice, Sarah Fishman, and Robert Zaretsky. *France and its Empire since 1870.* Oxford: Oxford University Press, 2010.

Cooper, Frederick. *Colonialism in Question: Theory, Knowledge, History.* Berkeley: University of California Press, 2005.

Corbin, Alain, Jacqueline Lalouette, and Michèle Riot-Sarcey. *Femmes dans la cité, 1815–1871.* Grâne: Editions Créaphis, 1997.

Cova, Anne. *"Au service de l'église, de la patrie et de la famille": Femmes catholiques et maternité sous la IIIe République.* Paris: l'Harmattan, 2000.

Curtis, David. "True and False Modernity: Catholicism and Communist Marxism in 1930s France." In *Catholicism, Politics and Society in Twentieth-Century France,* edited by Kay Chadwick. Liverpool: Liverpool University Press, 2000.

Curtis, Sarah A. *Civilizing Habits: Women Missionaries and the Revival of French Empire.* Oxford: Oxford University Press, 2010.

Darrow, Margaret H. *French Women and the First World War: War Stories of the Home Front.* Oxford: Berg, 2000.

Daughton, J.P. "Behind the Imperial Curtain: International Humanitarian Efforts and the Critique of French Colonialism in the Interwar Years." *French Historical Studies* 34, no. 3 (Summer 2011): 503–28.

———. *An Empire Divided: Religion, Republicanism, and the Making of French Colonialism, 1880–1914.* Oxford: Oxford University Press, 2006.

Davidson, Naomi. *Only Muslim: Embodying Islam in Twentieth-Century France.* Ithaca, N.Y.: Cornell University Press, 2012.

Davis, Diana. *Resurrecting the Granary of Rome: Environmental History and French Colonial Expansion in North Africa.* Athens: Ohio University Press, 2007.

Della Sudda, Magali. "Gender, Fascism, and the Right-Wing in France between the Wars: The Catholic Matrix." *Politics, Religion, and Ideology* 13, no. 2 (June 2012): 179–95.

———. "Socio-histoire des formes de politisation des femmes conservatrices avant le droit de suffrage en France et en Italie. La Ligue patriotique des Françaises (1902–1933) et l'Unione fra le donne cattoliche d'Italia (1909–1919)." PhD diss., Ecole des Hautes Etudes en Sciences Sociales, Paris, 2007.

Desan, Suzanne. *Reclaiming the Sacred: Lay Religion and Popular Politics in Revolutionary France.* Ithaca, N.Y.: Cornell University Press, 1990.

Diamond, Hanna. *Fleeing Hitler: France 1940.* Oxford: Oxford University Press, 2007.

Diébolt, Evelyne. "Les femmes catholiques: Entre Eglise et société." In *Catholicism, Politics, and Society in Twentieth-Century France,* edited by Kay Chadwick, 219–43. Liverpool: Liverpool University Press, 2000.

———. *Les femmes dans l'action sanitaire, sociale et culturelle, 1901–2001: Les associations face aux institutions.* Paris: Femmes et Associations, 2001.

Dobry, Michel. "Février 1934 et la découverte de l'allergie de la société française à la 'Révolution fasciste.'" *Revue française de sociologie* 30, no. 3/4 (July–December 1989): 511–33.

———. "La thèse immunitaire face aux fascismes. Pour une critique de la logique classificatoire." In *Le mythe de l'allergie française au fascisme,* edited by Michel Dobry. Paris: Albin Michel, 2003.

Downs, Laura Lee. *Childhood in the Promised Land: Working-Class Movements and the Colonies de Vacances in France, 1880–1960.* Durham, N.C., and London: Duke University Press, 2002.

———. "Each and every one of you must become a *chef*: Toward a Social Politics of Working-Class Childhood on the Extreme Right in 1930s France." *Journal of Modern History* 81, no. 1 (March 2009): 1–44.

———. "'Nous plantions les trois couleurs,' Action sociale féminine et la recomposition des politiques de la droite française: Le mouvement Croix-de-Feu et le Parti social français, 1934–1947." *Revue d'histoire moderne et contemporaine* 58, no. 3 (2011): 118–63.

Dueck, Jennifer. "The Middle East and North Africa in the Imperial and Post-Colonial Historiography of France." *Historical Journal* 50, no. 4 (December 2007).

Dumons, Bruno. "L'Action française au féminine; Réseaux et figures de militantes au début du XXe siècle." In *L'Action française: Culture, société, politique*, edited by Michel Leymarie and Jacques Prévotat. Lille: Presses Universitaires du Septentrion, 2008.

———. *Les Dames de la Ligue des femmes françaises, 1901–1914.* Paris: Editions du Cerf, 2006.

Dutton, Paul. *Origins of the French Welfare State: The Struggle for Social Reform in France, 1914–1947.* Cambridge, England: Cambridge University Press, 2002.

Echenberg, Myron. *Colonial Conscripts: The Tirailleurs Sénégalais in French West Africa, 1857–1960.* Portsmouth, N.H.: Heinemann, 1991.

Eichner, Carolyn J. "*La citoyenne* in the World: Hubertine Auclert and Feminist Imperialism." *French Historical Studies* 32, no. 1 (Winter 2009): 63–84.

Everton, Elizabeth. "Scenes of Perception and Revelation: Gender and Truth in Antidreyfusard Caricature." *French Historical Studies* 35, no. 2 (Spring 2012): 381–417.

Evans, Richard J. "German Women and the Triumph of Hitler." *Journal of Modern History* 48, no. 1. On Demand Supplement (March 1976): 123–75.

Ezra, Elizabeth. *The Colonial Unconscious: Race and Culture in Interwar France.* Ithaca, N.Y.: Cornell University Press, 2000.

Fanon, Frantz. *The Wretched of the Earth.* New York: Grove Press, 2005.

Fayet-Scribe, Sylvie. *Associations féminines et catholicisme: De la charité à l'action sociale, XIXe–Xxe siècle.* Paris: Editions de l'Atelier, 1990.

Fishman, Sarah. *We Will Wait: Wives of French Prisoners of War, 1940–1945.* New Haven: Yale University Press, 1991.

Fiss, Karen. *Grand Illusion: The Third Reich, the Paris Exposition, and the Cultural Seduction of France.* Chicago: University of Chicago Press, 2009.

Fitzpatrick, Sheila. *Everyday Stalinism: Ordinary Life in Extraordinary Times: Soviet Russia in the 1930s.* New York: Oxford University Press, 1999.

Fogg, Shannon. *The Politics of Everyday Life in Vichy France: Foreigners, Undesirables, and Strangers.* Cambridge, England: Cambridge University Press, 2008.

Fontaine, Darcie. "Treason or Charity? Christian Missions on Trial and the Decolonization of Algeria." *International Journal of Middle East Studies* 44, no. 4 (November 2012): 733–53.

Ford, Caroline. *Divided Houses: Religion and Gender in Modern France.* Ithaca, N.Y.: Cornell University Press, 2005.

———. "Reforestation and Anxieties of Empire in French Colonial Algeria." *American Historical Review* 113, no. 2 (April 2008): 341–62.

Forth, Christopher. *The Dreyfus Affair and the Crisis of French Manhood.* Baltimore: Johns Hopkins University Press, 2004.

———. *Masculinity in the Modern West: Gender, Civilization and the Body.* New York: Palgrave Macmillan: 2008.

Forth, Christopher, and Bertrand Taithe, eds. *French Masculinities: History, Culture, and Politics.* New York: Palgrave Macmillan, 2007.

Frader, Laura Levine. *Breadwinners and Citizens: Gender in the Making of the French Social Model.* Durham, N.C.: Duke University Press, 2008.

———. "From Muscles to Nerves: Gender, 'Race' and the Body at Work in France, 1919–1939." *International Review of Social History,* supplement 7, edited by Eileen Boris and Angélique Janssen, 44 (1999): 123–47.

Friedlander, Henry. *The Origins of Nazi Genocide: From Euthanasia to the Final Solution.* Chapel Hill: University of North Carolina Press, 1995.

Friedlander, Saul. *Nazi Germany and the Jews: The Years of Persecution, 1933–1939.* Vol. 1. New York: Harper Collins Publishers, 1997.

Fuchs, Rachel G. *Contested Paternity: Constructing Families in Modern France.* Baltimore: Johns Hopkins University Press, 2008.

Fulcher, Jane F. *The Composer as Intellectual: Music and Ideology in France, 1914–1940.* Oxford: Oxford University Press, 2005.

Furlough, Ellen. "Une leçon des choses: Tourism, Empire, and the Nation in Interwar France." *French Historical Studies* 25, no. 3 (Summer 2002): 441–73.

Gershovich, Moshe. *French Military Rule in Morocco: Colonialism and its Consequences.* London and Portland, N.H.: Frank Cass, 2000.

Geyer, Michael, and Sheila Fitzpatrick eds. *Beyond Totalitarianism: Stalinism and Nazism Compared.* Cambridge, England: Cambridge University Press, 2009.

Gilson Miller, Susan. *A History of Modern Morocco.* Cambridge, England: Cambridge University Press, 2013.

Gleyse, Jacques et al. "Images of Women in Literature on Physical Education and Sport: Representations of Social Transformation in France under the Third Republic, 1870–1939." *Sport, Education and Society* 9, no. 3 (November 2004): 327–45.

Goodfellow, Samuel. *Between the Swastika and the Cross of Lorraine: Fascisms in Interwar Alsace.* DeKalb: University of Northern Illinois Press, 1999.

Goodwin, Jeff, James M. Jaspar, and Francesca Polletta, eds. *Passionate Politics: Emotions and Social Movements.* Chicago: University of Chicago Press, 2001.

Gordon, Bertram. *Collaborationism in France during the Second World War.* Ithaca, N.Y.: Cornell University Press, 1980.

Gordon, Rae Beth. *Dances with Darwin, 1875–1910: Vernacular Modernity in France.* Aldershot, England, and Burlington, Vt.: Ashgate, 2009.

Gosnell, Jonathan K. *The Politics of Frenchness in Colonial Algeria 1930–1954.* Rochester, N.Y.: University of Rochester Press, 2002.

Gottlieb, Julie. *Feminine Fascism: Women in Britain's Fascist Movement.* London: I.B. Tauris, 2000.

——. "Right-Wing Women in Women's History: A Global Perspective." *Journal of Women's History* 16, no. 3 (Fall 2004).

Grayzel, Susan. *Women's Identities at War: Gender, Motherhood, and Politics in Britain and France during the First World War.* Chapel Hill: University of North Carolina Press, 1999.

Grazia, Victoria de. *How Fascism Ruled Women: Italy, 1922–1945.* Berkeley: University of California Press, 1992.

Green, Mary Jean. "The Bouboule Novels: Constructing a French Fascist Woman." In *Gender and Fascism in Modern France,* edited by Melanie Hawthorne and Richard J. Golsan. Hanover, N.H.: University Press of New England, 1997.

——. "Gender, Fascism and the Croix de Feu: The 'Women's Pages' of *Le Flambeau.*" *French Cultural Studies* vii (1997): 229–39.

Griffin, Roger. *The Nature of Fascism.* London: Pinter, 1991.

——. "Studying Fascism in a Postfascist Age. From New Consensus to New Wave?" *Fascism: The Journal of Comparative Fascist Studies* 1, no. 1 (2012): 1–17.

Gullickson, Gay. *Unruly Women of Paris: Images of the Commune.* Ithaca, N.Y.: Cornell University Press, 1996.

Ha, Marie-Paule. "'La femme française aux colonies': Promoting Colonial Female Emigration at the Turn of the Century." *French Colonial History* 6 (2005): 205–24.

Hale, Dana. *Races on Display: French Representations of Colonized Peoples, 1886–1940.* Bloomington: Indiana University Press, 2008.

Hallie, Phillip. *Lest Innocent Blood be Shed.* New York: Harper Collins, 1979.

Halls, Wilfred D. *Politics, Society, and Christianity in Vichy France.* Oxford: Berg Publishers, 1995.

Hanna, Martha. "Iconology and Ideology: Images of Joan of Arc in the Idiom of the Action Française, 1908–1931." *French Historical Studies* 14, no. 2 (Autumn 1985): 215–39.

——. *The Mobilization of Intellect: French Scholars and Writers During the First World War.* Cambridge, England: Cambridge University Press, 1996.

Harris, Ruth. "The Child of the Barbarian: Rape, Race, and Nationalism in France During the First World War." *Past and Present* 141 (Fall 1993): 170–206.

——. *Dreyfus: Politics, Emotion, and the Scandal of the Century.* New York: Metropolitan, Henry Holt, 2010.

——. *Lourdes: Body and Spirit in the Secular Age.* New York: Penguin Compass, 1999.

Harvey, Elizabeth. *Women and the Nazi East: Agents and Witnesses of Germanization.* New Haven: Yale University Press, 2003.

Hause, Steven C. "Anti-Protestant Rhetoric in the Early Third Republic." *French Historical Studies* 16, no. 1 (Spring 1989): 183–201.

Hause, Steven C., with Anne R. Kenney. *Women's Suffrage and Social Politics in the French Third Republic.* Princeton, N.J.: Princeton University Press, 1984.

Hawthorne, Melanie, and Richard Golsan, eds. *Gender and Fascism in Modern France.* Hanover, N.H.: University Press of New England [for] Dartmouth College, 1997.

Hecht, Jennifer Michael. *The End of the Soul: Scientific Modernity, Atheism, and Anthropology in France, 1876–1936.* New York: Columbia University Press, 2003.

Heineman, Elizabeth. *What Difference Does a Husband Make?: Women and Marital Status in Nazi and Postwar Germany.* Berkeley: University of California Press, 1999.

Heinsohn, Kirsten. "Germany." In *Women, Gender and Fascism in Europe, 1919–1945,* edited by Kevin Passmore. Manchester: Manchester University Press, 2003.

Hellman, John. *Emmanuel Mounier and the New Catholic Left, 1930–1950.* Toronto: University of Toronto Press, 1981.

———. "Vichy Background: Political Alternatives for French Catholics in the Nineteen-Thirties." *Journal of Modern History* 49, no. 1. On Demand Supplement (March 1977).

Herzog, Dagmar. *Sex After Fascism: Memory and Morality in Twentieth-Century Germany.* Princeton, N.J.: Princeton University Press, 2005.

Hesse, Carla. *The Other Enlightenment: How French Women Became Modern.* Princeton, N.J.: Princeton University Press, 2001.

Hilaire, Yves-Marie. "La sociologie religieuse du catholicisme français au vingtième siècle." In *Catholicism, Politics, and Society in Twentieth-Century France,* edited by Kay Chadwick. Liverpool: Liverpool University Press, 2000.

Holt, Thomas C. "Marking: Race, Race-making, and the Writing of History." *American Historical Review* 100, no. 1 (February 1995): 1–20.

Hopkin, David, Yann Lagadec, and Stéphane Perréon. "The Experience and Culture of War in the Eighteenth Century: The British Raids on the Breton Coast, 1758." *French Historical Studies* 31, no. 2 (Spring 2008).

Horne, Janet R. "In Pursuit of Greater France: Visions of Empire Among Musée Social Reformers, 1894–1931." In *Domesticating the Empire: Race, Gender and Family Life in French and Dutch Colonialism,* edited by Julia Clancy-Smith and Frances Gouda. Charlottesville: University Press of Virginia, 1998.

Horne, John. "Demobilizing the Mind: France and the Legacy of the Great War, 1919–1939." *French History and Civilization: Papers from the George Rudé Seminar* 2 (2009): 101–19.

Hunt, Lynn. *Inventing Human Rights: A History.* New York: W.W. Norton, 2007.

Husband, William. *Godless Communists: Atheism and Society in Soviet Russia, 1917–1932.* DeKalb: Northern Illinois University Press, 2000.

Hyman, Paula. *The Jews of Modern France.* Berkeley: University of California Press, 1998.

Irvine, William D. "Beyond Left and Right, and the Politics of the Third Republic: A Conversation." *Historical Reflections* 34, no. 2 (Summer 2008): 134–45.

———. "Fascism in France and the Strange Case of the Croix de Feu." *Journal of Modern History* 63, no. 2 (June 1991): 271–95.

Jackson, Julian. *France, the Dark Years, 1940–44.* Oxford: Oxford University Press, 2001.

———. *The Popular Front in France: Defending Democracy, 1934–1938.* Cambridge, England: Cambridge University Press, 1988.

Jenkins, Brian, ed. *France in the Era of Fascism: Essays on the French Authoritarian Right.* New York: Berghahn, 2005.

———. "Plots and Rumors: Conspiracy Theories and the *Six Février* 1934." *French Historical Studies* 34, no. 4 (Fall 2011): 649–78.

Jennings, Eric. "'Reinventing Jeanne': The Iconology of Joan of Arc in Vichy Schoolbooks, 1940–44." *Journal of Contemporary History* 29, no. 4 (October 1994): 711–34.

Jobs, Richard I. "Tarzan under Attack: Youth, Comics, and Cultural Reconstruction in Postwar France." *French Historical Studies* 26, no. 4 (Fall 2003): 687–725.

Kaddache, Mahfoud. *Histoire du nationalisme algérien.* Vol. 1. Paris: Editions Paris-Méditerranée, 2003.

Kalman, Samuel. "Le Combat par Tous les Moyens: Colonial Violence and the Extreme Right in 1930s Oran." *French Historical Studies* 34, no. 1 (Winter 2011): 125–53.

———. *The Extreme Right in Interwar France: The Faisceau and the Croix de Feu.* Aldershot, England, and Burlington, Vt.: Ashgate, 2008.

———. "Fascism and Algérianité: The Croix de Feu and the Indigenous Question in 1930s Algeria." In *The French Colonial Mind: Violence, Military Encounters, and Colonialism,* edited by Martin Thomas. Lincoln: University of Nebraska Press, 2011.

———. *French Colonial Fascism: The Extreme Right in Algeria, 1919–1939.* New York: Palgrave Macmillan, 2013.

———. "Parasites from all Civilizations: The Croix de Feu/Parti Social Français Confronts French Jewry, 1931–1939." *Historical Reflections* 34, no. 2 (Summer 2008): 46–65.

Kaplan, Marion. *The Making of the Jewish Middle Class: Women, Family, and Identity in Imperial Germany.* New York: Oxford University Press, 1991.

Kateb, Kamel. *Europeéns, indigènes, et juifs en Algérie, 1830–1962.* Paris: Ed. de l'Inst. National d'Etudes Démographiques, 2001.

Kéchichian, Albert. *Les Croix de Feu à l'âge des fascismes: Travail famille patrie.* Paris: Champs Vallon, 2006.

Keller, Richard C. *Colonial Madness: Psychiatry in North Africa.* Chicago: University of Chicago Press, 2007.

Kelly, Joan. "The Social Relations of the Sexes: Methodological Implications of Women's History." *Signs* I (1976): 809–23.

Kelly, Michael. "Catholicism and the Left in Twentieth-Century France." In *Catholicism, Politics and Society in Twentieth-Century France,* edited by Kay Chadwick. Liverpool: Liverpool University Press, 2000

Kennedy, Sean. "Accompanying the Marshal: La Rocque and the Progrès Social Français under Vichy." *French History* 15, no. 2 (2001): 186–213.

———. "The Croix de Feu, the Parti Social Français, and the Politics of Aviation, 1931–1939," *French Historical Studies* 23, no. 2 (Spring 2000): 373–399.

———. "The End of Immunity? Recent Work on the Far Right in Interwar France." *Historical Reflections* 34, no. 2 (Summer 2008): 25–45.

———. "Pitfalls of Paramilitarism: The Croix de Feu, Parti Social Français, and the French State, 1934–1939." *Journal of Conflict Studies* (Winter 2007): 64–79.

———. *Reconciling France Against Democracy: The Croix de Feu and Parti Social Français, 1927–1945.* Montreal: McGill-Queen's University Press, 2007.

Kent, Susan Kingsley. *Making Peace: The Reconstruction of Gender in Interwar Britain.* Princeton, N.J.: Princeton University Press, 1993.

Kerber, Linda K. "Separate Spheres, Female Worlds, Woman's Place: The Rhetoric of Women's History." *Journal of American History* 75, no. 1 (1988): 9–39.

Kershaw, Ian. *The Nazi Dictatorship, Problems and Perspectives of Interpretation.* 4th ed. London and New York: Bloomsbury Academic, 2000.

Kestel, Laurent. *La conversion politique: Doriot, le PPF, et la question du fascisme français.* Paris: Editions Raisons d'Agir, 2012.

Kiernan, Ben. *Blood and Soil: A World History of Genocide and Extermination from Sparta to Darfur.* New Haven, Ct.: Yale University Press, 2007.

Kimble, Sara L. "Emancipation through Secularization: French Feminist Views of Muslim Women's Condition in Interwar Algeria." *French Colonial History* 7 (2006): 109–28.

Kitson, Simon. *The Hunt for Nazi Spies: Fighting Espionage in Vichy France.* Translated by Catherine Tihanyi. Chicago: University of Chicago Press, 2008.

———. "The Police and the Clichy Massacre, March 1937." In *Patterns of Provocation: Police and Public Disorder,* edited by Richard Bessel and Clive Emsley. New York: Berghahn, 2000.

Koonz, Claudia. *Mothers in the Fatherland: Women, the Family, and Nazi Politics.* New York: St. Martin's Press, 1987.

Koos, Cheryl. "Engendering Reaction: The Politics of Pronatalism and the Family in France, 1919–1944." PhD diss., University of Southern California, Los Angeles, 1996.

———. "Fascism, Fatherhood, and the Family in Interwar France: The Case of Antoine Redier and the Légion." *Journal of Family History* 24, no. 3 (1999): 317–29.

Koos, Cheryl, and Daniella Sarnoff. "France." In *Women, Gender and Fascism in Europe 1919–1945,* edited by Kevin Passmore. Manchester: Manchester University Press, 2003.

Kramer, Alan. *Dynamic of Destruction: Culture and Mass Killing in the First World War.* Oxford: Oxford University Press, 2007.

Kramer, William. *Islam Assembled: The Advent of the Muslim Congresses.* New York: Columbia University Press, 1986.

Kselman, Thomas. "Catholicism, Christianity, and Vichy." *French Historical Studies* 23, no. 3 (2000): 513–31.

Kudlick, Catherine J. "Disability History: Why We Need Another 'Other.'" *American Historical Review* 108, no. 3 (June 2003): 763–93.

Lackerstein, Debbie. *National Regeneration in Vichy France: Ideas and Policies, 1930–1944.* Aldershot, England, and Burlington, Vt.: Ashgate, 2012.

Landes, Joan. *Women in the Public Sphere in the Age of the French Revolution.* Ithaca, N.Y.: Cornell University Press, 1988.

Laqueur, Thomas. *Making Sex: Body and Gender from the Greeks to Freud.* Cambridge, Mass.: Harvard University Press, 1992.

Larkin, Maurice. *France Since the Popular Front: Government and People 1936–1986.* Oxford: Clarendon, 1988.

Lebovics, Herman. *True France: The Wars over Cultural Identity, 1900–1945.* Ithaca, N.Y.: Cornell University Press, 1992.

Lerner, Gerda. *The Creation of Patriarchy.* Oxford: Oxford University Press, 1986.

———. *The Majority Finds its Past: Placing Women in History.* Oxford: Oxford University Press, 1979.

Lewis, Mary D. *Divided Rule: Sovereignty and Empire in French Tunisia, 1881–1938.* Berkeley: University of California Press, 2013.

Lorcin, Patricia M.E. *Historicizing Colonial Nostalgia: European Women's Narratives of Algeria and Kenya, 1900–Present.* New York: Palgrave Macmillan, 2012.

———. *Imperial Identities: Stereotyping, Prejudice, and Race in Colonial Algeria.* London: I.B. Tauris, 1995.

———. "Mediating Gender, Mediating Race: Women Writers in Colonial Algeria." *Culture, Theory, and Critique* 45 (2004): 45–61.

———. "Rome and France in Africa: Recovering Colonial Algeria's Latin Past." *French Historical Studies* 25, no. 2 (Spring 2002): 295–329.

Loubet del Bayle, Jean-Louis. *Les non-conformistes des années 30.* Paris: Editions du Seuil, 1969.

Lubac, Henri du. *Christian Response to Anti-Semitism: Memories from 1940–1944.* Translated by Sister Elizabeth Englund. San Francisco: Ignatius Press, 1988.

Machefer, Philippe. "Autour du problème algérien en 1936–1938: La doctrine algérienne du P.S.F.: Le P.S.F et le projet Blum-Violette." *Revue d'histoire moderne et contemporaine* 10 (1963): 147–56.

———. "Le Parti Social Français en 1936–1937." *L'information historique* 34 (1972): 74–80.

———. "Les Syndicats Professionnels Français (1936–1939)." *Le Mouvement social* 119 (1982): 91–112.

Machen, Emily. "Traveling with Faith: The Creation of Women's Immigrant Aid Associations in Nineteenth and Twentieth-Century France." *Journal of Women's History* 23, no. 3 (Fall 2011): 89–112.

Mann, Gregory. "What was the *indigénat?* The 'Empire of Law' in French West Africa." *Journal of African History* 50, no. 3 (November 2009): 331–53.

Marrus, Michael, and Robert Paxton. *Vichy France and the Jews.* New York: Schocken, 1983.

Massell, Gregory. *The Surrogate Proletariat: Moslem Women and Revolutionary Strategies in Soviet Central Asia, 1919–1929.* Princeton, N.J.: Princeton University Press, 1974.

Maza, Sarah. *Violette Nozière: A Story of Murder in 1930s Paris.* Berkeley: University of California Press, 2011.

McDougall, James. *History and the Culture of Nationalism in Algeria.* Cambridge, England: Cambridge University Press, 2006.

McMillan, James. *Housewife or Harlot: The Place of Women in French Society, 1870–1940.* New York: St. Martin's Press, 1981.

———. "Women, Religion, and Politics: The Case of the Ligue Patriotique des Françaises." *Proceedings of the Annual Meeting of the Western Society for French History* 15 (1988): 355–64.

Mendras, Henri, and Alistair Cole. *Social Change in Modern France.* Cambridge, England: Cambridge University Press, 1988.

Merkl, Peter H. "Approaches to the Study of Political Violence." In *Political Violence and Terror: Motifs and Motivations,* edited by Peter Merkl, 19–60. Berkeley: University of California Press, 1988.

Michel, Sonya, and Seth Koven. "Womanly Duties: Maternalist Politics and the Origins of Welfare States in France, Germany, Great Britain, and the United States, 1880–1920." *American Historical Review* 95, no. 4 (October 1990): 1076–1108.

Millington, Chris. "February 6, 1934: The Veterans' Riot." *French Historical Studies* 33, no. 4 (2010): 545–72.

———. "The French veterans and the Republic: The Union nationale des combattants, 1933–1939." PhD diss., University of Cardiff, 2009.

———. *From Victory to Vichy: Veterans in Interwar France.* Manchester: Manchester University Press, 2012.

———. "Political Violence in Interwar France." *History Compass* (2012): 1–14.

Millman, Richard. "Les Croix-de-feu et l'antisémitisme." *Vientième siècle* 38 (1993): 47–61.

———. *La Question juive entre les deux guerres: Ligues de droite et antisémitisme en France.* Paris: Armand Colin, 1992.

Milza, Pierre. *Fascisme français, passé et présent.* Paris: Flammarion, 1987.

Moi, Toril. *What is a Woman?: And Other Essays.* Oxford: Oxford University Press, 1999.

Moore, Brenna. *Sacred Dread: Raissa Maritain, the Allure of Suffering, and the French Catholic Revival, 1905–1944.* South Bend: University of Notre Dame Press, 2013.

Morton, Patricia. *Hybrid Modernities: Architecture and Representation at the 1931 Colonial Exhibition, Paris.* Cambridge, England: Massachusetts Institute of Technology Press, 2000.

Moses, Claire Goldberg. *French Feminism in the Nineteenth Century.* Albany: State University of New York Press, 1985.

Mosse, George. *The Image of Man: The Creation of Modern Masculinity*. Oxford: Oxford University Press, 1996.

Muel-Dreyfus, Francine. *Vichy and the Eternal Feminine: A Contribution to a Political Sociology of Gender*. Translated by Kathleen A. Johnson. Durham, N.C.: Duke University Press, 2001.

Munholland, Kim. "The French Colonial Mind and the Challenge of Islam: The Case of Ernest Psichari." In *The French Colonial Mind: Violence, Military Encounters, and Colonialism*, edited by Martin Thomas. Lincoln: University of Nebraska Press, 2011.

Nobécourt, Jacques. *Le colonel de La Rocque 1885–1946: Ou les piéges du nationalisme Chrétien*. Paris: Fayard, 1996.

Noiriel, Gérard. *Immigration, antisémitisme, et racisme en France, XIXe–XX Siècle: Discours public, humiliations privée*. Paris: Fayard, 2007.

Nord, Philip. *The Republican Moment: Struggles for Democracy in Nineteenth-Century France*. Cambridge, Mass.: Harvard University Press, 1995.

Northrop, Douglas. *Veiled Empire: Gender and Power in Stalinist Central Asia*. Ithaca, N.Y.: Cornell University Press, 2004.

Nye, Joseph S. *Soft Power: The Means to Success in World Politics*. New York: Public Affairs, 2002.

Nye, Robert. *Masculinity and Male Codes of Honor in Modern France*. New York: Oxford University Press, 1993.

Offen, Karen. "Depopulation, Nationalism and Feminism in Fin-de-Siècle France." *American Historical Review* 89, no. 3 (1984): 648–76.

———. *European Feminisms, 1700–1950: A Political History*. Stanford, Calif.: Stanford University Press, 2000.

———. "French Women's History: Retrospect (1789–1940) and Prospect." *French Historical Studies* 26, no. 4 (Fall 2003): 727–67.

Ory, Pascal, and Jean-François Sirinelli. *Les Intellectuels en France: De l'affair Dreyfus à nos jours*. Paris: Parrin, 2004.

Passmore, Kevin. "Boy Scouting for Grown-Ups? Paramilitarism in the Croix de Feu and the Parti Social Français." *French Historical Studies* 19, no. 2 (Autumn 1995): 527–57.

———. "Catholicism and Nationalism: The *Fédération républicaine*, 1927–1939." In *Catholicism, Politics, and Society in Twentieth-Century France*, edited by Kay Chadwick. Liverpool: Liverpool University Press, 2000.

———. "Class, Gender, and Populism: The Parti Populaire Française in Lyon." In *The Right in France: From Revolution to Le Pen*, edited by Nicolas Atkin and Frank Tallett. London: I.B. Tauris, 2003.

———. "The Construction of Crisis in Interwar France." In *France in the Era of Fascism*, edited by Brian Jenkins. New York: Berghahn, 2005.

———. "The Croix de Feu: Bonapartism, National Populism or Fascism?" *French History* 9, no. 1 (1995): 67–92.

———. "Crowd Psychology, Anti-Southern Prejudice, and Constitutional Reform in 1930s France: The Stavisky Affair and the Riots of 6 February 1934." In *The French Right between the Wars: Political and Intellectual Movements from Conservatism to Fascism,* edited by Samuel Kalman and Sean Kennedy. New York: Berghahn, 2014.

———. *Fascism: A Very Short Introduction.* Oxford: Oxford University Press, 2002.

———. "Femininity and the Right: From Moral Order to Moral Order." *Modern and Contemporary France* 8, no. 1 (2000): 55–69.

———. "The French Third Republic: Stalemate Society or Cradle of Fascism." *French History* 7, no. 4 (1993): 417–49.

———. *From Liberalism to Fascism: The Right in a French Province, 1928–1939.* Cambridge, England: Cambridge University Press, 1997.

———. "'Planting the Tricolor in the Citadels of Communism': Women's Social Action in the Croix de feu and Parti social français." *Journal of Modern History* 71, no. 4 (December 1999): 814–51.

———. *The Right in France from the Third Republic to Vichy.* Oxford: Oxford University Press, 2013.

———. "Theories of Fascism: A Critique from the Perspective of Women's and Gender History." In *Rethinking the Nature of Fascism: Comparative Perspectives,* edited by António Costa Pinto. New York: Palgrave Macmillan, 2011.

———, ed. *Women, Gender and Fascism in Europe 1919–1945.* Manchester: Manchester University Press, 2003.

Pateman, Carol. *The Sexual Contract.* Stanford, Calif.: Stanford University Press, 1988.

Paul, Harry W. *The Second Ralliement: The Rapprochement between Church and State in France in the Twentieth Century.* Washington, D.C.: Catholic University of America Press, 1967.

Paxton, Robert. *The Anatomy of Fascism.* New York: Random House, 2004.

———. *French Peasant Fascism: Henry Dorgère's Greenshirts and the Crises of French Agriculture, 1929–1939.* Oxford: Oxford University Press, 1997.

———. *Vichy France: Old Guard New Order.* Rev. ed. New York: Columbia University Press, 2001.

Payne, Stanley. *A History of Fascism, 1924–1945.* Madison: University of Wisconsin Press, 1995.

———. *The Spanish Civil War, the Soviet Union, and Communism.* New Haven, Ct.: Yale University Press, 2004.

Pedersen, Susan. *Family, Dependence, and the Origins of the Welfare State: Britain and France, 1914–1945.* Cambridge, England: Cambridge University Press, 1993.

Peer, Shanny. *France on Display: Peasants, Provincials, and Folklore in the 1937 Paris World's Fair.* Albany: State University of New York Press, 1998.

Pennell, C.R. *Morocco since 1830, a History.* New York: New York University Press, 2000.

Perkins, Kenneth. *A History of Modern Tunisia.* Cambridge, England: Cambridge University Press, 2004.

Perrot, Michelle. *Une histoire des femmes est-elle possible?* Paris: Rivages, 1984.

Perry, Matt. *Memory of War in France, 1914–1945: Cesar Fauxbras, the Voice of the Lowly.* New York: Palgrave Macmillan, 2011.

Peukert, Detlev. *Inside Nazi Germany: Conformity, Opposition, Racism in Everyday Life.* Translated by Richard Deveson. New Haven, Ct.: Yale University Press, 1987.

Pollard, Miranda. *Reign of Virtue: Mobilizing Gender in Vichy France.* Chicago: University of Chicago Press, 1998.

Popiel, Jennifer. *Rousseau's Daughters: Domesticity, Education, and Autonomy in Modern France.* Lebanon: University of New Hampshire Press, 2008.

Poulat, Emile. *Liberté, laïcité. La guerre des deux France et le principe de modernité.* Paris: Cujas-Cerf, 1988.

Preston, Paul. *The Spanish Holocaust: Inquisition and Extermination in Twentieth-Century Spain.* New York: W.W. Norton, 2012.

Prost, Antoine. *Les anciens combattants et la société française, 1914–1939.* 3 vols. Paris: Presses de la Fondation nationale des sciences politiques, 1977.

———. "Monuments to the Dead." In *Realms of Memory: The Construction of the French Past.* Vol. 2: *Traditions.* Directed by Pierre Nora, translated by Arthur Goldhammer, edited by Lawrence D. Kritzman. New York: Columbia University Press, 1997.

Prost, Antoine, and Jay Winter. *The Great War in History: Debates and Controversies, 1914 to the Present Day.* Cambridge, England: Cambridge University Press, 2005.

Read, Geoff. "'He Is Depending on You': Militarism, Martyrdom, and the Appeal to Manliness in the Case of France's 'Croix de Feu,' 1931–1940." *Journal of the Canadian Historical Association/Revue de la Société historique du Canada* 16, no. 1 (2005): 261–91.

Rémond, René. *Les Droites en France, de 1815 à nos jours.* 4th ed. Paris: Aubier-Montainge, 1982.

———. *Religion et société en Europe: La sécularisation au xix et xx siècle, 1780–2000.* Paris: Editions du Seuil, 1998.

Reynaud, Brigitte. *L'industrie rubanière dans la région stéphanois, 1895–1975.* St-Etienne: Centre d'Etudes Foréziennes, Université Jean Monnet, 1991.

Reynolds, Sian. *France Between the Wars: Gender and Politics.* London: Routledge, 1996.

Riley, Denise. *Am I that Name? Feminism and the Category of "Women" in History.* Minneapolis: University of Minnesota Press, 1988.

Roberts, Mary Louise. *Civilization without Sexes: Reconstructing Gender in Postwar France, 1917–1927.* Chicago: University of Chicago Press, 1994.

Rochefort, Florence, dir. *Le pouvoir du genre: Laïcités et religions, 1905–2005.* Toulouse: Presses universitaires du Mirail, 2007.

Rosenberg, Clifford. "The Colonial Politics of Health Care Provision in Interwar Paris." *French Historical Studies* 27, no. 3 (Summer 2004): 637–68.

——. "The International Politics of Vaccine Testing in Interwar Algiers." *American Historical Review* 117, no. 3 (June 2012): 671–97.

——. *Policing Paris: The Origins of Modern Immigration Control Between the Wars.* Ithaca, N.Y.: Cornell University Press, 2006.

Rousso, Henri. *The Vichy Syndrome: History and Memory in France since 1944.* Translated by Arthur Goldhammer. Cambridge, Mass.: Harvard University Press, 1994.

Ruedy, John. *Modern Algeria: The Origins and Development of a Nation.* 2nd ed. Bloomington: Indiana University Press, 2005.

Ryan, Donna F. *The Holocaust and the Jews of Marseille: The Enforcement of anti-Semitic Policies in Vichy France.* Urbana: University of Illinois Press, 1996.

Rymell, John. "Militants and Militancy in the Croix de Feu and Parti Social Français: Patterns of Political Experience on the French Far Right (1933–1939)." PhD diss., University of East Anglia, 1990.

Saada, Emmanuel. "The Empire of Law: Dignity, Prestige, and Domination in the 'Colonial Situation.'" *French Politics, Culture and Society* 20, no. 2 (2002): 98–120.

Saaïdia, Oissila. "Le cas de l'eglise catholique en l'Algérie avant la première guerre mondiale." In *Religions et colonisation, Afrique-Asie-Océanie-Amériques XVIe–XXe siècles,* edited by D. Borne and B. Falaize, 166–76. Paris: Les éditions de l'atelier, 2009.

Said, Edward. *Culture and Imperialism.* New York: Vintage, 1994.

——. *Orientalism.* New York: Vintage, 1978.

Sarnoff, Daniella. "Domesticating Fascism: Family and Gender in French Fascist Leagues." In *Women of the Right: Comparisons and Interplay across Borders,* edited by Kathleen M. Blee and Sandra McGee Deutsch. University Park: Pennsylvania State University Press, 2012.

——. "Interwar Fascism and the Franchise: Women's Suffrage and the *Ligues.*" *Historical Reflections* 34, no. 2 (Summer 2008): 112–33.

——. "In the Cervix of the Nation: Women and French Fascism." PhD diss., Boston College, 2001.

Sarti, Odile. *The Ligue Patriotique des Françaises (1902–1933): A Feminine Response to the Secularization of French Society.* New York: Garland, 1992.

Scales, Rebecca. "Radio Broadcasting, Disabled Veterans, and the Politics of National Recovery in Interwar France." *French Historical Studies* 31, no. 4 (Fall 2008): 643–78.

Schue, Paul. "Making Space for War: *L'Action Française, Je suis partout,* and French Right-Wing Understandings of the Spanish Civil War." In *France and its Spaces of War: Experience, Memory, Image,* edited by Patricia Lorcin and Daniel Brewer. New York: Palgrave Macmillan, 2009.

———. "The Prodigal Sons of Communism: *Parti Populaire Français* Narrative of Communist Recruitment for the Spanish Civil War and the Everyday Functioning of Party Ideology." *French Historical Studies* 24, no. 1 (Winter 2001): 87–111.

Schwartz, Vanessa. *Spectacular Realities: Early Mass Culture in fin-de-Siècle Paris.* Berkeley: University of California Press, 1998.

Scott, Joan. *Gender and the Politics of History.* Rev. ed. New York: Columbia University Press, 1999.

———. "Gender: A Useful Category of Historical Analysis." *American Historical Review* 91, no. 5 (December 1986): 1053–1075.

———. *Only Paradoxes to Offer: French Feminists and the Rights of Man.* Cambridge, Mass.: Harvard University Press, 1996.

———. "Unanswered Questions." *American Historical Review* 113, no. 5 (December 2008): 1422–1429.

Segalla, Spencer D. *The Moroccan Soul: French Education, Colonial Ethnology, and Muslim Resistance, 1912–1956.* Lincoln: University of Nebraska Press, 2009.

Sessions, Jennifer E. *By Sword and Plow: France and the Conquest of Algeria.* Ithaca, N.Y.: Cornell University Press, 2011.

Sghaier, Amira. *La droite française en Tunisie entre 1934 et 1946.* Tunis: Institut supérieur d'histoire du mouvement national, 2004.

Shapiro, Ann-Louise. *Breaking the Codes: Female Criminality in fin-de-Siècle Paris.* Stanford, Calif.: Stanford University Press, 1996.

Shepard, Todd. *The Invention of Decolonization: The Algerian War and the Remaking of France.* Ithaca, N.Y.: Cornell University Press, 2006.

Sherman, Daniel J. *The Construction of Memory in Interwar France.* Chicago: University of Chicago Press, 1999.

———. "'Peoples Ethnographic': Objects, Museums, and the Colonial Inheritance of French Ethnography." *French Historical Studies* 27, no. 3 (Summer 2004): 669–703.

Silverman, Dan P. "Fantasy and Reality in Nazi Work-Creation Programs, 1933–1936." *Journal of Modern History* 65, no. 1 (March 1993): 113–51.

Sinha, Mrinalini. *Colonial Masculinity: The 'Manly Englishman' and the 'Effeminate Bengali' in the Late Nineteenth Century.* Manchester: Manchester University Press, 1995.

Slavin, David. *Colonial Cinema and Imperial France, 1919–1939: White Blind Spots, Male Fantasies, Settler Myths.* Baltimore: Johns Hopkins University Press, 2001.

Smith, Bonnie. *Ladies of the Leisure Class: The Bourgeoises of Northern France in the Nineteenth Century.* Princeton, N.J.: Princeton University Press, 1981.

Smith, Leonard V. *Between Mutiny and Obedience: The Case of the French Fifth Infantry Division during World War I.* Princeton, N.J.: Princeton University Press, 1994.

———. *The Embattled Self: French Soldiers' Testimony of the Great War.* Ithaca, N.Y.: Cornell University Press, 2007.

Smith, Leonard V., Stéphane Audoin-Rouzeau, and Annette Becker. *France and the Great War 1914–1918.* Cambridge, England: Cambridge University Press, 2003.

Smith, Paul. *Feminism in the Third Republic: Women's Political and Civil Rights in France, 1918–1945.* Oxford: Clarendon, 1996.

Smith, Timothy. *Creating the Welfare State in France, 1880–1940.* Montreal and London: McGill-Queen's University Press, 2003.

Sneeringer, Julia. *Winning Women's Votes: Propaganda and Politics in Weimar Germany.* Chapel Hill: University of North Carolina Press, 2002.

Soucy, Robert. "Fascism in France: Problematizing the Immunity Thesis." In *France in the Era of Fascism: Essays on the French Authoritarian Right,* edited by Brian Jenkins. New York: Berghahn, 2005.

———. *French Fascism: The First Wave, 1924–1933.* New Haven, Ct.: Yale University Press, 1986.

———. *French Fascism: The Second Wave, 1933–1939.* New Haven, Ct.: Yale University Press, 1995.

Sowerwine, Charles. *Sisters or Citizens? Women and Socialism in France since 1876.* New York: Cambridge University Press, 1982.

Stephenson, Jill. *The Nazi Organization of Women.* London: Croom Helm, 1981.

Stewart, Mary Lynn. *For Health and Beauty: Physical Culture for Frenchwomen, 1880s–1930s.* Baltimore: Johns Hopkins University Press, 2001.

Stiker, Henri-Jacques. *A History of Disability.* Translated by William Sayers. Ann Arbor: University of Michigan Press, 1999.

Stoler, Ann Laura. *Carnal Knowledge and Imperial Power: Race and the Intimate in Colonial Rule.* Berkeley: University of California Press, 2002.

Stovall, Tyler. "The Color Line behind the Lines: Racial Violence in France during the Great War." *American Historical Review* 103, no. 3 (June 1998): 737–69.

———. "National Identity and Shifting Imperial Frontiers: Whiteness and the Exclusion of Colonial Labor after World War I." *Representations* 84 (November 2003): 52–72.

Sternhell, Zeev. *The Birth of Fascist Ideology.* Translated by David Maisel. Princeton, N.J.: Princeton University Press, 1994.

———. "Fascism: Reflection on the Fate of Ideas in Twentieth Century History." *Journal of Political Ideologies* 5, no. 2 (June 2000): 139–63.

———. "Morphology of Fascism in France." In *France in the Era of Fascism: Essays on the French Authoritarian Right,* edited by Brian Jenkins. New York: Berghahn, 2005.

———. *Ni droite ni gauche: L'idéologie fasciste en France.* Paris: Editions du Seuil, 1983.

Stites, Richard. *The Women's Liberation Movement in Russia: Feminism, Nihilism, and Bolshevism, 1860–1930.* Princeton, N.J.: Princeton University Press, 1978.

Stora, Benjamin. *Nationalistes algériens et révolutionnaires français au temps du Front populaire.* Paris: Editions l'Harmattan, 1987.

Stromberg Childers, Kristen. *Fathers, Families, and the State in France, 1914–1945.* Ithaca, N.Y.: Cornell University Press, 2003.

Surkis, Judith. *Sexing the Citizen: Morality and Masculinity in France, 1870–1920.* Ithaca, N.Y.: Cornell University Press, 2006.

Sweets, John. *Choices in Vichy France.* New York: Oxford University Press, 1986.

Tallett, Frank, and Nicholas Atkin, eds. *Religion, Society, and Politics in France since 1789.* London: Hambledon, 1991.

Thébaud, Françoise. *Quand nos grand-mères donnaient la vie: La maternité en France l'entre-deux-guerres.* Lyon: Presses universitaires de Lyon, 1986.

Theweleit, Klaus. *Male Fantasies.* Vol. 1. *Women, Floods, Bodies, History.* Minneapolis: University of Minnesota Press, 1987.

Thomas, Jean-Paul. "Les droites, les femmes et le mouvement sssociatif, 1902–1946." In *Associations et champs politique: La loi de 1901 à l'épreuve du siècle,* edited by Claire Andrieu, Gilles Le Béguec, and Danielle Tartakowsky. Paris: Publications de la Sorbonne, 2001.

———. "Les effectifs du Parti social français." *Vingtième siècle* 62 (avril–juin 1999): 61–83.

Thomas, Martin. *Empires of Intelligence: Security Services and Colonial Disorder after 1914.* Berkeley: University of California Press, 2008.

———, ed. *The French Colonial Mind: Violence, Military Encounters, and Colonialism.* Lincoln: University of Nebraska Press, 2011.

———. *The French Empire Between the Wars: Imperialism, Politics, and Society.* Manchester: Manchester University Press, 2005.

Tiersten, Lisa. *Marianne in the Market: Envisioning Consumer Society in fin-de-siècle France.* Berkeley: University of California Press, 2001.

Torrie, Julia. *For Their Own Good: Civilian Evacuations in Germany and France, 1939–1944.* New York: Berghahn, 2010.

Tostain, F. "Popular Front and the Blum-Violette Plan." In *French Colonial Empire and the Popular Front: Hope and Disillusion,* edited by Tony Chafer and Amanda Sackur. New York: St. Martin's, 1999.

Trumbell, George IV. *An Empire of Facts: Colonial Power, Cultural Knowledge, and Islam in Algeria, 1870–1914.* Cambridge, England: Cambridge University Press, 2009.

Tumblety, Joan. *Remaking the Male Body: Masculinity and the uses of Physical Culture in Interwar and Vichy France.* Oxford: Oxford University Press, 2012.

———. "The Soccer World Cup of 1938: Politics, Spectacles, and *la Culture Physique* in Interwar France." *French Historical Studies* 31, no. 1 (Winter 2008): 77–116.

Vauchez, André. "The Cathedral." In *Realms of Memory: The Construction of the French Past.* Vol. 2: *Traditions.* Directed by Pierre Nora, translated by Arthur Goldhammer, edited by Lawrence D. Kritzman. New York: Columbia University Press, 1997.

Vince, Natalya. "Transgressing Boundaries: Gender, Race, Religion, and 'Françaises Musulmanes' during the Algerian War of Independence." *French Historical Studies* 33, no. 3 (Summer 2010).

Vincent, Mary. *Catholicism in the Second Republic: Religion and Politics in Salamanca, 1930–1936.* Oxford: Oxford University Press, 1996.

———. "Spain." In *Women, Gender and Fascism in Europe 1919–1945,* edited by Kevin Passmore. Manchester: Manchester University Press, 2003.

Vovelle, Michel. "La Marseillaise: War or Peace." In *Realms of Memory: The Construction of the French Past.* Vol. 3: *Traditions.* Directed by Pierre Nora, translated by Arthur Goldhammer, edited by Lawrence D. Kritzman. New York: Columbia University Press, 1997.

Walton, Whitney. *Eve's Proud Descendants: Four Women Writers and Republican Politics in Nineteenth-Century France.* Stanford, Calif.: Stanford University Press, 2000.

Wardhaugh, Jessica. *In Pursuit of the People: Political Culture in France, 1934–1939.* New York: Palgrave Macmillan, 2009.

Weber, Eugen. *Action Française: Royalism and Reaction in Twentieth-Century France.* Stanford, Calif.: Stanford University Press, 1962.

———. "Gymnastics and Sports in Fin-de-Siècle France: Opium of the Classes?" *American Historical Review* 76, no. 1 (February 1971): 70–98.

———. *The Hollow Years: France in the 1930s.* New York: W.W. Norton, 1994.

———. *Peasants into Frenchmen: The Modernization of Rural France, 1871–1914.* Stanford, Calif.: Stanford University Press, 1976.

———. "Pierre de Coubertin and the Introduction of Organised Sport in France." *Journal of Contemporary History* 5, no. 2 (1970): 3–26.

Weil, Patrick. *How to be French: Nationality in the Making since 1789.* Translated by Catherine Porter. Durham, N.C.: Duke University Press, 2008.

Welch, Edward. *François Mauriac: The Making of an Intellectual.* Amsterdam, N.Y.: Editions Rodopi BV, 2006.

Whitney, Susan. *Mobilizing Youth: Communists and Catholics in Interwar France.* Durham, N.C.: Duke University Press, 2009.

Wilder, Gary. *The French Imperial Nation-State: Negritude and Colonial Humanism between the Two World Wars.* Chicago: University of Chicago Press, 2005.

Willson, Perry. "Italy." In *Women, Gender and Fascism in Europe, 1919–1945,* edited by Kevin Passmore. Manchester: Manchester University Press, 2003.

Winock, Michel. "En lisant Robert Soucy." *Vingtième siècle* 95 (2007): 237–42.

———. "Joan of Arc." In *Realms of Memory: The Construction of the French Past.* Vol. 3: *Traditions.* Directed by Pierre Nora, translated by Arthur Goldhammer, edited by Lawrence D. Kritzman. New York: Columbia University Press, 1997.

———. *Nationalism, Anti-Semitism, and Fascism in France.* Translated by Jane Marie Todd. Stanford, Calif.: Stanford University Press, 1998.

———. "Retour sur le fascism français: La Rocque et les Croix de Feu." *Vingtième siècle* 90 (2006): 3–27.

Winter, Jay. *Sites of Memory, Sites of Mourning: The Great War in Cultural History.* New York: Cambridge University Press, 1995.

Wood, Elizabeth. *The Baba and the Comrade: Gender and Politics in Revolutionary Russia.* Bloomington: Indiana University Press, 1997.

Wyrtzen, Jonathan. "Constructing Morocco: The Colonial Struggle to Define a Nation, 1912–1956." PhD diss., Georgetown University, Washington, D.C., 2009.

Zaretsky, Robert. *Nimes at War: Religion, Politics, and Public Opinion in the Gard, 1938–1944.* University Park: Pennsylvania State University Press, 1995.

Zuccotti, Susan. *The Holocaust, the French, and the Jews.* New York: Basic Books, 1993.

INDEX

Note: illustrations (indicated as "fig.1, etc.") are found after page 122. Page numbers followed by "t" and "n" refer to tables and endnotes, respectively; throughout the index, CF/PSF refers to Croix de Feu/Parti Social Français.

Abbas, Ferhat, 163–64
Abetz, Otto, 197
Abi-Mershed, Osama, 210n49
Action Française: Catholic Church and, 66; female membership, 61; integral nationalism of, 55; Joan of Arc fête and, 42t; LFF and, 15; pacifist congress attack (1931), 35
Action Libérale Populaire (ALP), 15
"Adapt and Assimilate" policy, 169–72, 204–5
Addams, Jane, 62
ADP (Auxiliaries to Passive Defense/Artisans du Devoir Patriotique): Allied liberation, provisional government, and, 198–200; cadres nomades, fixes, and locaux, 193–95; creation of, 181; disenchantment with Vichy, 191; early Vichy and expansion of, 185–88; evacuations, refugees, and, 182–85; Gestapo arrests of leaders, 197–98; Jews, resistance aid to, 195–96; Klan resistance and intelligence activities, 192–97, 201; moral quagmire of collaboration, 200–202; organization and structure of, 183, 186; Préval on "Army of the Good" and metamorphosis, 188–90; Préval's "true National Revolution" and, 189–91; PSF subsumed under, 182–83; Secours National partnership, 181–82, 186; welcome centers and aid stations, 181–82, 183, 187

Algeria: CF/PSF meeting attendance in, 159, fig.10; conquest centennial celebrations, 160–61; French conquest of, 3–4; Mitidja plain, 140–41; Popular Front and reform in, 161; recruitment of indigenous men in, 158–60; Soufflotines in, 138–43; Women's Sections and social program in, 149, 151–54. See also North African Croix de Feu/PSF; settlers in the French Maghreb
algérianiste movement, 6, 172
Algerian Muslim Congress, 161–64
Alibi network, 193
Les Allées convalescent home, Pau, 89–95
ALP (Action Libérale Populaire), 15
Les amis de La Rocque, 202
AMSJA. See Association Médico-Sociale Jeanne d'Arc
anticlericalism, 14–15, 40, 84, 106
anticolonial activism in the Maghreb, 160–68, 173–77
antifeminism, 21, 34–35, 47–48
anti-Semitism: Maghreb and, 172–73; Vichy, 195–96, 199
anti-southern prejudice, 126
Arab-Muslim nationalism, 162, 165–66
armistice celebration (Nov. 11), 41
Army of the Good, 188–90

d'Arras, Madame, 71, 72

Arslan, Emir Shekib, 165–66, 174

Artisans du Devoir Patriotique. *See* ADP

assimilationism and associationism: "Adapt and Assimilate" policy, 169–72, 204–5; Blum-Violette bill and, 164; CF/PSF, 12–13; civilizing mission and, 3; FEM and assimilation, 162; Iba-Zizen's "social harmonization," 170–71; La Rocque on Jews and, 195–96; North African vs. metropolitan, 10; religion, relationship with, 204; Soufflotines in Algeria and, 142–43

association. *See* assimilationism and associationism

Association des Ulama Musulmans Algériens (AUMA), 162

Association Médico-Sociale Jeanne d'Arc (AMSJA): autonomy and authority of women in, 98; creation of, 74; growth of medical centers, 63t; health clinic and Les Allées, staff issues at, 88–95; Javal and, 78; Maghreb, absence in, 148; physical education programs and, 117; Vichy period and, 183, 187–88

AUMA (Association des Ulama Musulmans Algériens), 162

Auxiliaries to Passive Defense. *See* ADP

Bard, Christine, 47

Barrachin, Edmond, 178–79

Barrucand, Mme., 188

bazaars, 97, 126–29, fig.7

beauty, 114–15

Bédarida, François, 191

Bellet, Hélène de, 137, 139

Ben Badis, Abd al-Hamid, 162–66

Bendjelloul, Mohamed-Salah, 158–59, 162–64

Berber Dahir, 161

Bernard, Jean, 82

Bernard, Mme., 103–4, 152, 153

Biehler, Gisèle, 195

Binet, Renée, 186, 197

Blum-Violette bill, 12, 161, 164, 167, 170

Borel, Mme., 94

Bouchedja, M., 159–60

Bouches-du-Rhone Civic Action, 102–3

Bourguiba, Habib, 166, 174–75

Bourrut-Lacouture, Mme., 196

boycotts of Jewish businesses, 172–73

Brasillach, Robert, 47

Briandism, 35

Briscards, 32, 32t

British Intelligence Services, 193–94

Brunschvicg, Cécile, 17–18, 20

Bruyas, J., 77, 79

budgetary problems, 96–98

Buisset, Mme., 62

cadres fixes, 193

cadres locaux, 194–95

cadres nomades, 193–94

Carlier, Mlle., 43–44

Carpano, Suzanne, 97–98

carte du combattant, 30

Cartel des Gauches, 20, 31, 213n100

Casanova, Mme., 102–3, 105

cathedrals, 40

Catholic Action, 24, 66, 76–78, 84, 204

Catholicism: Action Française and, 66; cathedrals, 40; CF/PSF social program and, 66–68, 76–78; French identity and, 10; Joan of Arc fête and, 42t; Maghreb and, 84–85; Mass of Marshals and, 40–41; pronatalist movement and, 18–19; social, 14, 53; Soufflotines and, 141; Soufflotines on Nazism and, 145; sporting clubs, 106; stripped of political power by Napoleon, 14; Vichy and, 188. *See also* ethnoreligious nationalism

cell theory, 112–13

Center for Physical Education, 116–17

CGTT (Confédération Générale des Travailleurs Tunisiens), 174

Chaillet, Pierre, 198–200

Chantiers de la Jeunesse, 121

Charaudeau, Georges, 193

charity bazaars, 97, 126–29, fig.7

Charter of Demands (Algerian Muslim
    Congress), 163

Chiray, Dr., 89

Chopine, Paul, 35–36, 46, 53–54

Chrastil, Rachel, 28

Christmas party, annual, 125

citizenship: Blum-Violette bill, 12, 161, 164,
    167; CF/PSF's reform delays, 24; integral,
    170; Jews and, 195–96; women and, during
    Revolution, 13

Civic Action (Action Civique), 75, 95–96,
    98–104

civic space, 50, 54, 57

Civil Code, 13–14, 17

civilizing mission: Arab nationalism and, 139;
    CF/PSF and, 9–13, 177, 204; conquest of
    Algeria, 3–4; Fête Coloniale and Tarzan
    narrative, 131–35; Fouché and, 71; Iba-Zizen
    and, 169; indigenous Algerians in PSF and,
    159; portrayal of colonial subjects and, 124;
    Soufflotines and, 142–43; Third Republic
    and, 4–5; universalism, assimilation, and, 3.
    See also assimilationism and associationism

Clancy-Smith, Julia, 11

class, 78–79, 148

"cloisters," 192

clothing depots, growth of, 63t

CNFF (Conseil National des Femmes
    Françaises), 18–19

Cole, Joshua, 158

collaboration: ADP and moral quagmire of,
    200–202; with ATP, 128–29; doctrine of
    collaboration of men, 86; with Muslims in
    the Maghreb, 157–60; post–D-Day purge of
    collaborators, 198; Préval on gender and,
    189; Vichy and, 178–80, 186, 191

colonialism: decolonialization, early stages
    of, 147–48; Fête Coloniale at World's Fair,
    130–35; social and cultural activities and,
    123; violence and racism of conquest, and

ethnoreligious hierarchies, 147; World's
    Fair colonial pavilion, 130. *See also* Algeria;
    civilizing mission; Morocco; North African
    Croix de Feu/PSF; settlers in the French
    Maghreb; Tunisia

Colonieu, Lucien, 151, 152, 153

combatant-noncombatant hierarchy in early
    CF and, 32–34

Le Comité de Vigilance des Intellectuels Anti-
    fascistes (CVIA), 74, 124

Commissariat General for Sports, 121

Commission for Indigenous Affairs, 168–72

Communist Party. *See* French Communist Party
    (PCF); Popular Front

Confédération Générale des Travailleurs Tu-
    nisiens (CGTT), 174

Conklin, Alice, 11, 111, 124

conscription laws, 106

Conseil National des Femmes Françaises
    (CNFF), 18–19

Cooper, Frederick, 9

coup d'état in North Africa, possibility of,
    154–55

Cova, Anne, 21–22

Croix de Feu, dissolution of (1936), 74

Croix de Feu, early (1927–34): ancillary groups,
    31–34, 32t; antifeminism vs. misogyny
    and, 47–48; combatant-noncombatant
    hierarchy, 32–34; culture of war and, 28–29;
    death's head symbol and, 27, 30; Joan of Arc
    fête and iconography, 41–45, 45t; La Rocque
    (François de) and, 31–36; as league, orga-
    nization, or movement, 207n1; masculine
    ideal in, 33–34; Mass of Marshal, 39–41; *Les
    Miserables* and, 27; name of, 27, 30; neigh-
    borhood sections, 30; paramilitarism and
    violence, 30, 34–37; purity ideology, 38–39;
    soup kitchens and women's participation
    in, 46–47; veteran's mystique and, 29, 35,
    37–38; womanhood, bifurcated conceptual-
    ization of, 45–46

Croix de Feu health clinic, Paris, 88–89, 94–95

Croix de Feu/PSF (Parti Social Français):
Allied description of, 179; assimilationism
vs. associationism and, 12–13; democratic
principles and, 25; dual character of Third
Republic and, 9–10; ecumenicalism in, 24;
ethnoreligious and gender hierarchy in
Greater France, historical context of, 2–9;
female membership of, 61–62; French
political culture, historiographic context
of, 21–25; historiographic context, 9–13;
influence of women, assessment of, 22–25;
as lone protector of national interests, 179–
80; number of women in, 22; as Pétainists,
178–79; reform delays by, 24; renamed Parti
Social Français, 74; renamed Progrès Social
Français, 185; success, reasons for, 58;
Women's Section, creation of, 23; women's
social and political action in metropolitan
France, historical context of, 13–21. *See also
specific topics, programs, and names*
Croix de Feu Soup Kitchen, 46–47
Croix de Guerre, 27, 44
cultural programs and entertainment: assimilation and association doctrines and, 125,
142–43; charity bazaars and integralism, 97,
126–29, fig.7; French cultural superiority
and, 78–79, 142; galas and soirées, 125; as
Left-Right battlefield, 78; World's Fair (1937,
Paris) and Fête Coloniale, 127–28, 129–35.
See also Soufflotines
culture of war, 28–29, 50, 81, 180, 215n4
CVIA (Le Comité de Vigilance des Intellectuels
Antifascistes), 74, 124

Daladier, Edouard, 51
Daujat, Jean, 67–68
Dauré, Mme, 103
D-Day landings, 198
death's head symbol, 27, 30
Debay, Alfred, 142, 155–56, 166, 168–69
Déléchant, Mme., 79–80
Della Sudda, Magali, 20

dependency and gender, 44–45, 98–100
Desmons, Mme., 103
Devaud, Stanislaus, 158, 171–72
Dieux, Father, 55, 57, 66
disability and disabled rights, 72–73, 206
disponsables (dispos) shock troops, 35–36,
46, 127
Downs, Laura Lee, 23, 79, 87, 190
Drieu la Rochelle, Pierre, 40, 46
Ducrocq, Madeleine, 88–96
Durleman, Pastor, 55, 56
Dutilh, Mme., 128–29
Duval, Marivic, 1, 139–42

ecumenicalism, 24, 54–55
El Okbi, 167
empire. *See* assimilationism and associationism; civilizing mission; colonialism
ENA (Etoile Nord-Afrique), 64–65, 162
entertainment. *See* cultural programs and entertainment
Entr'aide Français, 198–200. *See also* Secours
National
ethnoreligious nationalism: class integration
and, 78–79; colonial conquest and, 147;
gender ideology and, 84; Iba-Zizen and,
169; impact of, 203–4; Nazism vs., 146;
and secular feminism, hostility toward, 24;
Travail et loisirs and, 78–79; Vichy and, 188;
Women's Section inauguration and, 54–55.
See also Catholicism
Etoile Nord-Afrique (ENA), 64–65, 162
L'Etudiant Social, 81–83
eugenics, positive, 109–10
evolution, 110
exercise. *See* physical culture and physical
education
exhaustion of women, 95–96
Exposition artisanale (1938), 128–29

Faisceau, 20–21, 214n103
family, 18–19, 20

Fanon, Frantz, 69

Farrère, Claude, 80

fascism: Arslan and, 165–66; authoritarianism, borders with, 26; CF/PSF labeled as fascist by Popular Front, 39; contested memory over, 202; François de La Rocque as symbol of, 199; Kalman on colonial fascism, 6, 11; Nadine de La Rocque on republicanism and, 2, 206; North African CF and, 148, 149, 172; paramilitarism and, 36; political culture of interwar French Maghreb and, 147; of PSF settlers, 172–77; purity and, 39; race conceptions and conclusion that CF/PSF was fascist, 204; vs. communism at World's Fair, 130

fascist leagues: dissolution of, 74; hypermasculinity in, 20–21

Fascists' March on Rome (1922), 35

Fayet-Scribe, Sylvie, 14

Fédération des Elus Musulmans (FEM), 158–59, 162

Fédération Républicaine, 18, 213n102

FEM (Fédération des Elus Musulmans), 158–59, 162

femininity. *See* womanhood and femininity, constructions of

feminists: antifeminism, 21, 34–35, 47–48; CF/PSF contrasted with secular feminists, 24; on family, 20; history of feminist organizing, 16–18; Nord PSF at Lille conference (1937), 86–87; Radicals vs. conservatives, choice of alignment with, 17–18; structural subordination in Civic Action and, 98–99, 103–4; wider women's movement vs., 17

Femme Nouvelle, 18

Féraud, Germaine, 49, 54, 55, 57–60, 221n43

Fête Coloniale (1937 World's Fair, Paris), 130–35

Fils et Filles des Croix de Feu (FFCF), 31–32, 32t, 152

Le Flambeau (the Torch): bazaar publicity, 127; circulation of, 59; creation of, 30–31; gender ideology and, 31; Joan of Arc depiction, 43, fig.2; recruiting poster, fig.1; "What a Woman Should Know" and "For Her" (women's columns), 45; "What's Necessary to Know" (men's column), 45; Yver and, 46

La Flamme: on anticolonial coalition, 166; banned in Tunisia, 176; first issue of, 163; on Fouché, 85; on Judeo-Muslim bloc, 166–67; on nationalists, 174–75, 176; on Soufflotines, 142, fig.8; on threat to Greater France, 9; on Tunis riots, 176; on Ulama, 164

Fogg, Shannon, 198

Fouché, Suzanne, 69–73, 76, 85, 139, 148, 206, fig.6

Le foyer universitaire (The Foyer), 135–38. *See also* Soufflotines

Frader, Laura Levine, 73

Franco-Prussian War (1870–71), 28, 106

Free Federation of Republics of North Africa, 167

French Communist Party (PCF): CF/PSF seen as threat by, 52; on colonial independence, 124; *dispos,* harassment by, 36; *Le Flambeau,* competition with, 30; infiltration of CF/PSF by, 37; "Internationale" (song), 39; Joan of Arc and, 42, 44; provisional government and, 198; PSF social centers, violence at, 79–80; race and sport in, 107, 119; social workers and, 69; ultranationalist view of, 29; Women's Section, 61–62; women's youth group, 115; youth membership, 116. *See also* Popular Front

French identity. *See* national identity, French

French national identity. *See* national identity, French

French Revolution, women, and citizenship, 13

French Socialist Party (SFIO), 30

funding issues, 96–98

Garrigoux, Jeanne: ADP, German invasion, and, 183–85, 188, 201; Bouches-du-Rhone Civic Action and, 103; death of, 185; Exposition artisanale (1938) and, 128; Social Studies Bureau and, 75–76; Tunisian summer camps and, 96; women, essentialized view of, 101 gender: colonial dynamics and, 148–49; Mead, anthropology, and gender stereotypes, 113–14; Préval on metamorphosis and, 189; Social First! strategy and breakdown of separate spheres, 106; structural subordination of women in Civic Action, 98–104. *See also* suffrage, womens'; Women's Section, CF

gender ideology: CF ancillary groups and, 31–33; dependency and, 44–45, 98–100; leagues and, 19–20; misogyny vs. anti-feminism, 47–48; purity and, 38–39; sociocultural action and, 23–24; women's entry into Croix de Feu and transformation of, 83–84; women's rights during French Revolution and First Republic, 13–14; Yver, RNCF, and, 46. *See also* masculinity and hypermasculinity; womanhood and femininity, constructions of

geographical distribution of Women's Section, 60–61, fig.5

Gérus, Marie-Claire, 49, 54, 55–56, 186, 221n43

Goy, Jean, 86

Great Depression, 19

Green, Mary Jean, 22–23

Grey, Madeleine, 39, 125

Gros, Colonel, 155–56

Guillon, Armand, 175–76

Hause, Steven, 61

health clinics. *See* Association Médico-Sociale Jeanne d'Arc

Hébert, Georges, 110–12

Hermann-Paul, 34

H-Hour, 35

Hidieu, Thérèse, 46–47

Hitler, Adolf, 35, 47, 144, 155

Horaist, Mme., 118, 194, 197

Hugo, Victor, 27

hypermasculinity. *See* masculinity and hyper-masculinity

Iba-Zizen, Augustin, 159, 169–71, 241n116

iconography: *Croix de Guerre*, 27; death's head symbol, 27, 30; Joan of Arc, 43–46

identity, national. *See* national identity, French

immigrant communities in Paris, 64–65

integralism and integral nationalism, 55, 78, 126–29

intelligence gathering by the Klan, 192–95, 201

"Internationale" (song), 39

Islamic revivalism, 165

Javal, Mme., 78

J-Day, 35

Jean Mermoz centers, 187

Jeunesse Ouvrière Chrétienne (JOC), 66–67, 77

Jeunesses Patriotes: CF/PSF contrasted with, 24; female membership, 61; Joan of Arc fête and, 42t; membership of, 213n100; pacifist congress attack (1931), 35; Women's Section of, 20

Jews: anti-Semitism in the Maghreb, 172–73; "Judeo-Muslim" block, 166–68; La Rocque on, 195–96; resistance aid to, 195–96; Vel d'Hiv roundups of, 191, 196; Vichy anti-Semitism, 195–96, 199

Joan of Arc fête and iconography, 41–45, 45t, 137, fig.2

JOC (Jeunesse Ouvrière Chrétienne), 66–67, 77

Jouanneau, Marie, 197

"Judeo-Muslim" block, 166–68

Kalman, Samuel, 22–23, 172, 210n49, 231n36, 241n116

Kaplan, Rabbi, 55, 56–57

Kéchichian, Albert, 219n3, 219n83

Kennedy, Sean, 22–23, 148, 191, 197, 201

Kitson, Simon, 180, 193, 201

Klan resistance and intelligence activities, 190–97, 201

Kudlick, Catherine, 72

labor, forced, 134–35, 204

Labor Service, Nazi, 143–45

LADAPT (Ligue pour l'Adaptation du Dimiunué Physique au Travail), 69, 70, 72

La Rocque, François de: ADP and, 181, 183;
AMSJA and, 89, 91; antifeminism vs. misogyny and, 47; arrested by Gestapo, 197;
bazaars and, 127; Catholicism and, 66–68;
circular to Social Action Delegates, 99;
Commission for Indigenous Affairs and,
168–70; Croix de Feu ancillary groups and,
31–34; Debay on fascism and, 155; Exposition artisanale (1938) and, 128; Fouché and,
70; as French Intelligence head in Morocco,
192; German invasion and, 184–85; on
indigenous activism, 161; on Jews, 195–96;
Maghreb and, 147, 155–56; on Mlle. Carlier,
44; MSF and, 63–64; on Muslims, 166;
national reconciliationism and, 65–66;
at pacifist conference (Trocadero, 1931),
35–36; Parti Social Français renaming and,
74; post-Vichy provisional government
and, 199–200; Préval and, 49; provincial
background of, 126; on race and culture,
109; resignation of, 200; right-wing coalitions and, 180; Rivet on, 124; sanctions for
anti-Semitism, 173; *Service Public*, 53, 109,
161; on social program, 62; on Social Studies
Bureau, 75; social turn and, 219n3; Vichy
and, 185–86, 191–96; Women's Section and,
54, 59

La Rocque, Gilles de, 185

La Rocque, Jean-François de, 185

La Rocque, Nadine de: on republicanism, 2,
9–10, 52, 206; as Soufflotine ideal, 137

Latil, Jeanne, 112

Law on Associations (1901), 14–15

League against Imperialism and Colonial Oppression, 162–63

leagues and gender ideology, 19–20. *See also
specific leagues*

Le Beau, Georges, 159

Lecache, Bernard, 166–67, 168

Lefevre (Isère PSF section chief), 97–98

le Tanneur, Pierre, 192, 193

LFACF. *See* Ligue Féminine d'Action
Catholique Française

LFDF (Ligue Française pour le Droit des
Femmes), 18

LFF (Ligue des Femmes Françaises), 15

Liberty Front, 180

LICA (Ligue Internationale Contre l'Antisémitisme), 166–68

Ligue des Femmes Françaises (LFF), 15

Ligue des Patriotes, 42t

Ligue Féminine d'Action Catholique Française
(LFACF): Cardinal Verdier and, 66; Catholic
requirement in, 51; feminism vs. suffrage
activism and, 21–22; formation of, 15–16;
undermining of, 24

Ligue Française pour le Droit des Femmes
(LFDF), 18

Ligue Internationale Contre l'Antisémitisme
(LICA), 166–68

Ligue Patriotique des Françaises (LPDF), 15,
21–22

Ligue pour l'Adaptation du Dimiunué Physique au Travail (LADAPT), 69, 70, 72

localism, 73

LPDF (Ligue Patriotique des Françaises), 15,
21–22

Lyautey, Louis-Hubert, 35

Lyon Civic Action, 102

al-Madani, Ahmad Tawfik, 162

Madeleine (Soufflotine), 143–46

Maghreb, French. *See* Algeria; Morocco; North
African Croix de Feu/PSF; settlers in the
French Maghreb; Tunisia

Maire, Gaëtan, 108–10, 112, 113–15, 117–18, 187,
190, 193

Marin, Louis, 18

Marochetti, Simone, 63, 96, 130, 195
"La Marseillaise," 38, 39, 134
Martignier, Jeanne, 152–53
masculinity and hypermasculinity: Algerian social services bureaucracy and, 151–52; early CF and masculine ideal, 33–34; fascist leagues and, 20–21; Fête Coloniale and, 134; paramilitarism and, 35–37; physical education and, 121; social action, university centers, and, 81–83; SPES, Maghreb, and, 122
Mass of Marshal, 39–41
Mauriac, François, 69
Maurras, Charles, 66
Mauss, Marcel, 124, 129
Mazafran Women's Section, Algeria, 153, 157
Mead, Margaret, 113–14
medical centers. *See* Association Médico-Sociale Jeanne d'Arc
memory, collective, 38
Merle, Mme., 61
Mermoz, Jean, 82–83, 190, 194
Messali Hadj, Ahmed Ben, 162–64, 174
"metamorphosis," 189
Minguet, Dr., 70–71, 150–51, 175
Les Miserables (Hugo), 27
misogyny vs. antifeminism, 47–48
Mitidja plain, 140–41
Moreau, Marie-Thérèse, 20, 21
Moroccan National Action Bloc, 174
Morocco: Berber Dahir, 161; La Rocque as French Intelligence head in, 192; recruitment of indigenous veterans and elites, 157–58; security forces in, 154–55; social services policies in, 160; Women's Sections and social program in, 149, 150. *See also* North African Croix de Feu/PSF; settlers in the French Maghreb
Mouvement Social Français des Croix de Feu (MSF), 63–64, 74, 151
Munich Agreement, 138
Musée des Arts et Traditions Populaires (ATP), 127–29, 135

Muslims in metropolitan France, 64–65
Muslims in the Maghreb: pan-Islamism, Islamic revivalism, and Arab nationalism, 163–66; recruitment attempts and collaboration with, 157–60; Soufflotines and, 139–40
Mussolini, Benito, 35, 69, 155, 165

Napoleon Bonaparte, 13–14
National Front, 180
national identity, French: ATP and, 129; bazaars and, 126; cathedrals and, 40; Catholicism and, 10, 141; cultural superiority, 123–24, 129, 142; integralism and, 127; Mass of Marshals and, 40; "the social" and, 190
nationalism, ethnoreligious. *See* ethnoreligious nationalism
nationalism, integral, 55
national reconciliationism, 65–66
"National Reconciliation" slogan, 25
National Revolution, true (Préval), 189–91
Natural Method (Hébert), 111, 119
Nazi Germany: crackdown on PSF/ADP, 197–98; invasion of France, 184–85; Soufflotines visiting work-service camps in, 143–45; at World's Fair (1937, Paris), 130
Néo-Destour, 174–75, 176
Nobécourt, Jacques, 245n76
Nora, Pierre, 38
Nord PSF, 86–87
North African Croix de Feu/PSF: Catholic Church, obstacles to alignment with, 84–85; Commission for Indigenous Affairs, "Adapt and Assimilate" policy, and "social harmonization," 168–72; fascism of PSF settlers, violence, and repression, 172–77; Fouché's conferences, 71; historical background, 147–48; indigenous and anticolonial activism and racism, 160–68, 173–77; La Rocque directives on social service, 155–56; Muslim recruitment efforts and collaboration, 157–60; political-action pressure and

social organizing, 154–57; political culture and, 148–49; settler women compared to metropolitan women in, 148; social program and structural subordination of women in, 149–54, fig.9; Soufflotines and, 138–39; SPES, absence of, 121–22; Vichy and, 179 North African settlers. *See* settlers in the French Maghreb

Nouvion, Mme., 157

d'Orsay, Jean, 131, 190, 192, 193
Ottavi, Noël, 192, 193

pacifism: CF/PSF mission of protection against, 202; prohibition against violence in youth program, 81; purity discourse and, 38, 45; ultranationalists vs., 29; veterans and, 35
pacifist congress attack (Trocadero, Paris, 1931), 35–36
pan-Islamism, 163–64
paramilitarism: combatant-noncombattant hierarchy in early CF, 32–34; dissolution of paramilitary leagues after 1936 election, 74; early CF and, 30, 34–37
Parti Démocrate Populaire, 20
Parti Populaire Française (PPF), 21, 86, 214n103
Parti Social Français (PSF). *See* ADP; Croix de Feu/PSF
Passive Defense, 180–82
Passmore, Kevin, 20, 21, 23, 60, 126
patrie and paramilitarism, 35–37
Perrineau, Mme., 90–93
Pétain, Henri Philippe, 178–79, 185–86
Peyrouton, Marcel, 175
physical culture and physical education: CF/PSF/SPES physical education program, 116–21, 117t, 120t; defined, 230n11; disability and, 72–73; French history of, 106–7; gender stereotypes and, 113–15; growth of physical education centers, 63t; Hébert and, 110–12; La Rocque on, 109; Maghreb and, 121–22; Maire and, 108–10, 112, 113–15,

117–18; Mead and, 113–14; positive eugenics, 109–10; racial degeneration and racial rejuvenation, 107, 108–12; Ruffier and, 108, 112–13; social Darwinism, 110; Vichy regime and, 121; women, CF/PSF distinct approach to, 107–8, 112
Pinet, Antoinette, 192
Pius XI, Pope, 18–19, 68
political culture and early CF, 37–47
polygyny, 170
Pont de Beauvoisin PSF, 97, 98
Popular Front: Blum-Violette bill and, 164; CF/PSF, tension and conflict with, 73–74, 79–80, 127; CF Women's Section and competition with, 60–61; charity bazaars and, 127; colonial subjects, relative respect for, 124; dissolution of paramilitary leagues after 1936 election, 74; Madame Bernard on, 103–4; Maghreb reactions to election of, 173–76; misunderstanding of women's role in CF/PSF, 203; Musée des Arts et Traditions Populaires (ATP), 127–29; national reconciliationism and, 65; race and sport in, 107; riots of Feb. 1934 and, 52; settler fears, indigenous activism, and, 161; World's Fair (1937, Paris) and, 130
positive eugenics, 109–10
posters, recruiting, 34, fig.1
Pourquoit S'en Faire (Why Worry?) journal, 136–37, 138, 139
Pozzo di Borgo, Joseph Jean, 32
PPF (Parti Populaire Française), 21, 86, 214n103
Préval, Antoinette de: ADP and, 181, 183–86, 188–94; AMSJA, Les Allées, and, 88–95; on "Army of the Good" and metamorphosis, 188–90; background, 49, 126; bazaars and, 127; Bouches-du-Rhone Civic Action and, 102–3; Catholic Action coordination and, 77–78; Chopine on, 53–54; creation and organization of Women's Section and, 49–50, 54; death of, 202; exhaustion and illness, 95–96; Exposition artisanale (1938) and, 128;

Préval, Antoinette de (*continued*)
Fête Coloniale and, 130–31; Foyer and, 135;
Gestapo arrests and, 197; Jewish aid and,
196; La Rocque (François) and, 49; leadership of, 24, 53, 75; Maghreb and, 147, 150;
Pont de Beauvoisin PSF and, 97; post-Vichy
provisional government and, 199–200;
recruitment and membership and, 58–60;
on religion and women's activism, 57; sexual
immorality campaign, 92; Social Action and,
75; on "Social First!," 66; social program and,
53–54; social services network, creation of,
23; social work professionals, recruitment
of, 68–69; on SPES, 117; on suffrage activism, 24–25; Travail et loisirs and, 130; working classes and, 78–79
Préval hamlet, 202
primitivism, 110–11, 135
pronatalist movement, 18–19, 56, 101
propaganda: recruiting posters, 34, fig.1; songs
and, 39
Prost, Antoine, 35, 41
provisional government, 198–200, 203
PSF (Parti Social Français). *See* ADP; Croix de
Feu/PSF
purity, 38–39, 44

Quadregesimo Anno (Pius XI), 18–19

race: anti-Semitism in the Maghreb, 172;
common colonial stereotypes, 133; culture
as Left-Right battleground on, 123; ethnoreligious hierarchies, impact of, 204–5; ethnoreligious nationalism of Women's Section
and, 55; Fête Coloniale and, 131–32; more
extreme and explicit in the Maghreb, 205;
physical culture, racial degeneration and
racial rejuvenation, 107, 108–12; scientific
racism, 111, 124, 204; Soufflotines and, 141;
Soufflotines and cultural racism, 140. *See
also* assimilationism and associationism

Radicals, 17–18, 25
recruiting posters, 34, fig.1
Red Cross, 182, 186
Regnault, Mme., 93, 118
Regroupement National autour des Croix de
Feu (RNCF), 32–34, 32t, 46, 53
Reichsarbetsdienst (Nazi Labor Service, RAD),
143–44
Reichsarbetsdienst-weibliche Jugend (Women's
Labor Service, RADwJ), 143–44
religion: anticlericalism, 14–15, 40, 84, 106;
assimilation and, 204; CF/PSF emphasis on
compulsory religious practice, 67; ecumenicalism, 24, 54–55; ecumenicalism in CF/PSF,
24; Third Republic's assault on, 57. *See also*
Catholicism; ethnoreligious nationalism;
Jews
republicanism, French: dual character of, 9–10,
148; La Rocque (Nadine) on, 2, 9–10, 52,
206; Madeleine (Soufflotine) on, 146; Vatican's acceptance of, 14
Rerum Novarum (papal encyclical), 14
resistance: Algerian conquest and, 3; Chaillet
and, 199, 200; Iba-Zizen on, 171; Klan activ-
ities and Vichy-period resistance, 190–97;
Secours National collaboration as cover for,
201; Vichy disillusionment and, 180
Rey, Mme., 93–94
Richet, Charles, 19
rights, individual, 10
Rights of Man, 10
right-wing coalitions, 180
Rivet, Paul, 74, 124, 129
Rivière, Georges Henri, 128–29
RNCF (Regroupement National autour des
Croix de Feu), 32–34, 32t, 46, 53
Robert, Pierre, 192, 193
Roman Empire, ideal of, 140
Roux, Lisette, 195
Ruedy, John, 161
Ruffier, Jean Edward, 108, 112–13

Saint Ouen social center, 118, 194, 197

Sarrochi, Marcel, 173

scientific racism, 111, 124, 204

Secours National (later Entr'aide Français), 181–82, 186, 198–200

Section Française de l'Internationale Ouvrière. *See* Socialist Party

sénatus consulte (1865), 4, 12

Sept, 68

Service Public (La Rocque), 53, 109, 161

settlers in the French Maghreb: *algérianiste* movement, 6, 172; Charter of Demands and, 163; metropolitan vs. settler women, 148; political radicalism contrasted with metropolitan policy, 154–56; Popular Front election and fears of, 161; Soufflotines and, 139; universal individual rights, hostility toward, 10. *See also* North African Croix de Feu/PSF

sewing rooms, growth of, 63t

sexual immorality campaign by Préval, 92

sexuality and Joan of Arc, 44

SFIO. *See* Socialist Party

shock troops (*disponsables* or *dispos*), 35–36, 46, 127

Social Action (Section Féminine d'Action Sociale): autonomy and authority of women in, 98; Civic Action contrasted with, 99–101; formation of, 75; La Rocque's circular to Social Action Delegates, 99; in Maghreb, 148; Perrineau and, 90; physical education programs and, 117; summer camps, 96–97; Vichy period and, 183

"social action" as sociocultural action, 23

social centers: Catholic Church and, 77–78; in Compègne (Oise) vs. Antony, 76; growth of, 63t; intelligence activities and, 194; location patterns, 79–80; police appreciation for, 78; Saint Ouen, 118, 194, 197; transformed into welcome centers, 181; World's Fair children's shows and, 129–30

social Darwinism, 110, 121, 205

Social First! slogan and strategy: breakdown of separate gender spheres and, 106; creation and unveiling of, 23, 66; Maghreb and, 168, 169–70; university centers and, 82; Vichy and, 178

social harmonization, 170–71

socialism, social Catholicism in response to, 14

Socialist Party (Section Française de l'Internationale Ouvrière, SFIO): *dispos,* harassment by, 36; female membership, 61; *Le Flambeau,* competition with, 30; "Internationale" (song), 39; Pont de Beauvoisin PSF and, 98; provisional government and, 198; sporting association, 106. *See also* Popular Front

social program and social action movement of CF/PSF: advent of PSF and separate suborganizations, 73–76; Catholic Action, coordination with, 76–78; Catholics, campaign to engage, 66–68; civic space, women's social role in, 50; class and ethnoreligious integration, 78–79; Fouché's social sense conferences, 69–73; growth of, 62–64, 63t; La Rocque's (François) *Service Public*, 53; Maghreb, obstacles to Catholic alignment in, 84–85; male university centers and, 81–83; men and Préval's "metamorphosis," 189; national reconciliationism and, 65–66; neighborhood recruitment, immigrant communities, and, 64–65; in North Africa, 149–54, 155–57, fig.9; Popular Front, tensions and conflict with, 79–80; Préval leadership and structure of, 53–54; recruitment of social work professionals, 68–69; riots of Feb. 1934 and, 51–52; social turn, 219n3; Vichy and, 179, 185–88; women's entry and transformation toward, 49–50, 83–84; Women's Section inaugural speeches and ethnoreligious integration, 54–57; Women's Section membership growth and leadership and, 58–62. *See also* ADP

social sense, 70–71

Social Studies Bureau, 75, 117

Société de préparation et d'Éducation Sportive (SPES): autonomy and authority of women in, 98; establishment of, 74; Maghreb, absence in, 121–22, 148; organization and approach of, 117–20, 120t; Vichy and, 187

Solidarité Française, 21, 214n103

"Song of the Croix de Feu," 39, 139

Soufflotines: depicted as smiling tourists, 142, fig.8; Le foyer universitaire and, 135–38; intellectualism and, 137–38; name, origins of, 136; at Nazi work-service camps, 143–45; *Pourquoit S'en Faire* (Why Worry?) journal, 136–37, 138, 139; as tourists/emissaries in Algeria, 1–2, 138–43

soup kitchens, 46–47, 63t

sovereignty concept, 180

Soviet pavilion, World's Fair (1937, Paris), 130

Speer, Albert, 130

SPES. *See* Société de préparation et d'éducation sportive

SPES Study Bureau, 117

sport, 106, 115. *See also* physical culture and physical education

staff issues at health clinic and Les Allées, 91–95

Statut des juifs, 195–96, 199

Strohl, Mlle., 195

suffering, Fouché on, 72

suffrage, womens': feminism and, 16–18; feminism vs. suffrage activism, 21–22; interwar organizations for, 15–16; Préval on, 24–25; Senate refusal (1922), 17

Suire, Pierre, 83, 190

summer camps: Algeria, 152; depicted in "Youth and Family" show (1937 Worlds Fair, Paris), 130; funding issues, 96–97; growth of, 63t

Tarzan, 131–34

Tempucci, Mlle., 94

Thevenet, M., 110, 112

Third Republic: Catholicism, anticlericalism, and, 14–15; dual character of, 9–10; gymnastic and sporting societies in, 106; social action, compared to CF/PSF, 25; street riots of Feb. 6, 1934 and collapse of, 51–52

Thomas, Martin, 176

Tin Tin in the Congo, 132

Tixier, Adrien, 198–200, 203

tourism in Algeria, 1–2, 138–43

"Travail, Famille, Patrie" slogan, 25

Travail et loisirs (Work and Leisure): autonomy and authority of women in, 98; banned by Gestapo, 197; cultural activities, 125; ethnoreligious and class integration and, 78–79; Exposition artisanale (1938) and collaboration with ATP, 128–29; Garrigoux and, 76; Javal and, 78; Maghreb, absence in, 148; physical education programs, 117, 118; Préval and, 75; Saint Ouen social center, 118; Vichy period and, 182–83, 194; violence and, 80; World's Fair (1937, Paris) and, 129–35

Trumbell, George IV, 210n49

Tumblety, Joan, 107, 110–11, 117, 230n11, 231n36

Tunisia: conquest semicentennial celebrations, 161; recruitment of native Tunisians, 157; repression and violence in, 174–77; Women's Sections and social program in, 149, 150–51. *See also* North African Croix de Feu/PSF; settlers in the French Maghreb

Tunisian Social Action, 96

UFCS (Union Féminine Civique et Social), 16, 24

ugliness, 108–9

Ulama, 162–67

ultranationalism: Joan of Arc and, 41; physical culture and, 108; struggles of ultranationalist groups, 58; Women's Section and, 56

UNC (Union Nationale des Combattants), 86

Union Féminine Civique et Social (UFCS), 16, 24

Union Française pour le Suffrage des Femmes (USFS), 18

Union Nationale des Combattants (UNC), 86

Union Nationale pour le Vote des Femmes (UNVF), 16, 20

university centers, 63t, 81–83, 135–38

UNVF (Union Nationale pour le Vote des Femmes), 16, 20

USFS (Union Française pour le Suffrage des Femmes), 18

Vallin, Charles, 65

Vauplane, R. P., 40, 66

Vel d'Hiv roundups of Jews, 191, 196

Verdier, Cardinal, 66–67, 69, 77

Vérone, Maria, 18, 20

veterans' associations, 29–30, 35

veteran's mystique, 29, 37–38, 50

Vichy regime and period: anti-Semitism, 195–96, 199; armistice and establishment of government, 187–88; Catholicism and, 188; Chantiers de la Jeunesse, 121; Commissariat General for Sports, 121; D-Day landings and Allied liberation, 198; evacuations, refugees, and, 182–85; Klan resistance and intelligence activities against, 190–97; Passive Defense, 180–82; Pétain, 178–79, 185–86; provisional government following, 198–200; PSF's initial approval of, 185–86; Secours National and, 181–82, 186; social action, compared to CF/PSF, 25; sovereignty, culture of war, and, 180; "*Travail, Famille, Patrie*" slogan and, 25. *See also* ADP

Vieira, Mlle., 92

violence: anti-Jewish, in the Maghreb, 173; Communist-PSF conflicts and, 79–81; culture of war, 28–29, 50, 81, 180, 215n4; Popular Front vs. PSF and, 80–81; repression and violence in Tunisia, 174–77. *See also* paramilitarism

Violette, Maurice, 164

virginity and Joan of Arc, 44

VN (Volontaires Nationaux), 32–34, 32t, 151

Volontaires Nationaux (VN), 32–34, 32t, 151

voting rights. *See* suffrage, womens'

war, culture of, 28–29, 50, 81, 180, 215n4

Weiss, Louise, 18, 20, 86–87, 104

Wilder, Gary, 9

womanhood and femininity, constructions of: bifurcated concept in early CF, 45–46; bourgeois homemaker symbol, 45; Garrigoux and, 101; Joan of Arc and, 43–45, 44–45; "maternal mission" challenged by La Rocque, 53; "modern," 45–46; Nazism view, 144; pronatalism, 18–19, 56, 101; women's Croix de Fe participation correlated with feminist organizing, 61

women's activism, the Third Republic, and Catholicism, 14–16

women's involvement in CF/PSF. *See specific organizations and topics*

women's physical education, 107–8

Women's Section, CF: Center for Physical Education, 116–17; creation of, 49–50; geography of, 60–61, fig.5; growth of, fig.4; inaugural speeches, 54–57; leadership of local sections, 59–60; married and unmarried women in, 59–60, fig.3; name change to Social Action, 75; recruitment and membership, 58–60; reports from, 221n43

Women's Sections in North Africa, 149–54

Women's Sections of leagues, 20–21, 213n102

work-service camps, Nazi, 143–45

World's Fair (1937, Paris), 127–28, 129–35

World War I (the Great War), 15, 107

Wyrtzen, Jonathan, 160

Ybarnegaray, Jean, 65

youth: in Algeria, 152; Catholic-PSF relations and, 77; Communist Party and, 62, 115, 116; early CF and promise of, 29–33; Fête

youth (*continued*)
Coloniale and, 130–31; Jeunesse Ouvrière
Chrétienne (JOC), 66–67, 77; locat sections
and, 62; Préval on sexual morality and, 92;
purity discourse and, 81; "Song of Croix de
Feu" and, 39; summer camps, 63t, 96–97,
130, 152; Travail et loisirs and, 77; university

centers, 63t, 81–83, 135–38; violence, prohi-
bition against, 81. *See also* physical culture
and physical education; Soufflotines
"Youth and Family" show (1937 Worlds Fair,
Paris), 130
Yver, Colette, 39, 46, 48